MODERN ORGANIZATIONS

Organization Studies in the Postmodern World

Stewart R. Clegg

SAGE Publications

London • Newbury Park • New Delhi

First published 1990   Reprinted 1991

SAGE Publications Ltd
6 Bonhill Street
London EC2A 4PU

SAGE Publications Inc
2455 Teller Road
Newbury Park, California 91320

SAGE Publications India Pvt Ltd
32, M-Block Market
Greater Kailash – I
New Delhi 110 048

British Library Cataloguing in Publication data

Clegg, Stewart R.
  Modern organizations.
  1. Organization structure
  I. Title
  658.1

  ISBN 0–8039–8329–8
  ISBN 0–8039–8330–1 pbk

Library of Congress catalog card number 90–61987

Typeset by Photoprint, Torquay, Devon.
Printed in Great Britain by Dotesios Printers Ltd, Trowbridge, Wiltshire

Contents

Acknowledgements

All books have credits, as all ideas are necessarily shared. In the production of this book, apart from the many authors whose work is acknowledged in the text, the main sources of inspiration were several. First, I would like to acknowledge the contribution of David Dunkerley, with whom I wrote an earlier text on organizations (Clegg and Dunkerley 1980). Although this book differs in many respects from our earlier endeavours, having been there and done that once before in David's company made a solo trip much easier. Second, the guidance and example of David Hickson as a pioneer of a truly international organization studies has been a great source of inspiration. Third, being a frequent visitor to the University of Hong Kong Department of Management Studies over recent years, and working with Gordon Redding, helped me to develop a fascination for as well as a capacity to learn from East Asia (for example, see Clegg and Redding with Cartner 1990; Clegg, Dunphy and Redding 1986). Fourth, an occasion on which I was able to put some of this fascination and learning to the test was in the course of collaboration with Winton Higgins and Tony Spybey on an earlier piece which prefigures this text in many evident ways (Clegg, Higgins and Spybey 1990; see also Higgins and Clegg 1988). From Winton, in particular, I have learned a great deal, particularly about Sweden, and I am appreciative of the opportunities we have had for collaboration in the past: elements of all of these have entered into the construction of this book. Fifth, from Zygmunt Bauman's work I have found the framework for many of the ideas expressed here; for it is in this work, above all others, that the contours of transition from modernity to postmodernity begin to take a sociological shape. In an area where the debates are frequently somewhat arcane, one is thankful for his considered contributions.

The book had some other international antecedents. In the latter quarter of 1988 during a period of leave from the University of New England, Armidale, in New South Wales, Australia, where I was Professor of Sociology, I was fortunate enough to be a Visiting Professor in the Department of Management at the University of Otago, at Dunedin in New Zealand. During this period I taught some classes to the second and third year Management undergraduates. Some of the ideas that developed into part of Chapter 3 of this book were first developed in their company. Shortly thereafter, in the first three months of 1989, I had the pleasure of being a guest of the Department of Management at the University of Hong

Kong where I taught an MBA course in which some of the early applications of the material on East Asia were first developed.

After a most enjoyable period of leave, during which I worked on *Frameworks of Power* (Clegg 1989b), I returned to Armidale. Shortly after returning I began to work on the first draft of this book. At this time, without the institutional support of the University of New England and of key individuals within the Department of Sociology, including Trish Marshall, Roz Mortimer and Jim Bell, I doubt that I would have completed the first draft as easily as proved to be the case. In addition, it was also through the good auspices of the Department's 'Visitors Scheme' that Richard Hall was able to spend some time in the Department during the middle of 1989 and discuss aspects of these early drafts. The opportunities we had for discussion were much appreciated, as were the short comments he was later to make on a draft of the completed manuscript.

The book was completed after I had joined the University of St Andrews as Professor of Organization Studies and Chair of the Department of Management, from January 1, 1990. The facilities provided there – notably access to a Macintosh computer – greatly aided the completion of the book. Within the department, David Collinson, Mo Malek, Christos Pitelis and Fiona Wilson were kind enough to offer me some advice on aspects of the manuscript as it neared completion. The class of '89–90 on the postgraduate MEP (Management, Economics and Politics) course were stimulating sounding-boards and partners in exploration of the ideas which were taking final shape in the book. I hope that they enjoyed our exchanges as much as I did. They helped me think things through to a greater extent than would otherwise have been the case.

Some other acknowledgements to friends and colleagues of long-standing are also in order. Winton Higgins was one of the first people to read the manuscript and provided most encouraging and perceptive notes on it at that early stage. Jane Marceau also read the book through for me in early draft form and similarly made a number of useful comments, as did Richard Whitley for a later draft. Lucien Karpik was also kind enough to make supportive and positive suggestions on the manuscript during its genesis, as did Bill Ryan and Malcolm Lewis at a late stage of its development. Margo Huxley suggested some very useful references to me that I might consult in the journal *Society and Space* and provided me with access to the material that I could not otherwise easily have achieved. David Hickson and Peter Blunt offered challenging criticisms which forced me to try and make some aspects of the ideas clearer. Doubtless, there is still plenty of room for improvement on that score!

I would like to thank Stephen Barr for asking me to write for Sage again after his earlier work as editor on *Frameworks of Power*. Had he not asked me what the next one was going to be I might not have written it. It had many titles during its genesis, sometimes in one day! The title that we finally settled on has its allusions and, together with the subtitle, its equivo-cations. The allusions are unintentional, incidental and not meant to signify anything other than the title. The equivocations are more knowing and signify present postmodern possibilities perfectly. It was Zygmunt Bauman who first suggested that an interesting book might be developed from some of the ideas which framed the paper on '"Post-Confucianism", Social Democracy and Economic Culture', written with Winton Higgins and Tony Spybey (1990). Whether this book has turned out along the lines that he had in mind I do not know, but I trust that he will not object to being credited with a small contribution to its genesis. Finally, Figures 4.1 and 4.2 were adapted by permission of both Professor Mintzberg and Prentice Hall, Inc., Englewood Cliffs, New Jersey from Mintzberg's *The Structuring of Organizations* (1979: 20) and *Power in and around Organizations* (1983: 29). Figure 8.1 was adapted by permission of the journal *Industry and Labour*.

Above all else, during the production of this book I enjoyed the support of Lynne, Jonathan and William. Without them, the quality of everyday life would have been such that fulfilment would not easily have been found either in writing or in recreation away from the keyboard. The pleasures of the text do become tiresome, irksome, even life-denying when the day is beautiful and the sources of happiness are great. At such times they are far more easily set aside when there are such significant others to share life with. Finally, despite love and good fellowship from many kind people, it was I who wrote the book and thus I must take full responsibility for whatever infelicities, extravagant claims, wrongheaded assumptions and factual errors the book may contain. Books always do contain these – otherwise there would be no point in writing further ones!

1

Theoretical Contrasts and International Contexts

There are a great many existing texts on organization and management theory and this is yet another one. It is, however, one with claims to both difference and distinctiveness. In fact, its distinct claims to difference are several and will be briefly alluded to in this introduction. First, wherever possible the majority of the examples and case study material used are drawn from non-American and non-British material. Other books already provide material from these contexts and may well be of complementary use. The strategy of ranging further abroad for international and comparative perspectives should not only ensure more interesting and refreshing reading (not the same old cases trotted out yet again!) but will also serve a substantive purpose. Part of the argument of the book is that organization studies in the past, to their detriment, have drawn on both a range of materials and theoretical approaches which have been too restricted. Consequently, they have failed to reflect the complexity of the organizational world outside the limited range of empirical examples considered. Upon such a small slice of available reality some fairly large assumptions have been spread.

Conceiving the present simply in terms of modernity would hardly do justice to a world in which the 'postmodern' is such an avid topic for cultural discussion of all kinds. Yet it is by no means clear that modernity has in actual fact been superseded. Some writers talk of the present as an era of 'high modernism': others prefer the rubric of 'postmodernism'. We do not know what the outcomes of present practices and debates may be. These debates are of considerable significance for the study of organizations. Thus, a second distinct feature of this book is that it taps into important debates about the nature of modernity and postmodernity. These are complex terms and have been subject to considerable discussion. Rather than reflect all of the nuances of this complexity the discussion attempts to steer a simple and direct path through the debates linking modernity with postmodernity. It will do so by focusing on a common core component: that of the direction and the degree of 'differentiation' or division which characterize a period. Postmodernity, it is suggested, may be distinguished from modernity by its reversal of earlier tendencies to increasing differentiation.

The importance of the debate around modernity for organization studies is very simply proposed: organization theory is a creation of modernity, in particular in the debt it owes to Max Weber. However, current empirical tendencies in some international contexts may be such that organization practice may well have transgressed the limits to understanding which are framed by this modernist theory. The crucial hallmark of modernity is taken to be the centrality of an increasing division of labour. This will be referred to for economy as a process of differentiation. Recently it has been suggested that modernity may not be an endless process. Debate has focused increasingly on what happens 'after modernity', on what is termed postmodernity. It has been proposed, by contrast to the stress on increasing differentiation as the motif of modernity, that the crucial hallmark of postmodernity may be a decrease in differentiation. Within the world of organizations and work this might be economically translated as a process of 'de-differentiation'.

The two parallel oppositions of modernity/postmodernity and differentiation/de-differentiation thus form the narrative drive of the book, while it is the use of less conventional cases and material which guide it. Each is oriented towards the same end. The possibilities posed to modernity by the development of the postmodern may be seen to present a challenge for Anglo-American theory in much the same way as does the consideration of a much wider slice of reality than usual. Accordingly, it is argued that consideration of both a wider reality and a wider debate concerning the nature of that reality may be theoretically innovative.

There is a third distinctive feature to the book. The intersection of a text on organizations with arguments about disparate ways of managing modernity and postmodernity enables a dialogue to occur between frequently separated concerns. Obviously, these include debates in organization theory as well as debates around modernity/postmodernity. In addition there are a number of cognate areas which have been only partially related and which require greater connection. The substantive focus of these debates has been on social relations in and of production, seen not from the perspectives of organization theory but from those of industrial sociology, industrial relations and management theory, as well as a broader comparative sociology of economic life. The divisions between these enterprises, where they still exist, are in fact somewhat limited and arbitrary. The claim that this is so will become apparent in the use that the book makes of diverse materials drawn from these areas.

Organizations and modernity

If organizations are the form of our modern condition, one cannot help but note that this is frequently represented less as an opportune or benevolent phenomenon but more as something which is constraining and repressive. These elements can be attributed to a pervasive strand of modernist thinking, clearly articulated as a representative experience of modernity in the work of Max Weber and his vision of bondage, of the 'iron cage'. It is not surprising that it is from Weber that organizational modernism draws its most vital tap-root. To discuss organizations in any intellectual terms other than the most mundane necessarily is to draw strength from the well of Max Weber's intellectual legacy, even when it remains more implicit than acknowledged. Weber's legacy casts a long shadow over not only this text but also the whole field that any such text addresses. Of course, it is in the nature of a colossus to cast a large shadow. The shadow will be given a name: modernism.

There is no singular aspect to modernism and its play of light and shade across the field of vision. Indeed, organizations have been represented in various modernist terms. For instance, they have been imagined in terms of ideal types and their deviations, systems and their throughput processes, organizations and their contingencies, markets and their structures and failures, populations of organizations and their ecologies, cultures and their institutionalized myths and ceremonies, as well as the *realpolitik* of power. Many texts on organizations consider these topics in succession, as distinct enterprises as it were (for example, Morgan 1986). This text will consider them as competing hypotheses, capable of adjudication. Various perspectives will be considered in detail in the following chapters. In the course of this consideration one will gain a synoptic impression of the achievements and value of contemporary approaches to the analysis of organizations.

To speak of value begs the question of 'value for what' as well as 'value for whom'? Different conceptions of the appropriate answers to these questions distinguish and demarcate major cleavages in preferred modes of analysis. These are not purely academic but embrace a compass which takes in analysts stretching from the most prosaic consultant to the most precious critic. Within the vast range of perceptions encompassed, one would find many different notions not only of what the analysis of organizations entails but also of what it should be called. It is as well to attend to naming at the birth of an endeavour and this book will not break with such sensible precedent. The choices are many. In fact, the analysis of organizations as an enterprise has been called many things, including the sociology of organizations, organization theory, administrative theory and so on. In this text it will be called some of these things: mostly, it will be termed *organization studies*. The term is chosen not only because it provides as broad a conception of the enterprise as possible and one which finds a resonance in the title of one of the major journals in the field, but also because it is a term which has not yet been subject to polemical appropriation. Such polemic has been only too evident of late. The evidence is to be found in recent manoeuvres which have sought to demarcate 'Organization Theory' from 'Sociology of Organizations' and 'alternative programmes' (see Donaldson 1985a; Hinings et al. 1988). Organization studies, it is hoped, is unlikely to raise any hackles which might exist a priori. It is intended to be a broad designation for a big enterprise, albeit one pursued here on a small scale.

Organizations, in the form in which they were depicted so influentially by Max Weber as an ideal type of bureaucracy, were a modernist representation of archetypally modernist practices. Representational modernism consisted in the sketching of a singular set of empirical tendencies which were imagined to be irresistible and inevitable. These were the famous rationalization of the world, the success of which would be attributed to bureaucracy as the primary mechanism of its achievement. Its outcome was to be our imprisonment in the house of bondage – the iron cage of bureaucracy. This idea, in one form or another, has held enormous sway over the theorization of organizations by social scientists until the present day. Organization theory is in many respects a modernist discipline *par excellence*, springing as it does from Weber's modernist vision of the modernist world. It is in many respects a bleak and pessimistic vision, leavened only by the irony and intelligence of its progenitor and the undoubtedly ambivalent moral quality of his thought.

Weber was neither definitely for nor against the concept of bureaucracy. At different times he displayed quite distinct sentiments. There could be no doubting his stance on modernity, however. He was resolutely for modernity and against pre-modernity. As a strong liberal nationalist he interpreted pre-modernity in German terms as referring to a weak and divided set of states rather than a strong nation state. While for Weber all the arguments seemed to be for modernity and against pre-modernity, we live in different times and there lies the nub of the argument. Today, it may not be sufficient to be for modernity against the pre-modern images of the past. In addition, one needs to take a stance with respect to what has passed increasingly into currency as the postmodern.

Modernism frequently has taken an explicitly moral character. A key element in this morality play has been the role cast for bureaucracy. Although it is often reviled in the popular and populist consciousness this is less often the case for organization theorists. For these people bureaucracy has frequently been seen as a good thing, as something desirable. In the various editions of his *Complex Organizations* Charles Perrow has contributed most to advance the idea of bureaucracy as a moral project. Organizational rationality, expressed in terms of the principles of bureaucracy, is in this work taken as a guarantee against discrimination premised on particularistic aspects of identity, such as ethnicity, gender, age, religion and sexuality. The morality of bureaucracy lies in its implicit promise to treat each person according only to their status as an organizational member, irrespective of any other aspects of their identity. In a fully functioning bureaucracy, conceived in terms of this moral project, no other attribute of identity should have salient status unless it is formally represented as such in the constitutive documents and policies of the bureaucracy.

Undoubtedly there is much to recommend this conception of bureaucracy as a moral project. A conception of bureaucracy such as that advanced by Perrow is a liberal conception in all the very best senses of that term. It respects the individual's rights to be whoever or whatever they want to be outside of the determination of their status as an organization member. Should attributes of their status place limits on their ability to participate in membership then the existence of the principles of bureaucratic universalism are a first line of defence. These principles insist that one should be treated solely in terms of the rights, responsibilities, rules and duties appropriate to one's position as a member of an organization. Whether one is black or white, red or green, male or female, straight or gay, should be irrelevant. Organizations related to or derived from the modernist form thus place certain potential guarantees at the heart of the modern condition. Indeed, in some important respects, organizations are the form of our modern condition. Without a plurality of complex organizations there would be no possibilities of civility and citizenship, because it is only through organizational representation that the majority of people can achieve any form of interest articulation in a large scale, modern and mass society. Unions, parties, councils, governments, firms and other private and public organizations are the means through which we participate in modernity in other than the occasional drama and ritual of the formal political process. Public life is organizational life for most people.

An argument in several movements

The argument of the book unfolds in several distinct movements. The first encapsulates Chapters 2 to 4. These outline some arguments of mainstream contemporary positions in organization studies and indicate some analytical tests designed to differentiate between them. The second movement unfolds in Chapter 5 by posing some empirical limits which, it is proposed, currently influential theories of organizations fail to surmount. The theme of this second movement is that these theories are inadequate because even in their own terms they are not capable of dealing with the empirical variety of organizational realities which this text re-presents. Empirical realities are neither imaginary nor whimsical: they cannot be side-stepped. They serve as an embarrassment to certain generalizing and universalistic tendencies in organization analysis.

Chapter 5 is initially targeted at 'market' and 'efficiency' perspectives. Variation upon the theme which these approaches would have us play is achieved through the introduction of an element of critical dissonance. Such dissonance will be articulated through an empirical consideration of themes introduced as 'French bread', 'Italian fashions' and 'Asian enterprise'. Each of these themes undermines the assumptions upon which a universalizing and generalizing thrust in the analysis of organizations has developed. Let me elaborate the dissonance which they introduce.

According to Williamson's (1975) widely influential views, one would anticipate that French bread ought to be made in large, oligopolistic, vertically integrated and bureaucratically organized factories. It is not. The reason for thinking so is that it is invariably made that way in the United States and this case is taken as the paradigmatic framework for interpreting the modern organizational world. It is not only the artisanal mode of production of French bread which appears problematic for such chauvinism. Italian fashions, in particular those of Benetton, seem to contradict a great deal of the conceptual thrust of contemporary organization studies. Much of this activity is premised on the study of organizations as mechanisms that have been designed to handle a level of environmental uncertainty the totality of which they can never succeed in containing. Benetton, however, appears to come close to this containment. It offers a new conception of the management of organizations and markets. In the process it serves to pose a challenge to many of our ideas about the system boundaries of the organization. It is not only Italian fashion which poses fascinating puzzles for organization theory. In Japan, in South Korea and in overseas Chinese family businesses in countries like Taiwan and Hong Kong there are Asian enterprises which do not seem to be designed by people with a good grasp of the contingency design features of rational organizations. Despite this handicap they none the less appear to be rational and efficient in their functioning. Indeed, especially where Japan is concerned, it has increasingly become the case that this example is taken to prefigure what modern, perhaps even postmodern, management might be.

Can the distinctiveness of these cases be reduced simply to culture? It would be tempting to do so, particularly in the East Asian cases. Moreover, bearing in mind Crozier (1964), there are precedents for thinking similarly of the French case as well: *vive la différence!* Nor would this be merely an impulse of an earlier and now superseded social theory. In some recent and influential contributions, such as that of Berger (1987), there has been a tendency to see the success of East Asian enterprise, at least in part, in terms of a unique cultural configuration of values termed 'post-Confucianism'. These values are alleged to function as a source of entrepreneurial excellence, managerial acumen and organizational efficiency in much the same way that Weber (1976) saw the 'Protestant ethic' operating for nineteenth century European capitalism. Some critical distance will be taken from such views in this text. In fact, as Chapter 4 seeks to establish, the deficiency of universalizing theory premised on markets and efficiency is not easily rectified through a conception of culture which is equally essentialist in its reduction of explanation to one all-encroaching variable. It will be argued instead, following Granovetter (1985), that such reductionism makes too easy recourse to an 'over-socialized' view of economic action. Such a view is the direct antithesis of 'under-socialized' views, evident in universalizing, generalizing 'market' theories. Against these perspectives, Granovetter suggests, one must develop an 'embedded' view of the social organization of economic action.

Embeddedness refers to the configuration of those relations of 'relative autonomy' and 'relative dependence' which exist between forms of economic and social organization and the respective national frameworks of cultural and institutional value within which they are constituted. These configurations are an 'achieved' phenomenon. They are socially constructed, emergent, produced and reproduced. Consequently, forms of agency stand at the centre of the analysis. Agents are not necessarily people. Provided there are mechanisms in place for achieving effective subordination and control of individually effective agents, then agency may take either an organizational or a sub-organizational form. Agency wreaks its action on the world through the attempted accomplishment of projects which make sense in terms of the forms of calculation which agents have available to them. One of the important ways in which these vary will be in terms of the institutional frameworks within which action is lodged; in turn these will vary nationally. For instance, the forms of economic calculation which agents have available to them will be in part constituted and profoundly effected by nationally variable institutional phenomena such as tax regimes, accounting conventions, religious beliefs, formally constituted public policies in respect of matters of gender, equal opportunity, industry and regional policy and so on. Regarded in their totality we may use the term 'modes of rationality' to refer to attempts by agents to make sense of the potentially ambiguous, contradictory and uncertain nature of these available frameworks. Analytically, these are the patterned interpretations which can be made of the sense which agents appear to be making.

Unlike 'under-socialized' market views an embedded perspective does not operate with a pre-social or asocial version of agency. It makes no a priori assumptions about the nature or existence of specific forms of rationality privileged by the terms of neoclassical economic orthodoxy. In other words, an embedded perspective recognizes that there are likely to be a great many more salient identities available for assembly and use than merely that of the 'rational economic person'. Thus, it seeks to avoid the reduction of analysis to one identity, that of the market actor. This is the common economistic error. On the other hand it does not propose that the range of these identities will be given by the 'central value system' or core culture of a society. This is a common sociologistic error which it is also as well to avoid. Identities are not transmitted or read off from some over-arching culture. There is not some necessary relationship between culture and practice, although there may be contingent ones. It is important to resist any analytic impulse to reduce identities to one functionally efficient core culture. For instance, many things which might appear to be superficially similar in cultural terms, such as the organization of Asian enterprise in the common cultural space of 'post-Confucianism', are on closer inspection far more varied. That is, even within the common cultural frame there are significant variations which are not explicable in purely cultural terms. Moreover, they are so in ways which do not appear to be readily amenable to many of the concerns of contemporary organization studies. There appears to be something in each case which is over and above markets and culture. What is additional is not simply specifiable in terms of a common set of organizational properties which can be termed 'hierarchy' but is dependent upon the practical exigencies of agency and situated action.

Agents are practical experimentalists confronted by a potentially far more uncertain, ambivalent, contradictory and ambiguous world than any natural scientist might anticipate finding in the laboratory. Upon this chaotic canvas they will seek to impose their own 'circuits of power' (Clegg 1989b), configuring the field of action in such a way as to seek to realize the conditions under which their conceptions of their own interests, and the enrolment and translation of other agencies to these conceptions, may happen. A major mechanism for stabilizing the fields of force which they traverse will be the construction of relatively stable networks with only a limited number of ways or conduits through them, under the control of the agencies in question. Culture has often been regarded as such a conduit, particularly in the form of religious knowledges, beliefs and practices which apply to a whole population. Weber's (1976) analysis of *The Protestant Ethic and the Spirit of Capitalism* remains the classic text of this genre, with its conception of the formation of Protestantism as a conduit for meaning having the unanticipated consequence of producing a lifeline through which capitalism might also flourish.

Of late there have been interesting signs of a reprise of this intellectual strategy with respect not to Protestantism in the West but to 'post-Confucianism' in the East. Consequently, the third movement of the book opens up themes which are derived from East Asia. Considerable interest in East Asian economies has been expressed in the West in the last decade or so, not only with the nature of Japanese organizational practices, but increasingly with those of other significant East Asian economies. Many of the issues about markets and about culture may be seen with a specific thrust with respect to what has become the over-arching question: how and why are Japanese organizations so successful? The later chapters of this book, particularly Chapters 6 and 7, enter into this debate in detail, considering a broad-based literature about the nature of Japanese organization and enterprise. Certain propositions flow from consideration of this debate. Theories of organization which seek to use efficiency and effectiveness to explain the ascendancy of a limited number of organization forms are not quite as universalistic in scope as they might appear to be. Not only can one distinguish significant confounding examples, particularly in the economically successful East Asian cases; these conform to no one precise structural form. Rather than there appearing to be a convergence on any one dominant organization form, there appears to be a considerable range of what Cole (1973) once referred to, in the context of Japan, as 'functional alternatives'.

East Asian harmonic variations generate a further proposition, in the form of a null hypothesis. Neither over-socialized accounts of East Asian organizations which stress the importance of central value systems such as post-Confucianism nor those under-socialized accounts which stress market and efficiency factors are sufficient to encompass an expanded range of empirical cases. The conclusion which is drawn from this consideration is that organizations per se, conceived as the focal object of analysis, may not necessarily be the most appropriate theoretical object with which to construct an analysis of the management of economic action. The recourse to East Asian examples is thus a deliberate strategy rather than just recourse to some interesting travellers' tales that an Australian might have picked up travelling in Asia. Consideration of a wide range of empirical materials may serve to undermine not only that faith in bureaucracy which Perrow (1986) indexes but also the security of its organizational derivations as the central object of analysis. Just as it would be exceedingly unrealistic to regard the entity which corresponds to the legal definition of the person as the only appropriate object of social analysis, so it may be excessively restrictive to regard legally defined organizations as the necessary hub of organizational analysis. Clearly, in either social or organizational analysis, both persons and organizations will have a place, but not necessarily a privileged one. In each instance a key focus will be on the processes and mechanisms whereby forms of relative unity and disunity, organization and disorganization, will be accomplished.

On the one hand no reduction will be made to the person or to any of those accompanying notions which form part of the cultural baggage of that concept. If this may be taken as a theoretical reluctance to privilege people as conceptual prime movers, then the text is also resolutely anti-structural. It is equally reluctant to privilege conceptual aspects of organization structure as a necessary factor in the determination of organization practice. This puts one at odds with some mainstream currents in organization analysis which would construct a *cordon sanitaire* around the organization concept and proclaim 'thus far and no further!'. Such proclamations, in fact, have been made by colleagues such as Lex Donaldson (1985a) in the defence of a specific conception of organization theory. It is one which expresses what is almost an article of faith in the rightness and moral certitude of a particular way of doing organization analysis and management prescription. It should be clear that the author of this text has no such certainty. Two margins of uncertainty may be noted. On the one hand one seeks to pose some limits to the moral project of modern organization theory expressed in the liberal terms which Perrow articulates so well; on the other hand one attempts to resile from the much more limited moral project of theoretical absolutism with which Donaldson would replace it.

Organizations and postmodernity

A central part of the sociological legacy has been a focus on processes of differentiation as a core element of the modern experience. The division of labour has every right to be regarded as one of the central moral concerns of both classical sociology and political economy. After all, it was one of the central issues which bound otherwise disparate figures such as Adam Smith, Karl Marx and Emile Durkheim in their various concerns and passions: 'Smith's wonder at efficiency, Marx's wistfulness about artisanal labour, Durkheim's faith in the feudal *compagnonnes*' (Abbott 1989: 274). More recently it has been this emphasis on differentiation which stands at the core of sociological structural-functionalism. In its most important proponent in Talcott Parsons's (1966) evolutionary theory a moral component was quite evidently constitutive. More differentiation seemed to mean more modern and better societies.

Weber was every bit as moral in his concerns as these other eminent patriarchs of the social sciences. Weber's despair about bureaucracy, his concern with that iron cage within which '[t]he corporation, a fictive person, has replaced the company of equals as the legal scaffolding of work' (Abbott 1989: 273), clearly ranks in equal, if not greater, importance than Smith's pin factory or Marx's conception of the labour process. Organizations are indeed one of the great achievements of modernity. In fact they are the crucible within which processes of differentiation took place. Weber and his heirs in the analysis of organizations have made this abundantly clear. Today, we take such a judgement wholly for granted. It has not always been so.

Once upon a time before modernity, the division of labour was not a separate feature, it was not something which was worthy of attention in its own right. It was barely recognizable apart from the weave of what Abbott (1989: 274) calls

> the structure of occupations, the structure of work organizations and the pattern of staffing. These combined before modernity in such a way that the division of products was isomorphic with the relatively permanent partitioning of persons into occupations. Occupations themselves provided whatever social structure was required for work, and, since the division of products was a division of people, staffing was itself isomorphic with the division of products.

Modernity can thus be seen to be premised on processes of differentiation whereby this identity is broken. Task-differentiation implies a differentiation of occupation from organization in the move which Claus Offe (1976) has charted as the shift from task-continuous status organizations to task-discontinuous status organizations. Simply put, when tasks were less differentiated and more likely to be experienced as successive stages in a singular career in which one might achieve mastery of a trade, tasks and skills were more or less coterminous in terms of the managerial hierarchy. In a career as apprentice, journeyman and master one would move up the status ladder as one moved to a greater command of a range of skills. As organizations become more complex in their task structures then it is increasingly unlikely that any one person would have sufficient knowledge of all their processes to be able to control them in an adequate manner, even as they ascend the status order. At the same time, the break-up of the settled enclaves of pre-modernity, in which the ascription and surveillance of relatively fixed identities could flourish in equal measure, together with task-differentiation, made staffing a central problem for modern organizations. Not only did this involve the mapping of types of persons on to types of jobs, it also entailed the supervision and control of their discretion once they were in place (see Clegg and Dunkerley 1980; Clegg 1989b). Organizations became the primary frameworks linking these differentiations. Organizations, in the form of both '[c]ommercial corporations and administrative bureaucracies subdivided traditional tasks, transferring skill from workers to organization charts and relegating simple, repetitive, and laborious tasks to machines' (Abbott 1989: 276). Divisions of products and divisions of tasks no longer coincided nor were they related by any normative community. Instead, relations within organizations were largely constituted in hierarchical forms. Relations between organizations were increasingly mediated through mechanisms of market exchange and state regulation rather than through moral sentiment.

If modernity is characterized by processes of differentiation and their management as a central organizing principle, where does that place the notion of postmodernity? Postmodernity is literally that which comes after modernity. It has been suggested by Lash (1988), in line with the emphasis on differentiation in modernity, that postmodernity may well be premised on de-differentiation. Modernity, as the outcome of modernization, was premised on an increasing functional differentiation of phenomena. Postmodernization and postmodernity, on this account, would be distinguished by a reverse process. Lash (1988) conceives of this process as a blurring of the boundaries between what, under a more modernist impulse, would have been constituted as distinct phenomena. His examples are drawn from the world of culture but they serve to make the general point: de-differentiation is present in the postmodernist refusal to separate the author from his or her work or the audience from the performance; in the postmodernist transgression of the boundary (with no doubt greater or lesser success) between literature and theory, between high and popular culture, between what is properly cultural and what is properly social (Lash 1988: 312). It is for this reason that, in Lash's (1988) words, postmodern practices are premised on de-differentiation.

The management of modernity, in retrospect, appeared to be a straightforward matter. It consisted of devices and practices for managing the key process of differentiation. Born out of the secularization of rules for religious self-surveillance into the workhouses, the prisons, the asylums and eventually the larger factories of the Industrial Revolution, this management was based on supervision conceived literally as superordinate vision (Clegg 1989b: 167–78). Weber's model of bureaucracy merely codified and formalized some general rules for its accomplishment in tandem with the construction of a managerial career distinct from the ownership function. For this reason these earliest examples of management were derived from the public sector where the question of ownership made the issues of stewardship and management more problematic than in small owner-controlled factories. Later prescriptive developments by early management theorists on topics such as 'spans of control' and various approaches such as 'scientific management' augmented the analytical knowledge which Weber had already derived from the public sphere. (Clegg and Dunkerley [1980] discuss these early theorists of management in some detail.)

If an analysis of the management of modernity appears now to be relatively unproblematic, what of postmodernity? If the key feature of this process is the de-differentiation and disassembling of extant forms of the division of labour then this is tantamount to a deconstruction of some, at least, of the bases of modern management. Whatever postmodern management might be, it is unlikely that it would be based on the same organizational practices of differentiation as had been modern management. Recall that the general picture developed by Lash's account is one which characterizes postmodernism by its concern to de-differentiate whatever categorical canons, boundary markers and judgements of taste had been erected by modernism. Now this can cut several ways. Not only does it refer to the management of various mundane practices; it also has some important implications for the ways in which one might conceive of them analytically.

Postmodernism as a phenomenon emerged first in the arenas of architecture, aesthetics and art, and was rapidly seized upon by a number of influential theorists such as Lyotard (1984) and Jameson (1984). Despite widespread disagreement as to what constitutes postmodernism, as Albertsen (1988) discusses, some elements are clearly held in common across different conceptions. Amongst these is an argument concerning the decline of 'grand narratives', a term which Lyotard introduces. Lyotard's argument, very briefly, is that after the horrors of Auschwitz and Stalinism the grand narratives of the past, with their themes of progress, rationality and science, can have no credence. Not only could commandants and commissars enjoy Beethoven and Tchaikovsky as they despatched their horrific duties; the despatch of these was effected precisely through modern rational bureaucracy as their tool. The grand narratives of the past, licensed by Marx, by Science, by Reason, have become discredited as icons of emancipation and enlightenment in much contemporary thought (see Clegg 1989b). With the decline of modernism in practice there has been a decline of modernist theory, with its refrain of the meta-narrative. (Of course, there is always the problem that any account which points this out is itself, by definition, a meta-narrative!)

In organization theory the meta-narratives are many, and several of them will be encountered in this book: contingency determinism by size; the population ecology perspective; transaction cost analysis; and so on. Rather than use any one of these over-arching frameworks as a theoretical frame, something termed the 'modes of rationality' approach will be argued for which seeks to fuse elements of both the 'power' and the 'institutions' perspectives. The focus is on what agents actually do in accomplishing the constitutive work involved in organization.

Some prior assumptions have to be made, of course. Amongst these are a model of what is actually involved in managing and accomplishing organization: some such assumptions seem inescapable if any comparative purpose is to be served. One has to have an implicit conceptualization of what the objects are that one is appropriating. Other assumptions will also explicitly be made. For instance, it will be assumed that people and agencies in and around organizations are knowledgeable actors with a healthy regard for self-conceptions of their own and others' interests. It has already been argued that what they know is not purely idiosyncratic but is institutionally framed. It is because these institutional frameworks vary nationally in crucial areas such as accounting conventions, legal frameworks, occupational and skill formation and interest group association that we are able to identify broad patterns of organizational variation cross-nationally. A further assumption will be made that agencies and actors seek to act on the conceptions that they hold in everyday organizational life, tactics and strategy. They do this through recourse to whatever resources they can garner, within more or less complex situations whose rules will be more or less opaque, shifting, in their or some others' favour. It would not seem unreasonable to make the assumption that most of us, most of the time, are engaged in action with a practical interest in what one may be tempted to term a postulate of pragmatic utilitarianism. Other organizations and other agencies, however, frequently involve and implicate us against whatever terms we may have postulated.

Knowledge of countries whose practices are at the 'leading edge', variously defined, is important. It is from such knowledge that alternative frameworks to our own may derive. We may see the development of different rules and different agencies to those with which we may be familiar. Such differences offer inspiration for learning, guidance and possible feasible future projects for action, under the particular and more or less compatible local conditions which apply in specific national frameworks. Above all they function as powerful political shorthand. For instance, it will be argued that it makes a considerable political difference if, say, Sweden or Japan is held up as an icon of possible and desirable futures. Whether either one of them is a more or less feasible future is, of course, another matter. However, countries do learn, copy and adapt from each other and the major transmission belt for doing these things is their organizational carrying capacities – both public and private.

Modes of rationality, as an analytical construct fabricated out of the available resources, fixed in and through circuits of power and institutional knowledge which agencies find at hand, can be researched in many ways. It may be done through a well constructed questionnaire, a documentary analysis, an organizational biography of elites and others in the picture, through secondary analysis of the data of others, through discourse analysis of multiple accounts of organization realities and so on. It is because modes of rationality are constructed out of whatever materials are found at hand that 'culture' enters into the picture in important ways. It is out of such local cultural resources, amongst other things, that agencies will make what they will. (It should be clear that 'local' in this context indexes not so much the small, the inconsequential and the trivial as much as the close at hand, the available and the particular of the many localities and arenas within which action takes place.) For the same reason forms of institutional regulation through the state and its agencies, through trade unions, occupational and professional associations and so on are also important potential resources. Within these, where discourse and conceptions of interests function as necessary nodal points through which other agencies find they must pass, agencies whose strategic agency is thus secured may fulfil a Promethean role, enrolling other agencies in particular versions of the constitutive canvas upon which representations are stretched and within which they are framed.

Because the perspective that is recommended has a conception of power (Clegg 1989b) at its heart it is able to take on board many of the insights offered by other schools of thought. With institutional theory, for example, it is well aware of the strategic power of myth and ceremony in configuring the fields of force in which organizations operate, in which their managements and other actors seek to secure their agency. With population ecology it is well aware of the competitive pressure that organizations may sometimes operate under and the ways in which these may 'select out' and 'select in' certain organization forms. However, because of the ineradicably political nature of the analytical approach presented here, the argument offers no guarantees about postmodernity. It is a set of possible tendencies with no necessity attached to them.

In current debates, postmodernist aesthetics challenge the basis of existing modernist judgements. The existing differentiation of things into, let us say, the good, the bad and the ugly, is opened up for questioning (Clegg 1988). This questioning may be done through a de-differentiation of the objects of aesthetic or intellectual experience. Such objects may be deconstructed and reconstructed. In addition, the means for making conventional judgements of discrimination may also be questioned. Postmodernism challenges canonical bases for knowledge-discrimination. It opposes the relations of power/knowledge which these embody. Postmodernism is thus subversive of those modern practices which precede it.

A distinction may be drawn between an analysis of postmodernity and postmodern analysis. The latter has been widely disseminated of late through the work of a number of French writers who, in the dynamics of the English-speaking world, have gained considerable intellectual currency in the United Kingdom, the United States and elsewhere. Key journals such as *Theory, Culture and Society* have consciously acted as brokers and clearing houses for some of these ideas. In the analysis of organizations it is in the pages of *Organization Studies* that there has been a concerted attempt to translate some postmodernist theory into terms applicable to organization analysis (for example, Cooper and Burrell 1988). Wholesale importation into a discourse of writers who are icons of postmodernity such as Lyotard, Foucault or Derrida may be appropriate traffic for intellectual entrepreneurship in outlying entrepots of the social science trade. Such trade, however, is not in itself equivalent to an analysis of postmodernity. It does not produce an analysis of postmodern phenomena other than in its reproduction of what are already constituted as existing postmodern intellectuals and ideas.

A different tack may be used to steer a course. The specificity of empirical analysis of postmodernity need not be declined in favour of a generalized appreciation of postmodern theory per se. The contemporary theory of aesthetic debate is a fascinating object in its own right but it is unclear as to what extent its writ runs to the empirical issues canvassed in organization studies. Ultimately, for those of a postmodern sensibility, it would seem imperative to do as this text will seek to do; that is, to connect not only with debates of a similiar conviction but also with the discourse of everyday sites of life. It remains the case, for instance, that even postmodern consumers are dependent on the production of goods and services so signified. Hence, just as no theory of postmodernity can escape attending to the modes of signification within which goods and services are implicated, so it ought not to escape the insight that signification implies both organized signs and signs of organization as well as the organization of signifying sites. Postmodern theory requires a theory of organizational postmodernity.

Two options have been posed in the preceding. At issue is a clear choice about how one might take postmodernity on board in organization studies. The choice is between either a postmodern sociology or a sociology of postmodernity. The former would be an analysis which accepted the practice of postmodernity in aesthetics, in art and in culture as appropriate tenets for social analysis. Such a sociology would be theoretically and practically a self-contained, self-grounded and self-referential discourse. It would be resonant with Lash's (1988) 'figural' sensibility of sensation rather than one which is discursive and interpretative. A sociology of postmodernity would be an analysis of distinctive, emergent and possible postmodern practices.

The choices posed in the preceding paragraph refer to a distinction made by Zygmunt Bauman (1987; 1988a; 1988b; 1989). The distinction proposed is between a postmodern analysis and an analysis of postmodernity. In making the distinction he is arguing for the development of a postmodern sociology. For Bauman (1988b: 217) postmodernity is to be understood only in relation to the category of 'the intellectuals' and the extent to which it connotes their 'new self-awareness'. In Lash's terms, what they are aware of is the de-differentiation of a world built upon the value premises, categories and interpretations available to Western cultural experience. In the sphere of organizations and management these have overwhelmingly been cast in an American self-image of the age. More broadly, in terms of the overall Western project of modernity, such a world was clearly gradated: there were the modern and the pre-modern, the enlightened and the unenlightened, us and them, the civil and the uncivil. The latter parts of the opposition were a category which could be easily located, whether in the working class at home or the primitives, barbarians and savages abroad. The category of 'the other' in this Western scheme of things was a 'pliable, . . . malleable substance still to be given shape' (Bauman 1988b: 220). Such judgements were built on not just an overweening arrogance but also an overwhelming force of domination: of arms, of argument, of aesthetics, of values, conceived under the auspices of the Western project. From such auspices were articulated universal 'standards of truth, judgement and taste' (Bauman 1988b: 220).

Today, no one but 'the most rabid of diehards', in Bauman's (1988b: 220) words, believes in the prospect of universalizing Western rationality. The discourses of legitimation which modernist intellectuals provided have become unimportant (Bauman 1988b: 221; see also 1987). Once the modern world's citadels and categories became omnipotent the traditional role of legitimation which intellectual discourse played was no longer necessary. Thus, to return to the organizations theme, it was once the case that Max Weber's construction of bureaucracy had a paramount moral purpose as well as an analytical one. It helped to play a major part in the construction of an image of bureaucracy and of modern management. Today the heirs of Max Weber have less in the way of a constitutive and legitimating role to play in a wider society, although this has not hindered some aspirants from stating their definitive claims. Intellectuals no longer legislate easily on the meaning of the world; or if they do, hardly anyone takes any notice. Sure, there are a few minor squabbles about the correct order of things but these are just specialist games for a very limited audience. There are too many competing legislations and too few become necessary nodal points of discourse through which traffic must pass. Many fall by the wayside. Most intellectuals today serve mainly to interpret the world, not to make it or change it.

The fate of our times, one might think, would be such as to encourage a profound pluralism with respect to interpretation. Too many examples of practical atrocity and outrage have been committed in the name of too many absolute ideals. While the consequences of the monism which is sometimes attendant upon absolutism are frequently less awful in the sphere of ideas, its occurrence has been no less evident. Monism and tolerance are uneasy bedfellows. Yet pluralism need not mean nihilism: that anything is as good as anything else, that any interpretation will do. Indeed, it is part of the task of this analysis to argue that there are good reasons for choosing between competing representations of the empirical world, in other than an arbitrary legislation.

If one cannot rationally choose between competing representations of the nature of things, then it should not be surprising if the postmodern intellectual world of pluralities and complexities will appear as a crisis of and for modernity. In such situations, intellectuals are 'interpreters' between different lifeworlds, cultures, communities and traditions, as Bauman (1987) suggests. Interpreters simultaneously penetrate and translate between forms of life, giving rise to the articulation not just of a singular rationality but of diverse modes of rationality, *rationalities*. This is as true of cross-cultural research in the cross-national sense as it is in terms of mediating between the cultures of the academy and the everyday world. One thus makes the world more complex as one simultaneously reduces the divisions within which complexity was previously contained.

For all his unrivalled sociological vision and imagination Bauman has one blind spot in an otherwise acute conception of postmodernity. It is contingent upon the view, expressed in the earlier *Memories of Class* (1982), that relations of production are no longer of great analytic concern in the postmodern world: his focus shifts almost exclusively to consumption. In the sense in which conceptions of relations of production have been legislated in various categorical forms, or have been minutely inspected for those signs of crisis which lead not to postmodernity but to postcapitalism, this interpretation is, perhaps, an understandable response. However, in shifting the focus of a sociology of postmodernity almost entirely to a sociology of consumption Bauman (1989) risks missing the postmodern tendencies of the productive world. The task of managing modernity does not simply cease with the shock of the new. Postmodernity requires management. Organization does not simply fade away.

One writer who has used the term 'postmodern organizations' in passing is Wolf Heydebrand (1989: 327). Employing variables for the analysis of organizational form which focus on the size of the labour force, the object of labour, the means of labour, the division of labour, the control of labour and the ownership and control of the organization, a recognizably postmodern type of organization (which Heydebrand actually terms postindustrial) is sketched:

> it would tend to be small or be located in small subunits of larger organizations; its object is typically service or information, if not automated production; its technology is computerized; its division of labour is informal and flexible; and its managerial structure is functionally decentralized, eclectic, and participative, overlapping in many ways with nonmanagerial functions . . . [it] . . . tend[s] to have a postbureaucratic control structure even though prebureaucratic elements such as clanlike personalism, informalism, and corporate culture may be used to integrate an otherwise loosely coupled, centrifugal system. (Heydebrand 1989: 327)

Although the argument which Heydebrand (1989: 339) presents is not explicitly constituted in terms of postmodern tendencies, his conjecture that there are empirical tendencies which suggest '*a shift in the mode of administration* . . . rather than a monotonic continuation or increase in Weber's master trend of rationalization' is entirely consistent with the hypothesis of this study. Unlike a number of recent writers in the European literature Heydebrand does not hypothesize that changes in organization are contingent upon changes in consumption. If he had entertained this idea he would have found that an apparent paradox exists: differentiation and de-differentiation are dialectically intertwined in production and consumption. The postmodern world of consumption is based upon an increasing proliferation of differentiated items of consumption. It is upon this differentiation that the sociologically central processes of claiming 'distinction' and laying claim to elite 'positional goods' depend absolutely (see Bourdieu 1984; Hirsch 1978). Postmodern consumption is premised on an ever greater differentiation of the object-world of consumption. Such differentiation stands in sharp contrast to the modernist world of consumption, when in the era of Fordism you could have any colour car you wanted as long as it was black. Today it is not only colours which are differentiated but also model variations, to a bewildering degree by manufacturers such as Toyota. Yet the basis of this degree of differentiated consumption is a relative de-differentiation in production.

These new objects of consumption, like the more than one hundred models of Toyota, are produced in production practices which would have been unimaginable when all Fords were Model Ts and all Model Ts were black. However, it will be part of the argument of this study that the shift from modernity to postmodernity cannot be contained in a simple shift from a focus on production to a focus on consumption, contra Bauman (1989: 46). Production relations, seen in the envelope of organization, are themselves subject to major change. The changes appear to be in precisely the direction that Lash (1988) has suggested will characterize postmodernity: that is, towards de-differentiation. Differentiation would be reversed. The division of labour would no longer be inexorable.

Up to the present, with the exception of Heydebrand's passing reference, these issues have not been picked up in debates about either postmodernity or organizations. There has been a peculiar blindness. The nearest that debate has come to the matter is the wide discussion of post-Fordism and 'flexible specialization' which has been contingent upon the reception of Sabel (1982) and Piore and Sabel's (1984) work, as well as the important German debates centring on the work of Kern and Schumann (1984a), primarily in industrial sociology and industrial relations theory. These debates are addressed in Chapter 8. Post-Fordism, however, although an integral part of the tendencies that can be hypothesized as the possible postmodernization of organization forms, is only a part of the overall picture. It focuses debate upon the shop-floor, upon production relations proper, but rarely does it do so within the more encompassing framework of an organizational perspective. Nor has it focused to any great extent upon the context of social organization in which post-Fordism has been contained in its most evident example: Japan. In turn, the study of Japan in the broader comparative context of East Asia and other societies in the modern world is in its infancy.

Methodological modernism and postmodernism: objects of analysis

For reasons which are readily understood and just as easily justified, the focus of the sociology of organizations, of organization theory – indeed, of organization studies generally – has been on the *systematically bounded* world of organizations. What Bauman (1989: 53) notes as being true of the consideration of the nation-state in sociology as a whole stands as readily for the conception of organizations in this substantive corner of the social sciences. Organization, conceived in terms of its modernist antecedents, implies a degree of legal and moral normative unity, a single centre of calculation and classification, 'a relatively unambiguous distribution of power and influence, and a setting for action sufficiently uniform for *similar actions* to be expected to bring *similar consequences* for the whole and thus to be interpreted in a similar way'. Moreover, the modernist anchorage of the concept of organization allowed it to be situated in an endless play of determinations between inherent developmental tendencies, self-sustained and self-propelled, inexorably naturalized as being *inside* organization, such as 'size' and 'technology', and those factors *outside*, such as the 'environment', which have a precarious, contingent relation to these interior forces.

It has been clear for a long time that the theoretical conception of an organization as a bounded entity, a totality impervious to its environment, is an inappropriate conception: hence the popularity of the open systems perspective in organization studies. In its forms in the postmodern world organizational sovereignty loses credibility and conviction as a privileged space for economic action. What is most striking about the diverse organizations of East Asia, for instance, is that they rarely contain themselves within the organic form, but disperse through complex relations, of subcontracting, of kinship, of state sponsorship. Perhaps it is the same elsewhere and we just cannot see that it is so, being blinded by our frameworks of and for organization. Consideration of something from an unfamiliar culture can often make apparent what is opaque, even when it is under our nose: indeed, especially when it is under our nose. Part of the point about cross-cultural comparisons is to make the tacit evident. In doing this, however, we may not necessarily be attributing causality to cultural difference per se. It may simply be that cultural comparison is the vehicle for seeing important differences which we might otherwise overlook rather than culture itself being the prime mover behind the difference. Cross-cultural comparison does not necessarily commit one to cultural reductionism in one's arguments.

The 'modernness' of modern organizations resides in the ways in which they may readily be appreciated within a genre of more or less harmonious variations on the theme of Weber's composition of bureaucracy, in which differentiation was a key, although by no means the only, element. To suggest that in some respects organizations in Japan, for instance, might differ from this theme is not to say that they are not recognizably organizations. A postmodern building, such as the Hong Kong and Shanghai Bank in Hong Kong or the Lloyds building in London, is still recognizably a building. So it is with organization form. Postmodern organizations would be ones which, in at least some aspects of their design, find little resonance in either the modernist theory or practice of organizations. Taking Japan as the most materially advanced of the East Asian societies it is appropriate to regard aspects of organization design in this country as a hypothetical test-bed for a thesis of organizational post-modernity.

Before questions of the interpretation of the phenomenon of post-modernity in organizations can be considered the phenomenon itself has to be recognizably constituted as such. For as long as one's apparatus for theoretical cognition remains constituted out of assumptions which are prepostmodern – in a word, modern – then such issues of interpretation can hardly arise. One part of the argument of this book is that modernism is such a restrictive theoretical apparatus if we wish to have ways of seeing postmodern phenomena. Of course, the argument is one of 'theory-dependence'. We will only ever see what it is that our theories enable us to focus upon. All ways of seeing are simultaneously ways of not seeing. In these terms the project of a modernist analysis necessarily excludes at the outset consideration of those phenomena which might discomfit it. Consequently such a project could never be taken as a sufficient basis from which to reject the possibilities of postmodernist forms, as Maurice (1976: 6) has argued in another context. Astute readers will notice a certain 'double-edged' quality to this position. It cuts both ways.

A central question which is at issue in the consideration of Japanese methods of organization is whether or not they prefigure different principles of organization to those which have underlain the modernist representation of organizations. There has been a lively debate developed from both culturalist and economic auspices which suggests that something important and distinctive does characterize this figuration. The only way to address this question is by systematic comparison. That requires an instrument. In Chapter 7, a grid derived by Peter Blunt (1989) functions as such an instrument. (The initial ideas for this grid were developed as a larger number of criteria by Jacques [1989].) The instrument allows consideration of the question of whether or not there is anything distinctive about Japanese management and organization through a wide range of comparisons.

Some important considerations entered into the choice of this grid. It is designed in terms of functional problems. For some readers recourse to the idea that there may be underlying functions which organization has to address will damn whatever else follows. The prejudice against functionalism runs deep. However, it seems to be neither functionalist nor fallacious to propose that the mandators of organizations usually seek to achieve satisfactory resolution of certain basics in pursuit of whatever objectives they pose. The management of organizations is structured around a set of recurrent concerns. Needless to say, recurrent concerns may not necessarily entail endless repetition of the same answers every time and everywhere that they are posed. If it did, there would never be any possibility of competitive advantage accruing to management which differed from extant normative models of conventional practice. Moreover, as this book will argue, conventional practice in some places may not readily be measured against standardized normative metrics derived elsewhere.

At the base of postmodern phenomena, it will be argued, there would need to be the developments of new forms of de-differentiated organization. Such organization might be centred on a concern with 'flexible specialization'. If the postmodernist hypothesis is correct, these forms of organization would stand in direct contrast to the centrality of differentiation to the modernist project. Such postmodern organization phenomena may be viewed as possible sources for future isomorphism in organizational practice. They may become a model which will be widely imitated and diffused. There may well be ecological limits to this process of diffusion. Not all organizational niche-space will be favourable or appropriate for postmodern colonization. Consequently discussions of organizational post-modernity should not be read as a blueprint. For instance, the fact that some contours of postmodernity may be seen in contemporary Japan does not entail that they will find exact mimesis elsewhere. Knowledge *and* power are invariably implicated in the process of translation: this much at least should have passed into everyday currency in organization studies from one possible postmodernist (Foucault 1977; see Clegg 1989b).

One may propose that a postmodern organization studies will not be notably different in its approach, nor perhaps even in its methods, from more orthodox conceptions. Other versions of postmodernity and organization studies would not see it this way at all (for example, Cooper and Burrell 1988). In contrast to these other conceptions the notion of post-modern analysis which this text deploys is quite different. It proposes not so much to shock sensibilities reared in the good taste of modernist conventions as to augment them. Rather than constructing a distinctive postmodern organization studies on the basis simply of analytical style, one might instead be engaged in developing a study of postmodernist organization and management practice. To do so would be to engage in that sociology of postmodernity which Bauman (1989: 61) has seen as 'deploying a strategy of systemic, rational discourse to the task of con-structing a theoretical model of postmodern society in its own right, rather than a distorted form, or an aberration from another system'. There would be a primary difference between the objects of analysis of this sociology of organizational postmodernity and the past sociology of modernity. Postmodern organization, unlike that of modernity, is not containable within the system of the organizational form. The organization as such may not be a framework which is sufficient to capture the totality of economic action as it is organized under postmodern conditions. As Bauman (1989: 62) has said: 'This circumstance makes the task particularly complex; the reality to be modelled is, both in its present shape and in its plausible prospects, much more fluid, heterogeneous and "under-patterned" than anything the sociologists tried to grasp intellectually in the past.'

Not only is this reality less patterned; it is truly more contingent on the possibilities of political will, imagination and force. Postmodern management can be about choice. These choices do not appear to be epochal with respect to modernist themes. It is doubtful that postmodern organization will in any way transcend, overcome or annihilate previous forms. Indeed, it is improbable that any past can be so readily shrugged off. It would be most unlikely that the immediate future of postmodernism will be contiguous with postcapitalism. Even the most committed 'periodizers' such as Jameson (1984) do not go so far as to suggest that. Yet the choices that are available are not unimportant with respect to management of many of the particulars of most people's everyday worklife, matters of the capacity for skill formation, for community, for control. There are no guarantees, however. Postmodernity may well turn out in ways which serve to cramp rather than enhance capacities. Postmodernity is not a prognosis nor a prediction but it does seem to index some human possibilities. Against the rationalizing tendencies of recent modernity such small considerations may not go amiss.

Postmodern futures

Contrary to some people's hopes and some other people's fears, it will be argued that Japan is not the *necessary* vision of all our postmodern futures. It certainly is one possible and one highly successful route but it is not the only way. For instance, it will be argued towards the close of the book that there may well be some alternative routes which build upon the European traditions of social democracy and extended citizenship rather than the more restricted basis which is evident in Japan. A plausible argument can be mounted which suggests that a thoroughgoing postmodernization of organizations would not be focused solely on the de-differentiation of relations in production or organizations. It would also have to embrace relations of production and organization. Some will no doubt see in this the last gasp of an exhausted and *passé* modernist impulse, attributable to the socialist project which derived from Marx and focused on overcoming the divisions in and of labour as well as between labour and capital. Perhaps such an interpretation will occur anyway but it should not be imagined that this text is *intended* as a contribution to what, in the mainstream extensions of this project, have become wholly discredited Russian Bolshevik or Chinese Maoist experiments. (See the debates which have occurred between Clegg and Higgins [1987; 1989] and Shenkar [1984; 1989] in the pages of *Organization Studies*.) On the contrary. The traditions which are drawn on are quite different and, at the time of writing, seem capable of breathing new life into the discarded political husks of the Bolshevik shell in Eastern Europe. At their heart are expanded conceptions of what citizenship entails: not only political and civil rights but also economic rights vested in the world of work and organizations.

There are substantive examples and pointers towards an alternative organizational postmodernity which do not derive from Eastern Europe or mainland China. They come from a range of countries and practices developed within them, including Australia, Germany and Sweden. Some recent discussion of Swedish debates and events has suggested that these are evident signs of the death throes of organizational modernism (as Lash and Urry [1987] seem to suggest) rather than the development of anything which is particularly new (as Clegg and Higgins [1987] have suggested). It would be unfortunate if this were the case. Much of value would be jettisoned in consequence. What has characterized debates in Sweden is a political sharpness and a clarity of focus which have been singularly lacking in many other national contexts. In this book Sweden and Japan may be taken to stand for possible outer limits of alternative conceptions of prosperous postmodernist futures. This is not to deny that there may well be others, but these are the ones focused on here.

One important contribution which organization studies can make as an international field of enquiry is to facilitate translation between diverse 'outer limits' to understanding. What these outer limits entail is a task in which 'translation' is uppermost (Bauman 1989). Perhaps the most pressing task for such a sociology applied to the study of organizations will be to focus upon previously untranslated organizational forms. These are particularly evident issues with respect to the English-speaking reception of what 'Japan' and its organization and management entail. While it is not the case that Japan remains untranslated (or inscrutable, as it were), many of the translations appear to be marred by severe error and problems of comprehension: in a word, mistranslation. In particular, one thinks of the too-frequent recourse to accounts of Japan couched excessively in terms of a unique cultural difference as the locus of explanation. Moreover, the implications of Japan have not often been considered in the context of a text intended for use in courses in organization studies. Consideration may be given within a specifically Japanese or a broader context: not only that of other East Asian economies but also an appreciation of the responses to modernity of people elsewhere. It is one aspect of the distinctiveness of this text to approach that task of translation in such a broader context.

Conclusion

This book is not a minutely detailed and densely layered work, full of intense technical accomplishment. Such books will always have a central place and at the side of such masterworks the composition presented here may well seem slight. Yet, while this is a small book, it is one which seeks to paint a big picture with broad brush strokes, as befits a large topic. Necessarily it touches on many points which require greater elaboration than are allowed by the confines of this text. Nor by any means does it present an overview of everything there is to know about organization studies. Much of value and of interest has had to be sidelined for reasons of thematic development. There is a theme and that theme has both allowed and necessitated selectivity. In this respect it is less a normal textbook – one which blends all points of view – and much more one which has a definite argument to make. Finally, it would be disingenuous to pretend that no axe was ground in the honing of the argument. All arguments risk causing offence, and there is no reason to think that this is an exception. Indeed, I am sure it is not.

2

Organizations and the Modernization of the World

This chapter considers what has become a classic thesis in social science. It is one which inexorably links modernity and organization through the argument that modernity could only be accomplished by organization(s). Writers as diverse as Marx, Durkheim and Weber were in agreement on this much. While their views will be briefly considered, it should be clear that it was neither Marx nor Durkheim who did most to advance the thesis. The idea was to achieve its greatest specificity and most general diffusion through the reception and interpretation of Max Weber's work. Consequently, the bulk of this chapter is spent discussing Weber.

When Weber's work achieved wider diffusion in English after the Second World War it was not only in translation but also in the context of a subsequent series of independent empirical studies which qualified aspects of Weber's thesis. In Weber, it appeared as if the appropriate organization form for modernity was one which was rational, where 'rational' was given a quite precise definition. On the basis of some post-war landmarks in the analysis of organizations it can be argued that Weber's thesis was overdrawn. The following chapter will demonstrate that this overdrawn representation, one which seeks to equate rationality and efficiency in determinate and limited ways, has continued to prefigure the ground of much contemporary organization analysis. Consequently the classical scope of this thesis has been narrowed down somewhat into an argument which seeks to prescribe the limited organizational forms which modernity might adopt.

Modernity and organization

Sociology was conceived as that discipline which sought to understand the contours of modernity as they appeared in the nineteenth century. Invariably, modernity was understood as the history and future trajectory of a single process of modernization. Even as the process was recognized, disagreement existed as to what constituted its singularity. From these diverse nineteenth century representations modernism took intellectual shape.

Marx and Durkheim represent two significant reactions to moderniz-ation from within intellectually contrasting but sophisticated modernist positions. For Marx (1976) modernization meant the advance and eventual overcoming of capitalism as a dominant world-wide mode of production. In Marx's (1968) youthful writings, at least, this entailed overcoming the division of labour which earlier writers such as Smith (1961) saw as the very essence of capitalist rationality. Implicitly, the future fully modernist society would be characterized by simple organization structures, multi-skilled individuals, an absence of hierarchy and high degrees of job rotation.

Durkheim (1964) foresaw an increasing division of labour in societies. It was chiefly from this factor that his scenario of modernist organization, with a tendency to the 'over-development' of the division of labour, was developed. One consequence of this was what he saw as a potentially morally hazardous increase in the differentiation of available social identities. Differentiation was organizationally generated and contingent upon the relationship constructed between two key variables. These were the degree of marketization of social life, together with its political incorporation within authoritative, hierarchical forms. Thus, both hierarchy and com-plexity would characterize organizational modernity for Durkheim, as market society. Compared to Marx, Durkheim's (1957; 1964) view of modernization, although it stressed a process which was still economically embedded, conceptualized it as far less economically contained. Con-sequently, Durkheim focused on what he saw as the consequences for social disorganization of the extreme development of the division of labour (see Clegg and Dunkerley 1980: ch. 1).

Irrespective of their particular vision, what all the major nineteenth century social theorists shared was a similar 'universalistic' conception of modernization leading to modernity. The similarity of their views resided in their depiction of the imagined future. It was seen as being one in which there would be a 'gradual obliteration of cultural and social differences in favour of an increasingly broad participation of everyone in one and the same general model of modernity' (Touraine 1988: 443). The model was defined differently in each case, though always through similar processes of 'applying the general principles of reason to the conduct of human affairs' (Touraine 1988: 443). For most of these theorists the importance of 'organization' as purposeful goal-oriented action, encapsulated within routine, recurrent reproduction of social action, social relations and social structures (which we typically term 'complex organizations'), remained an implicit mechanism of social change. This would be as true of Marx's concern with the revolutionary impetus of changing productive forces and production relations as it would be of Durkheim's moral concern with the increasing differentiation of labour and identity in the modern world.

Organization as a process and organizations as an object of analysis are more or less implicit themes in the writings of the 'founding fathers' of sociology such as Comte, St Simon, Durkheim and Marx (as has been argued in detail elsewhere: Clegg and Dunkerley 1980). Despite the fact that they were undoubted witnesses to the birth of modernity, their work was not widely used to construct foundations for the systematic study of organizations as one of the cornerstones of modernity. Such distinction was to be granted to Max Weber's scattered observations on the nature of bureaucracy, on economic life more generally and on the role of the 'Protestant ethic' in facilitating the 'spirit of capitalism', work which became adopted as a foundation of the rigorous study of organizations (Weber 1948; 1976; 1978).

Max Weber and the analysis of organizations

Weber had evidently not intended to found a specialist field of organization studies: his comparative concerns were much wider than organizations per se. They ranged over a dazzling array of sources, questions and issues pertaining to the understanding of the major world-cultures and their relation to secular, rational modernity as these were expressed in the major world religions. None the less, when, in the 1950s, a number of scholars followed the traces of pioneers such as Philip Selznick (1943; 1948) and Robert Merton (1940) to begin the systematic sociological study of organizations as formal, complex constructions of human ingenuity, it was to the recently translated works of Weber (1947; 1948) that they turned. These were researchers such as Peter Blau (1955; 1956), Alvin Gouldner (1954) and Amitai Etzioni (1961).

There were other sources: for instance, the more pragmatic 'formal theories of administration' developed by consultants, engineers and successful managers such as Chester Barnard (1938) in the United States (see Perrow 1986) and Henri Fayol (1949) in Europe (see Clegg and Dunkerley 1980). In addition there was the body of work indelibly associated with Elton Mayo's (1933; 1975) critique of the 'industrial civilization' that had been constructed in the individualistic image initially developed for American industry by Frederick Winslow Taylor (1911) and subsequently picked up throughout the Western world (Maier 1970; Clegg and Dunkerley 1980; Braverman 1974; Littler 1982; Dunford 1988). This critique spawned a body of work which became known as 'human relations theory', work which stressed the importance of informal social organization within formal organization.

These and other sources were of considerable theoretical and practical importance. However, none of them shared the same academic status or distinction, the same honour, as did the much more intellectually demanding work of Max Weber. Indeed, it was in part the sheer magisterial quality, the depth of scholarship and the breadth of vision in his work which first attracted scholars who wished to differentiate their intellectual work from the far more mundane concerns of a Fayol or the instrumental visions of a Mayo.

As far as the analysis of organizations was concerned a process of selective attention occurred with respect to Weber's work as a whole. His broad-ranging concerns came to be increasingly interpreted far more narrowly by later organization theory. In this way he was constituted as a precursor of this field, as one of its legitimate forebears. It is hardly surprising: intellectual seed, once sown, may reap many a strange fruit.

Once constituted as a legitimate forebear, Weber could be seen to have

> analysed three general types of organizations stemming from the bases of wielding authority, and drew attention to the fact that in modern society the bureaucratic type has become dominant because, he considered, of its greater technical efficiency. In doing so he formed the starting point of a series of sociological studies designed to examine the nature and functioning of bureaucracy, and particularly to draw attention to the dysfunctions of this structural form which were left out of the original analysis. (Pugh 1971: 13)

It is not so much that this account is wrong in its focus on efficiency. There is no shortage of similar interpretation in the literature. Such interpretation is clearly selective in its focus, as Albrow (1970: 63) argues. Weber's evident insights were pressed into service in the context of a discipline which had neither framed nor generated them. The process was not inexplicable. It involved (to use a term which Weber [1976] derived from chemistry, via Goethe) an 'elective affinity'. Simply put, the notion of elective affinity means in this context that aspects of the two distinct discursive strands of Weber's sociology and the systematic study of organizations were sympathetic to each other. Arguments in one resonated with arguments in another. What was constituted as Weber's sociological vision and what became focused as the more efficiency oriented concerns of the burgeoning field of organization theory interpenetrated each other.

On Weber's side the affinity derived from his 'cultural pessimism'. From this perspective the 'rationalization of the world' would, he anticipated, produce for modernity a bureaucratic 'iron cage of bondage'. Organizations would become an essential and inescapable feature of whatever pathway modernity was to tread, whether it marched to an explicitly socialist or capitalist drum. This prognosis became incorporated into aspects of contemporary organization theory as it searched for factors which contributed to the efficiency of organizational design. It seemed that it was not so much organizations (in the plural) that constituted modernity, but that a particular form of organization would increasingly and inexorably become definitive.

'Modernity', the 'capacity to respond to a changing environment and to manage complex systems' (Touraine 1988: 452), and 'organization' were set on a fateful convergence, whereby a specific conception of the latter became the essence of the former. It was not to be a purely formal concept of organization as any means for achieving purposeful, recurrent and routine action, but a substantive concept which was to carry quite explicit values and meaning in its definition. To the extent that the capacity which is modernity becomes identified with a specific form of organization, then the nineteenth century Enlightenment project of imposing general laws of reason is implicitly adopted – albeit in a changed form.

It is worth recalling just what the Enlightenment project entailed, in particular for those who were deemed too ignorant to know that they ought to submit to what is inevitable. It might be said that such people were those who could be regarded as anthropologically estranged from the normative universe of the nineteenth century. Above all this was a universe defined in terms of conceptions of reason held by Europeans, by males, by the governing classes. Excluded from this definition, in general, were non-Europeans, however civilized they might appear to be; indigenous peoples in the world's wilderness areas; the industrial working classes at home, as well as the majority of women in toto. Literally, it meant the destruction of any claims to a form of life on terms other than those which were ascendant. At one extreme this frequently entailed something close to genocide (of the 'savages' of the Americas, Africa, Asia, Oceania and Australasia). Closely related to the destruction of these peoples was the attempted remaking of other 'exotic' cultures in a subordinate mould: not only the annihilation of indigenous peoples but also the loss of their languages and their land – cultural genocide. The armoury of moral reform could just as easily be targeted at the 'savages' abroad, as colonial subjects, as it could be at those indigenous aliens who took the form of the working classes at home. The same missionaries could be despatched to the East End of London with as much fervour as accompanied their adventures in East Africa. Alternatively, forms of life could be subject to a process of 'ghettoization' within the universe of the victorious civil society, such as the location of women in the bourgeois home.

Such destruction was not an explicit part of Weber's project. Weber's acute sociological vision was more closely focused than the preceding characterization of the implications of the Enlightenment project, even if it shared some of the same focus. The focus was not on gross annihilation but on the rationalization out of existence of less 'rational' forms of life. What was involved was a limiting of the social world of modernity, a narrowing down of the possible modes of existence. It is from this perspective that the elimination of difference can best be seen through the metaphor of 'the iron cage of bureaucracy'.

The iron cage of bureaucracy

In Weber's view the advent of modernity saw the 'discipline' of bureaucracy encroaching into almost every sphere of life. The cause of this encroachment was the irresistible spread of bureaucracy in the twentieth century. What made this advance inexorable was its 'purely technical superiority over any other forms of organization' (Weber 1948: 214). In many respects Weber regarded bureaucracy with a highly sceptical eye.

While it was indeed technically superior to other forms of administration it was still a human product. Yet, in his view, its humanity was fatefully compromised by its technical functioning. Although the efficient bureaucracy was a human creation it was one over which control was rapidly lost. What was unleashed was a human creation which could turn and devour the humanity that had produced it, as the following passage, taken from a speech Weber made late in his life, clearly suggests:

> Already now, rational calculation is manifested at every stage. By it, the performance of each individual worker is mathematically measured, each man becomes a little cog in the machine and aware of this, his one preoccupation is whether he can become a bigger cog . . . it is horrible to think that the world could one day be filled with these little cogs, little men clinging to little jobs, and striving towards bigger ones . . . this passion for bureaucracy is enough to drive one to despair. (Weber, in Mayer 1956: 127)

In Weber's view bureaucracy is to be regarded almost as if it were a scientific creation which has turned and devoured its human creators. Rational calculation has become a monstrous machine. All significations of humanity, those 'relationships which are important to us due to their connections with our values' (Weber 1949: 76), are devoured and denatured by this triumph of human ingenuity. What are left are 'cogs' as its chronicler despaired.

A common romantic myth of the nineteenth century had it that scientific ingenuity and creativity would unwittingly invite their self-destruction. The products of imagination turning on their producer was a popular theme for an age equally impressed by and anxious about the scope of scientific achievement. The myth is best known today in the form which Mary Shelley (1969) recorded as *Frankenstein*. Dr Frankenstein, a scientist obsessed with the creation of a technically perfect form of human being, creates an all too fallible creature. It is one which resembles humanity, but imperfectly so. Finally the creature turns in revenge and tragedy upon its creator and destroys him. An underlying theme of the story is clear. Nothing, it seems, can save us from the forces which rationality has unleashed.

Weber is in some respects replaying aspects of this myth, but with an important difference. No final act of revenge will be exacted by the technical form upon its human makers: instead, humanity will become ever more captive in the thrall and bondage of technical perfection. As Haferkamp (1987: 31) reminds us, for Weber bureaucracy was regarded as 'necessary', 'unavoidable', 'unstoppable', 'inescapable', 'universal' and simply 'unbreakable' (Weber 1920: 3f, 203ff; 1958: 318ff). It is these adjectives which serve to display Weber's 'cultural pessimism', in the simply irresistible but utterly unattractive face of the 'fate of our times'.

In the name of reason the nineteenth century saw an attempt to impose a philosophy of progress upon the world at large, and thus remake it in one image. The late twentieth century version of this tragedy differs markedly both from Weber's metaphorical entrapment and enveloping myth as well as from the viciousness of the civilizing process which imposed it upon recalcitrant subjects. However, as we shall see, within organization theory today there are some highly influential currents which would analytically annihilate the possibilities of variety in contemporary forms of organizational life. The elimination proposed will once more take place in the name of efficiency and effectiveness (Donaldson 1985a). It might just as well nail the flag of 'cultural pessimism' to its mast – at least, if it did, it would display the true colours of its genesis.

It has been suggested by Grumley (1988) that the work of Max Weber represents what is probably *the* most impressive intellectual attempt to come to terms with the sudden transition from pre-modernity to modernity. It was launched under particular conditions, those of Germany's national formation in and through the experiences of modernization, unification, industrialization and secularization. In Weber's work it is the theme of *rationalization* which threads these disparate experiences into a number of interlocking, contingent processes whose outcome is modernity as we have defined it: the capacity to respond to changing environments and to manage the complexity that this entails.

At the core of this modernist capacity was a unifying rationalistic principle. This principle could be seen in the rationalization of various institutional arenas such as the market, technology, law, the state. It could be seen in various general processes, such as the increasing depersonalization of social relations, particularly in work, the increasing importance of specialization for modern life and the concomitant intellectualization of all realms of knowledge, especially culture and scientific and religious life. The major mechanism of its transmission was the increasing differentiation of spheres of existence and of phenomena within them. What was wreaking these transformations as modernity was the growing pervasiveness of rational calculation in all spheres of life. It was this pervasiveness which created that phenomenon identified by Weber as the 'de-enchantment' or 'disenchantment' of the world. What he meant by these terms was a process whereby enchantment was stripped away from everyday life and belief. This was achieved through a progressive loss of faith in the unseen but enchanted movers of the human drama which had been provided by folk beliefs and by superstitions as well as by organized religions. These were not the only sources of enchantment, nor was it merely a historical phenomenon. In Weber's view contemporary parties organized on the basis of a putative universalizing 'historical subject', such as the proletariat, were captive to a more modern form of enchantment.

Disenchantment meant an end to ultimate values and to sacred meanings, together with an exposure to a world in which meaningfulness was never 'given' but had to be struggled for, had to be secured, even against the resistance of others. Only the rare charismatic leader, whose personal grace, sense of calling, duty and devotion to some ultimate ideal was unshakable, would in the future be able to impose this meaning on life. Even this would not smash the 'iron cage' of 'victorious capitalism', resting on 'mechanical foundations' (Weber 1976: 181–2) but merely make it meaningful for an efficient bureaucracy and a subordinated mass. Adrift from the meaningful frame of such superhuman powers more lowly beings could only hope to live their lives bereft of meaning, trapped within the iron cage of their increasingly rationalized, bureaucratized existence, wrenched from their traditional forms of life by the irresistible pull of modernity. In this way modernity was coeval with disenchantment: it was the latter which grounded the capacities for rational action of the former. Rational action consisted precisely in the capacity to respond to the new uncertainties of a world without meaning. The modern world was, by definition, an age of uncertainty. This applied equally whether or not the political system was totalitarian or democratic, the economy socialist or capitalist. Hence, the siren of rationality, in Weber's interpretation, would be the likely clarion call whatever the socio-economic and political system.

Uncertainty both defined and limited freedom. It defined freedom through posing the existential and environmental conditions under which rational action was possible. It limited freedom by imposing an ethic of calculation, as a totally objective rationality, upon this freedom to act. Henceforth, one could only ever hope to master uncertainty through the experience of modernity, yet this very experience of modernity entailed a loss of freedom as one submitted to the constraints of rationality. It also entailed a loss of faith: as one became free of the old dogmas one became condemned to the absence of any authoritative basis for one's life other than rationality itself. That rationality, if it was doing its work properly, would see to it that no other citadels of ultimate value could rise above itself in the mentality which it was crafting. The achievement of this rationality was to involve a profound emptying and opening up of the human condition as it battled to confront the nihilism of modernity. The process was always double-edged: new possibilities for cultural construction in all spheres of knowledge, now unyoked from dogma, were made available, yet no one of these could reunify the cultural spheres which had been liberated, because of the necessity of rationality, a constant witness against any new architects of domination.

In Weber's view rationality had only a limited number of sources. It might derive from those individuals who were forced to confront the world and choose how to impose value and meaning upon it. The world did not already confront such people as if it were set in concrete. It was not experienced as if it were resolutely, unyieldingly, already absolutely and unbreakably cast in a mould. There were precious few such people in Weber's vision, other than the charismatics and leaders, the 'Caesarists'. Most other people, one will recall, were trapped within the iron cage. On the other hand it is precisely this iron cage which is the instrumental, disciplined repository of rationality. The unfreedom of the many within the organizational apparatuses of modernity was the necessary foundation of the rationality and freedom for action of the few, a freedom and rationality achieved through the instrumentality of bureaucracy.

The iron cage is not only a prison but also a principle. As a principle it 'makes us free' to be modern. It makes us free because it is only through the purposefulness and goal directedness of organization that the uncertainties of disenchanted modernity could be coped with. Uncertainties were no longer explicable in terms of the enchanted but unseen, the knowing but unknown, the controlling but uncontrollable fates of divines, demons and devils – the bulwarks of those individual beliefs held against the uncertainties of an enchanted age. In Weber's view it would be only false prophets who would insist otherwise. Rational calculation would limit uncertainty to a world which was, in principle, manageable.

The freedom of modernity, experienced in the loss of entrapment within received meaning, is not something which is merely one-dimensional, something wholly positive. It is also something simultaneously experienced negatively – as a loss of freedom to organizational and rational constraint. For the foreseeable future, irrespective of the political values with which modernity was infused, Weber argued that 'the fate of our times' was such that the reproduction of this modernity was absolutely dependent upon the existence of vast public and private sector bureaucracies. The very existence of these would act as a further deepening of the rationalistic principle. Although large economic organizations would demand greater specialization within bureaucracy, this would not create greater individuality. Rational discipline would permeate all authoritative relations of modernity. The rise of the professional expert would greatly restrict the scope for individualism in any guise. 'Specialists without spirit', as the new breed of organization expert, yoked together with bureaucratic cogs, epitomized the future organizational trajectory of modernity for Weber. Its tracks were clear. Organizational servants would be required to subordinate personality to impersonal, objective rules and functions. Work was a sentence of bondage for prisoners in a vast mechanism and chain of command. To work was to be organized rationally, to obey prescriptions laid down from above and to meet the functional requirements of a system determined by objective, calculable rules for optimal performance, precisely as Grumley (1988: 30) describes it.

The variable tendencies of bureaucracy

Bureaucracy, for Weber, was a mode of organization. The concept of organization was such that it subsumed such differing substantive entities as the state, the political party, the church or sect and the firm. The defining characteristic of an organization was the presence of a leader and an administrative staff. These persons were ordered into specific types of social relationship, depending upon the type of rule to which action was oriented in the organization in question. Weber termed these rules 'the order of the organization', which he based upon different types of authority.

He contrasted three 'ideal types' of authority which were based upon: the ruler's charisma; the rule of tradition; and the rule of rational, legal precepts. An example of charismatic authority would be the special relationship claimed between, for instance, Christ and the disciples. Here the obedience of the disciples is premised upon the extraordinary grace and magnetism of Christ's personality. Weber regarded what he called the routinization of charisma as a particular problem. Where rule was based on charismatic authority there was always the problem of succession. How would the rule be maintained in the absence of the charismatic leader? Should the charismatic leader die, or be disgraced, how would the authority and rule of the order, the organization established, be maintained? Weber suggested that this routinization of charisma could take place in one of two ways. It might take place through the setting up of a traditional form of rule. Such traditional rule might be based upon notions of lineage and primogeniture, for instance: the idea that the extraordinary grace of the leader was passed down to the first born child, or more usually the first born son. These notions obviously sustained the traditional legality and the traditional rationality of kingship in much of European history down to the present day. Alternatively, and most powerfully, Weber believed, rule could be routinized through reference to rational legal precepts, bodies of abstract law, governing the social relations. In the long term he believed that this mode of routinization would be most prevalent. A prime example of this would be the modern state.

In an organization, whatever bases of order it might have, the administrative staff have a dual relationship to this order. On the one hand the behaviour of the administrative staff is regulated by rules; on the other hand it is the task of the ruling body to see that other members also adhere to the rules of the organization. These rules comprise an order governing the organization to which members are subject, by virtue of their orientation towards it:

> The validity of an order means more than the existence of a uniformity of social action determined by custom or self interest. The content of a social relationship will be called an order if the conduct is, approximately or on the average, oriented towards determinable maxims. Only then will an order be called valid if the orientation to all these maxims occurs among other reasons because it is in some appreciable way regarded by the actor as in some way obligatory or exemplary for him. (Weber 1968: 31)

Weber suggests that the reason why actors orient their actions to a similarly defined order is because their individual enactments are guided by collectively recognized rules. An order is not merely a form of codification of conventional and legal rules, but the existence of a dominant set of social rules more generally. Different types of rule exist in different orders to which one orients one's behaviour. They will thus afford differential probability that different types of command, under differing conditions of rule, will be obeyed. Such command will be authorized and made legitimate by reference to the rule. Submission to these rules would normally be called submission to authority. Different forms of belief in the legitimacy of authority are associated with different authority structures and hence with different organizational forms.

The most important of these from the point of view of contemporary analysis would be a situation in which people obey orders because they believe that the person giving the order is acting in accordance with the duties stipulated in a code of legal rules and regulations. Five related beliefs support such a claim. Following Albrow (1970: 43) we can summarize these in an abbreviated form as the following:

1 that a legal code can be established which can claim obedience from members of the organization;
2 that the law is a system of abstract rules; these rules are applied to particular cases, and administration looks after the interests of the organization within the limits of the law;
3 that the person exercising authority also obeys this impersonal order;
4 that only as a member does a member obey the law;
5 that obedience is due not to the person who holds authority but to the impersonal order which has granted the person this position.

Bureaucracy was not a distinctively modern phenomenon, yet Weber (1948: 204) argued that it existed 'in ever purer forms in the modern European states and, increasingly, all public corporations since the time of princely absolution'. Prior to this what had characterized the absolutist state were forms of patrimonial bureaucracy premised on patrimonial authority or domination. Weber thought that modern bureaucratic organization formulated on rational legal precepts was capable of sweeping other forms of organization before it: 'The decisive reason for the advancement of bureaucratic organization has always been its purely technical superiority over any other form of organization' (Weber 1948: 214).

The emergence of this modern bureaucratic form of organization rationality is not accidental. It is a necessary feature of modernity. 'The peculiarity of modern culture, and specifically of its technical and economic basis, demands this very "calculability" of results':

Today it is primarily the capitalist market economy which demands the official business of the administration be discharged precisely, unambiguously, continuously, and with as much speed as possible. Normally, the very large modern capitalist enterprises are themselves unequalled modes of strict bureaucratic organization. Business management throughout rests on increasing precision, steadiness and above all, the speed of *operations* . . . Bureaucratization offers above all the optimum possibility for carrying through the principle of specializing administrative functions according to purely objective considerations. Individual performances are allocated to functionaries who have specialized training and who by practice learn more and more. The 'objective' discharge of business primarily means a discharge of business according to calculable rules and without regard for persons. (Weber 1948: 215)

In his book *General Economic History* (1923) Weber enumerated what he took to be the peculiarity of modern culture. Its organizing principle is the existence of a capitalist market economy. Central to this are a number of factors. These include the existence of a 'formally free' labour force; the appropriation and concentration of the physical means of production as disposable private property; the representation of share rights in organizations and property ownership; and the 'rationalization' of various institutional areas such as the market, technology and the law. In particular, rationalization of the market depends upon the existence of an economic surplus and its exchange in monetary terms. Markets are the historical product not of reason but of might: 'money prices are the product of conflicts of interest and compromise' (Weber 1948: 211).

The outcome of this process of rationalization, Weber suggests, is the production of a new type of person shaped by the dictates of modern bureaucracy. Such a person, whether in business, government or education, is one with a restricted, delimited type of personality. Characteristically, this is the specialist, the technical expert who increasingly, Weber feels, will come to replace the ideal of the cultivated person of past civilizations.

Weber argues that rationalization is a process which affects almost all aspects of social life. Two notions of rationality are distinguished. First, means–end relationships, which are referred to as formal rationality. Formal rationality involves the attainment of definitely given and practical ends through increasingly precise calculation of means adequate to the achievement of those ends. The focus of this means–end rationality is very much on the means. The end itself is taken as given, as something which requires no explanation in its own right. The end, for instance, may be a religious or mystical end, or it might be genocide in concentration camps. Whatever ends may be served they could still be achieved in terms of rational calculable means.

Weber offers a second conception of rationality, which he terms 'substantive rationality'. This is the kind of rationalization that a systematic thinker performs on the image of the world: the increasingly theoretical mastery of reality by means of increasingly precise and abstract concepts. It was this aspect which we have seen Weber refer to as the de-enchantment or disenchantment of the world. It is the process whereby all forms of magical, mystical, traditional explanation are stripped away from the world. The world is laid bare, open and amenable to the calculations of technical reason. However, calculable means are connected to given ends. As Weber put it:

It is not sufficient to consider only the purely formal fact that calculations are being made on grounds of expediency by the methods which are amongst those available technically the most nearly adequate. In addition it is necessary to take account of the fact that economic activity is oriented to ultimate ends of some kind: whether they be ethical, political, utilitarian, hedonistic, the attainment of social distinction, of social equality, or of anything else. Substantive rationality cannot be measured in terms of formal calculation alone, but also involves a relation to the absolute values or to the content of the particular ends to which it is oriented. (Weber 1947: 185)

The 'absolute values' which Weber focuses on, in particular, were those which, he argued, initially sanctified capitalist activity, the religious values of Calvinism, especially the stress on 'this-worldly' asceticism (Weber 1976). However, he anticipated that ultimate values would be in inexorable decline with the advent of modernity, in large part because the 'calculability' of formal rationality progressively erodes values from the world. Such belief systems would no longer be necessary to sustain the technical rationality of contemporary life:

Since asceticism undertook to remodel the world and to work out its ideals in the world, material goods have gained an increasing and finally an inexorable power over the lives of men [sic] as at no previous period in history. Today the spirit of religious asceticism – whether finally, who knows? – has escaped from the cage. But victorious capitalism, since it rests on mechanical foundations, needs its support no longer. The rosy blush of its laughing heir, the Enlightenment, seems also to be irretrievably fading, and the idea of duty in one's calling prowls about in our lives like the ghost of dead religious beliefs. (Weber 1976: 181–2)

Clearly Weber was not a naive or unqualified proponent of bureaucratic rationality. However, he did not believe that despair in itself would be sufficient to see bureaucracy overcome. This was because of Weber's view of bureaucracy as an instrument or tool of unrivalled technical superiority. In consequence, given this instrumental nature, it was unlikely that despair could be turned to any alternative, more productive, channel.

In the political arena this theory of bureaucracy works itself out in the following terms. The political leader is engaged in a struggle for power. Such a person should serve ultimate values, ultimate ends (although this cannot be guaranteed with the rationalization of politics). In order to exercise power in the pursuit of such ultimate values the political leader must be able to call upon a reliable administrative staff as an instrument of authority. This involves a bureaucracy. Members of this bureaucracy must prove themselves by impartial performance, while political leadership proves itself in the competition for votes during elections and in heroic performances in the legislature. From such performances come the ultimate ends and larger policies which the bureaucrat has to serve in drafting the calculable means for the attainment of the politically sanctioned ends. Ideally, then, the bureaucratic organization as a whole is a simple tool in the hands of the political masters. It makes no difference in this conception whether the master is an elected president, a ministerial cabinet or a despot.

Weber was aware that such an ideal was rarely attained in practice. In reality, tensions are generated which condition the attainment of the ideal. The major tension is what we may refer to (after the British television series) as the 'Yes Minister' syndrome. The power position of the bureaucracy based on expert knowledge constitutes a major source of countervailing power to that of the political master. Such political mastery is premised in part on those sources and resources which the bureaucracy enables access to. Restricting access to these resources can always be justified by skilful bureaucrats through recourse to the rhetoric of secrecy, often under the format of technical or legal rationality itself, for instance an 'official secrets act'. Against this, political masters can try to control a bureaucracy by juggling internal struggles between bureaucrats, promoting this person, favouring that person, exploiting the competition for promotion which can enable them to control recalcitrance with the help of antagonistic colleagues.

Just as Weber discerned an ambivalence between political power, in the terms of leadership, and bureaucratic relations, so he discerned a similar tension between bureaucratic relations and democracy. To the extent that bureaucracy achieved formally rational means in terms of its own recruitment and administration through impersonal examination of formally free persons equipped with credentials and diplomas (what Wilson [1983] has referred to as the functional or scalar aspects of bureaucracy), then bureaucracy would seem to propose a certain degree of democracy in society. At this level one could argue that bureaucratization induces democratization. However, one could also argue the contrary. Insistence on credentials indirectly favours all of those who have the material means to undertake long periods of study in order that such credentials may be gained. In this respect it may be more accurate to characterize processes of bureaucratization as leading to meritocratization rather than democratization. Weber believed that democracy in any form of administration can only be achieved when the organization in question is of a sufficiently small size that the mechanisms of direct democracy can function. This would involve: a minimal division of labour so that administrative tasks can easily be assumed; little differentiation between the members of the organization; and a strong ethical commitment to the values of the organization. At the base of the bureaucracy are its members' beliefs in the legitimacy of its existence, its protocols, its personnel and its policies. Given these beliefs, and serving to reproduce them, there will exist a specifically bureaucratic form of administration and organization which is bureaucracy. It would be defined most precisely in terms of a number of tendencies.

1   Task discontinuity is achieved by functional specialization. Tasks are specific, distinct and done by different formal categories of personnel

who specialize in these tasks and not in others. These official tasks would be organized on a continuous regulated basis in order to ensure the smooth flow of work between the discontinuous elements in its organization: thus, there is a tendency towards *specialization*.

2   The functional separation of tasks means that the personnel charged with their despatch must have a level of authority and sanction available to them which is commensurate with their duties: thus, there is a tendency towards the *authorization* of organizational action.

3   Because tasks are functionally separated, and because the personnel charged with each function have precisely delegated powers, there has to be some relation of hierarchy between these: thus, there is a tendency towards *hierarchization*.

4   The delegation of powers is expressed in terms of precise contracts of employment which specify duties, rights, obligations and responsibilities: thus, there is a tendency towards a *contractualization* of organizational relationships.

5   Because officials are appointed on the basis of a contract, one which specifies what the qualities demanded for the job are, there is a tendency towards the specification of organizational qualities in terms of qualifications measured by formal credentials: thus, there is a tendency towards *credentialization* in organizations.

6   Differentially stratified credentials are required in order to enter different positions in the hierarchy of offices; thus, there is a career structure and promotion is possible either by seniority or by merit of service by individuals with similar credentials, depending on the judgement of superiors made according to the rules. Without the appropriate credentials one cannot be promoted to the next rung in the hierarchy: thus, there is a tendency towards *careerization* (striving to be bigger cogs in the machine) within organizations.

7   Different positions in the hierarchy are differentially paid and otherwise rewarded, with pensions, superannuation rights, travel allowances and so on. Thus there is a tendency towards a process of status differentiation in organizations. We may term this a process of *stratification* in organizations.

8   The hierarchy is clearly expressed in specific rights of control by superordinates, as well as specific powers to resist improper attempts at control on the part of subordinates: thus, there is a tendency towards a specific *configuration* of authority within the structure.

9   Functional separation, task-discontinuity and hierarchical relations require that the actual work of the organization and its superintendence should be formally rule-bound, either technically or legally, such that the rules can be followed without regard for persons; that is, without fear of offence. The rules serve to justify and produce legitimate action: consequently, there is a tendency towards *formalization* of rules in organizations.

10   The formality of rules requires that administration must be based on

files of written documents. Thus, the office, where these files are held and where they may be consulted by those with the right to do so, is the hub of the organization. A consequence of this is that organizational action assumes a standardized form – a tendency towards *standardization*.

11 The relationships in the organization are not just hierarchical. The centrality of the office develops communication, co-ordination and control which are routed through the hub: consequently, there is a tendency towards *centralization*.

12 Legitimate action within bureaucracy requires a sharp boundary between what is bureaucratic action and what is particularistic action by personnel. Thus, it is a requisite that the resources of the bureaucracy must be maintained as something quite separate from those which belong to and can be utilized by the members of the bureaucracy in their private capacity: thus there is a tendency towards the *legitimization* of organizational action.

13 Power belongs to the office and is not a function of the office holder. Office holders are bearers of powers which they cannot appropriate personally: thus, there is a tendency towards *officialization* of organizational action.

14 Because powers are exercised in terms of the office rather than the person there is a tendency towards *impersonalization* of organizational action.

15 This impersonalization occurs according to disciplinary systems of knowledge, both organizationally developed and adopted from external professional bodies of knowledge: thus, there is a tendency towards a *disciplinization* of organizational action.

Each of the fifteen tendencies of bureaucracy has been represented as a variable; that is, there may be more or less of a given process in any specific organization (for empirical instances of this in organization analysis see the work of writers such as Hall [1962; 1963], Hall, Haas and Johnson [1967], Pugh and Hickson [1976] and Hage [1965; Hage and Aiken 1970]). For instance, universities may tend to place a greater degree of emphasis upon the process of credentialization of personnel than may some other organizations less concerned with the categorization of knowledge per se. Weber (1978) used the notion of an 'ideal type' to capture this sense of a variable quality, by 'freezing' the qualities of bureaucracy in an idealized representation, one which provisionally alerts us to the kinds of empirical phenomena that we would expect to find if the organization in question had bureaucratic tendencies. As it has been put elsewhere, 'such types consciously and expressly accentuate value-relevant aspects of reality in an artificial model which serves as an interpretative and explanatory scheme' (Clegg and Dunkerley 1980: 38). However, rendering the central typical elements as processual variables provides one with a clearer idea of what Weber thought was important than does a precise reiteration of the type itself. Taken together, these processes represent his view of how the world will be turned into a complex of iron cages.

Loosening the iron cage

Weber's views have been deservedly influential, but require considerable revision in a number of respects. First, when empirical researchers began to study organizations using the Weberian ideal type of bureaucracy as their guide they quickly found that in the real world of modernity, rather than in Weber's theorization of it, bureaucratic tendencies did not always come together in a complete rational-legal package. One interpretation of Weber's model might have suggested that it was a guide for ideal practice. This would be one which proposed an obvious, if erroneous, interpretation of what an 'ideal type' is: that it is a model for perfect practice. We will briefly consider some of the more significant examples of bureaucratic practice which research discovered to be less than perfect.

Blau and Scott

Research by Blau and Scott (1963) suggested that it would make a difference to the way that one would think about organizations if one asked the question for whom were they rational, or 'who benefits' from them. It is not at all clear who would benefit from the 'iron cage' model of bureaucracy, except where there was a Caesarist, charismatic head of the organization. In circumstances other than these one has the feeling that nobody in particular would benefit from the tendencies towards bureaucratization once they were on the treadmill, inside the 'iron cage'.

In raising the issue of 'who benefits' Blau and Scott (1963) suggested that it was important to distinguish at least four categories of people who had an interest in any organization. These were the owners or managers of the organization; ordinary members in non-executive positions in the organization; clients, customers, inmates, suppliers of the organization – the 'public-in-contact' as they suggested that they be called; and the 'public-at-large' – the members of the society in which the organization was situated. Using these categories of beneficiaries or rationally interested actors they were able to come up with a schema which differentiated between, respectively, business concerns, mutual-benefit associations, service organizations and commonwealth organizations (Blau and Scott 1963: 43). The interests of the rationally committed actors will differ markedly in each case. While businessmen may be overwhelmingly committed to effectiveness and might decide that some of the strategies of the Weberian tendencies to bureaucratization were important to their achievement of this, it is unlikely that a mutual-benefit organization will agree with regard to variables such as impersonalization or hierarchization.

The business executive concerned to produce an efficient instrument for making a business profitable could well adopt these as adjuncts to business efficiency, while for the members of a co-operative of some kind these values would be anathema. They would tend to undermine the very point of their organization being as it is.

Etzioni

Organizations may serve different values. Not all values will be conducive to the hastening of bureaucratization. Some will be directly opposed. This point is underlined by Etzioni's (1961) revisions to the singular ideal type of bureaucracy. Weber does not address the question of compliance, of why members of a bureaucracy will submit to it, other than through recognizing that they may have few practical alternatives other than doing so. Given that Weber saw little alternative to bureaucratic organization there was no need to explore this issue, by definition. It was anticipated that only this one type would really exist under conditions of modernity. However, Etzioni (1961) enquires into both the nature of motivation in organizations, that is the type of involvement that people might bring to bear in their organizational life, as well as the different types of power that organizations might exercise over their members. The latter were something which Weber did consider in detail, focusing on the use of what we might now call 'disciplinary power' (Foucault 1977), the development of the whole organization as an apparatus of control and surveillance.

Etzioni seems to recognize that people might be persuaded to do things in organizations for at least three fairly basic types of motive. They might comply with organizational discipline for love, fear or money. These are termed normative, coercive and remunerative bases of power, deploying symbolic, physical or material means respectively. For example, a novitiate in a convent might submit to a regime of organizational discipline because of a love of God; a prisoner in a penitentiary might submit to the discipline of the chain-gang because of a fear of the jailer; while an industrial worker might submit to the discipline of the production line because of the incentive of the wages system which will reward effort in doing so. In each case the involvement will differ: for the novitiate it will be moral; for the prisoner it will, he says, be alienative; while for the worker it will be calculative. Etzioni believes that, typically, there tends to be a balance between involvement and power, so that coercive–alienative, remunerative–calculative and normative–moral couplings will be those which are most frequently encountered empirically.

On the basis of a cross-tabulation one would anticipate nine possible couplings. Balance would be achieved across the diagonal axis (1, 5, 9): see Table 2.1. (One aspect of Etzioni's having set up the contrasts in this way should be noted. By definition, any employee of any organization will tend to have a calculative involvement. As wage earners this is not surprising. However, there is also a tradition, deriving from Marxism, which tends to see wage earners as typically alienated workers, because they are waged employees, by contrast to a self-employed craftsman. However, in Etzioni's schema it will not be wage earners who are normally alienated but people who are in some way incarcerated against their will in coercive organizations such as prisons. This effectively cuts the legs out from under the Marxist critique of alienation [see Gamble and Walton 1973] because normally the involvement of the worker in work will be calculative: alienation becomes something which inmates of institutions such as the penal system will experience rather than employees of organizations. Whether this is a good or bad thing is not at issue: instead, one is simply pointing out what the implications are of seeing things this way.)

Table 2.1   *Kinds of power; kinds of involvement*

Kinds of power	Alienative	Calculative	Moral
Coercive	1	2	3
Remunerative	4	5	6
Normative	7	8	9

Source: Etzioni 1961: 2

Etzioni suggests that where we encounter balance in the way suggested by the diagonal axis then we will find more effective organizations; where we encounter substantively different organizations which belong to the same type then we would expect these organizations to be more like each other than organizations of other types. Organizations with 'similar compliance structures tend to have similar goals, and organizations that have similar goals tend to have similar compliance structures', suggests Etzioni (1961: 71). Moreover, there is a strain towards consistency according to Etzioni (1961: 14): 'organizations tend to shift their compliance structure from incongruent to congruent types and organizations which have congruent compliance structures tend to resist factors pushing them towards incongruent compliance structures'. It should be added that Etzioni (1975) was subsequently to adduce a considerable amount of evidence in support of his central propositions. Although they have been subject to some criticisms in the literature (for example, Allen 1975; Clegg and Dunkerley 1980: 145–56), these criticisms have not been empirical so much as theoretical. As Hall, Haas and Johnson (1966) show, the compliance typology stands up quite well to empirical scrutiny.

If the development of these typologies by Etzioni and Blau and Scott demonstrates that Weber's fears about the erosion of value under the conditions of modernity have not been realized, because there clearly are sensibly defined populations of organizations which, because of their value-basis, do not display the tendencies to bureaucratization in the heightened form which Weber had anticipated, then it is apparent that modernity is not the one-dimensional cultural experience which Weber predicted. The same point was to be made much later, incidentally, in Rothschild-Whitt's (1979) typological construct of 'collectivist organizations'. There remains more than one basis for organizing a response to a changing environment in order to manage complex systems, particularly where ultimate values come into play.

Merton and Selznick

An additional reservation against Weber's pessimistic thesis was also struck by some other research. Even organizations which strove for bureaucracy were not necessarily going to be efficient and effective. For instance, Merton (1940) demonstrated how executive pressure for reliability and predictability in the actions of organizational members would lead to considerable tendencies towards formalization and standardization. Members of the organization under such conditions would tend to become strict rule-followers, deploying a small range of specialized responses to whatever issues confront them. However, while this may ensure legitimacy of action for members, there may also be costs. Rigidity could come to characterize responses to new issues or challenges in the environment of the organization. Organization members may become locked into a self-reinforcing cycle of increasingly inappropriate actions, in the context of new questions or issues which might have arisen. From the point of view of the members, however, protecting the legitimacy of their actions, the repetition of standardized and formalized responses may be wholly appropriate. They cannot be sanctioned for following the rules, even if the consequences of doing so are catastrophic for their employing organization!

One way to try and produce a more responsive organization is to slacken tendencies to centralization, hierarchy and status-discrimination by seeking to devolve power and responsibility through delegation. There may well be costs in doing this in 'normal' decision-making circumstances, such as a shortage of time. Other consequences may follow. Selznick (1943) demonstrated that increasing the amount of delegation in an organization typically tends to increase the degree of both specialization and credentialization. This contributes to an organizational 'bifurcation of interests', as delegates develop their own agendas and goals rather than a commitment to the organization as a whole. He was subsequently to call this 'the problem of recalcitrance' (Selznick 1949) in organizations. Members of organizations, for whatever reasons, may not be compliant delegates of executive authority. Consequently, delegation means that considerable effort has to be spent on legitimizing those actions which the executive wishes organizationally to approve. As a corollary, just as much effort will have to be made on de-legitimizing delegate actions which are not executively desired.

Hage

It is clear from this brief consideration of the principles of bureaucracy, via the means of some classic studies, that the tendencies which Weber identified as those of bureaucratization do not necessarily always 'hang together'. They are not necessarily strongly inter-correlated nor internally consistent under all the contingent circumstances which organizations might face. This insight was seized upon by Jerald Hage (1965) in his 'axiomatic' theory of organizations. He chose to concentrate upon four central organization principles or tendencies and to relate them to four others, with the division between the two groups of four being premised upon the distinction between means and ends. The four means which he identified were conceptualized in terms of specialization (or complexity), centralization (or hierarchy of authority), formalization (or standardization) and stratification. One can see how easily these means could be derived from the list of tendencies identified in Weber. (It is not necessary to go into the definition of these in any complexity because their meaning is fairly self-evident. In addition, as well as Hage [1965], one may also consult the account in Clegg and Dunkerley [1980: 191–6].) The means which are chosen are seen to relate to the achievement of four ends, or organizational goals. These are defined in terms of adaptiveness (or flexibility), production, efficiency and job satisfaction. On this basis, assuming that the organization can be treated as if it were a 'closed system', immune to disturbances from outside, Hage is able to generate a number of testable propositions such as 'the higher the stratification, the lower the job satisfaction' (Hage 1965: 300). These demonstrate very clearly the trade-offs involved in implementing the full bureaucratization package. While intensifying one variable may be functional for some other variables, for yet others it may at the same time be dysfunctional. For instance, while high stratification is proposed to be inversely related to job satisfaction, it is also proposed that it is related positively to productivity. Bureaucratization as a whole may well be internally contradictory.

Although Hage's assumption concerning the closure of the organizational system may well make good sense as an analytic strategy, it is undoubtedly unrealistic as an empirical description of the majority of organizations which one is likely to encounter. Even in the most 'total' of institutions (Goffman 1959), such as a maximum security prison, it is extremely difficult to achieve total closure of the organization from the environmental conditions in which it is located. Moreover, these environmental conditions of the organization are of considerable importance, as a great deal of research in organization theory has demonstrated.

Burns and Stalker

While something approximating Weber's bureaucratic tendencies might be appropriate for some circumstances it would hardly be appropriate for others. Organizations may well attempt to achieve a degree of 'closure' on their boundaries, trying to 'shut out' disturbing or disequilibrating inputs from outside their domain, as Thompson (1967) argued. They might strive for rationality even when they are aware of the impossibility of achieving this closure. In an 'environmental' context in which the organization rarely met any phenomena that it could not readily process and deal with, according to rule, this striving for rationality might be highly effective. A predictable and relatively certain organizational environment could be handled by a relatively predictable and bureaucratic organization design. Such a design was termed 'mechanistic' by Burns and Stalker (1961). It corresponded to an organization which displayed relatively little openness to its environment. Where this was not characterized by high levels of change and uncertainty, where things were stable and rarely changed, this lack of openness might not matter. Under more turbulent circumstances the relationship between a closed structure and a more fluid environment would matter considerably.

Mechanistic organizations in stable environments, while not altogether closed, were able to operate with a relatively predictable and accurate model of the environment in which they operated. It was the nature of the environment in which they functioned which was important for the structure of the organizations. Those which operated in stable environments were able to develop highly bureaucratized structures – structures which Burns and Stalker found empirically in their study of the Scottish electronics industry. However, in the same industry they found a very different organization structure, which they termed 'organic'. Such organization structures were far less bureaucratized. Initially they were interested in explaining why it was that some firms were more successful than others. Eventually, an organizational explanation suggested itself. The crux of their explanation was that in different contexts different types of structure may be more or less appropriate. Those firms which operated in traditional markets, with traditional products, such that very little uncertainty surrounded the conditions under which the bureaucratic structure operated, were found to have a 'goodness of fit' between their structure and their environmental conditions. A bureaucratic structure and a predictable, relatively invariant environment seemed to 'hang' together. However, not every firm in the Scottish electronics industry displayed these characteristics. Moreover, those which were not heavily characterized by bureaucratic tendencies were not necessarily less efficient than those that were. On the contrary, it seemed as if these organizations were, in fact, highly effective, given the nature of their environment. Burns and Stalker (1961) termed these organization structures 'organic'; they differentiated these from the more bureaucratized structure which they termed 'mechanistic'.

The organic structure was seen to be most appropriate where the environment was constantly generating new questions, new problems and new issues. It was characterized by relatively low specialization, formalization, centralization, stratification and hierarchization within the organization. It tended to develop a more collegial structure, built on the common credential basis of the members, fostered by rewarding collective involvements and orientations rather than the more narrowly specialist and by recognizing the negotiated quality of problem and task structures. This occurred in firms which, unlike those with a characteristically mechanistic structure, were involved in extensive R & D in the electronics industry. It was interesting that these firms had not been 'designed' this way: often they had formally designated elements of a bureaucratic structure but they chose not to activate them. Organic structures dealt more effectively with uncertain and problematic environments.

Gouldner and Blau

One aspect of Weber's theoretical perspective was the resolutely 'interpretivist' basis of his approach. Bureaucratic rules were always something that the person oriented towards in Weber's framework. One researcher who particularly developed this aspect of Weber's work was Alvin Gouldner (1954). He focused on the emphasis on 'rules' in Weber, particularly the fact that rules always have to be interpreted and enacted by the members of organizations if they are to have any meaning. In doing this he made the important point that although the 'objective' structure of the rules may remain the same, what those rules might actually mean depends greatly on the context of their enactment. By focusing on questions such as who usually initiates the rules, whose values legitimate the rules, and whose values are violated by the rules being breached or enforced, he was able to distinguish three different 'patterns of bureaucracy'.

Where none of the protagonists within an organization, such as management and labour, accept the legitimacy of the rules which some third, external party seeks to impose upon them, then Gouldner suggests that this should be considered to be a 'mock bureaucracy' one in which no group of members either enforces or accepts the legitimacy of the rules, thus entailing not only a degree of collusion between members but also low levels of conflict. Empirically, such a situation might be encountered where an external authority sought to impose a safety-rule, for instance, which involved wearing uncomfortable safety gear. Another pattern of bureaucracy which also generates little overt conflict (although there may be some tension) is what Gouldner terms a 'representative bureaucracy'. Here, all parties to the organization accept not only the legitimacy of the rules, but also the legitimacy of managements imposing and workers accepting them. This is in marked contrast to the 'punishment-centred' bureaucracy. Here the rules are enforced by either one party or the other, that is by either management or the workers, while the other party seeks to avoid them. Not surprisingly, such a situation generates considerable tension and conflict. Ordinarily this is resolved by punitive action on the part of one or other of the parties, which the sanctioning party typically regards as legitimate while those sanctioned typically do not. Gouldner's stress on the meaning of the rules demonstrates clearly that the same objective bureaucracy may mean something different to, and thus be enacted as something different by, different people in different contexts at different times. Thus, changes in the environment or changes in personnel, particularly at a senior executive level, may transform the nature of the rules as a meaningful phenomenon and thus dramatically change the tendencies and the type of bureaucratization, as Gouldner (1954) explores with great verve.

Gouldner (1957) was later to explore a further aspect of bureaucracy as a meaningful phenomenon: that different types of members of an organization may hold quite different conceptions of their roles in it as a result of their different specialization and credentialization. These are not processes of interpretation which differ over time, as patterns of bureaucracy, but coexist as different orientations to the organization at the same time. The very processes of bureaucratization may have the seeds of internal incoherence built into them. This is a thesis which Gouldner explores by reference to the roles of 'cosmopolitans' and 'locals' within organizations: the former being the professionals who typically have a cross-cutting orientation towards their wider professional culture, while the latter are the bureaucrats whose careers are more closely focused upon their progression within their particular organization rather than within the wider professional community.

While Burns and Stalker (1961) suggest that too much bureaucratization may well be ineffective in particular environmental conditions, Gouldner (1954) demonstrates the importance of context more generally, when seen through the orientations of the members of the organization. Blau (1955) also focuses on the orientations that members of organizations have towards the rules of the bureaucracy. In the two governmental agencies which he researched Blau found that the organizations were more efficient when the members of the organization were consciously breaking, rather than following, the rules. Where they created an organization which was more decentralized, less hierarchized and less formalized, it functioned more efficiently, particularly where certain preconditions had been established. These included employment security, a developed degree of both careerization and credentialization, coupled with a standardized results-based evaluation system, as well as de-stratification towards a more collegial form. Not only are such organizations likely to be more efficient, according to Blau, they are also less conflictual.

Conclusion

Through the simple expedient of looking at some landmarks in organization studies which developed aspects of Weber's thought, we have been able to see that his pessimism concerning the necessary rationalization and bureaucratization of the modern world was misplaced, even in terms of his own system of concepts. They do not form a systematic, coherent package. Rather, they are a set of tendencies capable of accentuation in many possible ways (indeed, much as one might expect of an ideal type). They are not as easily conceptualized as a necessary correlate of modernity as might appear at first glance. Consequently, much of Weber's tragic vision relating to the iron cage of bureaucracy can be seen to be misplaced.

Rationalized, bureaucratized organization is not necessarily the most efficient, according to the findings of some classic studies. It appears as if plenty of scope remains for creativity and imagination. However, as we shall see in Chapter 3, these findings have not succeeded in dispelling that persistent pessimism which has been noted in Weber's foundations for organization theory. The latter, in an influential and sophisticated version, has irrevocably tied modernity to a particular concept of modernization, one carried by a particular substantive rationality of organizations, which Weber identified as the 'fate of our times'.

3

Why and Where did Bureaucracy Triumph?

Touraine (1988) captures a central and pervasive aspect of the understanding of modernity: it is a complex system embedded in a dynamic environment. The image is one of some body or entity seeking to create order out of the chaos of complexity. The ideas were first developed in the realms of natural science, particularly in biology (von Bertalanffy 1968). As a social scientific metaphor for modernity nowhere has this image received a more elaborated development than in the application of 'general systems theory' to the analysis of organizations.

General systems theory was introduced into organization studies in the decade after the initial exploration of Weber's ideas. Hence, its innovatory phase was the decade stretching from the mid-1950s to the mid-1960s, when writers like Boulding (1956), Katz and Kahn (1966) and, above all, Thompson (1967) developed the notion that an organization was like an 'open system'. The central idea was that organizations would attempt to create order in their own image by imposing 'organization' on themselves and their environments. Differentiating themselves and their processes from the environment which surrounded them, they would attempt to create their own specific boundedness through strategies designed to interiorize order. For instance, organizations would 'buffer' their core technologies by separating them from other functions of the firm. Subunits could be set up inside the organization which specialized in handling extraneous sources of 'uncertainty'. They would seek to 'absorb' and 'reduce' this uncertainty by being 'boundary-spanning' units whose function was to link organizations to their environments, leaving the technical core relatively free from extraneous influence except as it was organizationally 'smoothed' and processed. In other words, production could be left to the job of making things. An important aspect of organization would then consist in trying to smooth out uncertain demand schedules, obtained from the environment of customers, by locating a sales force in a separate marketing unit in order to regularize and routinize demand. Ideally, this would be achieved sufficiently so as to deal with exterior sources of disorder. Such an order could only ever be expected to be provisional, rather than complete, due to the inherent flexibility required by organizational behaviour when confronted with multiple and complex environmental sources of uncertainty.

Organizations conceptualized as systems

In the systems framework the organization is conceptualized as having a definite boundary through which flow environmental inputs and outputs. It strives to maintain this boundary in order to ensure its own distinctive survival as an entity. The entity is composed of a number of system components which exist together in a state of dynamic interdependency, processing throughputs and reflexively monitoring their environment through the re-entry of outputs as new inputs, a process known as feedback.

Systems ideas are now so much a part of the modernist consciousness that they barely require elaborate iteration (see Morgan 1986). Not only did they produce a major reconceptualization of organizations striving for orderliness in an otherwise chaotic world; they also successfully reinterpreted the past development of organization theory. Reading backwards from an open systems perspective, much earlier conceptions could now be interpreted as an excessively internalist and closed system account of organization structure and processes.

The ideal type of bureaucracy, with its affinities with early managerial and mechanistic approaches to organizations in writers like Taylor (1911) and Barnard (1938), could now be regarded as an example of a flawed closed systems approach to the analysis of organizations. Rather than conceptualizing the openness of the organization to the environment as a necessary corollary of its existence, these earlier theorizations had assumed that organization boundaries were fixed. What went on outside the organization was unimportant compared to the ability of those in positions of authority inside organizations to manipulate internal characteristics, such as employee morale, motivation and teamwork (Mayo 1975), in order favourably to affect output variables like productivity.

The open systems framework allowed for a far more dynamic conceptualization of organizations. A closed system, whether it be conceived as an organization or a machine, does not monitor and respond to the environment. By contrast, it is the very essence of an open system to do this. Its openness consists precisely in the capacity to import resources and energies from the environment, in order to use them for the benefit of the internal system. Open systems are inherently adaptive: like biological organisms their adaptive capacity is to be thought of in terms of the processes of differentiation and specialization whereby organisms evolve in changing environments.

Two of the key processual variables from the Weberian model, specialization and differentiation, could now be thought of within the framework provided by evolutionary biology and ecology. Organizations were just like other organic entities. The root metaphor triumphed. A new organicism was born in which the preservation of organic equilibrium and the maintenance of boundaries were the central drives for organization systems. However, because no organization can ever be a closed system, organic growth and survival require that boundary-spanning occur in order to secure resources; partly in consequence of this, different elements of the organization's internal system will be more or less functionally specialized on either internal or environmental processes and monitoring. The more environmentally oriented they are one would anticipate that the more 'loosely coupled' they will be vis-à-vis other elements of the organization system (Weick 1979). Complex organizations are thus characterized by the variable coupling of their sub-system elements.

One of the great advantages of this reconceptualization was that it easily avoided one of the substantive problems which the typological approach to organizations had encountered. To the extent that a specific substantive feature of organizations, such as rule-use or beneficiaries, was the basis for categorization then the population of organization types was always potentially incomplete. New bases for typologization were always empirically possible or could theoretically suggest themselves. By contrast, systems theory operated at a level of abstraction and generality such that the substantive qualities of specific organizations were of less conceptual importance. All organizations could now be conceptualized as creating structures and patterns of behaviour which enjoyed relative stability, were slow to change and could cope successfully with the uncertainties posed by environments, following Simon's (1957) and March and Simon's (1958) stress on organizations as the embodiment of pragmatic, bounded rationality. In this way common properties of organizations, irrespective of function, could be highlighted. Different functional types of organization which dealt with different types of environment might adopt similar patterns of behaviour to deal with them. A high degree of uncertainty in the environment, for instance, might lead to a reinforcement of credentialization and specialization as strategies for dealing with it. It only remained for the actual process of organization work to be de-substantivized, something achieved by thinking of it as the reduction of uncertainty. (Weick's [1979] stress on 'organizing' as the reduction of 'equivocality' is the classic case.) Now any organization could be abstractly compared with any other. On the one hand were its patterns of behaviour, built up out of the variable expression of Weber's tendencies to bureaucratization, supplemented from time to time by processes produced by new insights; on the other hand were more or less uncertain environments. Connecting them were system flows of inputs, throughputs, outputs and feedback. These were conceptualized as the sources of change in the patterns of organizational behaviour.

Scott (1981) has noted how a distinction made by Gouldner (1959) could be said to have overlain the historical construction of what was, by the

1960s, a burgeoning field of organization theory. The distinction was between 'rational' and 'natural' conceptions of organizations as systems. The 'rational system model' is one which 'views the organization as a structure of manipulable parts' (Gouldner 1959: 405), while the 'natural system model' is one which regards the organization as a 'natural whole', in which, irrespective of 'the plans of their creators', organizations 'become ends in themselves and possess their own distinctive needs which have to be satisfied. Once established, organizations tend to generate new ends which constrain the manner in which the nominal groups can be pursued' (Gouldner 1959: 405). While the rational model is an instrumental view, one which regarded organizations as human tools capable of more or less appropriate design for different purposes, the natural conception is altogether more organic: organizations are to be seen not so much as humanly shaped tools but as creatures with their own attributes and vitalism. As such, organizations conceived of as natural systems are likely to be regarded as primarily oriented towards a singular formal rationality, hierarchy, planning, impersonality, goals or efficiency, rather than to a plurality of modes of substantive rationalities, alliances, strategies, persons, needs or futures.

In terms of systems representations, early writers on organizations were overwhelmingly 'closed' and 'rational' theorists, whether they were sociologists like Weber (1978), management consultants like Fayol (1949) or engineers like Taylor (1911). From the 1930s until about the late 1950s the focus of analysis shifted towards conceptions of the organization as an evolving natural organism. It was one which was seen as having its own emergent properties, such as informal groups, which develop within the formally rational structure and which could be tapped into in order to increase the efficiency of the organization (Mayo 1975). The iron cage could now seemingly be made to reproduce its bondage from the only freedoms it contained: the freedom of informal group processes to flourish within it.

Inside the iron cage, enmeshed by unavoidable contingencies

The Aston studies

The iron cage of bureaucracy could have been built out of any of fifteen possible dimensions in terms of the earlier characterization of Weber's theoretical tendencies to bureaucratization. Actually, a lot less were used. In the early 1960s, using an open systems model, a number of researchers began to think systematically about Weber's variables and their relative weight in the structuring of organizations. Some went one stage further and commenced applying their systematic thought to the collection and analysis of empirical data describing organization structure. The most influential of these empirical studies of organization structures were what became known as the 'Aston studies' (Pugh and Hickson 1976). These studies derived their name from the place in which they were conducted: the University of Aston, located adjacent to the city centre of Birmingham in the West Midlands region of England.

The fifteen possible dimensions of organization structure located in Weber's variables were not all explored in the empirical study. Preliminary research by the Aston team suggested that organization structure was likely to be built out of just five of the dimensions: specialization, standardization, formalization, centralization and configuration, defined as follows.

> *Specialization*: the degree of division into specialized roles.
> *Standardization*: the degree of standard rules and procedures.
> *Formalization*: the degree of written instructions and procedures.
> *Centralization*: the degree of decision-making authority at the top.
> *Configuration*: long versus short chains of command and role structures, and percentages of 'supportive' personnel. (Pugh 1988: 128)

These variables were to be the key building blocks for one of the major landmarks in organization analysis. Intensive study of the prior theoretical literature on organizations as well as exploratory fieldwork carried out in a number of organizations in the immediate West Midlands region were the catalyst for its production. This remarkable research project has been elaborated at length in a collection of four monographs which contain all the major findings (see Pugh and Hickson 1976; Pugh and Hinings 1976; Pugh and Payne 1977; Hickson and McMillan 1981). In addition, Donaldson (1986a), in a paper which subjects the Aston data bank to re-analysis, is a useful source for the great many comparative studies which have been developed from the original research. (The project as a whole has been subject to 'cogently comprehensive' critique by Starbuck [1981], as Pugh [1988] suggests. An alternative critique may be found in Clegg and Dunkerley [1980].)

These five structural variables, arrived at from Weber's fifteen tendencies, and much more besides, were empirically derived from a far wider pool of hypothetical structural properties of organizations, and collected from a representative random sample of forty-six work organizations, stratified by size and product or purpose (Standard Industrial Classification) from the total population of West Midlands employing organizations. It was found that these five structural variables displayed certain consistent inter-correlations, or dimensions, which have been replicated many times, in many samples, derived from many countries (Donaldson 1986a). These dimensions were as follows.

- *Structuring of activities*: specialization, standardization and formalization are all highly related. Collectively, this package of correlationally consistent interrelationships was termed structuring of activities. It was found that this dimension was primarily related to the size of the organization, and secondarily to the degree of routinization of its technology. The larger the organization, defined in terms of the number of employees who were contracted to it in a stable employment relation, the more specialist, standardized and formalized it would be – in other words, the more highly structured its activities would be. These tendencies would be exacerbated particularly where the technology of the organization was highly routinized in terms of automation and integration.

- *Concentration of authority*: centralization is negatively related to specialization. This relationship is summarized by a single structural dimension called 'concentration of authority', a measure which increases as the dependency of an organization upon other organizations increases.

- *Line control of workflow*: this was a factor which comprised the percentage of superordinates and the degree of formalization and standardization of procedures concerning personnel decisions. Organizations with less routinized technologies tended to have a higher line control of the workflow.

The Aston studies found that size was the major determinant of these central features of organizational structure, a finding which has gained considerable support from other research programmes (for example, Blau and Schoenherr 1971). In particular it was found that larger organizations had their activities more highly structured; that is, they were more specialized, more formalized and more standardized than smaller organizations, although there was no strong relationship between size and either the concentration of authority or the line control of workflow.

Some informed commentators have questioned the central findings. On the basis of path-analysis of the original Aston data Aldrich (1972) suggests that the relationship with size is in fact more likely to be one with highly automated and integrated technology. The argument is that the technology leads to a requirement for a higher structuring of activities. The Aston researchers concede the importance of technology for structuring the 'technical core' of organizations – the work around the main technologically structured workflow – but reject its causal importance elsewhere. In doing this they are breaking quite sharply with an earlier tradition of organization theory established by Joan Woodward (1958; 1965; 1970).

Woodward

In the mid-1950s Joan Woodward studied about eighty industrial organizations in the south-east of England, mostly quite small firms compared to the range which the Aston researchers were subsequently to sample.

Whereas Woodward had few firms with over 1,000 employees (seventeen to be precise), the sample size of the Aston research was as high as 25,000 employees, with the smallest being 300. This discrepancy in the size of the units sampled probably had a great deal to do with the relative weight which each set of researchers was to ascribe to technology in the determination of organization structure (Hickson, Pugh and Pheysey 1969). Woodward found that the structural differences which the Aston researchers were to identify in terms of formalization, differentiation, centralization and concentration of authority formed a consistent pattern when the sample of organizations were grouped according to the pattern of their technologies as one or other of three groups:

1   Unit or small batch production, where the organizations make small runs of specially commissioned or designed articles.
2   Large batch and mass production, where there is a continuous standardized production process, such as an assembly line in a car factory.
3   Process production, where a long and continuous run occurs, using the same procedures over and over again, as in a petrochemical plant or oil refinery.

As one moved from group 1 to group 3 there was a corresponding increase in technical complexity. Together with this went definite structural changes. As the complexity of technology increased, the organization built around it became more and more amenable to co-ordination through standardization of the work processes. In mass production this produced a highly bureaucratized structure. By contrast, both unit and process production were less bureaucratized, but for different reasons. Unit production was less bureaucratized because it was a relatively simple structure based on personal surveillance and personnel skill. Employing less specialists, they were less specialized, with the relations between management and the workers tending to be less formal. In process production more specialists were employed but they were mainly incorporated into line management. Because of the high skill formation of the workforce, and the highly standardized nature of the work, the structure of the organization tended to be more flexible than the mass production bureaucracy, and to be one in which the stratification structure was more blurred. The mass production bureaucracy operated with the highest levels of standardization, the lowest levels of skill formation and the highest degrees of formalization and stratification.

The findings now seem remarkably commonsensical, although prior to Woodward's work they had not been grasped. It is clearly a measure of her achievement that they now seem so obvious. Batch production organizations will tend to be smaller, in part because they employ less specialists. Decision-making will tend to be taken 'on the job' for each item of production. It will tend to have product-specific rather than system-wide implications. An elaborate bureaucracy will not be required. The converse is true of mass production. The nature of the product demands less decisions to be actually made, but their consequences will be system-wide and have a longer-term impact, because production runs are fewer and bigger. The low levels of skill formation in the workforce mean that it requires more standardized and formalized mechanisms of co-ordination. Woodward thus provided not only a description but also an explanation of structural differences in organizations, one which has been subject to considerable subsequent support (for example, Harvey 1968; Zwerman 1970) and influence (for example, Blau et al. 1976; Hickson, Pugh and Pheysey 1969; Perrow 1967; Thompson 1967; Van de Ven and Delbecq 1974) as well as some criticism (for example, Marsh and Mannari 1981: 37; Tayeb 1988: 11–12).

The TINA tendency

Pulling together the Aston findings on the importance of size and the Woodward findings on the importance of technology in determining organization structure, several conclusions present themselves. First, that technology has the most impact on organization structure the closer to its technical core one moves (Hickson, Pugh and Pheysey 1969). Second, that the smaller the organization, then the more influence its technology will have upon it (Child and Mansfield 1972; Pugh and Hickson 1976: 154). Of course, there are notorious difficulties in sorting out technology from industry effects in these comparisons, as Child and Mansfield observed. Often the same technology will be used in organizations in the same industry and not in others. What exactly are the causal factors at work in such a situation?

Weber's cultural pessimism derived from the importance which he attributed to values, values which he saw being eroded inexorably by the rationalization of the world. What the Aston researchers and Woodward do is identify the mechanisms which are enclosing the iron cage around us. For Woodward they are the types of technology developed, chosen and adopted. For the Aston researchers technology has a more delimited role to play compared to the mechanism of organization size. Size becomes *the* determinant of the iron cage in these accounts:

> In all countries, big organizations will be the most formalized and specialized in structure. This is because everywhere growth means reaping economies of scale and expertise by dividing labour still further, and as the knowledge possessed by any one person of what is happening in the organization becomes a smaller part of the whole, so more formalized documentation of action and intended action is required for control. Non-formalized custom is inadequate to control large numbers in organizations with a turnover of personnel. (Hickson et al. 1979: 37)

> Simply stated, if Indian organizations were found to be less formalized than American ones, bigger Indian units would still be more formalized than smaller Indian units. (Hickson et al. 1974: 59)

There is a logic of organization. It is an inescapable logic. As organizations grow in the number of employees that they have then they will become more bureaucratized. It is not possible that it could be otherwise. There is no alternative to the increase in bureaucratization wherever there is an increasing size of organization. If one were of a whimsical turn of mind one might want to name this the TINA tendency within organization theory: *There Is No Alternative.* Or at least there is very little.

The TINA tendency is an organizational specification of one particular argument about modernity: the modernization thesis associated with Kerr et al.'s (1973) prognosis that there is a 'logic of industrialization' (as has been remarked elsewhere in Clegg and Dunkerley [1980: 247–51]). It is a straightforward argument. Modernization is driven by industrialization; in turn, industrialization takes place through the medium of large scale organization. The corollary of this, to adapt Michels, is that 'whomsoever says large scale organization says bureaucracy'. TINA. The iron cage has been shut, the lock bolted, the key turned. The lock is size, the key, it has been widely suggested, is efficiency.

Efficiency rules, OK?

Weber and efficiency

How and why did bureaucracy become dominant? To answer this question we have to step outside the framework of descriptive analytical theories of organizations, such as those of the Aston school, which tell us *how* organizations are. If we want to know *why* they are like that, another framework is required altogether, it would seem.

In what are probably the most frequently cited words that Weber ever wrote on the subject of organizations, it seems as if the 'why?' question is answered unambiguously in terms of efficiency:

> The fully developed bureaucratic mechanism compares with other organizations exactly as does the machine with the non-mechanical modes of production . . . Precision, speed, unambiguity, unity, strict subordination, reduction of friction and of material and personal costs – these are raised to the optimum point in the strictly bureaucratic administration, and especially in its monocratic form. (Weber 1948: 214)

Certainly, Weber has often been interpreted in this passage as offering a eulogy to bureaucracy (for example, Blau and Scott 1963). However, as Albrow (1970: 63) points out, 'It would be quite misleading to equate Weber's concept of formal rationality with the idea of efficiency.' What Weber realized only too clearly was that 'technical formal rationality' was not necessarily the equivalent of 'efficiency'. Not only was 'efficiency' a 'foreign' term to Weber (see Albrow 1970: 64), but, even in those terms he made his own, its achievement would have required more than sheer technique alone. It also required a normative, moral context of value which could only be given culturally, rather than instrumentally. Rather than the spread of bureaucracy being due solely to its instrumental efficiency, according to Weber, it would be more correct to point to the cultural conditions of 'rationalization' as the appropriate explanation. Such a cultural explanation points to the *institutionalization* of value as the overarching factor in interpreting the rise of particular types of organization. The iron cage is a cultural construct rather than a rational constraint.

Had Weber wanted to make an argument linking efficiency to bureaucracy he would certainly have found it easy to do so. He was, after all, thoroughly familiar with the tradition of Austrian marginalist economics (Therborn 1976: 290–5) in which such connections had been drawn. However, had he followed this path it is doubtful that the linkage would have been a positive one. Had Weber embraced an argument which linked bureaucracy to the achievement of efficiency it would have been necessary to mount a counter-argument to the marginalist position. From the perspective of marginalism what was most striking about bureaucracy was its inefficiency rather than its efficiency. Simply stated, this position regarded voluntary and reciprocally oriented transactions between individuals to be the maximally efficient form of exchange. Bureaucracy, rather than facilitating the market in these, instead interposes the heavy hand of centralized authority which overrides freely contracting individuals.

Hayek, markets and efficiency

From a marginalist economic perspective, order does not have to be organized: it is something which can emerge spontaneously, if it is not subject to interference. As Friedrich Hayek (1944: 21) argues, 'the commands as well as the rules which govern an organization serve particular results aimed at by those who are in command of the organization', as opposed to that 'spontaneous order' which the market can provide. Organizations, whether public or private bureaucracies (but particularly those of organized labour), distort the spontaneous order of the market (Hayek 1967). Against the necessity of organization which Weber argues for, Hayek would favour decentralization and de-authorization of action to aid the spontaneous formation of coalitions entered into by freely contracting subjects, untrammelled by the hands-on authority of any organizations.

For Hayek the market is a source of spontaneous order. It is the market which resolves the Hobbesian mystery. Social order is possible because of the myriad free and independent decisions to buy and sell on the market which the price mechanism allows. No system of central planning could achieve the same effects, he argues. Thus, organizations, as such systems, must be a second-best alternative to markets (and their very existence, of course, destroys 'fair' markets). The emergent basis of market order is premised upon the free decisions of many disconnected individuals, often based upon the most tacit and implicit of knowledge, who are brought into a relationship with each other simply through decisions to buy and sell, decisions effected through the 'price mechanism'. Planning could not hope to replicate the implicit, tacit and differentiated bases of this order. It could only ever be a stage on *The Road to Serfdom* (Hayek 1944).

Where planning fails, Hayek believes that a vicious cycle will set in, unless things are then left to markets. Otherwise, ever grander and more ambitious plans will seek to compensate for the failures of earlier ones. Such a fetish of planning will be doomed to failure. Planning fails because of the impossibility of any omnipotence capable of centralizing and synthesizing all the data necessary for decision-making. Besides, such omnipotence is unnecessary. According to Hayek the market can do whatever a plan can do so much more effortlessly and economically. The order which it produces does not need to be contrived. This uncontrived order is not purely a result of the serendipitious 'hidden hand' of the market: a moral order is involved as well. Hayek (1960: 62) writes that the freedom which is the market 'has never worked without deeply ingrained moral beliefs . . . coercion can be reduced to a minimum only where individuals can be expected as a rule to conform voluntarily to certain principles' (cited by Hindess 1987: 130).

Interestingly, Hayek, the advocate of freedom through the market, does not oppose the existence of enterprise organization per se. Hayek recognizes the existence of organizations as goal-oriented systems, at least where they are profit-oriented corporations. Whatever other goals an organization has ought to be rigorously subordinated to 'the profitable use of the capital entrusted to the management by the stockholders' in order to secure 'the single aim' of obtaining 'the largest return in terms of long-run profits'. Without this dedication 'the case for private enterprise breaks down' (Hayek 1967: 300, 312). Hayek makes an exception to the rhetoric extolling the pleasures of unbridled liberalism and the purity of the market as the most sacred of institutions. Large organizations are allowable as long as every aspect of their functioning is subordinated to the market principle of profit raised to an over-arching goal.

Hindess (1987: 127) notes that the central concept buttressing the market in Hayek's thought is that of 'liberty'. It is because planning reduces liberty that it is to be avoided; yet he does not regard the organizational basis of most enterprise calculation in the modern world as such a reduction of liberty. In this respect, as Hindess (1987: 129) observes, he is a far less astute and realist commentator than was Weber (1978):

> The fact that employees are not legally prevented from resigning and seeking alternative employment does not mean that they are not subject to coercion by their employers. The extension of freedom of contract in a society may well go hand in hand with the development of highly authoritarian relationships in the sphere of employment.

Exactly so. A certain blindness as to this issue is a peculiar affliction of all 'market' premised approaches to organization analysis in their delimitation of a sphere of efficiency other than the market.

Market perspectives on organizations

Hayek, as the most notable proponent of the 'market', is the patron saint of a panoply of theoretical approaches which have been enormously influential in 'New Right' advocacy in the past decade. They have done much to prepare an ideological climate more than just a little receptive to accounts constructed in terms of 'markets' and more than just a little mistrustful of organizations. One should not think, however, that all contemporary market-oriented accounts are necessarily convinced that organizations represent something akin to the devil's work. Some strive to 'explain' organizations, rather than dismiss them entirely as illegitimate entities. Chief amongst these have been some economists whose innovation has been to realize that the fictive phenomenology of the market, with its free, boundless and perfect rationality, makes a less than convincing account of the majority of economic transactions. An idea which corresponds rather less to the idea of free exchange and rather more to the idea of organized transactions is needed for these. Efficiency is the key concept for these theorists in a way in which it never was for Weber.

One thing should be clear about these economic approaches to organizations. These frameworks operate with a particular set of a priori values: these are that organizations are an aberration from a more natural form of economic activity. This more natural form is that of exchange on the market, conceptualized as both an economic primitive and, in principle, as an 'essential' category of analysis (Hindess 1987). The market is regarded as a fundamental principle. The beneficial effects of this principle, it is maintained, should be evident in any transactions which transmit and conform to this essential principle. These benefits, it is argued, are those of economic efficiency and personal liberty, virtues which markets maximize.

In this view there were markets before organizations. Markets need not be explained. The classic statement of this is Adam Smith's (1961) statement in *An Enquiry into the Nature and Wealth of Nations* that the market exists as a result of inherent propensities of human nature. Above all, these propensities are oriented towards 'regard' for 'self-interest':

> It is not from the benevolence of the butcher, the brewer or the baker that we expect our dinner, but from their regard to their own self-interest. We address ourselves not to their humanity, but to their self-love, and never talk to them of our own necessities but of their advantage. (Smith 1961: 15)

Smith also says that where butchers, brewers or bakers get together to organize the restraint of trade, they are far more likely to do so in order to erect organizational barriers to free trade in collusion rather than to plan how best to maximize the market. From Smith's perspective economic action is a natural phenomenon. Instead, the nature of this phenomenon is self-interested action by rational actors; these actors are individuals. This is a perspective which stresses 'an atomized, *under*socialized conception of human action' (Granovetter 1985: 483) which has been iterated endlessly in the classical and neoclassical traditions in economics (also see the critiques in Clegg 1989b; Clegg, Boreham and Dow 1986). From this perspective the deviation of organization from the market principle, as a principle based on 'hierarchy', is something to be explained. Among contemporary theorists it is Oliver E. Williamson (1975), who has done most to elevate an essentialist belief in the market to an axiom of organization analysis. This has been done by addressing the existence of organizations from a perspective which stresses the priority of markets. Where markets fail then organizations may triumph. (Note that this is to make certain assumptions about the nature of organization as necessarily hierarchical. These may well turn out to be every bit as essentialist as the assumptions about the market.)

Not only are we dealing with essentialism here; we also have a case of ideological affinity, as Granovetter (1985: 484) expresses clearly:

> It has long been recognized that the idealized markets of perfect competition have survived intellectual attack in part because self-regulating economic structures are politically attractive to many. Another reason for the survival, less clearly understood, is that the elimination of social relations from economic analysis removes the problem of order from the intellectual agenda, at least in the economic sphere. In Hobbes' arguments, disorder arises because conflict-free social and economic transactions depend on trust and the absence of malfeasance. But these are unlikely when individuals are conceived to have neither social relationships nor institutional context – as in the state of nature. Hobbes contains the difficulty by superimposing a structure of autocratic authority. The solution of classical liberalism, and correspondingly of classical economics, is antithetical: repressive political structures are rendered unnecessary by competitive markets that make force or fraud unavailing. Competition determines the terms of trade in a way that individual traders cannot manipulate. If traders encounter complex or difficult relationships, characterized by mistrust or malfeasance, they can simply move on to the legion of other traders willing to do business on market terms; social relations and their details thus become frictional matters.

From a perspective with these priorities it should be evident why organizations present an analytical problem. In the vast majority of the advanced industrial societies economic transactions take place either in or between organizations. The greatest volume in monetary terms are controlled by the very small number of very large organizations. Given this then the existence of organizations rather than markets as the major loci of economic action is a major embarrassment for the economics of neoclassicism. For one thing, where economic action occurs in organizations then the 'freedom' of the market as a solution to malfeasance or mistrust disappears. While one can easily transfer one's action from one horse-trader to another in a country fair or a bazaar, it is somewhat more complex (particularly under the labour market conditions of 'deregulation' favoured by neoclassical economists) as easily to reorder one's employment relations or to choose not to buy some essential from some monopoly or oligopoly supplier. Perhaps it is for this reason, amongst other more evidently ideological ones, that the public policy prescriptions of schools of theory such as 'public choice analysis' should so often consist of the nostrum that there should not be any *public* policy as such: instead what is public should be privatized, with decision-making left to the celebrated 'invisible hand' of 'market forces'. For the same sort of reasons the 'artificial' nature of organization generally, as opposed to the assumed 'naturalness' of the market, predisposes this school to regard the existence of organizations as a problem to be explained. Starting from the premise of the superiority and naturalness of the market, *the* problem of organization analysis for market-oriented theorists is why organizations should exist in the first place, when markets are self-evidently the most efficient means of ordering transactions.

There are two major specifications, from a market-oriented perspective, which seek to explain why it is that bureaucratized organization structures preponderate where and when they do. One derives from the economic historian Alfred DuPont Chandler (1977; 1984) and stresses the way in which organization was an efficient response to market pressure, while the other is derived from the 'transaction cost economics' of Oliver E. Williamson (1975; 1981; 1985), which stresses how organization is a response to market failure.

Contemporary market theorists: Williamson and Chandler

In Williamson's (1975) work the thrust of the essentialist assumptions which explain the shift from 'market' to 'hierarchy' turn out to be, in fact, a formal specification of the efficiency argument which has been wrongly attributed to Weber. There are large organizations, and thus there is bureaucratization, because 'efficiency is the main and only systematic factor responsible' (Williamson 1983: 125). It is only where markets fail that organizations should emerge. (Note the normative 'should': the more empirically neutral 'will' really does not capture the tone of liberal zeal which pervades this analysis.)

Chandler begins by looking at how pre-industrial, small scale, family owned and rudimentarily managed enterprises were transformed into large scale, impersonally owned and bureaucratically managed multi-divisional structures in the twentieth century United States of America. The story is that up until the advent of the continental railway system in America, business organizations remained typically small, usually under the control of merchants. The coming of the railway system from the middle of the nineteenth century changed this. The first change was due to the enormous geographic diversity of the railways themselves. The possibilities of control through the personal surveillance of an owner-controller were dissolved by the great spread of the operations of the organization. The railways had to develop some alternative if they were to prosper. The alternative was found in the adoption of military models of bureaucracy and a modern 'multi-unit' corporate form. The second change was occasioned by the markets that the railways opened up. The possibilities of a mass market could now be entertained, at least by those organizations which were able to increase the volume of their production.

Chandler argued that as businesses enlarged they found it more efficient to incorporate under one framework the multiple services which they had previously bought from commission agents on the market. These were services such as the purchase of raw materials, debt financing, marketing and distribution. Administrative co-ordination began to replace market exchanges as the major mechanism of control because it was a technically more efficient way of doing *a greater volume* of business. Productivity and profits were higher and costs were lower where organization through rudimentary bureaucratization replaced the fragmentation of markets.

Some other detail gives us an insight into how this growth was achieved. Although it takes place continuously – each time a firm hires more labour or buys out a competitor – it has been established that there are, in fact, distinct patterns of growth achieved through mergers (Aglietta 1979). Organizations don't just 'grow' into bigness: they frequently get there by virtue of assertive action vis-à-vis other organizations; they take them over. Thus, large organizations often acquire their bigness through takeovers. Aglietta (1979: 222–3) suggests that there have been several periods of heightened merger activity in the United States, with the initial peak occurring at the end of the nineteenth century. It was out of this wave of mergers that bureaucratized structures were to be consolidated.

At the end of the nineteenth century there occurred a wave of both horizontal, diversificationary mergers and vertical mergers which incorporated suppliers, marketing outlets and so on. The upshot of these was that what had been distinct family businesses were reconstituted under one centre of organizational control. Past family owners were often retained as more or less independent managers in the new organizations (Edwards 1979: 18). Their intimate knowledge of the local business was invaluable to the new owners, who frequently knew little of the specifics of the businesses they now controlled. Such people were able to exercise power personally on the basis of close technical knowledge of the work performed. Moreover, unlike the new owners, they had been in sufficient physical proximity to the workforce to be able to have an effective 'surveillance' (Foucault 1977) of the organization. It was a surveillance based on both technical knowledge and spatio-visual proximity. Fre-

quently, these conditions were replicated within newly merged organizations by incorporating elements of an internal market into the larger
organizations. The system for doing this is variously known as 'internal
contracting' (Littler 1980) and as 'inside contracting' (Clawson 1980).

This system will be briefly described here in terms which are close to
those of Chandler and Williamson. In Chapter 4 this material will be
reviewed in order to accentuate some of the features of the phenomenon
which might suggest themselves to someone looking at it from a 'power'
perspective. Unfortunately, even though the presentation here is designed
to illuminate aspects of the 'market' approach, realism dictates that on
occasion this will be complemented by a more explicitly 'power' perspective.

The internal contract system was widely used by organizations in the
nineteenth century, and into the twentieth century, in the major capitalist
nations of Britain, Japan and the United States (Littler 1982). Essentially
the system comprised an employer and owner of capital hiring a number
of internal subcontractors. These individual subcontractors would negotiate a lump sum payment with the capitalist in a contract in which they
would agree to provide a specific number of goods, by a specified date or
on a specified basis, by hiring labour to work within the organization, using
its technology, raw materials and so on to produce commodities only for
the organization.

The internal contract may be defined in terms of what Williamson (1985)
regards as the basic unit of economic analysis: an economic transaction,
defined as an exchange of goods and services across technological boundaries. The costs of the transaction were fixed by the capitalist in the initial
contract negotiated with the inside contractor. After that it was left up to
the internal contractor to determine how, by whom, at what profit or loss
to the contractor and in what way the transaction was accomplished. In
Williamson's terms, all the costs of the transaction seem to have been
displaced by the capitalist on to the internal contractor. Typically, this
person would manage through rudimentary direct surveillance of the work.

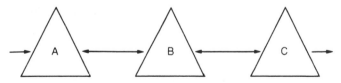

Figure 3.1   *Organizational co-ordination through external market
contract*

The system solved by default the problem of surveillance which was
likely to occur as the size of organizations grew beyond the spatio-visual
grasp of a single individual. We can conceptualize this readily (see Figure
3.1). A number of separate organizations in an industry, such as the steel

industry, might have been related to each other through a series of market transactions. The product of organization A becomes the material for transformation and fabrication by organization B, and so on. The exchanges are connected through the market as organization A contracts with organization B, using money as the medium of exchange and the contract as the medium of co-ordination. Subsequent to their horizontal integration through takeover the distinct organizations are subsumed within the framework of an encompassing organization, in which the medium of co-ordination is the internal contract (see Figure 3.2). It reproduced within single ownership organizations the exact possibilities for simple, personal control which had always characterized smaller organizations. It instituted the profit motive in the internal contractor: it was up to this individual, acting under the discipline of the contract and profit expectation, to achieve the transaction transformation. Exactly how this was done was up to the discretion of the internal contractor and the negotiation of the members of the 'work unit'. Sometimes the relationships were familial, under patriarchal authority; sometimes they would be highly exploitative, sometimes less so, under the informally hierarchical relationships of a 'gangerman' and 'gang'; occasionally they might be collectivist, under the rubric of what we might term 'self-management'.

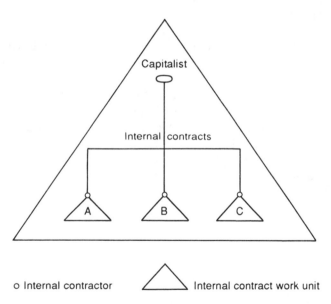

Figure 3.2   *Organizational co-ordination through internal contract*

From the capitalist's point of view the internal contract had a number of attractions as a system. It was flexible in terms of demand fluctuations and their impact on employment. It displaced risks inherent in the organization of work, quality of labour, raw materials and plant on to the contracting agent. It absolved the capitalist from detailed capital accounting through the mechanism of the fixed payment lump sum contract. It opened up possibilities for advancement by workers who might become contracting agents and it generated a mechanism whereby innovation might flourish in methods of work design and organization internal to the contract.

None the less, despite these evident advantages, internal contracting began to decline from the last quarter of the nineteenth century in both Britain and the United States, and in Japan from the early twentieth century. In Williamson's terms the costs of the transactions began to outweigh their benefits. These costs were those associated with the monitoring of the contracts. They offered little control over quality or pilferage, for instance. Some of the internal contractees acted 'opportunistically with guile', that is they did not do exactly what the capitalist and the contractor expected of them. This should hardly be surprising to anyone familiar with that large literature in industrial sociology which demonstrates how the rationality of action by different economic actors in the same firm is invariably constructed situationally (for example, Taylor and Walton 1971). One person's 'rationality' may well be another person's 'guile'. Resistance is quite normal behaviour in organizations (Clegg 1989b: 207–9). Some people may even be sufficiently guileful to the extent that they will join trade unions in order to try and improve their collective situation!

There was a situation – whether a problem of guile or not – in which were displayed resistant 'modes of rationality' on the part of workers in early twentieth century organizations. In addition, other rationalities, such as those of 'scientific management', were being developed by other agents in order to achieve a more efficient utilization of these workers' labour power. Such a utilization required a more regulated contractual relationship between the individual worker and the organization than the internal contract typically provided, particularly as the market conditions in the environment changed. It was the development of various types of 'rationalization' movement, such as scientific management, which led to the widespread bureaucratization of employment relations in organizations (Clegg and Dunkerley [1980: 84–6] go into this in some detail). Thus, for these various reasons strategically placed agents in organizations sought to replace the uncertainties of the internal marketplace through creating governance structures which internalized transactions, reduced their costs and thus, from the capitalist point of view, increased efficiency (Williamson 1985: 68–162). They also sought to avoid the uncertainties of external markets by buying out competitors, suppliers, marketers and so on.

Translating the specifics of economic history into the abstractions of economics, bureaucratization occurs when transaction costs can be minimized by internalizing them within firms rather than mediating them through markets. In this perspective, first there were markets and then there were organizations which grew as a response to market failures. The probability of market failure is higher the more complex and uncertain is the market – that is, the more it diverges from the ideal of perfect competition. All this is elegantly if occasionally somewhat unrealistically expressed by Williamson in terms of a few key concepts: the 'uncertainty' of markets, the 'opportunism' of economic agents, sometimes based upon their 'bounded rationality' (the fact that they have 'strategically contingent' [Hickson et al. 1971] skills with which to bargain), the 'asset specificity' of organization information about operating environments and so on. Different kinds of transactions will give rise to different kinds of organizations. Those that are most uncertain in their foreseeable outcomes, and which are substantially specific, as well as frequently recurring are the transactions most likely to find expression in organizations. The nature of organization diversity is to be explained through the complexities of markets. The organizations we have are, on the whole, the most efficient there can be, otherwise they wouldn't exist: this is the conclusion which this Panglossian logic draws us inexorably to. How else could the perfect fiction of the perfectly competitive market have been replaced in the first place?

Organizations derive from markets where contracts tend to be longer rather than shorter term; where the environment is more rather than less certain (actually a tautology, as the key variable affecting the certainty of the market is its perfectly competitive status – that is, its lack of organization; once organization is admitted, then the uncertainty of the environment begins to accrue, by definition); and where the barriers to entry for new agents are high (again, implicitly, these barriers are frequently organizational in that they concern the capacity to hire labour, raise credit, secure supplies and so on; these are less matters of individual ability and more of organizational contacts, networks and environmentally available resources). So the thrust of Williamson's theory is to argue that organizations grow when markets fail. However, in a sense what he is describing is a situation where markets fail because organizational conditions have begun to develop. Markets fail either because of the 'bounded rationality' which agents display when confronted with decisions which are contingent on complex long-term transactions or where agents display 'opportunism' – rational self-interest expressed in terms of a tendency to cheat on the conditions which have been contracted. While the latter conditions are not necessarily organizational, the former seem to be so. Where an argument proposes that markets fail because of organizational growth, then it would be injudicious simultaneously to hold that this failure should also serve as an explanation of the emergence of organizations. The effect would also be the cause.

Granovetter (1985: 494) identifies the transition from markets to hierarchies in terms of the mix of 'under- and over-socialized assumptions' which Hobbes deployed in *Leviathan*. The market, as we have seen, is conceptualized as if it were a natural state; the organization is regarded as a moral community in which hierarchical dictat (or 'fiat') can play a back-up role if the moral order fails and agents act 'opportunistically with guile'. Organization thus functions in a way which is similar to the mythical Hobbesian community and monarch in political theory more generally (Clegg 1989b): it internalizes conditions of both organic unity and hierarchical authority. One may find that it aids one in interpreting this argument if one keeps one's metaphorical tongue firmly in one's metaphorical cheek. Otherwise, one might conclude that the nature of 'membership' in organizations has nothing to do with that economic necessity to endure 'the dull compulsion to labour' of which both Marx and Weber wrote. For the majority of people the key calculus would seem to be which, if any, organizational employer they can hawk themselves to. Whether or not the transaction is then bathed in an ethos of morality is entirely an empirical question, depending in large part on the institutional framework within which the exchange is constructed. The same might also be said of recourse to hierarchy: no necessity adheres to either. In fact, the recourse to hierarchy in Williamson begs the whole issue of how it is that obedience is produced in organizations (see Biggart and Hamilton 1985; Clegg 1989a) as well as the 'embeddedness' of all organizational action within institutional frameworks (Granovetter 1985).

Williamson's approach is to argue that organizations grow when markets fail due to increased transaction costs. Note that structural failures, due to the growth of concentration, are excluded here. By contrast, Chandler, as we have seen, argues that they grow where they are market-driven. Both accounts tend to underplay the possibility that organizations are conduits, arenas and opportunities for power (Clegg 1989a). Organizations might better be understood as sites of power built from the *bricolage* of whatever materials might be available, including rational knowledge about their functioning, by whatever agents have an interest in and around them. Contracts are not incidental to this, as has been demonstrated empirically (Clegg 1975) and argued theoretically (Clegg 1989a) elsewhere.

Contingencies, adaptation and efficiency

The account which Chandler provides is in many ways compatible with a standard 'contingency theory' account, such as that which Lex Donaldson (1985a) develops, or that which we have already encountered in the contingency theory of the Aston school. There the chance, conditional, uncertain or contingent events which determined organization structure were the inescapable consequences of a growth in organization size. Not all contingency theorists would be in agreement with this version of the enterprise, it should be said. Some would probably find it an unduly restrictive conception; for instance, Mintzberg's (1983) more political version of contingency theory would not sit comfortably with the rationalist assumptions implicit in Donaldson's views. We shall consider Mintzberg in Chapter 4. For the moment we shall concentrate on Donaldson simply because he presents a very self-consciously 'orthodox' conception of organizational contingency theory. One should acknowledge that other, less orthodox versions are available.

Donaldson's (1985a) work demonstrates the fuller flowering of that rationalist and culturally pessimistic vision which Weber had first developed. In addition, it adds to organization theory a strong 'defence' of a particular conception, developed from contingency theory, of what organization theory *should* be. It would be fair to say that Donaldson is less interested in the full range of what it is that gets done under the general rubric of organization studies and more interested in demarcating and defending the superior legitimacy of certain aspects of it. In other words, organization theory is subjected to moral stipulation. Using the example of Popper's 'moral philosophy of science' the field is re-defined in a normative way to exclude much of what organization analysis has conventionally done (see the *Organization Studies* 'Symposium' [Hinings et al. 1988] on Donaldson's [1985a] text). The point of this restrictive re-definition is to privilege a discursive space in which 'organizational design', as a series of variations on a rationally limited theme, becomes the defining essence of what organization analysis should be. It is very clearly a moral project, as its own rhetoric leaves in no doubt (see the analyses in Clegg 1988; Colebatch 1988; Reed 1989).

Donaldson implicitly adopts Weber's cultural pessimism. Whereas in Weber this pessimism had an ironical, critical and cutting edge, in Donaldson it is constructed in an unreflective mode. It is a blunt instrument, bereft of other than instrumental social critique, keyed to one theme only. Even the best themes suffer from endless repetition. The theme stresses that things cannot efficiently be otherwise than allowed by a small range of determinate design options. If things are just so, rationally, then that is how they are and there is little or no point in worrying about it. As has been suggested, one might want to name this the TINA tendency.

The TINA tendency reaches its apotheosis with Donaldson's (1985a) work on strategy/structure models of divisionalized organizations, and the contingencies which correlate with divisionalization. In this respect it draws intellectually on the ideas of Chandler (1962; 1977) and Williamson (1975) to develop a perspective in which structural characteristics of organizations, such as specialization, standardization, formalization, hierarchization and centralization are linked to a number of contingent variables, including size. However, following Chandler's (1962) analysis of the emergence of the multi-divisional corporation, the contingency approach is taken one step further. The focus is upon how, when contingencies change, organizations make structural adjustments to regain an effective fit between their organizational form or structure and their performance function.

Organizations may be subject to some variation in the way in which their chief executive officers exercise their 'strategic choice' (Child 1972) as to how various sub-units are co-ordinated. Four 'pure' types of strategy concerning choice of structure-design are identified by Donaldson (1985a: 160–72). These are a functional structure (where an organization is composed of functional sub-units such as discipline departments in a university); a divisional structure, on either a product basis (where a university would be organized in sub-units which corresponded to the university 'products', such as degrees – faculties which would offer distinct degrees in Arts, Sciences, Education and so on) or an area basis (where a university has a multi-campus structure, and each campus is a sub-unit); or a matrix structure where there is differentiation by more than one criterion – say by area (multi-campus) and by product (faculties). The argument is that each one of these options (or their sub-options) will be a more appropriate strategy for certain situations rather than others. To determine an effective design choice Donaldson (1985a: 170) suggests that there are four key questions concerning, first, the degree of product diversity; second, the degree of geographical diversity; third, the relationship between the products, where it is not a single-product organization; fourth, where there are several related products, the degree of product innovation required. Posing these as questions, and using a 'decision tree' for selecting organization design, Donaldson (1985a: 171) reduces the whole issue of organization effectiveness to one of choice between thirteen different designs, each of which, it is argued, will be more effective where certain strategic conditions prevail. (Oddly, given the strictures against the 'strategic choice' perspective of John Child [1972] which are developed earlier in his volume, what Donaldson proposes is a tool for effecting such choices.) Donaldson's thesis would lead one to expect that efficient, successful organizations in similar industries, cross-culturally, would adopt the same type of strategy and structure. In this his argument would be consistent in its predictions with the outcomes postulated by Chandler, for both are efficiency-driven arguments that tend to minimize other phenomena. Strategy leads to structure in Donaldson's argument just as it does in Chandler's. This is seen most clearly in the account that they offer of 'divisionalization'.

Divisionalization is seen by Chandler (1962) to be the structural type which succeeds bureaucracy under certain industrial conditions. Divisionalization is a decentralized management structure in which firms are organized into product divisions, where each product division has a classically unitary, more bureaucratic structure. It is argued by Chandler that divisionalization will occur when an organization becomes more product diversified, where whether or not there is product diversification is largely determined by the industry the firm is in and by the propensity of its technology to develop related or unrelated products.

Williamson (1975) has argued, by contrast to Chandler (1962), that divisionalization is a response to increasing size of organizations, especially the number of employees. As organizations increase in size then the possibilities of control by the top managers becomes less. They approach the limits of their bounded rationality and are no longer able effectively to survey and control an expanded scale of operations. Consequently, other actors in the organization are inclined to see and to exploit an increasing number of opportunities for guileful behaviour – what Williamson also sometimes calls 'opportunism'. The divisionalization thus offers an opportunity to diminish the transaction costs of control by managers by reducing the scale of the arenas in which they have to exert their bounded rationality, thus making the possibilities of effective surveillance of business activity more likely. Whether or not size or diversification is more conducive to organizational divisionalization has been the subject of a sustained empirical debate (see, for instance, the Donaldson–Grinyer debate: Donaldson 1982; 1986b; Grinyer, Yasai-Ardekani and Al-Bazzaz 1980; Grinyer and Yasai-Ardekani 1981; Grinyer 1982; Child 1982). The current state of play in this debate is that the relationship between diversification and divisionalization is consistently stronger empirically than the argument which leads from size to structure (Donaldson 1986b).

Taken together the transaction cost and business history approaches of Williamson and Chandler represent a major axis of 'market' or 'economic' explanations of organizations. Recently these market approaches to the explanation of the spread and supersession of the bureaucratic by the divisional form have been re-specified in the perspective developed by Donaldson (1987). In this perspective the structural adjustments which organizations make to regain equilibrium, as they face changed contingencies, are the focus of study. It is hypothesized that 'a shift in the contingency variables leads to disequilibrium, this produces a decline in effectiveness that creates pressure for change, which causes structural adaptation producing a new structure and restoring effectiveness' (Donaldson 1987: 2). Rather than specifying either size or diversification as the variables leading to structural reorganization, the process is seen as 'contingency driven' (Donaldson 1987: 3). Little is gained analytically from this re-specification – the variables of size and diversification are simply re-titled as contingencies. In turn, these contingencies are regarded as impacting on organizations through moderator variables such as the degree of economic illiberality (a variable which can be gauged in terms of data pertaining to the industry-specific business cycle: see Donaldson 1985b).

What Donaldson (1987) does achieve is an empirical specification of the argument from contingencies. It is one which draws on a large data-set on the relation between the Chandlerian contingency of product diversification and the structural form of divisionalization. The data are drawn from five advanced industrialized countries (France, Japan, the United Kingdom, the United States and West Germany) and a wide number of separate studies (Channon 1973; Dyas and Thanheiser 1976; Suzuki 1981). The time-scale of the data stretches over two decades – the 1950s and the 1960s. The argument is developed against hypotheses derived from simpler contingency approaches which fail to specify that it is contingency change leading to *mismatch* which is important, as well as against arguments interpreted to suggest that the strategic choices of dominant actors in organizations can equally change structure as strategy. For the latter, the only consistent relations discovered are between diversification and structural change, mediated by mismatch and environmental illiberality. Strategy leads to structure; size does not do so to the same extent; structure does not appear to lead to strategy at all. The iron cage, interpreted now as not so much bureaucracy per se but the existence of a structurally limited range of organization types, appears to be constructed out of the dictates of economic efficiency on the basis of Donaldson's analyses. It will not necessarily achieve the same design in all contexts. There are iron cages rather than a single iron cage – but there are not many of them, and efficiency will drive all strategically similar organizations to make the same inexorable choices. To continue the Weberian metaphor, his argument is that we live inside a narrow range of iron cages because these options represent the best available design, where the criteria of good design are considerations of economic performance and efficiency.

Donaldson (1985a; 1985b; 1987) produces a strong and empirically well grounded argument in favour of the importance of efficiency-pressures in the determination of organization design. However, Donaldson's organizations are somewhat bloodless – one has no sense of them as arenas peopled by potentially plural agencies with multiple and conflicting conceptions of their own and other interests, conceptions which, often in the messiest way, can obstruct the pressure of efficiency. What we are presented with are organizations without operatics – no prima donnas here; efficiency without guile; agencies without antagonism; people without politics – these are the resonances suggested by structures driven by strategy and efficiency in the Donaldsonian scheme of things. Structural adjustment to regain fit does not appear to be a process in which any blood is spilt on the tracks of organization switching, disturbing the pursuit of efficiency and the appropriateness of design.

Conclusion

Weber has been interpreted by much organization theory as having had an 'efficiency-driven' view of the organizational future of modernity. It has been maintained in this chapter that in fact he did not have such a vision. The views that Weber did hold were bleak and deeply imbued with cultural pessimism. The bleakness of this vision was premised on the belief that life within organizations would become ever more one-dimensional. Even while not replicating the substantive focus of these views, much contemporary organization theory has been equally erosive of the possibilities of pluralism in the world of organizations. Such organization theory has persisted in developing radically truncated, if not one-dimensional, views. Moreover, in doing so it has helped maintain the belief that modernity itself confirms such a view. For some theorists the perspective is developed from a stance in markets; for others feet are firmly planted within the structures of organizations themselves. Either way the outcome is to make it appear as if only a narrow range of organization designs exist because they are the only ones that are efficient. Efficiency is the key concept. We have the iron cages that we have because of the pressure of efficient coping with pervasive contingencies. Chapter 4 will review studies which undercut perspectives derived from the contingencies of both markets and hierarchies.

4

Ecologies, Institutions and Power in the Analysis of Organizations

Donaldson is not the only researcher to have used a data-set detailing the spread of divisionalization as a means of adjudicating between competing theoretical perspectives. Another researcher who employs the same tactic on another data-set dealing with the same phenomenon (of the diffusion of divisionalization amongst organizations) is Fligstein (1985). The theories which he tests are in some respects different to those that Donaldson looked at, although they have in common the 'contingency' frameworks of Chandler (product diversification) and Williamson (size). However, they also open up for consideration issues of both power and institutions as well as ecology in the structuring of organizations.

Fligstein considers hypotheses derived from both 'population ecology' (Hannan and Freeman 1977; 1984) and 'institutionalist' (DiMaggio and Powell 1983) perspectives, as well as from a 'power' perspective (Karpik 1978; Perrow 1970; 1981; 1986; Pfeffer 1981; my own work would also fit this framework – for example, Clegg 1977; 1979; 1981; 1989a; 1989b; Clegg and Dunkerley 1980 – as would the account which Mintzberg 1983 provides). These contemporary approaches to organization analysis will be considered prior to looking at what Fligstein has to say about their usefulness for explaining divisionalization.

Population ecology perspective

The population ecology perspective is now well developed in organization theory; for example, consider Hannan and Freeman (1988). It draws heavily on analogies with biology. Organizations are regarded as if they were population species which inhabit distinct ecologies or environments. Organizations may thrive or decline under particular environmental conditions, much as may some species of flora or fauna. Ecological explanation attempts to explain the conditions which can sustain and inhibit particular forms of organizational life. Forms of organizational life are conceptualized in terms of coexisting and competing populations of organizations, where a population is defined in terms of the ecological niche which it inhabits in the environment. An extended use is made of the ecological metaphor which assumes that populations of organizations evolve in much the same way as a biological species might. Change *in* organizations will take place primarily through the change *of* organizations according to this perspective. It is the development of new populations of organizations which is significant. These represent new types of organizational form, some of which may flourish while others may decline, as the environmental conditions change. Change is likely to take the shape of 'punctuated equilibria', in which long periods of stability in organizational populations and forms will be disrupted by short bursts of innovation and creativity, as new forms are innovated and either selected 'in' or 'out'. These forms will inhabit more or less 'dense' population ecologies as organizations enter and leave the fluctuating population and populations grow or decline.

The process of population growth is not infinite but will be limited by the carrying capacity of the environment. The environment is not undifferentiated but is composed of specific niches. These could be thought of as being something like micro-ecologies in the overall ecology of the environment. Each niche, or micro-ecology, has a limited carrying capacity which can sustain life up to that number, but which is critically threatened if that number is exceeded. In the natural ecology, where the food supplies of a given micro-ecology are exceeded by the demands of the numbers of creatures competing for them, then not all the forms of life which are engaged in a struggle to survive in the particular niche will be able to do so. Some will perish; others may migrate elsewhere and chance their survival in a less familiar ecology.

Think of an ecology of competing organization forms instead of an ecology of competitive fauna or flora, in an ecological environment composed of variable market opportunities for sustaining various forms of organization life. This would represent what the population ecology theorists in organization studies are driving at. Just as species of natural phenomena evolve in distinct patterns of development, so, it is argued, will organizations. One can look at, for instance, the frequency with which new organizations in a population are founded or cease to exist. With respect to the founding of organizations, this will tend to accelerate from the initial founding, if there is a niche space for the form (if not, initial entrants will quit the population through either the death or the non-reproduction of the founders). Acceleration cannot be indefinite. Niches will become saturated or overcrowded, and not all the entrants which sought to settle in that niche will survive. A 'shake-out' occurs. The rate of founding falls and the population will stabilize. As the total number of organizations of given forms specific to a niche reduces, then the forms which best fit the niche will become more evident. Certain forms of organization will become preponderant, acquire legitimacy in a given niche-space and be the design patterns which newer entrants would seek to emulate. There will, however, be far fewer newer entrants as the field becomes more dense. Quitting or 'mortality' rates will increase as the number of organizations in a population grows beyond the risky exploratory stage of development when entrants have few precedents as to how they might design their organization form. Later, as this becomes more evident knowledge, then there are more survivors. Later still, as saturation of the niche-space occurs, the mortality rate will increase once more. Only those forms which best fit the conditions of survival in the niche will continue. A consequence of the scenario that Hannan and Freeman (1988) sketch is that as populations of organizations age they become more stable and thus the organizations which comprise them have a greater probability of survival. They are also less likely to change and adapt. Innovation is more likely to come from the creation of new organizations than it is from the redesign of existing ones. Older organizations are more likely to continue to live longer than emergent newcomers: there is a 'liability of newness' which younger organizations will suffer from. These assets and liabilities of age will be enhanced by those of size: large organizations have larger amounts of spare resources or 'organizational slack' with which they can try to withstand diminishing munificence from their environments. Organizations within a population will also be affected differently according to the extent to which they attempt to be specialists or generalists within the niche-space. Generalist organizations which offer a wider range of services and products appear to do better under variable conditions than do more specialist organizations: these flourish best in more stable cyclical conditions.

Recently the population ecology perspective has been subject to some critical scrutiny in the literature (Young 1988). Prior to this the ecologists had enjoyed a remarkably clear run, their work being prolifically published without much sustained criticism being devoted to it. In some respects this is peculiar, because beneath the surface of extended ecological metaphor there appears to be a far more familiar discourse at play – this is the talk of the market. (Robins [1985] makes this apparent in his 'lesson' for ecological theory.) It is competitive pressure which drives the ecological theoretical system as surely as it does the more obviously economically indebted contributions to organization analysis.

An initial point of criticism of the population ecology arguments of Hannan and Freeman (1988) that is made by Young concerns the delineation of a 'population' of organizations – by which, as she says, they seem to mean 'species' of organizations. 'A species is collection of forms – in biology, one that can interbreed, that is, constitute a gene pool. A population is a frequency distribution. To use the word population where species is meant is confusing' (Young 1988: 2). Hannan and Freeman (1977: 935) regard differences in formal structures as equivalent to species differences; but, as Young (1988: 2–3) notes, they do not advance any clear rules for differentiation. Certainly, there are several imprecise suggestions; but the nature of their imprecision is either unilluminative (differences in formally available descriptions of the organization; patterns of activity in the organization; the organization's normative order), circular (look for the boundaries between species) or apparently operationally meaningless (for example, 'the bag [*sic*] of variables that covary as a result of differential net mortality': Freeman [1982: 9]).

No less central in the adoption of ecological terms is the role that 'niche' plays in organizational applications of population ecology theories. In the host discipline of ecology the concept of niche is usually defined in terms of 'a set of constraints in abstract space that are sufficient to maintain a species' (Young 1988: 5), an idea which typically implies that there is a limit to the occurrence of a niche. Otherwise there would not be any competition for niche-space. In the parasite discipline, unfortunately, because of the implicit conception of niches as markets, it is unclear what the limits are: markets, even for seemingly quite useless things, seem capable of almost infinite expansion.

Other substantial problems of definition arise. It has been suggested by Freeman (1982: 9) that species should be defined differently for different studies. Such a strategy would also raise the issue of limits: does this mean that the same species can freely transcend the limits of a particular niche-space, or that organizations could be easily subject to re-definition? A related issue arises with conceptions of 'species change' or 'speciation'. Technology appears to be conceived of as an autonomous, exogenous and determining variable (for example, Brittain and Freeman 1980: 295–6), in the familiar and well criticized mode of 'technological determinism' (Clegg and Dunkerley 1980). Not only is there the problem that technology clearly is not a neutral and autonomous variable (which is not to deny it may well effect determination, through setting limits within which variation may occur). There is also a question concerning the interrelation of niche and species:

> niches are identifiable only if we know the species that occupy them; they are meaningful only in such a specific context. And, in fact, it is possible that the same niche is suitable for several species that have not yet competed to decide on the survivor. We would be sorely mistaken to give these future competitors the same identification. Thus, definitions of species and niche, two key concepts, are both basically lacking, since they are defined only in terms of each other. (Young 1988: 5)

There is a confusion of levels of analysis present in the population ecology perspective. Population ecology perspectives conceptualize that organizations can 'quit' a species, something which Hannan and Freeman refer to as mortality. In the world of natural species, death is usually unambiguous – not so in the world of organizations. Young (1988: 8) suggests that in these ecology models almost any change in organization form becomes equivalent to the 'death' of that form and the 'birth' of something new – hence, the bias towards stasis in the ecology model's conceptualization of intra-organizational process (Hannan and Freeman

1984) and the confusion which Young (1988: 8–10) identifies in their conceptualization of change. The question of level of analysis arises when one considers that the ecology metaphors are drawn from a host discipline whose theoretical object is not the members of a species, but the species itself. As Young (1988: 10–16) remarks, drawing on the ironical possibilities of the extended ecological metaphors, the usage seems to enjoy a parasitic half-life, by turns feeding off the host or deriving supplementary nurture elsewhere. The hypotheses derived are, not surprisingly, as hybrid as the nurturing process which sustained them. The parasitic usage maintains the metaphors but does not apply them to the concept of a species. Instead, they are applied not to the notion of species as a consciously constructed and analytically abstract 'theoretical object' but to specific organizations. The latter may well be actually existing empirical objects but they do not have the same rigorous theoretical form that the concept of species demands.

Treating concrete entities as if they were analogous to abstract concepts such as species is, from an ecological point of view, erroneous. The birth and death of particular empirical objects – organizations – do not signal the birth and death of the putative species which are constituted as the theoretical object. Given the complexity of the formal, legal constitution of organizations under diverse conditions of calculation and ownership, then the appellation 'species' must remain putative. As Young (1988: 12) notes with a wit which is more than a trifle acid:

> The smallest bug or goldfish or wood mouse is an independent actor, but the largest Sears Roebuck branch has little to say about its fate. Is not studying branch plants, associated and affiliated organizations, and government agencies as if they were independent actors similar to studying frogs' legs as if they were independent of frogs?

One might also note that no goldfish, wood mouse or frog, let alone the smallest bug, is an agency in which competing and frequently contradictory discursive rationalities, embodied in various human and administrative forms, struggle for control of the arena in which the entity's organic behaviour is determined. It is a rare organization indeed which can empirically operate as if it were an integral, organic and instinctive entity bereft of contradiction, ambiguity and conflict (see Clegg 1989a).

The population ecology perspective clearly has some major problems (not all of which I have addressed here; for instance, the empirical studies have not been discussed at all. Had they been, then a number of additional points of criticism would be in order, as Young [1988] develops). None the less, Fligstein (1985) felt that hypotheses were derivable from it.

Recall that the Chandler/Williamson 'market' perspectives on organizations suggest that bureaucracies develop where contracts are internalized, and that in turn, divisionalization will be likely to succeed bureaucratization as a structural form under certain conditions. They disagree about these conditions. Chandler stresses diversification while Williamson proposes size. Grinyer lends support to the arguments from size, while Donaldson argues that Chandler's account is empirically better grounded. The arguments from size and diversification do not, unfortunately, exhaust the range of explanatory options. As we might anticipate, given the stress on the change of organization forms through 'mortality' which we find in population ecology, relevant hypotheses may be derived from this genre of analysis. These apply to the transition from bureaucratization to divisionalization.

As a new form one would expect divisionalization to be carried by new organizations rather than by existing bureaucratic ones, according to organizational ecology. This is the hypothesis that Fligstein (1985: 379) derives: 'one would expect that younger and smaller firms would be more likely to adopt the MDF [multi-divisional form] than older and larger ones'. Irrespective of the ecological auspices and coherence of such a proposition, it is one which should stand alone as capable of decisive testing. It is clear that if the majority of divisionalized (or MDF) organizations in a sample over a period of time were not the youngest and smallest organizations then the hypothesis would be disconfirmed.

While the rival Chandlerian and Williamsonian 'market' perspectives are one axis of an explanation which stresses 'competition' as a key environmental pressure, and the ecological perspective is another, there are other perspectives which are far less amenable to the rhetoric of competitive pressure and efficient adaptation than any one of these perspectives would suggest. The key to explanation for each of the perspectives that have been considered thus far is that of efficient adaptation: whether to niches, market structures or size constraints. In this respect, although no one of these models is anything like Weber's view of organizations, they do share one similarity with the received (but incorrect) wisdom about Weber's analysis. They seem to stress efficiency. Not all organization theory does so and it is important to recognize this fact. In particular, there are two loosely organized schools of thought, which may be called the 'institutionalist' and the 'power' perspectives, which are inclined to treat efficiency arguments with some scepticism. It is to these that we shall turn next.

The institutionalist perspective

Whereas other theories considered thus far would tend to see the environment as a source of disorderly 'uncertainties', expressed in the form of 'opportunism', 'technologies', 'product markets' or 'niche spaces', they simultaneously play down the disorderly conduct of organization affairs. Hierarchies are established, contingencies coped with, organizations survive or die – in short, organizational order is established. However, in every case this theoretical determinism is achieved at the expense of the 'agency' aspects of organizations.

Choice is minimized for the ecologists by the necessity of large samples, which means studying mostly small organizations with little effect on environmental conditions: hence environments determine. For both the transactionists and the strategy/structure theorists, organizations are structure-takers not structure-makers – the difference between them is not whether or not organization structures are determined but what the source of the determination is. Contingency theorists such as Donaldson differ on this: on the one hand they deny 'strategic choice', but on the other they write of organizations 'selecting', 'making', 'reorganizing' and 'recentralizing', contingent on 'the search for enhanced growth and product innovation, . . . cost economies [and] resource allocation into new products' (Donaldson 1985a: 166). Unless the seekers are blind, which would seem to be a metaphorical impossibility, then they presumably have to make choices, otherwise 'selecting' could have no purchase in this context. That they select structure is admitted elsewhere (Donaldson 1987); that these structures are sometimes systematically capable of manipulating environments is also well documented with respect to large and powerful organizations. One may look to studies of the oil industry, for example. Sampson (1976) has chronicled the way in which the major British, Dutch and American oil companies have had an effective role to play in determining and delivering foreign policy in their respective arenas of influence for much of their history. This licence was broken only when OPEC (the Organization of Petroleum Exporting Countries) was able to restructure the environment of the big oil companies through its own effective organization as a cartel with its own foreign policy objectives in the wake of Arab defeat in war by Israel (see Harrington 1977: 236–74).

There are several other studies which demonstrate how some organizations can causally determine salient aspects of their environments. For instance, one thinks of Crenson's (1962) well known study of organizations in the steel industry in two Lakeside cities in the Great Lakes region of the United States (see also Lukes 1974). The strategic choices studied concerned whether or not these organizations would continue polluting the local ecology in ways which were technologically unnecessary. The organizations in the two cities were structurally similar; they had the same technology; they operated in the same product market; the means to avoid pollution were equally available to them. However, in Gary, Indiana, the steel organizations did not act until 1962 whereas in East Chicago they acted in 1949. What precipitated the action in each case was local government legislation. The reason why this was much slower in shaping the strategic choice whether to pollute or not in Gary was because in this city the ownership of the steel-making organizations was vested in just one company – US Steel; effectively, Gary was a company town. In addition, the local government was dominated by one political party. In East Chicago the steel mills were not all vested in one set of ownership relations nor was local politics dominated by just one party.

The explanation which Crenson offers for the difference is that under the conditions of monopoly organization and politics the environment could literally be subject to strategic choice to pollute it. The organization, US Steel, had strategically chosen to construct a company town. In this company town they could strategically choose to pollute the environment. This is a fairly clear-cut case of an organization manipulating its environment in order to suit its strategic purpose. Legislation was held at bay for thirteen profitable years compared to the situation of competitors in East Chicago. After this time the situation changed: the environment, even when chosen, may still be a potential source of uncertainty for organizations. The point is that instances of organizations determining environments are hardly rare in the annals of history, even if they are in those of certain predilections in organization theory.

Some implications flow from this downplaying and denigrating of the agency of organizations, together with the acceptance that organization environments, even where subject to systematic choice, may still be generative of future uncertainties which cannot be controlled. The salience of future uncertainties will be particularly acute for those organizations which have the characteristics of a 'risky business'. Such organizations operate with tightly coupled structures, where the activities of the constituent parts are highly interdependent; they have highly uncertain technologies which exist in a state of complex interaction with each other, and they deal with an inherently dangerous or risky process for whose potential problems no optimal solutions exist. These are precisely the organizational characteristics which tend to produce 'normal accidents' – with nuclear reactors, for instance (Perrow 1984). The system of the organization of a nuclear power plant, for example, is so tightly coupled and so highly complex that if several things go wrong simultaneously the 'dysfunction' can rapidly amplify throughout the system, out of control. This is the case even though there may be individual back-up components and fail-safe elements. It is the complexity and tightness of the interdependencies which render these relatively useless in a situation of breakdown. The implications are that uncertain environments, certain forms of tightly coupled organization agency and multiple contingencies will render only a weak determination of organization structures and practices. This is one reason why such organizations are typically subject to complex, if sometimes co-opted, regulatory controls from the state (another body which is largely noticeable by its absence from many more conventional organization theory accounts).

Against the current of this determinism (and in the case of Donaldson [1985a] a possible semantic confusion over what is entailed by 'strategic choice' as Child [1972] specified it), institutionalist theorists would agree with Child (1972) that strategic choices do occur and with Weick (1979) that they are enacted. They would add the rider that the enactments which occur arise because of the way in which they conform to culturally valued 'rational myths' about how things should be organized if they are to pass critical scrutiny, from a regulatory agency or whatever. The environment of the organization thus becomes conceptualized by 'the elaboration of rules and requirements to which individual organizations must conform if they are to receive support and legitimacy' (Scott and Meyer 1983: 149). Organizations conform to certain forms not because of any intrinsic instrumental efficiency per se, even though it may be the case that a particular form is efficient in some of these terms, but because they are obliged to or are thus rewarded for doing so, in terms of acquiring greater legitimacy, resources and survival capacities than might otherwise have been the case (Scott 1987: 498; Meyer and Rowan 1977).

Institutional theory has its roots in sociological approaches developed by Selznick (1957), Hughes (1939) and Berger and Luckmann (1967), as Scott (1987) elaborates. Institutionalists argue that where organization structures tend to become similar this will be because of neither ecological nor product market pressure, nor because of immanent determinism by contingencies of size or technology. On the contrary, the argument is that organizations will be as they are largely because they are cultural objects which are infused with value. They are produced and reproduced that way by people engaged in constructing institutional reality out of the cultural fabric which is available to them.

Four variants of institutional theory have been distinguished (Scott 1987), with some suggestion that as far as current work in the field is concerned, these can be safely reduced to just two varieties (Zucker 1988). One of these stresses, after Perrow's (1986) espousal of Selznick's (1957) work, the institutional environment of organizations as a storehouse of cultural examples which may be adopted in structuring organizations. Currently this is associated with the work of contributors such as DiMaggio (1988; DiMaggio and Powell 1983), closely linked to the institutionalist tradition of Selznick, through the influence of Perrow. While researchers in this tradition have primarily had an East Coast location in the United States, another tradition has institutional affiliation with the West Coast. At the centre of the latter concerns is a focus on how organizational actors are involved in cognitive processes of reality construction, processes which are embedded within taken-for-granted aspects of everyday life, whereby its facticity and objectivity are accomplished. The links with Berger's 'sociology of knowledge' perspective are evident, particularly in the work of Zucker (1977; 1983; 1988) and Meyer and Rowan (1977). While Zucker's work concentrates on the common understandings which may be culturally embedded in an organization, Meyer and Rowan are more concerned to chart the loci of those 'rational myths' which are institutionalized.

Meyer and Rowan (1977) focus on the processes whereby institutionalized rules become constituted, and the ways in which they frequently function as if what were institutionalized served only technically rational ends rather than culturally valued purposes. In fact, they are far more inclined to believe that the latter is the case; hence, institutional elements can become so institutionalized and taken for granted that they function as rational myths.

Rational myths are simultaneously not only affirmations of value, in as much as they tell us about culturally prescribed forms, but also denials of value, in as much as the *rational* element is stressed. They become *myths* which deny value in as much as it is argued that organizations must inescapably adopt certain forms under certain contingencies. Undoubtedly, the latter position is an argument for a value. However, the apparent inescapability of the value elected for outlines the value-infusion visible in the otherwise inscrutable mask of technical reason: TINA. Where a policy, a programme or a structure achieves the status of TINA, once clothed in the imperial robes of this rationality the reproduction of its values will be highly favoured (Clegg and Dunkerley 1980).

It has been proposed that institutional pressures towards conformity may be classified as producing isomorphism premised on coercive, mimetic and normative practices (DiMaggio and Powell 1983). These isomorphic pressures are increasingly seen as being regulatorily shaped by organizational bodies of the state and of the professions, as privileged sites of production of what become constituted as rational myths. The iron cage is seen to be composed of rules which enmesh organizations. As Scott (1987: 508–9) suggests, those deriving from state organizations will typically centralize discretion at the apex of organizations while those deriving from professional bodies will 'generally prefer weaker and more decentralized administrative structures that locate maximum discretion in the hands of individual practitioners' (Scott 1987: 509). At the same time it can be expected that state organizations will tend to have greater recourse to coercion and to organization, while professional organizations will more likely turn to mimetic and normative pressures. In addition, Johnson (1972) has hypothesized that professional projects launched from less elite social auspices will have greater recourse to the state in securing their legitimacy than has been the case with more traditional professions, such as the law or medicine, although Chua and Clegg (forthcoming) suggest that this account requires some qualification by gender.

The power perspective

The 'power perspective' is in many ways the *bête noir* of those researchers who stress efficiency. Both Donaldson (1985a) and Williamson (1985) rail against those theoretical persuasions which tend to use 'power' as a constitutive property of their model of organizations. For Williamson the adversary is primarily Perrow (1981; 1986), while for Donaldson it is Clegg and Dunkerley (1980). However, it is doubtful that there is a single power perspective, any more than there is a single institutionalist perspective. For Fligstein, the power perspective is primarily constituted in terms of the 'strategic contingencies' (Perrow 1970; Hickson et al. 1971; Hinings et al. 1974), 'resource dependencies' (Pfeffer and Salancik 1978; Pfeffer 1981) and 'political economy' (Zald 1970a; 1970b; Walmsley and Zald 1973) approaches. Such a list is by no means exhaustive (see Clegg 1989b).

However, at the very minimum, there is something in common between these and some other approaches such as Mintzberg's (1983). It is the view that organizations and environments should be conceived as arenas. Within these arenas differentially valued resources are competed for by differentially powerful agencies, exercising differential control of these resources, in complex games with indeterminate rules which each agency seeks to exploit to its advantage. Power perspectives will typically stress control of valued resources such as capital, skill, information, ownership, networks and information. The more sophisticated versions will tend to see this control deployed in complex and shifting games with indeterminate rules, in which the rules themselves become the focus of analysis. (These issues have been discussed elsewhere in detail in a number of contexts: for example, Clegg 1975; 1977; 1979; 1988; 1989a; 1989b; Clegg and Dunkerley 1980.)

As we have noted, one important perspective which Fligstein (1985) does not refer to is that of Mintzberg (1983), a writer who has developed a model of the contingency framework in which the politics of organizations are pervasive. He has done so through developing a systematic set of 'peculiar pictures' representing the basic components of organization structure. The peculiarity of the pictures resides in the way Mintzberg rings the analytical changes on a basic representation of organization – one which to my eyes looks somewhat like a stylized model of the lungs and digestive tract of the human body. Look at the basic shape in Figure 4.1 and see what I mean.

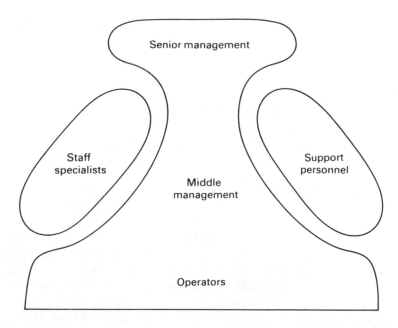

Figure 4.1 *The physiognomy of the organization according to Mintzberg (Mintzberg 1983: 29)*

It is instructive to use the basic framework of Mintzberg's analysis, blended with other elements of a power perspective deriving from Clegg and Dunkerley (1980) and Clegg, Boreham and Dow (1986), to reconsider the basic data which both Williamson and Chandler discuss. In this way one can gain some purchase on how the same descriptive processes can be subject to quite distinct theoretical specification. To do this one can build on the earlier discussion of the emergence of some predominant modern organizational forms.

At this point we may reconsider the internal contract system, already encountered in Chapter 3. How and why did this develop when it did? A power perspective would stress some different aspects to those already encountered, focussing in particular on aspects of control. From this perspective, internal contracting was devised to handle problems of surveillance and control which emerged with new conditions of production contingent on changes in the ecology of organizations (note how the terms of rival perspectives are not incompatible with a power perspective). The ecology of organizations changed as a result of the merger wave which occurred at the end of the nineteenth century, particularly in the United States. In turn, this was contingent on 'long waves' (Aglietta 1979; Kondratieff 1979; Mandel 1975; Rostow 1978) in the movement of capital accumulation in the business cycle.

Capital accumulation has been shown to have a distinct rhythm to it, when looked at through a time-span of over a century or more. There are two phases in the cycle, an upswing and a downturn, lasting around twenty or more years each. During the ascendant or upswing phase, capital accumulation is buoyant; increasing surpluses and good profits are made. Towards the end of this phase of the cycle, however, the rate of surplus appropriation and redeployment begins to slow down and the rate of new investment consequently declines. It is at this point, when equipment is becoming obsolescent and organizations begin to be under-capitalized, that mergers typically occur. They are also likely to occur at the end of a downswing because of the under-capitalization which exists in this phase of a recession. What happens, in ecological terms, is a survival of the fittest – those firms with the stronger asset base and more predatory strategies will tend to gobble up other firms. Organizations thus become more centralized.

Centralization is contingent upon a wholesale change in ownership relations as a result of the 'massive destruction of capital' (Aglietta 1979: 219) which occurs during merger periods. Organization environments change radically. However, it is not these environment changes which cause the births and deaths of organizations. The environment changes are the births, transformations and deaths of organizations. These occur because some organizations (which, *post hoc*, can always be defined as the fittest, thus they survive) actively intervene in and destroy existing organizations as legally separate entities of ownership relations. They are taken over. The elimination of what must be defined as less efficient organizations (less efficient because they did not survive), and the related centralization of economic activity, establishes new competitive relations and possibilities for a renewed upswing in capital accumulation of an increasing surplus on the part of the surviving organizations, organizations which will now control a greater amount of economic activity than they did previously. To this scenario Williamson and Chandler add accounts of where these mergers are likely to occur, in terms of what organizational and industry condition. (We shall see in Chapter 5 that although these accounts may have some plausibility for the United States' nineteenth and early twentieth century history, they are not the basis of a general theory. Only one counterfactual would be required for them to be undercut and, as we shall see, such counterfactuals can be readily adduced by entering into a more comparative perspective.)

Towards the end of the nineteenth century a great many small organizations of a petty bourgeois form (that is, under the ownership and practical surveillance of a small business-person) disappeared. Initially, the subordination of these many smaller organizations to the larger organizations created, organizations with legally more centralized ownership relations, was more formal than real. Within the newly merged plants the previous owners would frequently continue to direct the work (or to control the labour process as power theorists would typically put it). However, they would now be doing this as more or less independent managers, directing, evaluating and disciplining work (Edwards 1979: 18). Their methods of doing this were much as they had traditionally been. Patriarchal family autocracy and paternalism (such as Hobsbawm [1975: 216] describes for Britain) went together with the detailed technical knowledge of the labour process that the previous 'masters' had acquired. As Offe (1976: 25) argues, where enterprise organization was traditionally premised on a 'task-continuous status organization' (that is, one where the status hierarchy and the knowledge hierarchy coincided – the higher up the organization hierarchy one was then the more complete would be one's mastery of the organization's whole activities), then the past masters, or people who had been under them in the previous status hierarchy, really were the best people available to organize the work, because they had the most complete mastery of the knowledge involved in the organization. It was organized in such a way that this would be so. Each level of the task hierarchy presupposed a mastery of all the lower levels. The higher the level of skills mastered, the higher the level of status. Position in the skill structure was coterminous with position in the status structure.

When organizations were primarily task-continuous in their structure there was a close correspondence between the organization property relations and the organization power relations. Power would most frequently be fused with property *and* with mastery of the organization as a skill structure. These power relations would be reinforced by the relatively tight discipline of a product market in which there were a large number of small competitive firms and by a largely unorganized labour market – at least, outside the craft unions, which would have effective control over entry to the craft. Edwards (1979: 18–19) has described the power relations that would have existed in the following terms:

> A single entrepreneur, usually flanked by a small coterie of foremen and managers, ruled the firm. These bosses exercised power personally, intervening in the labour process often to exhort workers, bully and threaten them, reward good performance, hire and fire on the spot, favour loyal workers, and generally act as despots, benevolent or otherwise. They had a direct stake in translating labour power into labour, and they combined both incentives and sanctions in an idiosyncratic and unsystematic mix. There was little structure to the way power was exercised, and workers were often treated arbitrarily. Since work-forces were small and the boss was both close and powerful, workers had limited success when they tried to oppose his rule.

Such close surveillance methods of control were of much less value once enterprises developed into large scale organizations. At the end of the nineteenth century not only were larger organizations being formed as a result of merger, but new types of much larger organization were also being founded. In the steel industry, for instance, many small firms had previously been linked through markets, as they transacted exchanges based on semi-finished products in a complex product cycle. However, mergers frequently incorporated these different types of production process and their marketing under a single centre of ownership relations. Nominally, these centres would be unified sites of calculation and control. However, the fact that the new types of organization were now necessarily frequently *not* continuous in their status/knowledge organization posed problems for the realization of unified calculation and control. The continuity of the status hierarchy and the task organization no longer held. Organizational structures were becoming increasingly 'task-discontinuous' (Offe 1976). The unity of simple, direct and personal surveillance, ownership and control, premised on an intimate mastery of all the tasks at hand, no longer held. It was in this situation that internal contracting developed as the predominant regime of discipline and control.

Internal or inside contracting (Clawson 1980; Littler 1980) was well established in many countries by the end of the nineteenth century, particularly so in the textiles, metalworking and mining industries. It became particularly well entrenched in the USA. It comprised a simple solution, in the short term, to the problem of controlling the greater complexity of merged, centralized task-discontinuous organizations. The system comprised an employer and owner of capital hiring a number of internal subcontractors. Frequently these internal subcontractors would be the masters or senior overseers of the earlier independent organization. Some similarities existed between internal contractors and independent subcontractors. However, there was a major exception. Internal contractors were not legally separate organizational entities but employees of the subcontracting organization, working inside the organization, using the organization's machines, materials and equipment to produce commodities for sale only to the employing organization. As employees they would receive a lump sum for which they would contract to provide a specified amount of a specified product by a specified time. The internal contractor was free to hire and fire employees, to set wage rates, determine methods of production and exercise discipline over the workers. The internal contractor thus had a very strong interest in ensuring that the costs of the production process did not exceed the lump sum, because the difference between the two represented the contractor's profit or loss.

The internal contracting system thus reconstituted the conditions of a task-continuous organization within the changed context of a task-discontinuous organization. Internal contracting operated through the mechanism of a lump sum payment. It achieved the devolution of control, discipline and surveillance to a context of intra-organizational conditions which resembled older task-continuous organization. Lump sum contractors served to mediate changed conditions of ownership and control contingent upon merger. They stood between a greatly more centralized set of ownership relations and a set of knowledge relations which had become far more discontinuous. The set of formally subordinated labour processes that comprised the knowledge-base of merged organizations were far less subject to a unified centre than had been the case when they were independently linked through market rather than hierarchy. Previously they were diverse status systems, subject to no unified powers of surveillance. Although the power of ownership was vested at the centre of the new merged organization, this was not coterminous with authority in a singular status system born of mastery. Now, once the organization structure had become task-discontinuous, no one person could ever achieve this kind of mastery, with its associated status and authority. However, any single set of centralized ownership relations could, using the internal contract system, subordinate as many diverse knowledge practices vested in sub-organizationally specific labour processes as it chose. In effect, it would be displacing the issue of control and surveillance to the internal contractor's discipline, leaving only the very simple function of calculation to the centre, a task made simple by the reckoning of the costs of the various lump sum contracts against other costs and anticipated profits from anticipated sales. What went on in the various sub-organizational labour processes, with their diverse skills and knowledge-bases, was not a matter for centralized concern, as long as the contractor delivered.

In the early days of the internal contract system the organizations involved in it were fairly simple. Workers (Mintzberg calls them operators), under the watchful eye of the internal contractor, produced a product for disposition by the owner (or CEO: chief executive officer). The watchful eye might be more or less fraternal (in co-operative craft relations), more or less patriarchal (in familial relations) or more or less merely contractual. Clawson (1980) has suggested that in many work-settings control may have been largely premised on self-control, or self-management, conducted by workers who shared the brotherhood of the craft. Other accounts stress that notions of craft fraternity or patriarchal familialism are not only somewhat romantic but 'could often be a cloak concealing ugly relations of exploitation and ill-treatment' (Littler 1980: 157).

Internal contracting solved by default the problem of surveillance and control of an increasing scale of operations. The increase in the scale of operations, as we have seen, was contingent upon merger. The solution by default simply extended pre-existing forms of direct, personal control, premised on the mastery of an intimate knowledge of work practices and surveillance, into the larger embrace of a more centralized organizational form. It instituted, and in many cases continued, an appreciation of the profit motive in a subaltern order of quasi-entrepreneurs whose calculations concerned the labour power utilization of their workers – how to get the most out of them in the available time for the least outlay.

Internal contracting was attractive to the owners of the centralized organization – people whom it is conventional to call capitalists, because they have control of capital – for a number of reasons. It was flexible in terms of demand fluctuations and their impact on employment. No risk was entailed by the capitalist(s) due to defects or variety in the raw material characteristics, as only finished products were accepted. As a fixed payment was made for the finished product, the employer was saved the risk of capital accounting and actual costs becoming misaligned. Capital risks could be determined easily. It also had attractions for the workers as well. In Littler's (1980: 161) words, 'it provided financial incentives, and a path of upward mobility, for key groups of workers'.

Why did internal contracting not survive as the historically predominant form of organization in certain industries? Its decline seems to be linked to certain problems of control. From the capitalists' point of view, the major source of uncertainty with the internal contract system was that some organizational processes were, literally, out of their control. The system was not reliable in terms of time or quality parameters; it was one in which fraud and embezzlement of the capitalists' property were rife, particularly the illicit use of raw materials and the subsequent sale of the product. Where workers became organized in trade unions, as they increasingly did during the last decade of the nineteenth and into the twentieth centuries, then a first line of organized resistance (or, from other perspectives, 'guileful behaviour') mobilized around the wildly divergent conditions of employment which flourished under diverse internal contracts. Workers doing similar tasks in the same industries could do so under quite divergent employment practices.

The transformation of internal contracting took several directions. In Britain, for instance, the internal contractor was rapidly changed into a more direct employee, such as a foreman or a chargehand. In Japan, the changes wrought to the system of internal contracting, according to some accounts, laid the foundations for the post-war development of paternalist labour market practices in the core corporations of the post-war economic miracle. In the United States, the process was different again. Here the changes were focused by the application of engineering principles to human movement and work design through the techniques known as systematic or scientific management. These techniques developed a routinization, standardization and formalization of work roles. According to one influential account this was to result in a relative 'de-skilling' of craft work and its recomposition under diminished craft and increased managerial control (see Braverman [1974] for the *locus classicus* of this account; Clegg and Dunkerley [1980] for a discussion of it from an organization theory perspective; for an empirically informed and critical perspective which debunks the view of 'de-skilling' as a singular, uni-directional historical tendency, see Attewell [1977]).

As conditions changed, with variable periodicity in different industries and countries, the limits of simple surveillance and internal contract as a system of control became apparent. The solution that we now know as 'middle management' became widely diffused. In some instances this new layer of management was premised on the development of 'scientific management', with its formalization of the supervisory and subordinate functions. In other instances the development was less systematic. As these people became more numerous so we can speak of the growth of an extended administrative layer in the organization structure. These are people who are basically responsible for controlling the work of others. As organizations grew larger this administrative layer could become elongated – a hierarchy or a line of 'authority' would be developed. (It is usually assumed in organization theory that the fact that people are appointed to superordinate positions is sufficient to ensure that they have 'authority' by virtue of the position that they occupy. This need not be the case, of course – many people will be able to think of organizations where those 'in' authority 'have' very little real authority, and their instructions frequently are undermined, ironicized, demeaned, avoided or even aborted. Just being in a position does not mean that one necessarily 'has' all the power and respect of that position. Such capacities are easily lost and frequently hard to establish.)

According to the account which is implicit in the structural perspective on organizations of the Aston researchers, as size and complexity increase further, then organizations typically adopt more standardized methods to deal with the increased range of issues entailed. Standardization ensures that an organization develops a collective memory, capacity and basis for dealing with matters which are rarely unique and can often be assimilated to a standard response. In contemporary organizations an example of this would be a word-processed letter which is computer-generated when an account falls overdue. Of course, once an organization has things like computers inside it, unless extensive subcontracts are entered into, it will generally be the case that staff specialists are hired to look after the methods of standardization (Mintzberg 1983). Consequently, accountants, computer specialists, production engineers, quality control managers and so on are inserted into the structure of the organization, along with the operatives and the middle management who stand in a supervisory relationship to the workers. The staff specialists tend to take over from management certain responsibilities for co-ordination by instituting various methods of standardization which are supposed to serve either to complement or to supersede more direct supervision. Buttressing the line managers on the other side are the support personnel who provide services to other parts of the organization: they clean, cook, type, file and otherwise contribute to the reproduction of the organization's activities and its members (Mintzberg 1983). Typically these workers are predominantly female, recruited from a quite distinct labour market segment (see Loveridge and Mok 1979) to the staff specialists and management.

At the base of the organization are the workers or operatives: people who typically earn less and have less comfortable and often physically more demanding jobs (not necessarily harder – they could just be more boring, noisier, dirtier, more dangerous, more insecure of tenure, have less fringe benefits and so on). These are the people who form what Thompson (1967) terms the 'technical core' of the organization or those whom Mintzberg (1983) refers to as the 'operative core': they make things or provide its basic services. In the middle are the administrators. There are three types of these: the line management (who are inside the gut of the organization in Mintzberg's picture) and the staff and support personnel (who, to continue the representational metaphor, are together the lungs of the organization). Some of the people in both the staff and support function will be occupants of positions which are not markedly different from those of many of the workers, at least in some aspects of their jobs. One would be referring to aspects such as wage levels, tenure and so on. One difference might be that 'white collar' workers may frequently enjoy a more pleasant work environment than their brothers and sisters 'on the shop-floor'. As a rough and ready rule, in organizations such as those which Mintzberg's picture represents, the higher up the organization one looks the more attractive are the rewards and remuneration of the job. At the apex of the organization are the senior management, the peak of whom is the chief executive officer (or CEO). Such a person, if they do stand in an ownership relationship to the organization, may well be an absolute boss; otherwise they will more likely report to, advise and be advised by an executive board.

Where there is either product or regional diversification, according to Chandler and Donaldson, we would anticipate that this structure would be replicated across the divisions, with the apex of each structure overlapping and radiating from the 'hammer-head'-shaped centre: the structures would stretch into any number of peripheries on this basis. A centre–periphery model would thus overlap with and form a common hammer-head. Actually, in such a centre–periphery divisionalized model, elements of both the support staff and the staff specialists would be likely to be found at the central apex as well.

Mintzberg (1983) regards organizations as sites of power games in which 'influencers', or a 'cast of players', make an appearance. Some of these players are inside the organization: these he calls the 'internal coalition', the most likely members of which we have just met. Others are outside, representationally 'around' the organization; these he calls the 'external coalition'. The term 'coalition' is intended to summon the sense of a group of individuals who bargain, negotiate, even engineer a certain distribution of organizational power amongst themselves. There are ten possible groups of influencers: four in the external coalition and six in the internal coalition. Enclosed now in what appears to be an under-inflated radial

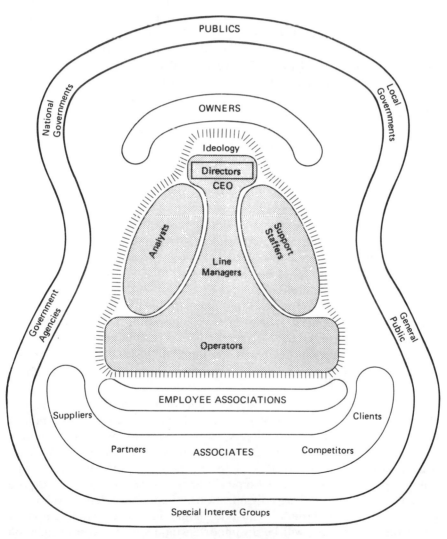

Figure 4.2 *Mintzberg's cast of players: or framing organization physiognomy (Mintzberg 1983: 29)*

tyre, the 'cast of players' is represented by means of some embellishments on the familiar picture – see Figure 4.2.

Ownership can be thought of as variable in a number of diverse ways. While something may be owned in any of several ways (by, for instance, a single individual, several or many individuals, a family or families, an institution or constellation of institutional interests or a charter) the relationship can be conceptualized as varying in terms of dimensions of 'concentration–diffusion' and 'detachment–involvement'. Consequently, unless actual legal title to ownership is coterminous with some mechanisms securing concertation and involvement of ownership, it will be unlikely that actual ownership will provide effective control. From this empirical possibility has developed a long-running debate about the nature of ownership and control of business organizations (discussed in detail in Scott 1979; Clegg, Boreham and Dow 1986: 105–31; Mintzberg 1983: 34–5; the debate originated from the work of Berle and Means [1932]). Today it is widely held that effective control of an organization can be held with relatively small amounts of legal title, if the remaining title is sufficiently detached or dispersed. Often this effective control is in fact held by senior or chief executives within the internal coalition. As we shall see in Chapter 5, there is significant variation between different national economies in terms of the typical degrees of intervention and detachment practised by members of the external coalition, which can have major institutional effects on organizations.

Associates, suppliers, clients, partners and *competitors* are agencies outside the organization with which they may stand in varying degrees of resource–dependence relationship (Pfeffer 1981), being more or less strategically contingent upon each other (Hickson et al. 1971; Hinings et al. 1974). Strategic contingency is determined by looking at factors such as how 'substitutable', how 'central' and how 'concentrated' the relationship between organizations and associates and so on is. Again, as we shall see in Chapter 5, there are important comparative implications in the way institutional frameworks enable these relationships to be constructed, particularly on a contractual basis.

Employee associations are representational bodies such as trade unions and professional societies. In some countries, such as Sweden, just about everybody in every organization would chose to be in a union right up to the very senior executives in the organization (Lawrence and Spybey 1986), while in other similarly advanced industrialized and capitalist countries, such as the United States, many organizations would be 'union free', particularly if they were small businesses, with only a few large organizations in certain sectors of the economy having any widespread union representation. Indeed, some firms exist there whose sole purpose is to exorcize unions from organizations: 'Union problems? Who you gonna call – unionbusters.' Thus, it should be evident that union or employee associations will be an important and variable contingency on the freedom of action of both the strategy and structure of organizations, in ways which will be subject to important comparative variation, as we shall see in Chapter 5. This is an important insight from the power perspective which is often missed by accounts which do not specifically consider the presence or absence of countervailing powers in and around organizations.

Publics are external organizations such as governments, special interest groups and those general 'public interest' bodies such as the media and churches. Of these, governments are undoubtedly the most important because they directly effect the 'rules of the game' in which all organizations are involved through their actions, particularly those which are regulatory and legislative. Much of the action of other agencies in the public arena, such as special interest groups and ecological, animal rights, feminist or producer organizations, will be oriented towards persuading governments to change these rules in some way which they favour. Often these will be competing groups with conflicting aims, such as exist between Friends of the Earth and bodies representing producers or unions in environmentally sensitive areas like logging, where each is aiming to influence both governments and specific organizations.

Mintzberg (1983: 45–6) identifies the complexity of the contingencies that the external coalition raises:

> Thus organizations exist in potentially intricate fields of influencer forces. These forces come from a great variety of groups – owners, suppliers, clients, partners, competitors, unions, professional societies, newspaper editors, family and friends, governments at different levels, including a myriad of departments and agencies, and a wide range of special interest groups. Each has its own set of distinct needs to be satisfied by the organization. But perhaps more interesting than their needs is how they are able to bring their external basis of power to bear on the organization, that is, how they are able to evoke the outcomes they desire when they must function from outside the regular decision-making and action-taking processes of the organization.

The means whereby external influences may act on organizations vary enormously. Mintzberg (1983: 47–97) suggests a continuum leading from influence which is most diffuse and relatively powerless (the most regular, general and detached) to that which is most specific and powerful (the most episodic, focused and personal), extending through social norms, formal constraints, pressure campaigns and direct controls, to board membership. While the latter is the primary conduit for specific external influence to occur in an organized fashion, it is not the only one. However, the nature of the board composition as representing either a 'dominated', a 'divided' or a 'passive' external coalition is of particular importance. The progression from one to infinity of the number of independent external influencers traces the movement through the three types of external coalition in the sequence suggested (Mintzberg 1983: 96–110).

Where a board is subject to a dominated external coalition (which in turn dominates it), where, for instance, there is really only one powerful external agency such as a founding family or individual, or a dominant shareholder, either individual or corporate, then the relationship of 'goodness of fit' between strategy and structure may be achieved relatively effortlessly. Where there is a plurality of powerful external actors, then the possibilities of a divided coalition with differing strategic aims having diverse structural implications follows. In the passive external coalition, where power is clearly diffused amongst many agencies, then the opportunities for the type of contingency pressures and scenarios sketched by Donaldson (1985a) are most probable – *if* power is relatively concentrated and firmly held within the internal coalition.

The elements of the 'internal coalition' are, as we have seen: at the apex, the chief executive officer of the board (the CEO); the operators; line managers; the technostructure of staff specialists; the support staff and 'ideology'. This is all pretty straightforward, except perhaps for the ideology of organizations being a basis for internal coalition formation. By this Mintzberg (1983: 29) seems to mean what many other writers have referred to as the distinctive 'organization culture': 'the set of beliefs shared by its internal influencers that distinguishes it from other organizations', although elsewhere he refers to it as 'a kind of aura' which is 'emanating from the organization' (Mintzberg 1983: 30). As we will see in Chapter 5, he is indeed correct in this assumption: the values, culture and ideology of an organization, particularly when viewed in a comparative national-cultural context, are decisive in the way they allow for assembly of the institutional framework within which the power relations amongst and between both internal and external agents can develop.

Unlike Donaldson's (1985a) contingency-design perspective, or Williamson's (1981) transaction-cost approach which positively rails against the analytical existence of anything called 'power', the perspective which Mintzberg develops has power in centre field (although, as has been argued in detail elsewhere, the specific *concept* of power which is deployed by Mintzberg is hardly exhaustive of the observations one could make from within a power framework: see Clegg 1989a; 1989b). While Fligstein's (1985) framework is nowhere near as elaborated as Mintzberg's (1983), it is not incompatible with it. Mintzberg sees the impact of power relations within either the internal or the external coalition. Different types of organization form are hypothesized as likely to arise from different configurations of power. These give rise to different games, with different rules and likely different winners and losers. Depending on the nature of the games in progress, power will be of greater or lesser importance to the determination of action within the organization. The Bradford studies of decision-making by David Hickson and his colleagues (1986) demonstrate this clearly. Organizations may be configured by different structures of decision-making processes, some of which will be far more imbued with power-play than others. Fligstein (1985: 380) is necessarily less developed than these lengthier studies, but some of the central aspects of a power perspective are focused when he argues 'that in different historical periods, different departments are likely to control large firms for different reasons'.

In the early years of the twentieth century control became likely to be vested in entrepreneurs and manufacturing personnel. It was these people who were capable of co-ordinating large scale production processes. Many of the early wave of mergers produced organizations which were not successful (Kolko 1963). This was because the people in control of the organization could not handle the co-ordination problems which mergers produced. The success of the entrepreneurs and manufacturing personnel in doing so led to their rise to power. However, once production issues became successfully routinized, Fligstein (1985: 380) argues that power shifted to 'sales and marketing personnel as the key issue for the organization becomes growth'. This is a similar argument to that of Perrow (1970). The rise to dominance of sales and marketing as organization strategies focusses on extending market penetration and developing innovation through product-related strategies. However, the dominance of these issues and interests was not immutable. Its decline can be related to two phenomena in the United States: first, governmental concern with increasing product-line concentration, which led to legislation restricting it (the 1950 Cellar–Kefauver Act); second, there was a shift to product-unrelated and merger strategies leading to conglomerates, as a consequence of the legislation:

> The emergence of conglomerates and the possibility of enormous growth through mergers further affected business strategies in the early 1960s. Finance departments are natural heirs to power in this kind of situation because investment decisions are made primarily on financial criteria. This is because firms have little expertise in evaluating product lines that are quite different from their primary lines. The only persons in the organization who can make claims to evaluate such purchases are those who have a criterion of evaluation and finance personnel are in that position. (Fligstein 1985: 380)

As the rules of the game shifted historically, then different issues became critical for considerations of organization strategy. Each set of critical issues stood in determinate relationships privileging specific forms of occupational knowledge in the organizational division of labour. With different critical issues then different personnel had the advantage of the organization field, in terms of the rules of the game. The rules were nationally specific and shaped by the institutional framework structured by that specific nation-state. The latter is an important point which will be returned to in Chapter 5. It points to the way the 'power' and 'institutional' perspectives are interpenetrated. What facilitates power is rules; rules are institutionally structured.

The interpenetration of power/institutions

From the perspectives which have been considered thus far, it seems that when we study the question of why it is that organization structures are as they are, the answer is likely to be far more complex than the simple surmise that they are subject to efficiency and effectiveness pressures. This is not to say that organizations will not be subject to criteria serving this remit. Frequently this will be the case. However, the criteria can obviously vary enormously. For instance, one may be simply concerned with the quantitative expression of the 'bottom line' profit and loss account, in the case of a business enterprise. It is always easy to show a profit in an accounting period by simple expediencies such as not investing some of the surplus for the future. The efficiency imperative can rarely be untangled from the institutional framework within which calculations both of what efficiency is and of how it is to be achieved are made. Elsewhere, in a university for instance, one might be concerned with the criteria of quality and quantity of departmental publications or the ratio of graduating students per staff member over a period of time. Whether or not a university department judges itself and is judged by the efficiency of its graduate output, or its research output, or both, will necessarily be a highly political matter. At the same time it will be specifically institutional. Consider the case of a departmental member who seeks to follow norms of research productivity acquired in the ethos of an outstanding graduate school. Such a person may find that in the context of first employment in an institution which is overwhelmingly dedicated to teaching, but which wishes to recruit the 'best' talent available (where the institutional norms of research are predominant in the definition of 'best'), the achievement of efficiency in local institutional terms is not at all unproblematic in terms of the institutional ethos in which their identity had previously been forged.

Increasingly, current organization theory is aware of the interpenetration of power, institutions and efficiency. In part these questions become more clearly seen as interpenetrated when organizations are viewed over time instead of just cross-sectionally. For instance, Marsh and Mannari (1989) researched the well known relationship between organization size and the administrative component of bureaucracy in the same forty-eight Japanese organizations which they sampled both in 1976 and then again in 1983. This was a period of rapid change in Japanese organizations as they adapted to the post-1973 oil crisis and the worst post-war recession in Japanese history. The institutional framework of Japanese organizations (which will be considered in detail subsequently) was one in which particular Japanese-style employment practices were 'partly responsible for averting larger-scale employment adjustments through American-style layoffs' (Marsh and Mannari 1989: 93). None the less, these practices of greater security of employment tenure in the core of the labour market did not prevent between 5 and 15 per cent of the labour force being laid off (Shimada 1977: 9; cited in Marsh and Mannari 1989: 93). However, during the recession Japanese firms accepted lower rates of return on total assets than did United States firms (Marsh and Mannari 1989: 93). It was this, in part, which enabled the overall rates of unemployment in Japan to be considerably less than in most of the other OECD countries during this recession (see Therborn 1986). Hence, the institutional framework within which calculations of efficiency were made was quite dissimilar to those current in otherwise similar organizations in other, higher-unemployment countries during this period.

Where the organizations which Marsh and Mannari (1989) studied did change in size during the period between 1976 and 1983, not all of them declined in size – some grew. For those organizations which were in decline they found that members of the administrative component successfully resisted erosion of their ranks to a greater extent than did the members of the production component, a finding consistent with other longitudinal data (Ford 1980). Decline does not mirror growth. During periods of growth, according to Blau and Schoenherr (1971), the economies of scale will be greater than the costs of complexity, and thus increases in size will not be positively correlated with administrative intensity. Large organizations, it is argued, actually have proportionately fewer administrative members than do smaller ones. In this view, very influential in Australian tertiary education public policy circles in the late 1980s, large organizations will be more efficient and effective than will smaller ones, because they swallow up less overhead costs.

Blau and Schoenherr (1971) worked from cross-sectional data. On the basis of this data one might anticipate that just as the growth curve is supposed to bring efficiency savings in administration so the decline curve should see the administrative component shed at the same rate at which it grew, in order to maintain these efficiencies. A contrary argument has in fact been advanced by Freeman and Hannan (1975), following Inkson, Pugh and Hickson (1970), who suggest that the relationship between growth, decline and the relative size of the administrative and production components has a 'ratchet effect' in which, on the downturns, the administrative component is much more lowly geared than the production component.

The predicted ratchet effect in the direction proposed was confirmed by Marsh and Mannari (1989). The Japanese organizations they researched were slower to shed administrators than they had been to employ them. Moreover, they shed them less rapidly than they did the production workers, even under Japanese institutional conditions. From a power perspective one would simply note the greater 'stickiness' of administrative workers relative to production workers due to the fact that the former exercise greater control over the latter, hence they, as managers, are in a better position to protect their own interest in continued employment than are the workers. One could argue (as Marsh and Mannari [1989] do) that the greater stickiness of managers is due to efficiency criteria, because

> When an organization unit A of size N with one supervisor begins to reduce its numbers of workers, its one supervisory position cannot be eliminated until such time as unit A's remaining workers are so few in number as to make A no longer viable as a separate unit. When unit A is consolidated into another unit, B, which already has a supervisor, we have a more critical test of the power vs efficiency explanations. (Marsh and Mannari 1989: 92)

While agreeing with the criteria for a 'more critical test' it is difficult to accept the first part of the argument. A power explanation would seize precisely on the supervisor–supervised relationship as the crux of this arena of organizational power (for example, Braverman 1974) in contrast to a situation of 'self-management', for example (Stanton 1989). That there are supervisors and supervised points to a structural context of control which managers are clearly able to use to greater advantage in securing the reproduction of their own, as opposed to workers', jobs. Considered from the power perspective, this is bureaucracy.

It is clear that the same phenomena can be viewed easily from more than one perspective and that the perspectives cannot be hermetically sealed off from each other. None the less, a degree of analytical separation is necessary if some comparative test of the explanatory potential of different perspectives is to be attempted. Fligstein (1985) provides such a test.

Comparing perspectives: an empirical test

Donaldson looked at comparative data drawn from five countries over a span of two decades. Fligstein's data is one-country specific, drawn from the USA only, but covering a longer time-span, from 1919 to 1979. The period thus spans the era both before and during the spread of the divisional form. Lists of the 100 largest non-financial firms by asset size were collected over this period, studying changes in organization form over the decades from 1919 to 1979. The dependent variable was whether or not a firm switched to a divisional (or MDF) structure over this period. For every firm that appeared on the list, as its composition changed over the period, data were collected on the time point at which the firm entered and, if relevant, exited the list. Reasons for exit were coded in terms of lack of growth, merger, bankruptcy or 'unascertainable'.

The perspectives were operationalized by stripping each one down to some central or core propositions compatible with the data upon which they were to be tested. We can briefly discuss each in turn.

1 *The argument from the strategy/structure perspective.* Chandler (1962), it will be recalled, laid stress on product diversification strategies as the causal factor explaining why divisionalized structures developed. To

test out this hypothesis Fligstein coded strategies as one or other of products dominant (where one product accounts for more than 70 per cent of their output), related (where there are substantial, multiple and related product lines, in which no one product is dominant) or unrelated (where firms are engaged in unrelated businesses with no dominant line). In addition, he anticipated that another measure of strategy would be the number of mergers, because they could be seen as reflecting a growth strategy, whether product related or not, which would necessitate the MDF as an organizational form (Fligstein 1985: 383).

2   *The argument from the transactions cost perspective.* Williamson's (1975) argument stressed that the overhead costs of co-ordinating transactions in organizations of increasing size would lead to the development of a divisional or MDF structure for organizations. Thus, from this perspective, the crucial independent variable would be measures of organization size and growth. Fligstein (1985: 383) measured changes in size using the per cent changes in organization assets expressed in millions of dollars over a decade, standardized in 1967 dollar values.

3   *The argument from the population ecology perspective.* Hannan and Freeman's argument stressed that transformations in organization form, such as the development of divisionally structured organizations, were most likely to occur through the creation of new organizations rather than through transformations in older, existing ones. As organizations age they become less likely to change their formal properties in this perspective. Thus, if the population ecology perspective is correct, then the divisional form will more likely be found among younger organizations over the time period of the study.

Certain problems are acknowledged by Fligstein in his test of the population ecology perspective. Hannan and Freeman's emphasis on youth and smallness of size as sources of innovation would not be easily picked up by a study which only looks at the largest one hundred organizations. One can note, however, that the divisional form was *not* an innovation of either new or small firms historically. It originated with DuPont and General Motors, as Chandler (1962) observed: neither was small or infant at this stage in its history. Fligstein (1985: 385) also suggests that the sample is not a population in Hannan and Freeman's (1984) terms. As these terms are themselves somewhat suspect (Young 1988) this will not detain us here. In fact, in so far as the test which Fligstein proposes conforms to the criterion of studying large and significant organizations – what Collingon and Cray (1980) term 'critical organizations' – rather than the relatively small and insignificant organizations which population ecologists have often studied, such as restaurants, there is much to recommend it.

4   *The argument from the institutional perspective.* As Fligstein (1985: 384) notes, the institutional argument is not an easy one to operationalize: 'The issue is how to capture a mimetic effect.' Obviously any attempt at measurement would have to capture some sense of the way in which a form

available in a given environment becomes increasingly pervasive in its adoption by the majority of organizations within that environment. One way of gaining some insight into this would be to use industry as a proxy for environment. Thus, using Standard Industry Codes (in this case at the two digit level), if one were to record the percentage of firms in each industry category which had made the transition to the divisional form at the beginning of each decade, then this would be a reasonable approximation to the events that institutional arguments suggest would occur. (Actually, it is a little bit more complicated by the necessity of certain statistical procedures which enable one to estimate the odds that any organization which is in the decade-sample would change structure; this would not be stable over the period as some organizations would enter and others leave, but these need not concern us here: see Fligstein 1985: 384.)

5 *The argument from the power perspective.* The power perspective would suggest that where organizations change form, then the likely cause would be that certain strategic actors had succeeded in changing the rules of the game regulating the reproduction of that organizational entity. Thus, typically it would assume that the new rules of the game would be those which favoured the continued ascendancy of these strategically inclined players in the organizational game. Fligstein (1985: 380) suggests that as 'the MDF could be viewed as a mechanism which allows for growth through product-related and -unrelated strategies, its implementation would be favoured by those who stood to gain the most from those strategies, i.e., sales and marketing, and finance personnel'. If these players are ascendant to a greater extent in divisional than in non-divisional organizations, then this would seem to favour explanations proffered by the power perspective. It is not difficult to operationalize this perspective using readily available biographical information. Having determined who the CEO was for each of the time points at which an organization appeared on the list, the occupational/functional identity of this person could be determined in 90 per cent of the cases by using this biographical material. These identities were coded as manufacturing, sales and marketing; finance; general management; entrepreneur; lawyer; and unable to ascertain.

When Fligstein (1985: 385–8) analysed the data he found that it displayed a clear bimodal distribution: firms either stayed on the list throughout the period of analysis or were on for only a relatively short period. Throughout the period the percentage of firms having a divisional form increased from 1.5 per cent to 84.2 per cent, with the largest increase occurring in the 1948–9 period. Generally, with the exception of the period from 1959 to 1969, there was no significant difference in organization form between firms which entered or left the list. For this decade, however, staying on the list and entering it, as opposed to leaving it, were positively associated with the MDF organization.

On an industry basis the distribution of the MDF was much as one might have anticipated from Chandler's (1962) argument:

Industries where product-related strategies dominated, like machine, chemical, and transportation industries, adopted the MDF in large numbers relatively early; while industries that were more likely to be vertically integrated, like mining, metalmaking, lumber and paper, and petroleum, adopted the MDF later and to a lesser extent. Except for mining, metalmaking, and miscellaneous industries, all industries had high rates of adoption by 1979 . . . [O]rganizations actually come to resemble those around them. Food, lumber and paper, and petroleum industries all adopt the MDF, though they do so at a later date. (Fligstein 1985: 386)

The data lists at decade intervals the one hundred largest non-financial firms, broken down by industry and whether or not they had adopted the MDF during that decade. In the first decade only the two 'pioneers', General Motors and DuPont, had adopted the divisional form of organization. During the second decade firms with product-related strategies (Chandler) were more likely to adopt a divisional form, a relationship which persists through the decades. Another strong relationship is between organizations having CEOs from a sales, marketing or finance background (power perspective) and the adoption of a divisionalized structure, a trend which also continues through the decades of data. (In 1929–39 sales, marketing and finance are all powerful; in 1939–49 it is sales and marketing which count; in 1949–59 it is finance; in 1959–69 either sales or finance is powerful. From 1969 to 1979 there remains a positive and statistically significant relationship between a finance CEO and the adoption of a divisional form.) In a contradiction of the population ecology perspective it was the older, not the younger, firms which were most likely to have adopted the MDF. No support was found for the explanation from growth, as advanced by Williamson. In fact, throughout the decades, with an exception only for the period from 1939 to 1959, no support at all could be found for the arguments from increasing size as predicted by Williamson. Nor does the population ecology perspective fare well. It is consistently the older rather than the younger firms which adopt a divisional structure throughout the decades in question. As the decades advance there is a consistent positive effect that as other firms in an industry change to the divisional form, then any remaining firm is more likely to do so (Fligstein 1985: 387). This is confirmation of the mimetic processes stressed by the institutional perspective.

Donaldson (1987) favoured a model which saw divisionalization as efficiency driven by the Chandlerian contingencies of product-mix. In the light of Fligstein's research (1985) it is clear that (with the important qualification that this may apply only for the United States), the model requires broadening. These findings suggest a model of organizational behaviour in which 'those in control of large firms acted to change their organizational structures under three conditions: when they were pursuing a multiproduct strategy; when their competitors shifted structures; and when they had a background in the organization such that their interests reflected those of the sales or finance departments' (Fligstein 1985: 388).

With respect to the 'moderator' variables which Donaldson considered, it would seem that one must also refer to aspects stressed by the power perspective, such as the occupational identity of the CEO, as well as to the fact that the diffusion of the MDF may be as likely to be as driven institutionally as by efficiency. One could counter that efficiency determined that CEOs in sales and finance were best able to run divisional organizations, and that it was the pressure of efficiency which caused laggard organizations to follow the leaders in an industry in adopting the divisional form.

The structural changes which occurred are subject to the greatest specification when described in terms of the putative mechanisms advanced by institutional and power theory. If the pressures from efficiency were as strong as Chandler and Donaldson suggest then it really ought not matter what the occupational identity of the CEO was – CEOs would simply have to respond to efficiency pressures or their organizations would cease to survive. The power perspective suggests, as Fligstein (1985: 388) argues, that certain organization actors formed in specific occupational identities, 'who have the resources to implement their point of view on appropriate corporate strategy, and hence structure, would choose to implement the MDF as a structure that would enhance and extend their power'. In doing so they watch their competitors for strategies which they can legitimately adopt in order to enhance their strategicality and hence contribute to processes of institutional isomorphism.

For the future, research would be well advised to try and construct an account of the various historical organization rules and games, in their institutional specificity, which enabled the ascendance of particular types of occupational identity. Thus, any further research in this area would need to see, as part of an overall multivariate research strategy, how the powerful CEOs rose to dominance: did they get there in a discontinuous manner through boardroom coups in the face of efficiency pressures or was the process far less crisis-driven? If the latter, then this would seem to be a further weakening of arguments from efficiency. Although one could argue that efficiency drove the outcomes, given that the crises were caused by inefficiency in the first place, this is a fairly roundabout argument. Why is it that certain types of occupational identity are far more likely to end up as strategically powerful than others? Rather than suggesting a relatively ineffable process whereby efficiency works its purpose on organizations, it is clear that what is constituted as optimal economic efficiency is always subject to social embeddedness (Granovetter 1985).

In different social contexts different institutional frameworks for economic action will lead to diverse 'modes of rationality', rather than just one framework for evident economic efficiency. Modes of rationality have to be constructed by strategic actors out of available resources or stocks of knowledge. These will include not only those stocks of knowledge that have been acquired as a matter of occupational identity but also those practices which appear to enjoy a widespread legitimacy in the environment of action. Thus, the institutional perspective orients one to the search for variations in institutional frameworks. As we shall see in Chapter 5, these do occur at the level of national variation. At the same time an institutional perspective also orients one to the necessity of identifying agents who are sufficiently strategic to be in a position to be able to strive to reproduce their preferred modes of rationality. To strive is not always to succeed. There is no necessary circuit of power to rationality and efficiency. Agents can and frequently will be seen to make mistakes, when they are reviewed with the benefits of hindsight. What is important is to appreciate not only that efficiency requires intermediation by dominant organization actors but also that diverse conceptions of the concept will enter into the ways and means through which they strive to reproduce their dominance.

Conclusion

Fligstein's (1985) contribution enables one to consider both systematically and empirically a number of recent influential perspectives in organization analysis. Not all theorists would see the necessity of doing this – of being quite so 'positivistic' in one's argumentation. However, there are good reasons for compromising in this way. Although there are many directions and competing fields of force in organization studies it would be fair to say that its present centre of gravity is as an empirical science premised on quantitative data. There is a research ethos which the culture fosters. It is macho, where theoretical mastery can only ever be ceded to those who control their numbers. If one's argument is not going to be subject to disdain and lack of acknowledgement, because it is 'theoretical', then it is important to disarm this criticism. (In passing, it is odd that theory and measurement should have reached this impasse, if my diagnosis is correct.) There are those circles in which 'theory' is a term of abuse unless it is accompanied by multivariate equations. It is rather harder to be abusive to an argument which accepts the culturally appropriate premises. Thus, the article served as a peg on which to hang consideration of the competing theoretical perspectives of transaction cost analysis (Williamson); the strategy/structure perspective (Chandler); contingency theory (as developed by Donaldson); the population ecology perspective (developed by Hannan and Freeman); institutional theory (in the framework offered by DiMaggio and Powell); and the power perspective (which has been developed by Mintzberg, Perrow, myself and many others). It enabled systematic empirical testing of these perspectives with an historical and reliable, if nationally specific, body of data. Moreover, it allowed for some adjudication of these theoretical perspectives. Neither the transaction costs nor the population ecology framework survives the encounter particularly well. Theoretically, the interpretation of the data suggests the useful intermediation of the institutionalist and power perspectives as an overlay to the basic narrative account provided by Chandler and conceptualized in contingency terms by Donaldson.

A strategy of analysis suggests itself for the next chapter of this book. The Donaldsonian gloss on Chandler argued for organization form being derived from the contingencies of the product market affecting intra-organizational processes of efficiency adaptation. If these are contingencies one would expect to find that they are indeed industry specific. Not every large firm would necessarily adopt the MDF by virtue of being large. However, where an industry sector in one of the advanced societies becomes characterized by the MDF, then one would anticipate that, on a global basis, in so far as the industry is widely distributed, firms in that industry ought to adopt the same form across the advanced societies. Hence, if one were able to find some counter-factual examples from an industry which elsewhere was characterized by the divisional form, then this would be a strong argument against contingency theory as a determinate explanation. Following the logic of the analysis of this chapter, where one did not find the contingency argument supported, one would instead seek to explore the institutional framework and power processes specific to the exceptional cases for clues as to why the deviant cases should have occurred. Should one be able to construct a plausible account of these exceptions in terms of power and institutions, then it will be that much harder to accept the generalized contingency theory account with its strict adherence to norms of efficiency as the only important value. It would be allowed that organizational modernities contained a number of diversities, rather than a more limited horizon of possibilities.

To reprise the Weberian theme of the iron cage, it would seem that several observations are in order after the review of this chapter. First, there clearly is no single iron cage of bureaucracy. Numerous organization forms have been developed and diffused on the path both to bureaucracy (internal contracting) and subsequently to divisionalization. Second, the evidence seems to suggest that these variable organization forms are less the result of inexorable adaptation to population ecology, increasing size and product market and technology structure than they are to culturally defined criteria of what a 'dispositional good' might be in terms of organization structuring and the ability of certain strategic actors to constitute these in ways which reproduce their strategicality. The form of the 'iron cage' thus begins to look somewhat more like a nifty piece of political opportunism than it might otherwise have done. Nor are the politics merely those of the observed: they are clearly also evident in the preferences of the observers as they seek to enhance the cultural capital of their preferred views of what organization analysis is – or should be.

5

French Bread, Italian Fashions and Asian Enterprise

I have just returned to my study from lunch to start typing this text. I had some cheese, pickles and bread – the type of thing which a clever marketing executive with the M&B Brewery in Britain coined as a 'ploughman's lunch' in the mid-1960s. Had I been in Hong Kong, perhaps, it would more likely have been steamed fish and boiled rice or green vegetables, lightly stir-fried, perhaps with noodles, preferably with chillies – lots of them! I quite enjoy all of these foods; my tastes are rather catholic. At lunchtime, however, I prefer bread to rice and noodles.

The lunchtime preference for bread is not unqualified; it depends on the type of bread that is available. For instance, on the basis of limited sampling, I have yet to eat a bread in the United States which I enjoy. Invariably I find it too sweet and too refined. In my limited experience I would hypothesize that 'bread' is not a term which signifies a unitary category of foodstuff. What kinds of bread are there? Brown bread, white bread, black bread, sweet bread, sour bread – the list can proliferate rapidly, as new distinctions are added and further categories created.

What does this brief excursus on bread have to do with a book on organizations? Actually, it has a great deal of relevance. Odds are that most readers of this book who have shared my lunch pattern today, at least if they are outside the 'Latin' European countries, will have eaten what Daniel Bertaux and Isabelle Bertaux-Wiame (1981: 155) term 'industrial bread': that is, 'industrial food wrapped in a shroud of cellophane which is sold in the supermarkets of the Western world under the somewhat euphemistic label of "bread"'. It is this industrial bread which accounts for almost all the bread sold in the United States, Canada, Australia, New Zealand and much of Europe – particularly in Britain, as I recall. The reasons for the supremacy of this 'industrial bread' are evident from what we have learned from Chandler (1962). It is usually one product-line, often produced from within a division, of a giant food conglomerate, such as Goodman Fielder Wattie or Rank Hovis McDougal, formed by merger and based around vertical integration from flour milling to bread and related food retailing. It is a classic case of an industry in which, as organizations merged and became conglomerates, divisionalization occurred and products diversified. This product diversification is typical of the industrialized foods industry.

One of the characteristics of Chandler's (1962) account is that it is specifically about the United States. If the thesis that he advances were to be the basis for a scientific generalizing account of how and why organizations have the structures they do, as Donaldson (1987) suggests, then a single appropriate counter-factual would serve to demonstrate that it had a more limited utility than might otherwise be thought. According to Donaldson's view of the Chandlerian thesis, efficient and successful organizations in similar industries, cross-culturally, would adopt the same type of strategy and structure, irrespective of their location. Another way of thinking of this would be to say that the organizational characteristics of an industry which has divisionalized in the United States ought to be the same for the organizations in the same industry making the same product in an economically similar advanced capitalist country.

French bread

So, how is French bread possible? How has the market dominance of conglomerate oligopoly bread manufactured by firms like Goodman Fielder Wattie or Rank Hovis McDougal been avoided? Why should it be that in France the equivalent of these 'manufacturers' control only about 10 per cent of the market whereas in other countries, such as Britain and the United States, it is far closer to 100 per cent? It was this question which generated one of the more entertaining studies in social research. Its entertainment value is particularly marked in contrast to a great deal of organization theory. Perhaps for this reason, or because of the bibliographic habitat of many organization theorists, one has rarely seen it cited in the annals of those interested in the study of organizations (Marceau 1989 is an exception). The article is called 'Artisanal Bakery in France: How it Lives and Why it Survives', by Daniel Bertaux and Isabelle Bertaux-Wiame (1981).

What is French bread? Visitors to and residents of France know it as a crusty *baguette* or half-pound loaf. It looks good and it tastes good. However, to describe it does not tell us what French bread is. It is clearer, perhaps, if we determine what it is not. First, it is not a standardized, easily transportable, mass-produced product, one whose quality is, as Bertaux and Bertaux-Wiame (1981: 159) say, 'invariable (or invariably poor)'. It is not capitalist bread. It is not the product of a capitalist mode of production. It is not a heavily marketed, brand-identified, size-invariant, shrink-wrapped and sliced product sold identically in virtually similar supermarket chains throughout the country. It is not an easily transportable commodity capable of being mass-marketed and distributed. It is the result of an *artisanal* rather than a capitalist mode of production. Consider the conditions of its production:

France has now about 52 million inhabitants and 50,000 bakeries; one bakery for one thousand people, this is the average ratio. And it means, quite obviously, a very decentralized scattering of small, independent bakeries – the bread, before being put on sale, is firstly *made* on the spot. Not only bread but also cakes, croissants, and so on are *produced* by the baker (who is by training and function, an artisan rather than a shopkeeper) and by his workers, when there are any. The shopkeeper here is the baker's wife, and the couple is the real economic unit, man as artisan, woman as shopkeeper, and the bond of marriage between them functioning somehow like a relation of production.

The 50,000 bakeries employ about 80,000 workers, and this says a lot about the small size of most bakeries: on average they employ less than three workers. What is more, 40 per cent of these 'workers' are under 20 years old, they are in fact *apprentices* (aged 15 to 17) or young workers aged 18 to 19. The age-pyramid of the male population is quite unusual; it has a tremendously large base, composed of these young men. Such a structure means that most of them leave the trade some time between 20 and 25, that is soon after returning from military service (which is compulsory for all men, starting at age 20 and lasting at least one year).

To indicate with rather more precision the structure of this branch of trade, we have to use detailed statistics, the most recent of which date from 1962. In this year, the total number of bakeries was 48,000. Of these 13,000 did not employ anybody other than family members. The husband at the oven, the wife at the cash register, maybe a child helping to sell on Sunday mornings or market days, or a young girl from a neighbouring family working there as a non-registered salesgirl: this was all the labour power of these very small bakeries.

In 1962, 28,000 bakeries still employed only one or two persons, usually one worker and either an apprentice or a salesgirl. And if one adds the 5700 bakeries employing from three to five persons and the 13,000 without employees, the total comes to 46,700, that is almost the totality (97 per cent) of the bakeries. In the midst of an industrialized society, the existence of such a scattered branch of production looks like a socio-historical aberration.

The remaining 3 per cent of the total (1300 bakeries with more than five employees) employ 45,000 persons, which means 40 per cent of the salaried workforce of the bakeries (in 1962). It seems huge, but this percentage is misleading because the artisans and their wives should also be included in the workforce; taking this into account, the largest bakeries employ no more than 20 per cent of the total workforce.

Not all these bakeries are of the industrial type. Actually most of them are large boulangeries-patisseries, making not only bread and viennoiserie (croissants, petits pains), but various kinds of cakes and pastries which require much labour. The number of really industrial bakeries was small in 1962 (thirty-three establishments employing more than twenty persons, out of which four employed more than 100, and one more than 500). In 1978 their number is still small, and their share of the bread market is under twenty per cent.

As far as we know, there has not been any drastic change since 1962. For instance, the number of bakeries has remained stable; in fact it increased between 1962 and 1966 (from 48,000 to 55,000), thus following the increase of French population at this time. Their numbers have been diminishing since, but quite slowly (53,700 bakeries in 1970, 51,000 in 1977). (Bertaux and Bertaux-Wiame 1981: 156–7)

Hidden in these figures is a change in location of these artisanal bakeries, if not in their form. The recent decrease masks two tendencies. First, there is the decline of many of the poorest businesses in depopulating urban areas and deserted villages. Second, there is the emergence of new, larger (employing ten to fifteen people) bakeries making bread for markets as large as 10,000 to 20,000 people in newer suburban areas. However, these are the same kind of artisanal bakeries, making the same kind of artisanal bread, using the same methods of production. It is apparent that the artisanal form is not in present danger of extinction.

Why is it that the huge bread factory, a division of a even huger merged conglomerate food producer based on flour, distributing its standardized, industrialized product across the nation, why has such a firm not exploited the efficiencies of the divisional form to colonize the French market for bread and, in so doing, make the science of organizations truly generalizable, truly universal, truly a positive science? Do the French not know their contingency theory?

It is not just a matter of the culture of France, as one might think. After all, as Bertaux and Bertaux-Wiame (1981: 158) note, despite the famed *gastronomie* of the French and their penchant for long lunches, this has not stopped other areas of the national culture being undermined: 'No doubt, the French used to like good wines, good poultry, good cheese and that did not prevent all these foods from becoming food products, industrialized, standardized, homogenized; dead things. Still the French eat them, albeit with a grimace.' What is so special about bread?

It is not as if the normal forces of the market, from which Chandler and Donaldson would make a theory, have not occurred in France. They have – but the outcomes have been different. In the 1950s a campaign was waged against traditional (artisanal) bread on a broad front – it was fattening, it was claimed, in comparison to dietarily desirable rusks (a charge which research commissioned by *Le Syndicat de la Boulangerie* did not support). During the 1950s, perhaps in part in response to this campaign, the staple product of *les boulangers* changed from a one-pound loaf to the crustier half-pound baguette. 'More crust, less crumb', as the researchers put it. The *baguette* was a major success. It possessed an inherent quality of 'freshness'. It was not a stable industrial product which could be easily transported through space and time. It was a perishable product, one whose intrinsic, positional value was that it was fresh, that it did perish and that it could not be bought other than on a daily basis. It incorporated everything that industrial bread could not be.

In 1966 the largest flour-milling group in France, which had a virtual monopoly of the supply of flour to the Paris market, was rumoured to be preparing a huge bread factory close to the Seine in order to supply industrial bread to the French market. Given the support that *les boulangers* enjoyed for their *baguettes* it would first be necessary to batter down the bakers with whatever artillery (or 'resource dependency') came to hand. The monopoly was the evident answer. One day, without warning, the flour-milling company changed the terms of trade: henceforth, only full truckloads would be delivered, a crippling blow to bakers who had neither the market nor the storage capacity to warrant such an amount. However, after a week of panic the small bakers discovered

> that some small mills were still functioning in the rural regions surrounding the Paris area. These mills were on the verge of closing down, as they were only working at 20 per cent of their capacity. They were, of course, extremely happy to accept the orders of the small bakers, and thus to reach full capacity. After one month of groping about, it appeared that the new network could quite possibly function smoothly. The big flour-milling company understood it had lost the fight; it went back to its previous policy of retail delivery, lowered its prices to get back its former customers, and put the plans for the factory back in the safe where they are waiting for the next opportunity. (Bertaux and Bertaux-Wiame 1981: 161)

Hence, the survival of the small bakers is not achieved without struggle. Not only is this struggle of an occasionally dramatic kind against those forces which would rationalize the world of French bread, scenting a profit and an opportunity to internalize a potentially profitable transaction. The workday life of the small baker is also a daily struggle, and it is in this struggle, in particular, that the organizational form of French bread is reproduced and *les boulangeries* survive all efforts to achieve their structural adjustment to a more efficient form.

It is not a rational life, baking bread. It has always been hard work for small returns. Before the war the working day would often start as early as midnight, or earlier, with the preparation of the first batch of dough. The oven had to be warmed next, so wood had to be cut, the fire lit and so on. At around two in the morning the first batch had to be cooked and so on in successive batches through to noon. Lunch and sleep followed till four, when the baker and the young apprentice would load up the cart and attend to their rural rounds delivering bread to the farms. Returning home from this later that evening they would have time for a few hour's sleep until midnight and the quotidian round recommenced.

Well, things have improved a little. In 1936 the state decreed that all baker's shops had to shut for one day a week, which meant that on the previous day the baker worked twice as hard to make double the bread for loyal customers to take them through the day off. This batch was known as *le doublage*. Nowadays wood no longer has to be cut and dried; much of the process of production has been mechanized, and the baker has to start the working day at 'only' three or four in the morning and work 'only' nine or ten hours, albeit more intensively than in the old days, as there are now machines to be kept up with. *Le doublage* still remains. Despite laws against it, these hours are usually the hours of the apprentices as well, for how else will they learn the trade?

What of the bakers' wives? Their day is also long and their role important. The shop opens from eight in the morning, or seven in working class districts; it may shut from one till four and then reopen, closing finally at eight, a long day's work 'which by the way gives no salary, no social rights whatsoever, and no property rights either' and to which 'they must add the work of any housewife and mother. The closing day is used not for rest or leisure, but in making up for the accumulated backlog of cleaning, washing, shopping' (Bertaux and Bertaux-Wiame 1981: 163). Yet, in the whole process whereby the artisanal bakeries have been reproduced in France while in most other places they have been rationalized out of existence, it is the wives who are the most important actors. The baker's wife is the street-level worker, the front-line marketer. Good bakers bake good bread but it is good wives who sell it, who create a regular custom attracted to a particular bread and a particular shop. Not only the marketer and salesperson, the wife is also the accountant, cashier and trusted confidante. A good wife will not cheat a good husband, one who is also a good baker. While wives who become widows can hire bakery workers to continue the business, husbands who have become widowers or whose wives have left them find it difficult to continue in the business without an unpaid and trustworthy partner. Anyone else cannot be trusted not to cheat; besides, they have to be paid. Good wives are good investments in more ways than one. It is to the wives' judgement that the reproduction of this whole enterprise falls. It is the wives' judgement which preserves for the French their bread and provides this fascinating counter-factual to the efficiency ethic of some colleagues in organization theory.

Once upon a time, bakers were born into the trade. The professional organization of bakers saw to it that in almost every case the only way to become a baker was to be born the son of a baker. The role of the wife was literally to reproduce the next generation to mind, manage and eventually take over the business. These days, with enhanced possibilities of occupational and social mobility, few parents who are bakers would want to see their children destined for the same end, and few children who have seen what is entailed at close quarters would want to end up like their parents. 'Today's bakers are not born bakers; this is the key discovery' (Bertaux and Bertaux-Wiame 1981: 164). Given the nature of the trade, only someone who had been apprenticed in it could possibly run the business. Most of the present-day bakers were former bakery workers who had become self-employed at an early age (recall the odd age-demography of bakery employees). Initially, this discovery was puzzling. Where would a lowly paid worker in a low-status trade, in all probability with no collateral, raise the 100,000 francs necessary to buy even one of the smallest going concerns? Certainly not from a bank.

There are two sides to any transaction. Consider an old couple whose life has been their bakery, who want to retire. They have no children to hand the business on to; perhaps they are childless or their children have gained other skills and followed other opportunities. How can they retire? Only if they can sell the business as a 'going concern' complete with 'goodwill' to someone who will continue to use the premises as a bakery.

Only if the bakery is to be continued as a bakery can that 'goodwill' (a set of stable customer relationships with a specific local population) return an appropriate monetary value, which the machinery, frequently worn out, will not. Premises are invariably rented. The only people who can take over the trade are the young men who have been apprenticed in it. Not only are they the only ones who 'know' the trade and its skills, they are also the only ones who make themselves available. Usually these young men (and their brides) are from a rural background, for whom the prospect of arduous work for low rewards, but together with the 'freedom' of being their own *patron*, is an inducement few others would accept.

For those young men who stay in the trade after military service has broadened their occupational horizons (many quit, as the demographics show), becoming a self-employed baker consummates the hard union of their apprenticeship, long hours and low pay. It is this ever present project which makes *existing* as a lowly worker not equivalent to *being exploited* as a miserable proletarian. It is a temporary state of affairs en route to the *petite bourgeoisie*.

Still, two aspects of this puzzle remain to be completed. First, how are these bakery workers able to afford to become honourable proprietors in *Le Syndicat de la Boulangerie?* Second, what is distinctive about France which allows this to happen, which saves the French from the dubious delights of industrial bread and disconfirms those contingency theorists who, on the basis of an industry, a technology, a product, a market, would predict a certain scale and mode of organization?

The wife is the key to the whole enterprise, it has been said. We shall see in what way this is so. First, how do bakery workers become proprietors and old couples retire from the trade? The retiring couple *lend* the money which is necessary to the bakery worker. For the incoming baker and his wife it means eight years of relative hardship and privation as they save to repay the value of the goodwill (based on the value of an average month's sale of bread). For the retiring couple it means placing tremendous trust in the new couple, for the turnover may be a risky business: if they do not succeed in the trade then they cannot repay the loan. Actually, the trust is placed not so much in the couple, for the bakery worker is expected to 'know' the trade on the basis of his ten years' or so service. The trust has to be placed in the young wife who is entering the trade. She is the secret of the future success of the *boulangerie* – has she got what it takes to be a good shopkeeper? Can she tolerate the long hours of work during the day and the emptiness of the nights as her husband toils in the bakery? Does she know what being a baker's wife means and entails? Will she resent the customers who, arriving after hours, will none the less disturb her because they want, expect, fresh bread? As the researchers note, 'it is extremely interesting to observe the practices of the two couples during the crucial period of *passage*. Pretending to show the young lady how to behave as *boulangère*, the experienced woman will also check her spontaneous reaction and try to uncover her fundamental values'

(Bertaux and Bertaux-Wiame 1981: 167). A good baker needs a good wife as well as money to succeed. If he does not have the former it is unlikely he will make the latter. A baker's marriage is not just a transaction between marital partners; it is also a transaction between an artisan and a shopkeeper who are bonded together.

The second and remaining piece of the puzzle is, why should it be that these social relations and this bread have survived in France (and some other Latin countries such as Spain and Italy)? The clue to this is the largely rural background of new entrants to the trade. The bakeries as an artisanal pursuit have for most of their history (the past ten centuries) been an urban phenomenon. Peasant women typically baked their own bread up until the early years of this century. Today this is no longer the case. According to the most authoritative source (one hesitates to call it a 'cookery book', for it is far more than such a simple text of recipe-knowledge),

> The average French household does no yeast baking at all except for *babas*, *savarins*, and an occasional *brioche*. It certainly does no bread making, and there is no need to because every neighbourhood has its own *boulangerie* serving freshly baked bread every day of the week but one, usually Monday, when the *boulanger* takes his day off. Thus you cannot even find a bread tin in a French household store, and there are no French recipes for home-made bread. (Beck and Child 1978: 84)

It is only in the late nineteenth century that rural bakers appeared, sometimes by diffusion from urban areas, sometimes through local millers using newer technologies to extend their trade to capture what had previously been done as domestic labour, other than in rural-industrial areas where they emerged with the mills. During the early twentieth century a dense ecology of bakeries developed, each one serving about 500 to 1,500 people and with it a new pool of labour was tapped from the ranks of the independent peasantry, a peasantry embodying a fierce individualism and a commitment to good husbandry, to a job well done. These people were the vital part in the continuity of the *boulangerie*.

The baker's sons disappeared as recruits for reproduction of the artisanal form. In France, with its peculiar peasant structure located in the post-Napoleonic settlement and reproduced even in the contemporary structure of rural life, potential bakery workers embodying peasant values were available to take over the enterprises that the owning families vacated. Over the course of the apprenticeship, embodied peasant values become overlain, interpenetrated and nurtured by a new set of rhythms acquired as a constitutive part of the job:

> the trade penetrates the body . . . you have to transform your body completely. Its natural rhythm has to be reversed, the body must learn to sleep during the day and be awake in the dark hours of the night. The speed of movements have to be augmented . . . It means a trained body, which lives on its nerves; and the

training, the restructuring of the body is what apprenticeship is all about. So it may be said that while bakers make the bread, the bread also makes the bakers; if the population needs bread to live, the artisanal form needs the bakers' bodies in order to survive. The relations of production produce the people who will reproduce them . . .

[T]hrough competition between bakers, this rhythm becomes the rhythm of the whole trade, and if one considers not only one bakery but fifty thousand with their long opening hours and the hard work which takes place around the ovens, all this for relatively low economic rewards; if one considers the amount of work invested, then one understands better why it is so difficult for industry to take over the market for bread. (Bertaux and Bertaux-Wiame 1981: 175–6)

The space in which industrial bread could be made – the space, that is, in which it could be consumed, because the alternative had disappeared – never occurred in France. The reason the form was able to survive was precisely because it was able to reproduce, due to the survival of the French peasantry into the twentieth century, a survival contingent on a complex of state actions and public policies from the post-revolutionary settlement to the present day. One should be clear: in a text which otherwise has postmodernity as a theme the choice of French bread as an example of the limits of a mode of organization analysis points not so much beyond modernity but to the reproduction within of something seemingly pre-modern.

It has been a long and complex tale, one I wish that I had written myself, rather than being merely the transcriber, yet I believe that it teaches us some profoundly important things about organizations. First, organizations are composed around a core of 'value imperatives', as the institutionalists have argued. At every stage where the *boulangerie* might have been annihilated at the hands of industrial bread and its organizational form, the resources of deeply embedded cultural values were there to enable resistance. Resistance is grounded in the cultural resources which people have available to them in any specific institutional context. For the *boulangerie* of France these resources were a supply of potential *petits bourgeois* drawn from the ranks of an independent peasantry which elsewhere the transition to modernity had almost eliminated or which had never been fabricated in anything like the same form (Moore 1968). Second, organizations are embedded within a complex field of force laced together by the capillary power of culturally embedded ways of doing, ways of being and ways of becoming (Clegg 1989b). Sure, there are contingencies, transaction costs and pressures of efficiency. We saw how the industrial flour-millers sought to exercise power and dispense with the regrettable contingency that French consumers would not and will not willingly purchase the kind of industrial bread that they could make. Sure, the transaction costs are expensive and inefficient for all concerned. The customers have to shop for bread every day; with industrial bread the transaction costs could have been minimized to just one weekly supermarket trip. For the bakers the costs are even higher. They have to endure a long, arduous and unremunerative apprenticeship; they have to borrow heavily at the beginning to become proprietors and to lend heavily at the end to become retirees; they have to take extraordinary risks that at the end of their lives the transaction costs associated with retirement may never be recouped; they leave themselves open at the most vulnerable stage in their lives to the transacting party operating both opportunistically with considerable guile or foolishly with insufficient acumen. They place their fate in the hands of a transacting party that they may never be sure to trust in a transaction which has no guarantees. Yet they still do all these things. They choose to be bakers. In addition, their customers choose to eat baker's bread rather than its industrial counterpart.

Perhaps it would be more efficient if the French government simply invited some major United States organization theorist to conduct a consultancy into the efficiency and effectiveness of the system for the production and distribution of bread. It is certain that such a person would be appalled at what they saw (though they might be surprised by what they ate). One could anticipate that they would recommend dismantling the inefficient supply system that exists (50,000 bakeries!) in order to achieve proper economies of scale, reasonable transaction costs and an appropriate contingency-designed organization form to deliver it. They might – indeed, probably would – recommend inviting in Goodman Fielder Wattie or Rank Hovis McDougal for a slice of the action. But would a government that did this ever dare face the electors again?

Conceptions of action and economic embeddedness

The preceding analysis of 'French bread' is a testament to what Granovetter (1985: 481–2) has termed the 'embeddedness' of economic action: 'the argument that the behaviour and institutions to be analysed are so constrained by ongoing social relations that to construe them as independent is a grievous misunderstanding'. Granovetter attempts to correct this 'misunderstanding' by focusing on the central role of networks of social relations in producing trust in economic life. Seen from this perspective, the reproduction of the *boulangerie* is not only a mode of organization but also a complex of cultural and economic practices. In its exclusion of forms which are, from certain influential perspectives, transactionally more efficient, contingently more appropriate and organizationally more rational, not to mention more rationalized, it is a classic case of embeddedness. One consequence of an embedded analysis is a perceptible transformation in the object studied. The focus of interest is shifted from concrete empirical objects, such as the 50,000 small bakeries, to the network of social relations in which these organizations are constituted, embedded and reproduced. It enables one to appreciate that 'small firms in a market setting may persist . . . because a dense network of social relations is overlaid on the business relations connecting such firms' (Granovetter 1985: 507). Granovetter's emphasis on 'embeddedness' is quite at odds with the conventional conceptions of most proponents of an efficiency perspective on organizations. In the terms which he proposes such theorists operate with an 'under-socialized' conception of action in their models and analysis, one modelled on the abstractions of 'economic rationality'.

It might appear that the example of French bread with its seemingly implicit appeal to culture, is an invitation to accept an 'over-socialized' account instead of one which is under-socialized. Enduring precedents for these over-socialized views of economic action were contributed by Weber's cultural reflections on the foundations of modernity. Weber's cultural pessimism, a characteristically modernist yet retrospective vision, echoed a sense of gloomy foreboding, a creative despair at the advent of mass society and the domination of the machine which was to be found across the human sciences, aesthetics, cinema and other visual arts in the texts of his near contemporaries such as Walter Benjamin, Charles Chaplin, Georg Simmel and T. S. Eliot. Modern times, dominated by objects produced in and by the age of machinery, were articulated, in what were taken to be some of their most representative experiences, as a meaningless wasteland. By the 1950s and the 1960s this aesthetic experience had become the normal science of modern sociology, encapsulated in works such as W. H. Whyte's (1956) *The Organization Man* and Herbert Marcuse's (1964) critique of *One-Dimensional Man*. In organization theory it was evident in the widespread use of functionalist arguments throughout its development (Burrell and Morgan 1979). Later, the nihilistic emphasis was to join ranks with romantic currents in the modernist project, culminating in Braverman's (1974) wholesale critique of 'the degradation of work in the twentieth century', giving rise to a 'labour process debate' through which William Morris's ghost might just, sometimes, be visible in the value placed upon the romance of craft labour.

Meanwhile, outside the aesthetic mainstream and the representations of the world which expressed its concerns, there was an undercurrent of solid industrial anthropology in both Europe and America which was less inclined to accept the modernist prognosis of cultural denudation than were the 'normal science' heirs of Weberian rationalism. In Europe writers like Jacques (1951) in *The Changing Culture of a Factory* and Crozier (1964) in *The Bureaucratic Phenomenon* had plumbed the depths of bureaucratic despair and found them to be, in contrast to the received wisdom, rich and fertile grounds of human imagination, purpose and achievement, even if this occurred within the more general bureaucratic bondage. In the United States researchers like Roy (1958) were coming to similar conclusions: within the iron cage, whether its frame was cast from a capitalist or a bureaucratic shell, culture was alive and well, and meaning existed. The radical twist to modernism saw this occurring in spite of the iron cage of capitalist relations even as it irrevocably reproduced them (Burawoy 1979; Willis 1977), while more conservative prognoses saw in this discovery of culture the 'salvation' of capitalism, its revitalization, its holy grail of 'excellence' (Peters and Waterman 1982). The news was out: culture is good for business. At the macro-level of whole societies Berger (1987) cheerfully retailed the news, while at the level of specific organizations and their culture the running was made by Peters and Waterman (1982). It is doubtful whether or not some of those who realized this 'good business' would be too happy with the analysis of the *boulangeries* presented earlier in this chapter. While it is evident that culture was captured in centre-field, outside of niche marketing there would appear to be little profit in *baguettes*, nor much future in even attempting to replicate the conditions of French bread where divisionalized and industrialized bread is king.

Granovetter focuses on the central role of networks of social relations in producing trust in economic life. Seen from this perspective, the reproduction of *les boulangeries* is not only a mode of organization but also a complex of cultural and economic practices. These practices are quite distinct from the predominant models of economic action which have been considered elsewhere (Clegg 1989b: 41–6). In such views, those who are transacting do so in a context in which whatever impediments to neoclassical economic rationality exist are to be regarded as functionally efficient solutions to the fundamental problem of a theoretical world populated by autarchic and atomized individuals. This fundamental problem is the 'possessive individualism' (Macpherson 1962) of excessively egoistic actors, actors whose actions are so premised on self-interest that they have no basis for other-regarding action, as they simply cannot trust others to be any less self-interested than they are themselves.

The under-socialized approaches of economics can be contrasted with the views of those theorists who operate from the opposite pole of an 'over-socialized' conception of action. In sociology one is familiar with such accounts being presented in functionalist theory. The work of Talcott Parsons (1951) is the best known of such accounts. Here the emphasis is on 'society' as moral order – a unified normative sphere which coalesces around a 'central value system'. Action is produced by agencies inculcated with the 'values' of this system. Agents acquire these values through the transmission of institutionally located and defined meanings in diverse settings such as the family, the polity, the economy and education. Such meanings are expressed in organizational terms through 'the primacy of orientation to the attainment of a specific goal' (Parsons 1956: 63), where the goals are defined institutionally and organizations, defined in terms of their formal orientation to goal-achievement, are the means of their transmission and reproduction. Recently, as we have seen in Chapter 4, some of this concern with the institutional features of organizations has re-entered organization analysis – but, as Richard Hall (1989) has observed, without benefit of the Parsonian reference.

The concern with the cultural embeddedness of French bread should not lead one to think that a straightforward transfer from an under-socialized and economistic to an over-socialized and culturalist account is being proposed. Such culturalist accounts are available and it is worthwhile considering them in order to show the ways in which the account proffered here differs.

Recently there has been a significant rediscovery of a culturalist axis in what Berger (1987: 7) has espoused as a concept of 'economic culture': 'the social, political, and cultural matrix or context within which particular economic processes operate'. At base what Berger (1987) argues is that some cultures, which are nationally specific, may be more 'efficient' economically than are other cultures. The outcomes which are valued by efficiency theorists, it is argued, can be achieved through the means which are ordinarily the focus of more institutional theory. The culture and the means turn out to be those of a relatively unbridled 'capitalism'.

Berger (1987) is not alone in seeing this concern with culture as having a particular efficacy in explaining how and why successful enterprises have in the recent past developed in both form and location outside the patterns of an earlier history. At the beginning of the twentieth century Weber (1976) also charted the role of culture in the explanation of economic organization. The more recent specification by Berger (1987) of the contemporary existence of culture and meaning institutionally fused in the economic code of modern capitalism would have been an agreeable paradox for Weber. Agreeable, because his basic conception of economics was not one which stressed it as a natural science, concerned purely with criteria of efficiency. Instead, he regarded it as a cultural science. The paradox would arise because it was Weber's view that although the foundations of modern industrial capitalism had been forged in the heat of religious values and culture it would henceforth be firmly set in a mould from which these sources of meaning had drained away. His nightmare was that the pan-cultural value of rational action would transform the contours of modern capitalism to a uniformity in which cultural value was absent.

Ideas such as these were at the crux of the Weber (1976) hypothesis concerning the 'Protestant ethic'. In this work he implicates the specific cultural embeddedness of Protestantism as a major causal agency in the genesis of modern capitalism, an analysis which is elaborated and extended rather than undercut in his later work (Weber 1923; see Collins 1980). *The Protestant Ethic and the Spirit of Capitalism* is the original locus of that metaphysical pathos which has so frequently characterized thinking about organizations. As we saw in Chapter 1, it posited a gloomy view of Weber's future and our present. Weber anticipated an horizon of meaninglessness, an iron cage of bureaucracy entrapping us as little cogs in a vast machinery of effort expended to no higher purpose and to no other cultural ideals than those of dull compulsion, necessity and relentless striving.

An additional legacy from Weber to contemporary organization analysis may also be established. At the base of the whole sociology of organizations and organization theory which have developed from Max Weber has been the assumption both that the organization is the object of analysis and that, as such, its 'essence' is constituted by simple contracts of employment. As an employee of a firm, one belongs to it; one is 'inside' it; one is a member and can be counted as a statistic in determining its size. Indeed, when we consider the importance which has been attached to size as a determining force in structure, in the research programmes of both the Aston school as well as the transaction cost analysis approach, we can see how decisive has been this simple assumption that organizations are an envelope which one enters by being an employee. Simply by being hired by an employer, or being fired, one may be contributing to the structuring of modernity!

Consider a model in which organizations grow or decline in size simply by taking on or shedding labour and in which size is a determinate and independent variable related to a number of dependent variables, such as formalization and standardization. It is assumed that organizations are unitary centres of calculation to which a number of other relationships, including the employment contract, are subordinate. An organization has a boundary defined by the sum of its contracts of employment. If it grows it opens more contracts with additional people; if it shrinks it terminates present contracts with existing employees, or simply does not replace people when they leave its employment. Thus, if one named a firm like the Ford Motor Corporation one could have a nationally specific picture of it as an enterprise composed of a number of sites, containing a number of people, people who were defined as employees by their contracts of employment. If it grew it hired more people and this had effects for the administrative carrying capacity of the firm. Of course, there were always complex interdependencies with subcontractors, but these did not affect the size variable. These were separate entities with separate employees and were subject to separate analysis – even where the firm in question might be effectively 'captured' by Ford, producing a component entirely for it. The latter would then become an issue for inter-organizational analysis.

Employment relations do not need to be enveloped within the corporate form of a singular organization. It has merely been conventional that this should be the case. One of the strengths of the transaction costs approach is that it enables one to see clearly that economic activity might be organized by the envelope of a formal, recurrent hierarchical structure, or it might be left to a series of transactions on the market. In considering economic activity which is not contained within the envelope of the formal organization it is useful to have a concrete example to hand. The one I have in mind is derived from the world of Italian fashion.

Italian fashion: the united colours of Benetton

'The united colours of Benetton' is a captivating slogan for a firm which now has an upmarket presence in many cities around the world, selling brightly coloured and co-ordinated casual clothing in highly fashionable designs, for both men and women as well as boys and girls. Benetton fashions are oriented primarily at an affluent and style-conscious market. Many readers have probably seen Benetton shops; some may even have bought things there, but how many people know the organizational story behind the brightly coloured retail façade?

> Benetton, an Italian family firm described as 'one of the most successful clothing companies in Europe', is organized in a flexible network of production and distribution. At the market end it has 2,500 national and international outlets, furnished with specially designed electronic cash registers that transmit on-line full data about which items are being sold, their sizes and their colour. This information is centrally received and processed for decision-making at the design and production end. There, the output mix flexibility of the main production facilities is complemented by a network of 200 small firms in a sort of 'putting out system' that provides additional flexibility regarding volume, although possibly at the expense of these indirect workers. Allegedly the response time to market change is reduced to 10 days. (Perez 1985: 454)

What is the organization that we refer to as 'Benetton' in this system? Does it include the 2,500 retail outlets, for instance? Not really, because these are retail franchises – but they sell only Benetton products. However, employees of these franchises are not Benetton employees – but they are utterly dependent on Benetton. Is Benetton the design and production facilities located in the north of Italy? Well, certainly it is this – but is it just this? On a 'contract of employment' basis it would certainly be just this, but would not this be isolating only a part of a network? What about the 200 small firms involved in something approximating a 'putting out system' – are these part of Benetton? Are they really a 'putting out system', some kind of primitive anticipation of a modern organizational form in which the work will once more be brought under the surveillance of an internal contractor, and eventually, perhaps, the hierarchy of complex organization? Or, with Benetton, are we dealing with something completely different to a traditional organization? Is Benetton perhaps better thought of less as an organization per se and rather more as an organized network of market relations premised on complex forms of contracting made possible by advances in microelectronics technology? What sense does it make to write of an organization coping with uncertain contingencies when it nests in a system whose major virtue appears to be that it has just about minimized whatever uncertainty there was in what was once a highly uncertain environment? The combination that is Benetton is indeed complex, but is it a singular complex organization?

Consider the following elements: instantaneous market signals from the point of purchase are electronically transmitted to Benetton headquarters; a precise knowledge of what lines to ship to which retail outlets is provided; flexible manufacturing can rapidly respond to product design changes determined by the precise market knowledge of 'what lines are selling where' which this instantaneous market signalling allows; extensive sub-contracting allows for smaller production runs and the rapid shifting of production schedules as demand varies. All these advantages, plus the fact that there is no direct competition at the point of sale, seem to signify a very different type of organization in the fashion industry to the large corporation such as Levi Strauss in the late 1970s, with its different product lines organized divisionally: over here 501s, over there shoes, here shirts and so on. Benetton appears to have subverted the basis for those conventional assumptions which have been implicit in organization theory about the employment relations involved in manufacturing and marketing a commodity. In so doing, is it perhaps heralding the limits of a scientific enterprise defined by an empirical object which may well be in the process of relative extinction? By posing the question this way one raises the possibility that the conventional organizational form, which grows by taking more people on to its payroll, in which its size (measured in terms of numbers of employees) will always correlate positively with its bureaucracy (measured in terms of formalization, standardization and so on), may be a historical moment rather than an eternal verity. Indeed, the fate of some times, perhaps, but not necessarily our times. If this were the case then the analytical strategy of focusing on 'transactions', irrespective of the particulars of how it is done, may be a sounder strategy.

What makes Benetton distinctive is the combination of several things. First, at the core of Benetton is a highly modern information technology. Second, Benetton operates a retailing system based entirely on franchising. It is not a system of franchising based on highly formal regulation (as is McDonalds, for instance) nor is it one in which the retailers have to pay royalties to the Benetton organization. However, a Benetton shop is entirely a Benetton shop – it is not allowed to sell any other make of product. Nor does Benetton retail its products other than through these outlets. 'In essence it exports the entire selling strategy: not only its products but also the Benetton style, shop organization and marketing strategy' (Belussi 1989: 119). Third, the strategy is based on well established putting-out methods, which, rather than being an innovation, built upon the basis of local practice in the Veneto region of north-east Italy, where Benetton began in 1965. In this region the extensive use of sub-contracting had never been wholly superseded by the factory organization of production.

Subcontractors are involved in all the labour-intensive phases of Benetton production: that is, in assembly, ironing and finishing. Four categories of subcontractor have been identified by Belussi (1989: 119): financially subordinated firms which are effectively controlled by a Benetton holding company; 'affiliate' firms; independent firms and homeworkers. Affiliate firms belong either to former Benetton employees or to present managers and clerks. Such firms have been 'grown' by Benetton through guaranteeing orders in the start-up phase. Extensive subcontracting has two major benefits: first, it uses external managerial resources in whom the managerial and financial controls are located, rather as in the internal contract system. As in this system it is the ability of the subcontracted management to control the pace and intensity of work tightly which delivers the benefits for Benetton. Second, it significantly reduces by about 40 per cent the unit labour costs that Benetton would otherwise experience (Belussi 1989: 120). Subcontractors are exclusive to Benetton. The agreement to subcontract is attractive because it guarantees both demand and profit margins (the latter at about 19 per cent for work undertaken).

The Benetton information system has a crucial nodal point in its circuits of power. This nodal point is routed through the 'sales agents'. Their function is to present the Benetton collection to shop operators in their own territory and to collect orders for the initial stock and subsequent re-orders, as well as to co-ordinate extensive advertising for 'The colours of Benetton'. These agents, of whom Belussi (1989: 120) advises there were thirty-five in late 1982, will frequently supervise and hold an interest in a number of stores, each one of which is recognizably Benetton by its colours, design, displays and open shelves. The latter are very important. There is nothing to a Benetton shop that the customer does not see. All the stock is on the shelves. The use of information technology enables the retailers to use a retailing philosophy of 'just enough'. No stock is carried other than what is on show. Benetton's production, warehousing and retailing form a tightly coupled system with rapid feedback responses built in to minimize error. The rapidity of the feedback depends upon the combination of new forms of organization, premised on the subcontracting system, with new forms of information technology.

The use of information technology links together production and distribution. Almost the whole of Benetton's production is made in response to retailers' orders. These are collected initially by agents and updated by shops feeding back through the computer link information on what sizes, colours and models are selling where and when. No production is for stock. Inventory and warehousing costs are slashed to a minimum. Re-orders can be supplied within about ten days. It may be said, with Belussi (1989: 128), that we have in this case 'the domination of the market by the firm'. However, it is a domination premised on an entirely new set of strategies to those which in the past consisted of domination through size. (On the strategies in more detail see Belussi 1989: 128–9.)

It is worth noting that Benetton is not some exotic and rare example of the impact of new technology on enterprises. For instance, Lorenz's (1988) study of small and medium size French firms in the engineering industry revealed that substantial 'downsizing' of these organizations had occurred at the same time as a sharp increase in sales during the early 1980s. In part this was contingent upon improvements in productivity wrought by the adoption of new forms of computer-controlled machine tools, but it was largely due to 'a substantial increase in their use of subcontracting for intermediate component production'. Subcontracting was not novel: few firms 'were of sufficient scale in their operations to warrant investing in plant for such specialized tasks as gear grinding or heat treatment' (Lorenz 1988: 195). Moreover, because of French redundancy laws, subcontracting was an attractive strategy for dealing with temporary fluctuations in demand requiring extra capacity. More than this was involved, however:

> It was a shift to subcontracting on a permanent basis for such standard operations as turning, milling, and drilling. It allowed the firms to avoid making investments in up-to-date machine tools and was frequently the occasion for a reduction in capacity, with some existing plant being sold off. While the general type of operation subcontracted was not specialised or specific to the particular firm in question, the design and specifications of the components were. Thus it was not a case of substituting in-house production for standardized components available in the market: rather, components were being machined (turned, milled, etc.) by subcontractors according to firm-specific plans produced in the design offices of the client firm. (Lorenz 1988: 195)

Microelectronics appear not only to be contributing to the transformation of design, production and distribution and the way these are linked together but also to be raising questions about the appropriate objects of analysis for economic sociologists interested in organizations. The questions are normative vis-à-vis the subject-matter of the specialism. Rather than the organization per se, perhaps the focus should be the network in which organizations are embedded? Organizations similar to Benetton may be witness to the decline of a model of organization based on a number of sharp distinctions. The distinctions in question would include being 'in' and 'of' the organization as opposed to being 'out' of it, as well as between conception and execution. A complex functionally differentiated internal hierarchy, the classic Weberian bureaucracy in the superstructure, based upon an equally classic 'Fordist' substructure, may be being subject to replacement with what Perez (1985: 453) terms 'systemation': 'the new trend towards merging all activities – managerial and productive, white and blue collar, design and marketing, economic and technical – into one single interactive system'. We shall return to the implications of this 'new flexibility' in Chapter 8. Let us note just one thing for the present – under conditions of a new flexibility, organization design may well allow more variation than has hitherto been anticipated in contingency theory.

The Benetton model presents a clear example of one type of embeddedness of an organization form whose size and complexity would be somewhat obscured by application of criteria premised only on a 'focal' model of the organization. The Benetton we see is quite different if we look only at the focal firm or if we look more broadly at the social relations in which it is embedded. What makes Benetton possible, in part, is a sophisticated application of 'telematics' to enable a far more flexible manufacturing system than an older, labour-intensive organization could have achieved.

Benetton differs markedly both from an older 'sweatshop' model of 'putting out' in the garment industry by design-houses and from the divisionalized structure of other well known 'brand-name' manufacturers in the fashion industry. Its most distinctive feature, from the perspective of an interest in organization analysis, is the way it confounds assumptions about what the appropriate unit of this analysis should be. Without entering into this in detail, it is clear that some aspects of the Benetton story are specific to the fabric of social relations in the 'Third Italy' of the Emilia–Romagna region. Lest it be thought that with embeddedness one is dealing with a purely local datum, specific only to this region, to the fashion industry or, mindful of Lorenz's (1988) analysis, only to 'high-tech' French engineering, we shall consider the case of East Asian enterprise. It will be seen that similar characteristics of embeddedness structure the complex diversity of organizational relationships which characterize economic action in the Newly Industrialized Countries (NICs) of East Asia.

The protagonists of the 'culture' literature, such as in Peters and Waterman (1982), were responding to an economic threat which they perceived as emanating from Japan. In their response what we find is a quest for patterns of transformational leadership which would enable managers to walk tall and be authentically *American*. It was the perceived difficulties of American business in the face of the Japanese challenge which spurred the renaissance in studies of 'organization culture' during the 1980s. To many observers it seemed as if 'corporate culture' might be what gave the Japanese their competitive edge and that was good reason enough for its study. It was the 'threat' from Japan which captured 'culture' as a marketable item. During the 1970s and into the 1980s, as conventional economic criteria failed to capture the reasons for the economic success of Japanese firms, this success increasingly became understood in terms of specifically cultural phenomena.

We shall see that these culturalist accounts prove to be theoretically somewhat deficient, precisely in terms of their over-socialized conceptions. Now, this does not require proposing an under-socialized account in their stead. What is required, in fact, is a re-specification in terms which are far more explicitly embedded. It once more becomes evident, just as it did in looking at the story of French bread, precisely what is at stake in this switch to a more embedded perspective. It not only involves shaking off Weberian cultural pessimism. It also means abandoning the framing assumption of the iron cage, as a specific organization, as the object of analysis. It is this fixation on concrete organizations as objects of analysis which has had such a hold on our analytical imagination, like a gridlock, for so long.

Variations of organization form in East Asian enterprises: the limits of 'under-socialized' accounts of economic action

Chandler's (1962) argument was constructed from historical materials specific to the United States. Implicitly, it was a convergence theory: other societies, as they developed the economic infrastructure of the USA, would, with specific market variations, come to adopt the same sorts of solutions to common business problems. Hamilton and Biggart (1988: S64) find that Japan, South Korea and Taiwan are very similar in terms of the variables that Chandler stresses:

> First, in all three countries internal transportation and communication systems are well developed, modern and certainly far beyond what they were inside 19th century America . . . External transportation and communication systems are also well developed. Second, the three countries possess substantial and growing internal mass markets, which have already risen above the level of early 20th century America. But more important, all the countries have vast external markets. Third, Japan, South Korea and Taiwan use, have available, or have developed, the most advanced technologies in the various industrial sectors. This level of technology, of course, is far advanced over that discussed by Chandler. Fourth, business enterprises in all three countries operate on principles of profit in the marketplace. By any definition, they are capitalist enterprises; they practice cost accounting, depend on free labor, develop through invested capital, and, if unsuccessful, may go bankrupt.

These countries are far more advanced in terms of Chandler's crucial variables than was nineteenth century America; they are all broadly similar, yet they differ in quite diverse ways. Large Japanese enterprises are closest in form to the Chandlerian model. However, they have been that way from the beginnings of Japanese industrialization: they did not emerge *with* industrial development but were the form which carried it from the outset as the *zaibatsu* developed from merchant activity generated under the feudal shogunate of the Tokugawa era, or from enterprises founded after the Meiji restoration. In many respects one could say that the inter-market groups were a pre-capitalist and early capitalist rather than developed capitalist form.

In South Korea the leading role played by the state makes the market explanation difficult to accept. The large organizations of the *chaebol* were creations of the state rather more than of the market. Their origins appear to be in the period of Japanese imperial control of South Korea, prior to the Second World War, when aspects of Japanese industrial policy and organization structure were the subject of institutional 'borrowing'. In the South Korean context, as Lee (1987: 12–13) has observed, it is in part because the state has had an extensive involvement that the number of business groups has remained small. It is easier for the state to deal with a small number of very large actors in the economy than with a great many small ones, especially where state direction has been high and public trust in capital market investments has been low. An ability to have a close interpretation of government policy has been important for doing business in South Korea. It may well be, as Lee suggests, that the South Korean *chaebol* of today are more properly compared with the Japanese corporate landscape during the 1930s and 1940s.

While the size and divisional aspects of both Korea and Japan could be said to fit the Chandler thesis, this is not the case in Taiwan. One finds instead of vertical integration and oligarchic concentration a far more dispersed network of business overlain in part with kin relationships, such as is characteristic of overseas Chinese business throughout the Pacific (Redding 1990). A complex web of contracting relations, which are rarely formalized as such, connect firms making different component parts of a finished product, through market relations rather than through hierarchical subordination. For instance, two industries in which Taiwan has a large share of world trade are bicycles and televisions, both of which are fabricated through organizational relations premised on private family control, curb market financing on an informal money market, loose group integration and flexible short-term subcontracting, under the control of patrilineal networks, suggest Hamilton and Biggart (1988). In addition, vertical integration is in part 'blocked' by state and governing party (the KMT nationalist party) ownership and operation of an industrial complex which has monopoly control of upstream industries (Numazaki forthcoming).

There is some debate as to the extent to which some of these characteristics are as pervasive as Hamilton and Biggart (1988) suggest. The data which they consider are drawn from the 1985–6 edition of *Business Groups in Taiwan*. In this respect the researchers are very much dependent upon the coding decisions made by its editors. Change the percentage amounts of cross-share holdings or definitions of kin designed to register the existence of *jituanquiye* or group enterprises and the data are subject to very different interpretation. Patrilinealism as a business principle in Taiwan, it has been suggested by Numazaki (1987: 18), may be an effect of the data-emphasis of *Business Groups in Taiwan*. In addition, existing networks are not only familial. Equally as important, suggests Numazaki (1987: 20–1), are networks constructed around common regional or village village localities. These form inter-group networks cross-laced together by complex webs of partnership arrangements, often fostered by the rules of inheritance which stress partition between brothers, dispersing stock ownership across the second and subsequent generations.

In Taiwan it appears to be rare for a successful family business to attempt vertical integration in order to try and control the marketplace. The typical strategy is instead to 'diversify by starting a series of unrelated firms that share neither account books nor management' (Hamilton and Biggart 1988: S66). These authors cite 1985 research by the China Credit Information Service, Zhonghua Zhengxinso, which shows that of the ninety-six largest *jituanquiye* 59 per cent are owned and controlled by family groups. In addition to those which are family controlled, many enterprise groups are family connected, comprising a coalition of what are frequently family-centred partnerships rather than family-dominated groups of firms (Numazaki 1987: 18–19). Many of these firms actually owe their existence to dollars pumped into them as a part of the anti-communist

bulwarks which United States aid programmes sought to construct after
the Second World War and after the creation of the People's Republic of
China on the mainland. Although firms may be characterized by elements
of patrilinealism, Numazaki (1987: 19) remarks that this has not been
inconsistent in the past with huge inputs of overseas capital – nor is it
inconsistent in the present when investment is flowing in increasingly from
Japanese multinationals such as Matsushita (in Taiwan's National Electric
Group) and Nissan (in the core corporation of the Yue Loong Motor
Corp.).

If Taiwan is a further counter-factual to the arguments from Chandler,
it is also inconsistent with those from Williamson (1975). Irrational and
inefficient transaction costs abound in Taiwan.

> In the first place, a normal pattern by which business groups acquire firms is to
> start or buy businesses in expanding areas of the economy. Often, these firms
> remain small to medium in size, are not necessarily integrated into the group's
> other holdings (even for purposes of accounting), and cooperate extensively with
> firms outside the holdings of the business group. As such, firm acquisitions
> represent speculation in new markets rather than attempts to reduce transaction
> costs between previously contracting firms.
>
> Second, uncertainty is a constant feature in Taiwan's economic environment.
> Family firms, many no larger than the extended household, usually do not have
> either the ability or the means to seek out or forecast information on demand
> in foreign export markets. They produce goods or, more likely, parts for
> contractors with whom they have continuing relationships and on whom they
> depend for subsequent orders. The information they receive on product demand
> is second- and third-hand and restricted to the present. In fact, misinformation
> and poor market forecasting are common, as is evident in the high rate of
> bankruptcy in Taiwan. (Hamilton and Biggart 1988: S67)

If one were to follow Williamson, one would predict, given these inefficient transaction conditions, that there should be a clear tendency
towards the emergence of vertical integration, particularly on the part of
the larger family firms. Hamilton and Biggart (1988) can find no evidence
that this concentration is occurring. Nor is it the case that one is dealing
with a regionally dominant variant of the standard organization form. If
one considers the archetype of successful Asian enterprise, without doubt
it would be one of the famous large Japanese firms. When one considers
the structure of large Japanese enterprises one finds that they differ
considerably from that divisional form which Chandler (1962; 1977),
Williamson (1975) and Donaldson (1985a) have detailed from the United
States model, as Clark's (1979) account demonstrates. Moreover, as
Hamilton and Biggart (1988) have demonstrated, they differ markedly
from the structure of other East Asian enterprises.

In the leading edge areas of the Japanese economy it would be quite
inappropriate to regard the unit of analysis as 'the organization', in the
singular sense. Organizations do not stand alone as legal entities com-

prising an unambiguous population of employee-members. Clark (1979: 95–6) refers to the embeddedness of Japanese organizations in a network of institutional relations as being like a 'society of industry' which envelopes them entirely. As Hamilton and Biggart (1988: S36–7) observe, 'The important point here is that, if one looks only at individual firms, one misses the crucial set of social and political institutions that serves to integrate the economy.'

The basic unit of analysis for Japanese enterprises is the 'interrelated network of firms' (Hamilton and Biggart 1988: S57; this source will be drawn on considerably for what follows) within which each enterprise belongs. These are known as 'enterprise groups' (Caves and Uekusa 1976), of which two sub-types may be identified. First, there is a set of relations which occur horizontally among a range of large firms. These firms will differ in size and prestige, although all will be relatively large and prestigious (Clark 1979: 95). Dore (1983: 467) regards the network characteristics as being 'relational contracting between equals' where the organizations span a number of diverse markets and industrial sectors (Vogel 1979: 107). Second, there is a 'dual structure' of 'relational contracting between unequals' (Dore 1983: 465) in which small and medium sized firms are related to a large firm. 'Both types of enterprise groups make centrally located firms and associations of large firms the principal actors in the Japanese economy' (Hamilton and Biggart 1988: S57).

One type of enterprise group has at its core the *kigyo shudan*, or 'inter-market' groups, the latter-day equivalents of the pre-war *zaibatsu*. These are normally composed of groups of firms in unrelated businesses, inter-connected by central banks or by trading companies (Clark 1979; Caves and Uekusa 1976; Hamilton and Biggart 1988). Prior to the post-war reconstruction of Japan these had been controlled by the founding family via holding companies. Today there are six major groups centred on Mitsubishi, Mitsui, Sumitomo, Fuyo, DKB and Sanwa. Another type is the vertically linked set of relations which exist between what Abegglen and Stalk (1985) have analysed as the *kaisha* and their related subsidiaries. These *kaisha*, or independent groups, are constituted from the big-name companies which comprise the major manufacturers. They are linked through extensive subcontracting to smaller independent firms which serve to 'buffer' the larger organizations. The *kaisha* and the *kigyo shudan* comprise the dominant centres of 'large, powerful, and relatively stable enterprise groups' (Hamilton and Biggart 1988: S59). (Incidentally, Ueda [1987], who is one of the leading authorities on Japanese enterprise structures, suggests that the independent and enterprise groups are not as easily collapsed into the same terms.)

It is within these enterprise groups that stable sources of finance and shareholding are organized, as well as more general matters of strategic policy. Of particular importance will be the institutional relationship between the capital market and manufacturing activity: manufacturers need access to long-term credits and new equity to finance strategic investment and to maintain a favourable debt-to-equity ratio. Typically, as dealers in money or liquifiable assets, financial institutions will seek to lend short term at high rates of interest, against securities that can be liquidated at any time; whereas manufacturers need inexpensive long-term credits or stable venture capital. From the manufacturers' point of view, this problem calls for institutional measures that subordinate financial logic to manufacturing. In Japan, the appropriate relation has in the past been achieved through straightforward regulation of banks, channelling semi-public funds directly into manufacturing, and through the strong institutional links that are provided by the *kigyo shudan* groups. These include a system of 'stable shareholders' who take up new share issues in manufacturing firms and undertake not to trade in them. In recent years these relationships have become somewhat weaker than they were during the earlier period of post-war reconstruction and growth. Many firms have begun to rely more on the stock market and on internally generated funds (Kosai and Ogino 1984). However, both bank and internal sourcing ensure that continuity can be constituted in and through the forms of economic calculation which are available at the enterprise level. Relative success in this was clearly evident in the behaviour of the Tokyo market subsequent to the October 19, 1987 stock market crash.

A similar integration is achieved in South Korea with different mechanisms. Here the enterprise groups, known as *chaebol*, are usually owned and controlled by a single person or family, and generally operate in a single industrial sector. They do not rely on stable subcontract relations but vertically incorporate most component producers. While control is associationally negotiated in Japanese firms, in the South Korean enterprise it is familiarly unified. It also appears to be subject to strong political steering. Strong state support is preferentially associated with the ability to raise loan capital from the banking sector. During the 1970s this state steering pushed forward the growth of large, new capital-intensive industries (Jones and Sakong 1980: 106–9). While financial stability is achieved in Japan by highly organized joint stockholding, in Korea it is achieved by family control and financing, together with board links to government-controlled financial institutions, the major source of externally generated capital. Thus the state, through the banking sector, is vital. The informal economy of the curb market is not unknown here either: recent estimates suggest that it is the source of about 35 per cent of total bank loans (Numazaki forthcoming). Hamilton and Biggart (1988: S59) report that by 1985 there were fifty *chaebol*. Between them these exerted control over 552 firms. The four largest of these *chaebol* controlled 45 per cent of GNP in the same year. During the previous year the top fifty *chaebol* controlled 80 per cent of GNP.

Family or individual control of the *chaebol* ensures continuity of purpose and ownership, through the intermediary of central holding companies. These holding companies are not wholly autonomous centres of economic calculation, in the way in which the Japanese enterprise groups are. 'Instead, they are directly managed by the South Korean state through planning agencies and fiscal controls . . . [they] rely on financing from state banks and government-controlled trading companies' (Hamilton and Biggart 1988: S59–60). Unlike in Japan there are large public sector enterprises, few large successful firms outside the *chaebol* and far less subcontracting between firms.

Family control also characterizes Taiwan. Firms are known either as *jiazuquiye*, where they are family enterprises, or *jituanquiye* where they are business groups. *Jiazuquiye*, the family firms raised through family sources of finance, are of more importance. Orrù, Biggart and Hamilton (1988: 22), for instance, report that over 60 per cent of capital is derived from family and friends. Consequently, *jituanquiye* enterprise groups are familially interlinked through individual family members holding positions in multiple firms. These often form a network which is controlled by a single family, consisting of 'conglomerate holdings of small, medium and a few modestly large firms' (Hamilton and Biggart 1988: S61).

Firms are on average much smaller than the larger Japanese or still larger South Korean enterprises, usually being small to medium in size (defined as having fewer than 300 employees or total assets of less than US $20 million by Hamilton and Biggart 1988: S60). These firms are frequently linked through informal contracts constituting production, assembly or distribution networks, while some firms subcontract for larger organizations. The small size factor can be explained primarily through inheritance laws which fragment assets generationally. Unlike in either Japan or South Korea, there are 'relatively low levels of vertical and horizontal integration and a relative absence of oligarchic concentrations' (Hamilton and Biggart 1988: S60).

There appears to be sufficient evidence to suggest that there is considerable diversity in organization form across these three East Asian cases. This diversity does not appear to be the result of different specifications of any 'efficiency' variables due to societal differences. One appears to be dealing not with three variations on the same underlying set of variables but with three distinct societal responses to the organization of economic action. In one instance, that of Taiwan, familism appears to be uppermost in the response; in another, that of South Korea, it appears to have been the role of the state; in Japan, it was the re-emergence of pre-war networks. The market-premised explanations are not sufficient to grasp the nature of East Asian enterprise structure in South Korea, Japan and Taiwan. They make no reference to the institutional processes so clearly at work in South Korea in its mimetic modelling on Japanese lines by a colonial state. The very different conditions of state formation and penetration of business in the three cases is not considered. In Korea the state has fostered large private business groups, while the Taiwanese state has not. There the state has formed public rather than private enterprises. In Japan neither of these strategies has been followed, the path of indicative planning being favoured. The important role of the state and of state power in the creation of very large South Korean private enterprises, and the important role of kin and trust-based relations in the much smaller Taiwanese private (as opposed to public) enterprises, has to be considered. While the Korean and Taiwanese enterprises are clearly post-war in their formation, the modern organization forms of Japan have a clear pre-modern origin.

The Confucian tradition applied to East Asian enterprises: the limits of 'over-socialized' conceptions of economic action

Many advocates of the importance of culture for an understanding of economic organizations, including Berger (1987), have been impressed by the economic growth rates of Japan, Hong Kong, Singapore, South Korea and Taiwan. Economic explanations alone seem inadequate to addressing the question of why it was these countries, rather than other Asian, African or Latin American nations, which became the NIC powerhouses (Clegg, Dunphy and Redding 1986).

The limits to economic explanation have already been broached in perspectives developed on organization analysis from an 'efficiency' perspective. However, a wider ambit of economic explanations may be considered. For instance, economic explanations which intuitively stress cheap labour, government subsidies or the inexpensiveness of transport costs to major markets as explanatory factors in East Asian economic success do have a certain plausibility in explaining economic performance: but it is one which is limited. On these criteria there is no reason why the currently debt-ridden nations of Latin America would not have seemed a better proposition for economic growth than did those of East Asia in the immediate post-war period.

The East Asian NICs are often presented as being extremely market-oriented economies tightly organized around the price mechanism, having liberal doses of entrepreneurialism, high domestic savings and 'free' labour markets. Although these factors are not applicable across the board, such elements would seem to conform precisely to a liberal conception of economic practice. Consequently, market conditions have invariably been paid most attention, stressing phenomena such as labour-intensive export-oriented policies and free trade conditions existing for exporters, policies underlined by specific frameworks of interest rate, agricultural, educational and anti-labour support. While consideration of these issues would offer some explanatory purchase on how these East Asian economies were able to industrialize rapidly they do not specifically focus on their successful export-orientation.

Some considerable ingenuity has been exercised in explaining this successful export-orientation: it was due to factors in scarce supply, such as a lack of natural resources, of land and of a large domestic market, at least where the city-states are concerned. The 'advantage' of a total lack of natural resources has often been regarded as a factor in Japan's success. The ingenuity is only exceeded by the implausibility of these explanations. Although the idea of countries not having the luxury of options and being forced to export or perish is intuitively attractive, there are still many countries where the same might apply and apparently does not. Having explored and run up against the limits of economic factors many explanations of this success have sought instead to understand it in terms of purely cultural factors (for example, for Japan consult Abegglen 1958; Benedict 1946 is an early example of this cultural explanation).

The focus has been on the East Asian cultural context in which successful economic husbandry has occurred; the specificity of this context has been defined in terms of the embeddedness of a highly specific economic culture. What characterizes these arguments is the use of long-standing and pervasive cultural attitudes and institutions which are identified as the source of East Asian success. In the East Asian case this explanation has come increasingly to be made in terms of what has been called the 'post-Confucian hypothesis'. The post-Confucian hypothesis was first explicated by Herman Kahn (1979), who proposed that the success of organizations in Japan, Korea, Taiwan, Hong Kong and Singapore was due in large part to certain key traits shared by the majority of organization members which were attributable to an upbringing in the Confucian tradition. The traits stressed are those of familism and obedience. The general argument, which draws out the implications of a common post-Confucian heritage, can be gleaned by consulting sources such as Redding (1980; 1990) on the 'overseas Chinese', Silin (1976) on Taiwan and Saha (1989–90) on Japan.

The ancient Chinese sage Confucius (551–479 BC) was the progenitor of Confucianism. Classically, a key notion of Confucianism was that of *chün-tzu*, a concern for the courteous and correct conduct of one's duties, particularly towards the family, based on a profound respect for social conventions. Character was to be built around the key principles of Confucianism. These were not transmitted in chapel, church or sect. Confucianism was not an organized religion (although, historically, during the thirteenth century elements of Taoist and Buddhist belief became fused into a religious synthesis known as neo-Confucianism), nor did it contain any conception of a deity or an absolute being. Confucianism was based purely on the rules of conduct which were the essential attributes of the mandarinate, the governing class, in China. For this class Confucianism provided the basis of an appropriate education. Confucianism, in its concern with ritual, order, imperial patrimonialism, service and the meritocratic achievement of these virtues, was profoundly anti-individualist: it legitimated a corporate, bureaucratic elite unified around the highly developed monopoly of complex literacy enjoyed by the mandarinate.

Neo-Confucianism developed in Tokugawa Japan between 1600 and

1868 under the patronage of the shogunate. It was the emphasis on social order, harmony and loyalty in neo-Confucianism which attracted a governing class seeking to pacify the country. Consequently, neo-Confucianism was developed as an authentically indigenous movement, in spite of its roots in mainland China. Some authorities suggest that it was re-invented or at least rediscovered after the Meiji restoration of 1868 overthrew the Tokugawa, but this time by emergent industrialists seeking an ideology with which to counter the conflict fostered by rapid capitalist industrialization. The 'organicist' and harmonious edicts of neo-Confucianism were appropriated for the task. This was particularly so after the adoption of the early Factory Acts in Japan in 1911 limited their capacity for unbridled exploitation. After the end of the First World War existing conflicts were exacerbated by the emergence of socialism and labour unionism against which the neo-Confucianist stress on a family spirit and harmonious social relations was once more pressed into service by entrepreneurs, both moral and industrial, such as Shibusawa Elichi (1840–1931), who founded *Kyochokai* or the Conciliation Society. It would be wrong to assume that neo-Confucianism was the only managerial ideology in circulation: there were other elements including classically liberal ideas such as those promoted at the Keieo Business School. In the post-war era, some Japanese elites once more turned in a time of adversity to Confucianism, after an initial retreat from ideas discredited not only by defeat but also by the modernizing managerialism imposed by the victorious occupying US forces. It is this post-war variant, initially in Japan and latterly elsewhere in East Asia, which has been termed post-Confucianism.

One might, in view of this characterization, be tempted to think that the only commonality between classical Confucianism and post-Confucianism is a shared stress on familism, collectivism defined in terms of the family, and a meritocratic stress on education as the means collectively to consolidate family wealth. The elite, ascetic, other-worldly characteristics appear to be lacking. The stress is far more on the cardinal virtues as these are defined by Confucianism, cardinal virtues whose mastery and practice might be expected to contribute towards the achievement of a stable social order.

Confucianism is a living tradition. Redding (1990) notes that it is still transmitted in overseas Chinese communities in both the family and the school. In the family it is evident in the child-rearing strategy whereby for the first five years the children are greatly indulged; a high level of dependence is created. After the age of 5 the pattern becomes far more disciplined and strict. The gravest threat for the child is of the withdrawal of affection for transgressions of the family code, a code which is loosely derived from Confucian principles and is centred on the importance of filial piety. Confucian principles are also taught in school as a means to achieve that social finesse which is synonymous with social grace for a Chinese person. The principal sanction learned and applied here is the loss of 'face':

the learned acquisition of a capacity to feel shame in the light of one's having been seen to have transgressed the moral code. One who lives one's life according to Confucian philosophy would seek to cultivate inner harmony and exterior grace, striving to present a decorous face to the social world. At the centre of this face is the web of meanings and obligations which are woven through the family. Society, as a social order, is a fabric spun from the threads of filial piety, familial responsibility and kinship obligations, reaching out to the clan, to the locale of village or neighbourhood and to the wider associational civil society. At the core one trusts one's family absolutely, one's clan only somewhat less, one's friends and acquaintances in as much as 'face-work' (Goffman 1959) allows one to and others not at all. The weave of this fabric exhibits all the tensions that one might anticipate from such pervasive yet unavoidable intimacy and mutual dependency coexisting with outer relations of extreme indifference and lack of trust and is marked, not surprisingly, by a high degree of formality and power-distance as a major coping strategy.

While considerable insight into the nature of contemporary Confucianism in its stress on 'face' and what has sometimes been referred to as 'utilitarian familism' can be gleaned from the contemporary novel by Timothy Mo (1978), *The Monkey King*, a more orthodox social science source would be Bond and Hofstede (1988). It is here that the most significant application of the post-Confucius hypothesis is to be found. Bond and Hofstede (1988) define culture as the collective programming of the mind which distinguishes the members of one category of people from another; implicitly in this line of work the categories of people are equated with national populations, or at least samples drawn from and mapped on to national populations. Culture is assumed to vary with national boundaries, within common cultural heritages which may sometimes map on to clusters of countries which display similar empirical configurations of data collected on cultural traits. The common Confucian heritage of certain East Asian nations is seen as providing such a cluster.

Methodologically these common clusters, where they can be observed, are seen to derive from similar patterns of responses to standard questions on cultural traits administered to matched samples of people from across a range of nations, where the patterns are revealed by factorial analysis. The research programme had its impetus from Hofstede's (1980) path-breaking study of *Culture's Consequences*. Four dimensions of high to low power distance, individualism to collectivism, masculinity to femininity and high to low uncertainty avoidance were described by Hofstede (1980) as cultural universals on which national variances might be arranged. Consequently, using some fairly heroic assumptions of cultural homogeneity and national integrity, various nations could be taxonomically arranged on these dimensions. Extension of the research programme to East Asia, through the development of an independent set of questions in 'the Chinese values survey', threw up another cultural configuration on samples of students across twenty-two countries. This time, however, it

was not a universal value but something which was seen particularly to
characterize East Asian nations. Whereas three of the four dimensions
which Hofstede had found in his massive survey data (derived from IBM
personnel files) were replicated in this study, another factor altogether
was isolated. Uncertainty avoidance, related to the search for absolute
values like 'truth', was missing. Instead, a dimension which was named
'Confucian dynamism' was isolated. It appeared to be related to values
distributed around orientations to core aspects of contemporary interpretations of Confucian teaching in its future-oriented aspects. Its positive
pole stressed a dynamic future-oriented mentality, while its negative pole
stressed a more static, tradition-oriented mentality. (Although the distribution of the values was not specific to Confucian cultures, high positive
scores on them were.) Those countries which scored high on this dimension
were also the countries which had enjoyed the highest rates of economic
growth over the past twenty years. Whereas none of the previously isolated
values associated with economic growth, this Confucian value did. At the
core seemed to be a marked concern for the importance of 'status order'
in the constitution of social relations, a stress on perseverance and thrift,
together with a strong sense of shame. These were seen to be significant
in the economic success of Japan, South Korea, Hong Kong, Taiwan and
Singapore, within the context of laissez-faire politics and markets. Uncertainty avoidance is uniquely Western, while Confucian dynamism is
uniquely Eastern. While the former is seen as dealing with the search for
truth, the latter deals with the search for virtue. According to Bond and
Hofstede, while the search for the former was once a societal advantage,
in the recent past it has become a liability, compared to the pragmatic
search for virtue in things which work rather than things which incorporate
or reflect timeless absolute truths. Thus East Asian economic achievement
is attributable to deep-seated and culturally given social facts.

Confucianism may promote individual self-control, perseverance and
thrift, it may facilitate societal and organizational obedience by stressing
the necessity of dutiful conduct to one's superiors, drawing on the wider
duty to be an honourable family member, but as a social or even
organizational explanation it necessarily operates at a high level of
generality. Where it will work best is in explaining economic action which
is embedded in a network of family enterprises. Thus, it has greatest
applicability for overseas Chinese family businesses (Redding 1990), where
familial trust, premised on Confucian obligations, inclines entrepreneurs
to appoint family members to executive positions. It does not operate as
well outside the familial web when applied to firms. Nor is it sufficiently
specific for cross-national analysis, when applied to an understanding of
the differences between East Asian economic organizations. It is too
general a level of analysis.

Some aspects of the post-Confucian argument are appealing in precisely
the same terms as were Weber's similar ideas about the role of Protestantism
in forming a 'capitalist ethic' in nineteenth century Europe and America.

This is that in the initial stages of capitalist development, either ethic could provide at least some of those conditions of capital formation which are necessary for initiating sustained production and accumulation. To re-invest capital to the glory of God or to that of the family will, if diligence, application and market conditions allow, achieve the same end of deferred consumption and increased investment leading to greater productivity. There is a sting in the tail, however. Precisely to the extent that such ethics are capitalistically successful, their success will begin to undermine the conditions that first produced them, as Weber was well aware in his prognosis for the future of the Protestant ethic:

> Where the fulfilment of the calling cannot directly be related to the highest spiritual and cultural values, or when, on the other hand, it need not be felt simply as economic compulsion, the individual generally abandons the attempt to justify it at all. In the field of its highest development, in the United States, the pursuit of wealth, stripped of its religious and ethical meaning, tends to become associated with purely mundane passions, which often actually give it the character of sport. (Weber 1976: 182)

It is not simply the character of the meaning structure which regulates economic activity in its drive, its production, which can serve to undercut an economically cultural ethic. As Marcuse (1964) observed, the very conditions for successful mass production are those least likely to repro-duce the ascetic conditions of the initial economic success. Mass pro-duction, at least in its early twentieth century form, was premised on mass markets and mass consumption. Against this orchestrated conformity of consumption Marcuse imagined that the hedonism which it unleashed would lead to an eventual revolt, not of mass producers, but of those excluded from a mass society and whose life-style was consequently no longer shaped by an ethic of asceticism. However, although the most recent era has witnessed a 'revolt into style' it has done so not as a spectacle of rebellion but as one of highly differentiated consumption premised on ever more fine-grained flexible production and niche marketing, within the mass form. Japan, in particular, has been in the vanguard of these new forms of flexible production. The implications of this are important for the general cultural explanation of post-Confucianism.

While it can be seen that a norm of *ascetic* individualism would seem destined to wither with the full flowering of an era of mass consumption, a collectivist, familist ethic would appear to be much hardier. For one thing, mass consumption, centred on the familial household, would serve to reproduce these households as the appropriate social unit of consump-tion. The very social forces that undermined a Protestant, ascetic ethic while leaving its individualism with relatively unbridled opportunities for hedonistic development could serve to reproduce an ethic based on the collective, familial household. However, the sting is not entirely absent.

East Asian economic success, particularly that of Japan, has been in large part premised on a keynote of flexibility in producing highly specialized variants of basically mass produced goods. These have depended upon pin-point accuracy in differentiating and positioning commodities in the market. Any contemporary visitor to the highly fashion conscious centres of Hong Kong, Singapore or Tokyo cannot fail to be impressed by the success with which advertisers have created an individualist ethic of consumption in these post-Confucian heartlands. One does not have to be a latter-day Marcuse (1964) to ask whether or not mass marketing, demographic analysis and urban density will produce conditions which may not reproduce the initial conditions posited for the economic success: familism, deferred consumption and disciplined order can be and are undercut by marketing strategies oriented to individual differentiation. Evidence in support of this proposition may be drawn from a cross-national survey of youth from 18 to 24 years of age which the office of the Prime Minister of Japan conducted in eleven countries. Japanese youth came out as more 'highly egoistic, self-centred and oriented to personal interests' and with the highest 'levels of frustration against family and school' among the nations surveyed, as Sugimoto (1986: 66) reports from the *Mainichi Shinbun* of February 12 and 13, 1984. The sting is evident: if the post-Confucian hypothesis is to be accepted, then the highly differentiated consumption characteristic of its success would appear to undermine the productive basis of this post-Confucian economic culture's core-values of familism, deferred consumption and disciplined order – that is, if one accepts that these values play the role that has been suggested for them by the culturalists.

What conclusions can be drawn from this 'cultural' and 'economic' explanation? Well, if one were a non-Confucian who was persuaded by the post-Confucian hypothesis, one might take comfort in imagining that in the longer term East Asian managers will confront precisely the same social fabric and workforce characteristics that European and American managers presently face. But this would be false comfort, I will argue, because, contrary to popular consensus, the success of Asian business cannot be attributed so simply to cultural factors, despite the stress on these in the literature.

A representative example of this literature can be culled from one of the most recent of its exponents. In his treatment of the 'Shadow of Confucius', Ketcham (1987: 106), in illustrating the nature of 'groups' in the workplace in Japan, depicts the following world of work:

> the crux is a pervasive, emotional commitment to the group as a group. Everything depends on the closeness and assurance of the bonds within the group, and the willingness of everyone in it to share its tasks and accept the moral and emotional responsibilities that go with prolonged intimate association. The group develops a keen sense of camaraderie and commonly spends long hours together, day after day, at work and in relaxation. Individuals are valued and trusted, all speak up and make important contributions, each member knows the abilities and weaknesses of the others, personal idiosyncrasies are

acknowledged, and the needs of all are attended to thoughtfully – yet the essential verticalness is never relinquished. All are deeply aware of, utterly imbued with the clear hierarchies of every relationship within the group.

This representation has echoes of a distant drum. In the nineteenth century the fading blush of conservative dreams of a cosy, warm, intimate *Gemeinschaft* could only be constructed as a moral retrospect, functioning discursively in much the same way as the Marxian Utopia of a dawn prior to the division of labour (Clegg and Higgins 1987). Which is to say: mythically. In the 1980s the mythology rises like a phoenix in the East, clothed in ideographic characters, kindled from the ashes of Confucianism. Although such views are widespread in much of the literature dealing with Japan, we are inclined to regard such depictions as more ideological than literally empirical in function. The search for moral community has rarely been absent from the more explicitly conservative social analysis, even in areas as pragmatic as organization theory (Clegg and Dunkerley 1980). Japan has become the contemporary vehicle of its expression, one may suggest. The stress on 'groupism' functions in part as a means of ideological wish-fulfilment, as well as being the mechanism of an over-socialized conception of economic action. (However, one would not want to dismiss the cultural explanation entirely: some aspects of primary socialization in the family do seem to be of importance in producing competitive workers who are also compliant.)

Amongst some Japanese scholars, such as Murakami (1986), a cultural explanation is adopted but given a different specificity than in the general post-Confucian case. Japan, he suggests, should be differentiated from other Confucian societies. The cultural specificity of Japanese industrialization was premised not on a religious ethic but on distinctively pre-industrial patterns of social organization:

> Its unique characteristic was the preindustrial basic unit of social group formation called *ie*, which had exceptional compatibility as a production unit in industrial society (Murakami 1984). The *ie* had exhibited strong capabilities for expansion, efficiency, and achievement, as well as for creating and thriving within a system of functional hierarchy. However, a basic group unit similar to the *ie* is rarely found in other agricultural societies. Therefore, I argue that the *ie* has been one of the main reasons Japan could adapt its indigenous culture to industrialization with extraordinary rapidity. This also is the reason Japan should be distinguished from other societies of the China periphery type and why in all likelihood it will remain a unique case among societies achieving industrialization. (Murakami 1986: 229)

Stressing the *ie* social group formation locates Japanese groupism not in Confucianism but in forms of samurai-led agro-military organization, the key aspects of which were stable authority structures capable of guaranteeing the land rights of local peasantry. Murakami (1984; 1986: 230) argues that central features of this social organization survived successive transformations into the present day, including functional rather than kin membership, membership homogeneity rather than stratification and a consequently functional hierarchy rather than one of class or status discrimination. What is crucial for accounts such as Murakami's (1984; 1986), Ketcham's (1987) and Nakane's (1973) is a focus on the 'group' qualities of Japanese employment and social relations.

Japanese organizations in historical perspective

It is worth noting that it is only relatively recently that the cultural specificities of Japanese practice have been viewed positively. Prior to the 1970s in the English-language literature Japanese organizations and management were frequently regarded as a deviant case which was merely slow in converging on current Western (United States) practice, as Dunphy (1986: 344) demonstrates. Japanese writers shared this view, often referring to distinctive aspects of Japanese organization culture in terms of 'pre-modern' 'inefficiency', 'irrationality', 'pathologies' and 'collective irresponsibilities' (Dunphy 1986: 346–7; see Takezawa 1966; Yamada 1969; Odaka 1963; Takamiya 1969; Imai 1969). Following a lead of Vogel's (1979: 134), it appears as if it was not until the mid-1970s that it became part of the elite currency of debate in Japan that there might be something positive in features like *ringi-ko* decision-making, the seniority and tenure employment system and other features of what has become known as the Japanese model (Dunphy 1986: 347). This is significant because there is evidence from the extensive literature review which Dunphy (1986: 367) conducted to suggest that the 'unique characteristics of Japanese enter-prises' might best be understood 'in terms of conscious problem solving on the part of key elites in Japan'.

The solutions sought do not appear to owe their existence to a felt need to preserve some ancient and special culture. Indeed, with some minor exceptions, they do not appear overly to derive from such a culture. The highly segmented labour market, for instance, is not particularly cultural, but it does appear to be important in Japanese economic success. It was Abegglen (1958) who was first responsible for introducing Western obser-vers to the idea that a central aspect of this segmented labour market, the system of core lifelong employment, was some kind of ancient moral idea derived from feudal times. However, subsequent writers have painted a picture in which tenure or lifetime employment was in fact instituted during the transition from internal contracting to modern bureaucracy which occurred in Japan between about 1910 and 1930. This was a period of growing labour militancy and high labour turnover. During this time the system of internal contract was stabilized and incorporated into Japanese enterprises on the basis of a compromise weighted towards the preservation of aspects of the *oyakata* system of internal contracting. Large firms in a strong oligopolistic position sought to create labour commitment by preserving aspects of the *oyakata* system in job security and regular progression up a pay hierarchy (Littler 1982). Lifetime employment does not mean that there are no redundancies, particularly during recession. Suzuki (1981) describes the practices of *madogiwa-zoku* and *genryo-keiei*. The former practice involves placing people 'near the window' without assigning them a job, while the latter describes the dismissal, transfer or demotion of underemployed managers. Some writers, such as Wornoff (1982), regard these practices of underemployment as sources of major inefficiencies in Japanese enterprise. It is only constant attention to production engineering, he suggests, which provides the counterweight to this inefficiency. Given the fact that these practices apply only to that small percentage of employees in the internal labour market, it is possible that Wornoff (1982) overstates his case.

In contemporary times, at least, the Japanese succeed not only on the backs of highly segmented workers but also in part because they pay a great deal of attention to factors directly related to particular performance measures. Work practices are subordinated to these, especially with respect to quality controls. The percentage of final output inspected correlates most highly with productivity level, followed by attention to various aspects of machine technology (like computer usage), utilization of plant capacity and budget accountability. Characteristically, major enterprises in Japan have married successful quality control with enterprising innovation (Dunphy 1986).

These performance measures and the segmentary work practices may well be at the root of Japanese economic success, rather than an economic culture which stresses post-Confucian values of consensus and group harmony. Groupism variables in Japanese organizations are not associated positively with performance (or, as in the case of morning ceremonies, they may even be negatively associated with performance). This suggests that such practices have been systematically overrated by those Western observers who have advocated cultural sequestration in order to increase performance. Such practices may well be culturally compatible and decorative additions to the Japanese economic machine, rather than its essential mechanism, much as Dunphy (1986) suggests.

Further evidence of the non-essential nature of culture in producing Japanese productivity is what happens to it in subsidiary overseas operations. While there is evidence that some important and distinctive features of Japanese personnel policy (such as participative decision-making) are transferable to other cultures, Japanese firms tend to drop many of these practices in their overseas operations. Some features are more easily transferred than others. Ichimura (1981), for instance, found that there were problems in the employment of local managers in overseas operations, because of the tight Japanese control of strategic apices both at home and abroad. (The problems that Japanese corporations have in employing indigenous managers in overseas operations have also been discussed by Ishida [1981].) These problems can be demonstrated by considering the example of Japanese firms in Singapore. Milton-Smith (1986) has documented the difference between Japanese business ideology and practice in Singapore. Difficulties are experienced by the Japanese in operating in a different business culture to that of Japanese ethnocentrism. Personnel and labour management, often cited as the cultural locus of the organizational expression of post-Confucianism are, in fact, the weak points of Japanese management overseas. In particular, the increasing integration of subsidiaries into the global marketing strategies of the Japanese parent mean that these strategies predominate over concern for the welfare of local employees. In addition, the exclusion from decision-making of non-Japanese, locally hired, subsidiary managers would suggest that Japanese companies will experience increasing difficulty in hiring and retaining bright, ambitious local managers (see also Tsurumi [1976], who explores the same phenomena from the point of view of union organization). Thus many of the much debated Japanese personnel policies may prove to have no real impact on organizational performance in Japan and to be a handicap in adapting cross-culturally, even in East Asia. This would be a significant problem in view of Japanese industries' increasing direct investment abroad as a result of the strong yen.

Managerial skill in relating organization variables, such as technology or semi-autonomous work groups, to productivity increases, product quality and innovation appears to remain crucial. The organization of the labour market into both an internal labour market in the big companies and a highly unprotected and secondary sphere outside it is a vital adjunct of this. The contribution made by various aspects of personnel policy to performance at the enterprise level remains controversial. It is not clear to what extent various aspects of personnel policy contribute to performance, detract from it or are merely cultural accretions of ethnographic interest but of no relevance to performance. What does appear to be clear is that particular aspects of personnel policy may contribute to performance at home but be non-exportable without some 'functional equivalent' for the material, institutional underpinnings. If exportable, they may, nevertheless, become a liability in another cultural setting. Research in Thailand into the presence of Japanese organizations suggests that this is the case. A system which recruits indigenous labour only for lower level work within the organization, and which rewards seniority, thus slowly replacing expatriate labour when local labour has been thoroughly trained and socialized, will be seen as 'colonial' by the indigenes (Taira 1980). Given the historical record of Japanese colonialism, particularly in the 'greater co-prosperity sphere' of East Asia, such resonances will be particularly unpleasant.

It is not just Dunphy (1986) who suspects that Japanese management practices may be the result of 'conscious problem solving' by Japanese elites. Other writers have had a sceptical regard for this 'group-centred' 'Japan-model', as Sugimoto (1986) and Sugimoto and Mouer (1985) have termed the variant of functionalism which attributes Japan's success to a unique configuration of values. From their perspective much of Japanese 'groupism' and 'consensus' is an effect not so much of culture as of control from above, an element of control missed by those Western scholars whose research only samples the elite and their institutions in the Japanese context. In this regard they come down heavily on the side of power theory. (The myth of consensus, they suggest, should be regarded as an elite construct; as Berger [Berger and Luckmann 1967] counselled long before *The Capitalist Revolution* [Berger 1987], the social construction of reality should never be regarded as a disinterested affair.) One way of testing this hypothesis, that the culture of consent and groupism is an effect of elite control of the mechanisms of ideological transmission, rather than being more deep-rooted within Japanese life, is to consider the historical record. If Japan's economic success since the Meiji restoration of 1868 is due to a unique economic culture rooted in post-Confucian consensus and groupism, then the historical record of Japanese labour relations should display this fact.

It is worth considering just how unique the putative achievement of a mature industrialization without conflict would be. Probably a majority of sociologists, outside of either extreme functionalists or extreme Marxists, would not accept the 'dominant ideology thesis' (Abercrombie, Hill and Turner 1980). Instead, judged on the empirical record, industrial societies have come to be regarded as having fragmented and diversified cultures, as displaying a plurality of world views and experiential frameworks rather than an all embracing unitary culture or dominant ideology or hegemony. The sociology of deviance (Taylor, Walton and Young 1974) would also seem to confirm this hypothesis: modern societies are composed of loosely coupled and relatively insulated subcultures rather than a singular, all embracing coherent normative order.

The study of Japanese industrial relations (Gordon 1985) appears to offer a striking disconfirmation of any historically rooted Japanese national consensual culture. Instead, the standard struggle attendant on the 'making' of a working class from a traditionally recalcitrant peasantry was as typical of Japan as it has been elsewhere (Vlastos 1986). There is little evidence to support the argument that Japanese practices are somehow culturally 'set' in a unique mould. Shirai and Shimoda (1978), for instance, looking at the historical evolution of unionism and the industrial relations system, suggest that the most important characteristics were fabricated in the post-war era. For whatever reasons of ideology or scholarship, a certain interpretation of this period has become widely known in the West which focuses on a few institutional features, embraces a cultural history to 'explain' them and, writers such as Sugimoto (1982: 19–20) suggest, systematically occludes understanding by focusing on what are idiosyncratic features of the totality.

The idea that Japanese organizations can rely on particular qualities of loyalty and consensus on the part of their employees, qualities which are culturally deep-rooted, as Abegglen (1958; 1973) has suggested, is challenged by the historical record. Taira (1961), for instance, in an early rebuttal, demonstrated that over the preceding one hundred years from the Meiji restoration the stability of Japanese labour had fluctuated widely in response to changing management tactics, which themselves were conditioned by the changing economic climate. At the inception of Japanese capitalism peasants were hijacked from the fields and virtually press-ganged into forced labour in the factories.

If the myth of consensus has any historical root it is to the 1930s and 1940s that we must look. In the 1930s, as Japan prepared for war, a combination of government legislation, a strong police force, factory owners and their hired gangs of factory-employed thugs succeeded in creating an apparently calm industrial relations atmosphere. Trouble, defined in employers' terms, was largely eliminated by the simple expedients of efficient coercion and repression. However, issues raised in the inter-war era, including tenure guarantees, wage payment methods, the relative status of workers and staff specialists and their role in organizational decision-making, were, Kenney and Florida (1988: 126) suggest, to re-emerge in the post-war era. As part of the United States programme of the post-war democratization of Japan, trade unions, which had been repressed entirely during the war, were once more allowed. During 1946 the membership of the trade unions grew rapidly from nil to five million, and the unions quickly developed a political role, with their political allegiances being split between the socialist and communist parties. However, they also engaged in more direct forms of democracy. Workers took over factories, expelled bosses and managers and during the first six months of 1946 practised workers' control (Moore 1983). This occurred in 255 factories involving 157,000 workers (Gordon 1985). It did not last for long: the occupying American forces together with the Japanese Government drastically weakened the labour movement; tough anti-labour legislation was introduced and in 1950 12,000 workers were expelled from the Japanese industrial system's core enterprises because they were considered to be communists.

However, the union movement was not without some success. One of the demands of the left-wing unions in the post-war era was for enterprise-wide unions which would include both operatives and staff specialists. This demand arose out of the workers' control movement and the occupation of the factories. It was hoped that the enterprise-wide unions might be transformed from 'factory councils' to 'workers' control', in the familiar model of the 'soviets', as in the Turin workers' movement after the First World War (see the discussion of Gramsci in Clegg and Dunkerley 1980). By 1949 over half the workforce had been unionized, a total of six and a half million workers. Unions negotiated worker–management joint councils through which they were able, temporarily, to obtain a significant role in enterprise decision-making.

Progress was also achieved on the wages front where the principle of a 'need component' in the wage package was fought for and achieved

(Gordon 1985; Kenney and Florida 1988: 127). Wages took on a tripartite character composed of an element of seniority, base and merit components. The merit components were fought for by management, while the unions were able to preserve the 'need' elements of base and seniority.

Gordon (1985: 424) describes the immediate post-war era as a time in which, at the enterprise level, the balance of power between workers and management was finely negotiated. Policies which might later be reconsidered to have been unilaterally management-initiated ideas frequently were not; often they were attempts by management to strike with a policy pre-emptively before it was further radicalized by union demands. The initiatives were not all on one side, of course. The 'human relations' precursor of today's groupism was introduced under American tutelage. There was a massive employers' counter-offensive in 1949–50 in which an important weapon was the creation of more conservative and human-relations-oriented enterprise unions, once the communists had been expelled. With the loss of the radical leadership, management regained the ascendancy in the power-play which was going on at enterprise level. As Kenney and Florida (1988: 128) put it, 'The undermining of radical forces made it easier to transform many worker gains into the evolving framework of capitalist accumulation.'

Not all of the concessions which the unions gained were won back, however, as Kenney and Florida (1988: 125) note: 'enterprise unions had to deliver on demands raised in previous worker struggles; capital was thus unable to re-establish the prewar rules of the game'. Among the achievements of the radical labour movement which were not defeated was the demand for tenure of employment. As Kenney and Florida (1988: 128) point out, this was just as well, because with enterprise unionism, dismissal meant union shrinkage with little prospect of replacement of lost membership. Consequently, even the tamest of the enterprise unions which the employers had established had an interest in supporting tenure demands. They were hard to resist, given the enterprise base of unions and strikes, because this allowed unions to pick off recalcitrant employers one by one. Few firms could afford a prolonged firm-specific strike which their competitors avoided by a concession. Moreover, enterprise unionism promised to resolve the turnover problems which had been endemic in inter-war Japanese enterprises (Clark 1979). In addition, enterprise tenure would ensure that the employers who invested in the training required to rebuild post-war industry would at least retain the fruits of their investment and would not have their trained labour poached elsewhere. Consequently, 'guaranteed employment for male workers in core firms became a fundamental feature of postwar Japan, with dismissals falling largely outside routine management prerogatives' (Kenney and Florida 1988: 128). Subsequently these rights were to be recognized in labour law. It was on these bases that the post-war 'economic miracle' was constructed in some Japanese enterprises.

What are some of the characteristics of post-war Japanese enterprises?

First, there is a pronounced split between those workers integrated into the 'company world' of the internal labour market, with its seniority wage system and lifetime employment, and other workers. Those within the 'company world' of Japan amount to less than one third of the industrial labour force: these are the members of the enterprise unions, whose main function is as 'an auxiliary to management in the personnel sector' (Kawashini 1986: 156). They are to be found in the enterprise groups (Orrù, Biggart and Hamilton 1988) and big name firms which dominate the peaks of Japanese enterprise. Within these, core workers within the individual enterprises will belong to enterprise-specific unions: each company has its own local wage scales premised on managerial evaluation of the skill requirements of a labour capacity which is itself constituted within the 'company world'. These are the elite of Japanese industrial workers, held securely in place by the 'golden chains' that the company proffers (Muto 1986).

Enterprise unions may be the prevalent pattern but there are also some corporations which are characterized by a 'plural-type' union situation, in which there is not only a majority union but also a breakaway minority union born after some decisive event in the previously enterprise union. About 12 per cent of unions which belonged to *Sohyo* (the 'left wing' union peak organization, with particular strengths in the iron and steel, chemical and machine-manufacturing industries and the public sector; Deutschmann 1987b: 468) are plural-type unions, amounting in 1982 to 768 unions. Such unions generated a disproportionate percentage of labour disputes handled by the Central Labour Relations Committee (*Churoi*) in the private sector, some 41 per cent in all (Kawashini 1986: 141). Such plural-type unions are particularly evident in the public sector. Outside the core workers in the enterprise groups, organized into enterprise or (more rarely) plural-type unions, there are a great many medium and small size companies which do not form part of the 'company world'.

The contemporary union picture in Japan is rapidly changing. Institutional arrangements such as those depicted in the sphere of union peak organization by Deutschmann (1987b) no longer exist. In November, 1987, the private sector trade unions became unified under a single umbrella organization known as *Rengo* – the National Federation of Private Sector Unions. *Domei*, the other main union peak organization, and *Sohyo* are now incorporated under this new umbrella structure, having been formally dissolved in November, 1987. Speculation has been widely entertained that with the establishment of *Rengo* as a peak organization, leaving out only *Toitsu Rosokon* with its links to the Japanese Communist Party, the hitherto fragmented socialist and social democratic opposition parties may be closer to achieving unity in the future (see *Far Eastern Economic Review*, January 14, 1988: 16–18). In the light of the defeat of President Uno in the polls during mid-1989, after leading members of the government were embroiled in a series of sex and bribery scandals, this appeared nearer than at any time during Japan's post-war democracy, albeit that the appearance has since faded.

In spatial terms, big name companies and their 'company world' will sometimes dominate whole towns, like Toyota, Hitachi, Kawasaki Steel and the Chisso Corporation do. The big name companies also cast a contractual shadow over the employment scene. Whether or not towns are literally company towns, the enterprise groups dominate whole areas of employment through a vast number of subcontract firms. Although formally independent these are highly structured and semi-formalized and enjoy ongoing relations with the big name and enterprise group core companies. Effectively, in Muto's (1986: 135) phrase, they are 'vassals' of the big companies. In turn, many of the subcontracting firms themselves rely on work subcontracted out to smaller subcontractors who in turn subcontract to female domestic outworkers who work on piece-wage rates far removed from those of the enterprise union members. In the Japanese automobile industry, for instance, 75 per cent of work (as compared to 50 per cent in the United States) is sourced outside the big name firms to primary subcontracting firms, which in turn may subcontract to secondary firms, which in turn may subcontract to tertiary outworkers, who will be paid at a fifth of the rate of workers in the larger subcontract firms (Muto 1986: 135). In the smaller secondary subcontract firms, those with less than 100 employees (which provide 68.7 per cent of all employment and over 50 per cent of GNP), the wage rates have been roughly about 70 per cent of those which prevail in the big name firms, although there are indications that these are now equalizing somewhat (Kenney and Florida 1988: 130). Small firms also employ a disproportionate share of minority workers and older workers who have been forced to retire from the core companies.

The Japanese labour market is highly gender segmented (see Brinton 1989). It is not that women are less likely to participate in the labour market in Japan than elsewhere: the participation rates are broadly comparable, with Japan having greater female workforce participation than many Western European countries, although not as much as Scandinavia or North America. What is at issue is the pattern of this participation. Women in Japan are far less likely to be employees and far more likely to be, as Brinton (1989: 550) terms them, 'unpaid family enterprise workers in small-family-run businesses or farms'. Where they are in employment, in every category women receive lower rates of pay which are age related in their impact. Younger women in the 16–20 age group are at the relative peak of their earning power, receiving only about 15 per cent less than males. By the time that they are about 35 this will have been reduced to about 50 per cent. These earnings rates parallel the participation rates: participation is highest amongst women in the younger age categories (20–4), declining monotonically except for a slight increase in the 40–4 age group, consistent with the cessation of childcare responsibilities. While men and women have broadly the same propensity to enter the core organizations of the Japanese economy, they do not have the same propensity to stay there (Brinton 1989: 551). A two-fifths decline or shift in female participation occurs in the core sector over the life cycle from age 20 to 49. Women thus tend to end up in the 'external' labour market to those in which career ladders are to be found. The low level of female executive success in joining the managerial ranks in Japan demonstrates this, where only 13 per cent of management is female. This contrasts with a figure of 68 per cent in the United States, for example. It is also apparent in male/female wage differentials. Japanese women in the aggregate earn the lowest percentage wages compared to men in the OECD countries. The average aggregate monthly rate is 55.5 per cent of the male rate.

A double bind exists in Japanese employment practice in the core corporate sector. Women are frequently encouraged by their employers to quit in their mid-twenties in order to have children. At the same time the same employers will point to this propensity to quit as sufficient reason why women should not be trained (Brinton 1989: 553). This framework of meaning and institutionalized practice seems to be behind the results that Brinton (1989) discovered from the workforce survey she conducted in three urban locations in Japan in 1984. Inside the core organizations which men and women have a broadly similar propensity to enter when they commence employment, there is a marked difference in pattern. Seventy-one per cent of the men in the sample entered career track positions in large core organizations; only 23 per cent of the women did. Most women enter low-level non-career track 'assistant clerical' positions. Of overall employment, while 22 per cent of all men start their work lives on a career ladder, only 7 per cent of women do. This initial handicap does much to explain the different outcomes (Brinton 1989).

There is a life cycle pattern visible in the employment of those women who do not enter career ladder opportunities. When they return to work after the cessation of 'family responsibilities' they are more likely to enter small firms in which tertiary outwork is concentrated. In fact, tertiary outworkers are most likely to be women. Female employment outside the core sector is highly concentrated in outwork and also in part-time and temporary jobs which are most vulnerable to recession (see Kenney and Florida 1988: 130–1). Some subcontracting workers may well work within the big name firms' factories, on a modern-day version of 'internal contracting' (see Clegg, Boreham and Dow 1986: 93–7; Littler 1982): the *oyakata* system, where subcontracted labour is provided for a lump sum. Alongside them may be temporary, seasonal workers, frequently drawn from the agrarian sector (disproportionately large in Japan due to deliberate government policy of tariff and quota exclusion of imports and of subsidies to primary producers) or from the ranks of part-time workers, usually housewives. Their ease of recruitment and dismissal is a major basis of Japanese flexibility, together with the enterprise base of the unions themselves. Data from 1970 show that 12 per cent of the workforce employed in large companies of more than 500 workers, in major industries such as steel, shipbuilding, automobiles and construction, were such temporary workers, compared to only 2–3 per cent in companies employing 30–99 employees (Muto 1986: 136).

The firm will proceed to train those core workers fortunate enough to have gone to the elite schools and universities favoured in recruitment by the big name firms and whose personal background passes scrutiny (see Rohlen 1974). At this level a particular 'corporate culture' does seem to come into play. Training is firm specific; it not only is oriented to 'functional qualifications' but is also 'a process of moral socialization into the community of the firm' (Deutschmann 1987a: 45). Indeed, Deutschmann suggests that the corporate culture in this respect does build on more general cultural phenomena in terms of the primary socialization role of the family, a family conceived as a co-operative community (Deutschmann 1987a: 44). To Western observers it seems to be an extremely patriarchal (in an older sense of the term) system. The scope of the system can best be seen in the extent to which work time and work relations are routinely organized into the time and space outside of work. Lifetime employment is the cost and the benefit of this system. Cost, because it precludes any external labour market options for most workers. They are simply not trained for other enterprises and would not consider or be considered for such employment. In so far as it does deliver employment security (which it does not always achieve and is less likely to in the future with the rapidly changing role of Japan in the world economy) then lifetime employment is indeed a benefit, at least until age 55, when retirement normally occurs. However, this security is of employment, not employment status: marginalization and downgrading do occur. Moreover, the less than generous state pension scheme is not available until age 65. In these last ten years personal labour market 'flexibility' becomes an acute consideration.

Conclusion

The point of entering into this institutional fabric in some detail for Japan has been to stress that consent, where it is achieved, may well have rather more of a material than a cultural basis alone. Whether the origin of the latter is attributed to a Confucian or to a samurai ethic, the outcome is the same. Far too much reliance is placed on order produced through 'over-socialized' mechanisms than either the empirical record or theoretical sophistication should allow. The proposed singularity and coherence of post-Confucian culture cannot be sustained upon detailed investigation (Hamilton and Biggart 1988). Culturalist explanations in Confucian terms are too general, too unspecific. Consider the vast canvas of East Asia. While culture can explain some common patterns across the East Asian societies, such as familism, it cannot explain the variations within and between these societies. These are of considerable importance at the enterprise level (Hamilton and Biggart 1988). Moreover, if the cultural factors are deep rooted in the historical 'collective consciousness', why do they only become effective in the post-war era and under certain, diverse institutional conditions? It is an irony of contemporary sociology that factors which an earlier generation of scholars, such as Weber, saw as inimical to rational, efficient capitalism should now be seen as central to its very essence!

While culture does have a role to play in explanation it is not the role that adherents of the post-Confucian ethic have proposed. In the terms which Granovetter (1985) adopts from Wrong (1961) they are constructing an over-socialized conception of human action, one which assumes too much about the strength and determinacy of cultural transmission. This does not mean, of course, that one should instead have recourse to an under-socialized conception of economic action which accepts as necessarily sufficient explanation by purely market forces. For one thing, it was the insufficiency of these in the first place which led to the explanation from culture. This is not to deny a role for market explanations: in the East Asian context at least, they are certainly correct in emphasizing phenomena such as deregulated labour markets, a highly educated population, an export-orientation and a high level of domestic savings for investment. However, why this particular mix of phenomena should have occurred in these East Asian countries is less clear. Reference is invariably made to the role of government in devising appropriate policies. The appropriateness of these policies varies with the commitments of the commentator: some will make reference to more market-oriented aspects (for example, deregulated labour markets), others to the more politically oriented aspects (such as the role of Japan's Ministry of International Trade and Industry), depending on their ideological elective affinities.

This chapter has ranged widely through geographical space, from the bread of France through the fashions of Italy, to the enterprise of Asia. Its analytical focus has been consistent, however. On the one hand it has explored the insufficiencies of under-socialized conceptions of economic action and organizations, whether these are located in the contingencies of markets, size or technology. On the other hand it has opposed over-socialized conceptions. These replace the previous contingencies with that of culture. Whether the contingencies are those of culture, size, markets or technology, explanation has remained oriented towards efficiency. Against this the chapter has endorsed an orientation which draws on Granovetter's (1985) conception of economic embeddedness, a conception which clearly fuses the institutional aspects of culture with aspects of explanation far closer to power theory. It makes reference to culture but seeks to context and locate it in its institutional specificity. In organizational terms culture works through framing the assumptions that agencies are able to operate with. It frames and it enables; it enables and it constrains. The crucial factor is not that a manager or an organization is Japanese rather than American or Australian. It is what being Japanese makes available in terms of normal ways of accounting for action, of calculating strategy, of constituting rationalities, of mapping cognitively, which is important. These matters are not *just* cultural: they depend upon distinct and nationally variable institutional frameworks. By such frameworks one is referring to nationally specific, hence variable, conditions within which managerial and organizational action is constituted. Action is never unbounded. It is framed within more or less tacit understandings, as well as formal stipulations, which enable different agencies to do not only different things but also the same things distinctly in diverse contexts. An embedded concept of culture looks to the ways in which these resources are available and utilized and the differential consequences entailed.

A stress on culture as institutionally framed and nationally diverse does not mean that efficiency is unimportant. Its importance resides precisely in its value. Efficiency is one of the highest cultural values of modernity. As such a value it cannot enter into explanation of those forms which exist in other than a tautological way. Yet, as such a value, it will frequently play a key role in analysis. Few people would want to be seen to be endorsing inefficiency. Not to be for efficiency is tantamount to being against modernity! To be efficient is to be modern; it is to bask secure in one of the self-images of the age.

A number of things are involved in countering the construction of explanations based on efficiency arguments. First, one has to construct an account in such a way that it is clear that one is not placing a normative value on inefficiency (or conversely efficiency). Hence the best line of critique is empirical and the appropriate strategy is one of falsification. If the arguments from efficiency predict a certain state of affairs, such as the triumph of divisional organization structures in certain product markets or industries, then the provision of just one case which contradicts this argument is sufficient to destroy the generality of the theory. Of course, it may still well be a good 'regional' theory when applied to the United States, for instance. Thus, one way of undercutting efficiency arguments is through furnishing falsifying cases. The analysis of French bread, it is suggested, provides such a case. Bread was a product in an industry which throughout most of the advanced capitalist world confirmed the outcomes one would predict from efficiency theory. However, France is different and this difference serves to undermine the generality of efficiency theory as a universalizing enterprise. The production of a staple product of advanced industrial capitalist societies, bread, is capable of diverse modes of rationality in its production. The case of French bread on its own would not be sufficient to undermine the claims to scientific generalizability of arguments derived from an efficiency perspective, but it would certainly raise some questions about the contingent factors which have to be taken into account. At the very least it should serve to suggest the need for serious revision of the theory.

In the analysis of organizations the major thrust of efficiency arguments has been towards predicting a convergence in the range of organization forms to be found in modernity. It is anticipated that the pressure of efficiency will lead on a global basis to more and more organizations becoming less and less different from each other. Diversity, in this respect, would be an indication of 'underdevelopment'. Clearly, if one were to establish a significant number of organization forms which were unquestionably 'of' and 'in' modernity, and which were at the same time distinctly different from the form that one might predict from an efficiency perspective, then this would represent a further undercutting of the argument from efficiency to modernity as something which gives rise to rather a limited range of organizational experience. I take it that the material from East Asia provides such an argument.

Familiarity with aspects of East Asian enterprises and capitalism not only raises some question marks concerning the applicability of under-socialized arguments which stress the efficiency aspects deriving from markets or transaction costs. It also raises issues relating to the role of over-socialized explanations which derive their focus from culture. Cultural explanation has recently had a resurgence in the analysis of economic life in the work of Berger (1987), in particular. In this case, a particular aspect of his analysis has been to explain the efficiency of East Asian capitalism in cultural terms, as part of a more general account of capitalism as the most efficient system available to modernity. The argument of this chapter opposed any understanding of East Asian capitalism in the over-socialized terms which Berger and others have proposed. The diversities which exist between the organizational structuring of the major East Asian economies also serve as further empirical evidence against the efficiency perspective.

Organizations are embedded in ways which the conventional distinction between organizations as focal objects of analysis and their environments does not sufficiently capture, as was apparent in the analysis of French bread, as well as in the analysis of Benetton and in the diversity of East Asian enterprises. Had one studied French bread through an analysis purely of its 'small business' organization form, in a cross-sectional framework, it is doubtful whether one would have arrived at the insights which Bertaux and Bertaux-Wiame (1981) were able to generate from their deeply embedded account. One would have looked to a whole range of other phenomena 'outside' the organizations in question. Where organizations find their expression in institutionally framed and culturally embedded terms of relationships which structure the field of force in which they are constituted, then the appropriate object of analysis is composed of the diverse rationalities of these relationships, rather than the structural features of a central but limited element of them. Again, this aspect comes out clearly in reference to the East Asian materials, particularly those from Taiwan.

At the centre of analytical focus one finds the cultural and institutional frameworks which facilitate the diverse forms of calculation and modes of rationalities within which are constituted networks of organizational relations. The actual form that organizations take occurs within the specification of these features.

6

Organizational Diversities and Rationalities

Organizations are human fabrications. They are made out of whatever materials come to hand and can be modified or adopted. Organizations are concocted out of whatever recipe-knowledge is locally available. Thus, a contingency framework certainly appears to be appropriate for organization analysis, but it would be one where 'context-free' contingencies vary not only organizationally but also in terms of national institutional patterns. The variation in the latter, it will be proposed, may be such as to 'over-determine' the former.

In the early stages of modernity it was quite natural that organizations should have been built out of locally available materials. Fabricators of organizations would have drawn from the material culture of their immediate institutional environment. Such environments are frequently constituted in national terms and instilled with value in cultural terms (Anderson 1983). For instance, the values of the peasantry in France, their peasant culture, were important for the reproduction of the *boulangerie* into the late twentieth century in not only an urban but also a rural location. The characteristic values derived from this peasant background formed the strategies and modes of rationality of *les boulangers* and enable the French to have their *baguette* and eat it.

We have seen clearly that if *les boulangers* were unable to trust their loans to the potential next generation of breadmakers then the *baguette* could hardly be taken for granted. This premise of trust is actually not at all unusual in organizational action: as Lorenz (1988: 198) puts it, 'If transaction costs are thought of as friction in the economy, then trust can be seen as an extremely effective lubricant.' Organizations operate in uncertain environments deploying the calculations of agents whose rationality can never be unbounded or unlimited. These problems of boundedness and uncertainty are compounded when organizations externalize their recurrent routines and relations to agencies which are outside their control or authority. Under such conditions trust becomes more than usually expedient. It is what makes forms of action calculable as elements in modes of rationality constructed as responses to uncertain environments and limited knowledge.

A central issue has been specified by Child and Keiser (1979) for the substantive concerns of any comparative organization studies. The terms proposed are those of a choice between adopting a culture-free perspective as against one which stresses cultural specificity. Within organization studies the strongest proponents of the former are contingency theorists such as the Aston school (for example, Donaldson 1985a) who provide an organization-level specification of the thesis of convergence (see Clegg and Dunkerley 1980: ch. 6 for a general discussion). The latter position has been associated with writers with more of an anthropological than a managerial or sociological orientation, perhaps because they are more disciplinarily attuned to difference. Crozier (1964) is probably the best known example in mainstream organization analysis.

One study which sought to test the extent to which cultural specificity enters into organizational contingencies was the comparison of German and British organizations conducted by Child and Keiser (1979). Briefly, they found that on standardized Aston data a sample of German organizations were consistently more centralized than the British ones, something which they put down to specific cultural effects. It was suggested that these effects over-determined more generalized institutional effects such as the impact of models of good and efficient practice retailed by international consulting agencies. Models derived from this provenance should tend to produce more of a convergence as they erode the value-basis of cultural specificity, in this case a German predisposition towards more centralized control.

The institutional frameworks within which organizations are embedded may frequently contain quite divergent and contradictory pressures, as Child and Keiser's (1979) research suggests. It will be a matter of local detail, the depth of cultural resistance and the prescriptive power of external regulative agencies as to the resolution of these institutional pressures in specific settings. One might anticipate that convergence on the context-free contingencies of organizational design will be lower where cultural resistance is high, where agents are able to draw on cultural reserves of great specificity. Alternatively, where institutional frameworks and pressures of regulation (in particular, by professions such as law and accounting, and by government and the state) have a highly developed specificity, then context-free contingencies may well be shaped in nationally specific ways.

Back to basics: economic embeddedness, institutional frameworks and modes of rationality

By common consent, the basics of organization analysis start from Weber's conceptualization of the sociological categories of economic action, the title of the second chapter of *Economy and Society* which deals with the vexed relationship between formal and substantive rationality. A good deal of the force of Weber's analysis derives from his exploration of the differentially distributed powers of control and disposal over productive resources that underpin the characteristic form of a modern market economy, which is defined as 'a complete network of exchange contracts in deliberate planned acquisitions of powers of control and disposal' (Weber 1978: 67). Not only does this characterization put paid to economic-liberal representations of freedom and equality in a contractual universe, such as those of Williamson (1975), which at best present only one side of the social process involved, but it also sets the stage for the conflict between different modes of economic rationality as well as demonstrating the often implicit trust which is embedded in economic action.

Organizations exist by virtue of the fact that, in all probability, 'certain persons will act in such a way as to carry out the order governing the organization' (Weber 1978: 49). In other words, organization is premised on an expectation of trust in the obedience of others. It is out of this trust and obedience that the order which is the effectively functioning organization is constructed. In Weber's terms this order refers to the 'structure of dominance' under which the organization is constituted. Structures of dominance are cultural in context. They are always substantive sources of rationality, substantive sources which may, of course, be constructed in such a way as to be indistinguishable from formal rationality. This identity would occur if the formal categories of a purely accounting notion of efficiency were to be the dominant element shaping organization designers and elite judgements, for example. In such a situation a specific cultural value – efficiency, defined in terms of the categories of a particular form of knowledge – would have been raised to the status of an 'ultimate value' to be culturally prized for its own sake, as an end in itself, as something in which we trust.

For Weber, economic action is *formally* rational to the extent that it rests on the best technically possible practice of quantitative calculation or accounting. No such precise notion of *substantive* rationality is possible, however, as this is a generic concept designating goal-oriented action where the goals are variable. Economic action is substantively rational to the extent that it is motivated and assessed according to an ultimate goal of some sort. Such a substantive orientation, Weber notes from the start, may lead the actor to see formal, quantitative calculation as unimportant, or even inimical to the achievement of ultimate ends. The probability that this will be so is lessened the more that the world approximates to a formally rationalized ideal of capitalist accounting in which ultimate ends hardly figure (Weber 1978: 165). Ironically, of course, this denial of ultimate ends in the face of technical rationality elevates technical reason itself to the value of an ultimate end. It becomes 'iconic'. It is no longer in obedience to God that we place our trust but in obedience to the rational techniques that He once sanctified.

The immediate lure of formal rationality in a money economy is the fact that money itself is the most rational formal means of orienting activity. It can be used as more than a medium of exchange: it apparently offers a universal measure of quantification and calculation for all elements of capital, including heterodox physical capital and present and future monetary claims, obligations and expectations. Working from real or fictional transactions both between enterprises and within them, accountancy offers the formal possibility of global assessments of gross and net capital worth at selected moments now and in the future, and thus the (equally formal) possibility of calculating profit and loss.

Weber's discussion of accounting practice suggests something of a relapse into marginalist economics' quasi-objectivist problematic, a suggestion that is confirmed rather than scotched by his repeated proviso that the formal rationality of monetary calculation rests on 'real' prices, that is, prices achieved on an unfettered market. The ideal rationality of economic enterprise per se is then conflated to the economic system in toto. Weber was not unaware of having done this. He observes that there is an unavoidable element of irrationality in all economic systems, evident in the fact that their operations are always conditioned by a 'structure of dominance', something substantively alien to purely technical rationality (Weber 1978: 942).

Ironically, it is at this highest level of formal rationality that Weber (1978: 108) begins to note the systematic entry of elements of what from a purely technical interest would be constituted as substantive irrationality: the possibility of diverse modes of rationality. He isolates three circumstances in particular where the ramifications of monetary calculability induce this 'irrationality'. The first of these is the relevance of autonomous and antagonistic enterprises, which produce according to no other criterion than arbitrarily distributed demand. The second concerns the environmental conditions upon which capital accounting depends. The latter presupposes absolute property rights over capital goods, a purely commercial (as opposed to technical) orientation of management, and favours speculative behaviour based on these unfettered rights. Capital accounting thus approaches technical optimality under ideal economic-liberal conditions, to wit: unqualified proprietorial prerogatives and market freedom, including control over appointment of managers; freely available labour and an unfettered labour market; complete freedom of contract; mechanically rational technology; formally rational administration and legal system; and a complete divorce between enterprise and household organization. Weber singles out the exclusion of workers from control over capital ownership as well as from its returns, together with their subordination to entrepreneurs, as a specific form of substantive irrationality (Weber 1978: 129, 138, 161–2; see also Clegg, Boreham and Dow 1986: 60–1).

The third circumstance in which Weber sees formal rationality being compromised is where the economic organization becomes prey to the calculations of outside interests: it becomes, in effect, a potential locus of contradictory calculations rather than being a single discrete calculating subject (Cutler et al. 1979a; 1979b). 'Expropriation of workers from the means of production' and the concentration of control in proprietorial interests are in fact the entry points for external influences of two kinds – credit and financial institutions, and predators who acquire the issued share capital for speculative purposes. Either way, the outside interests pursue their own business interest, 'Often foreign to those of the organization as such' and 'not primarily oriented to the long-term profitability of the enterprise' (Weber 1978: 139; see also the discussion in Clegg, Boreham and Dow 1986: 61–2). This problem becomes acute when these interests 'consider their control over the plant and capital goods of the enterprise . . . not as a permanent investment, but as a means of making a purely short-run speculative profit' (Weber 1978: 140). Familiarity with the gamesmanship, argot and institutions surrounding corporate takeovers (Hirsch 1986) only serves to underscore the contemporary salience of these aspects of Weber's account of the substantive bases of mistrust, despite their relative neglect in the organizations literature.

Chapter 2 has traced how that concern with formal rationality and efficiency which pre-dated Weber's translations, in Barnard (1938) for instance, effectively structured the context within which Weber's work was assimilated into the sociology of organizations. What was lost in this process was the broader comparative concerns with the religious roots and societal consequences of rationalization, as well as the central focus on substantive sources of rationality and their existential tension with formal rationality. A narrower focus on bureaucracy prevailed, one in which an instrumental concern with efficiency overshadowed the historical, institutional, political and economic sociology of the market which Weber (1978) had pioneered. By 1968, when the first translation of the whole text of *Economy and Society* appeared, the sociology of organizations was already constituted as 'normal science' (Kuhn 1962; and see Donaldson 1985a) in which Weber's broader concerns found little resonance.

Weber's problematic did not go entirely unheeded, however. It is to be found in aspects of both an institutionalist and a power perspective. In the former it is to be found in the emphasis on institutional iconicization, as one might term it, and it is necessarily central for proponents of the power perspective, if they are to match Weber's sense of *realpolitik*. In France, for instance, Lucien Karpik (1972a; 1972b; 1977; 1978) developed a critique of what he took to be the thrust of Marx and Weber's writings on organizations. In so doing he resuscitated themes in Weber's work which organizational sociology had neglected. The organizational theory of the firm (Baumol 1967; Marris 1964; Cyert and March 1963; Williamson 1963) was coupled to the concern with the organization as an arena which individuals attempt to dominate, in concert with others, as a locus of calculation and decision. These attempts at capture proceed through coalitions engaged in competitive bargaining for organizational resources and positions, in order to enforce their own ends on the organization. Within this arena organizationally dominant coalitions appropriate the organization, from time to time, through various forms of strategic calculation. They are able to consolidate 'structures of dominance'. In crypto-Foucaultian anticipation of later themes in the study of power/knowledge, these coalitions are analysed through the study of various forms of strategic practice, modes of rationality sometimes termed 'logics of action' (see Karpik 1972a; Clegg and Dunkerley 1980: 502). The organization is conceptualized as a multiplicity of centres of power (see also Clegg 1989b). Within the organizational arena agents with varying strategies are seen to struggle to constitute the capacities of the organization in policy terms which represent their conceptions of their interests. In so doing, they will bargain with whatever resources can be constituted as strategic. Such resources may be located either within or without the organizational arena. It is not just that there are resources waiting to be activated: rather, these are constituted in struggles which may be represented discursively as diverse ways of being rational in Weber's sense of substantive rationality. Hence 'modes of rationality'.

Structures of dominance articulate around more or less abstract cultural values and achieve their expression through organizationally situated actions and vocabularies of motive (Mills 1940). These are the normal ways of accounting for action (where 'accounting' is not being used in the technical sense of the discourse of accountancy). It is through such accounting that one may make reference to the socially available and publicly accountable complexes of reasons with which one might seek to justify organizational actions. Such rationalities when considered collectively may be seen as modes of rationality. No assumption of unity or coherence should be read into this designation. It is quite conceivable that organizations, and the agents located in and around them, may construct diverse and simultaneous rationalities which cohere neither across space nor through time.

Modes of rationality are built out of locally available conceptions which embed economic action. These conceptions will be derived from local custom and practice, as these have been shaped either by a broader culture or by the institutional framing of available vocabularies of motive. Consider an example taken from the construction industry in Britain. There is a dominant mode of rationality of the key agents involved in the contractual relations which constitute the construction site. The contract is central to any understanding of what occurs on site. It stands as the reason for the site organization's existence, because if there were no contract there would be no site. The contract also determines the categories of occupational action one will encounter on the site, as well as the nature and types of activity, working to what plans and what schedule, using what material and so on.

The contract provides for just about everything other than its own interpretation. Its meaning is never exactly clear. It is rare indeed that a contract can be read without the need for interpretation of what ethnomethodologists call the 'indexical particulars'. These are aspects of the interpretation of the documents which cannot depend upon their interpretation by 'disinterested' agents. Those who are involved in interpretation will have an interest in securing particular interpretations over and above the particularly interested interpretations of others. Agents such as the contractor, subcontractor, consultants, architect's office and client will routinely seek to interpret the inherent 'indexicality' of the contract to their advantage. The fact is that understanding the contract is never a self-evident process. The contract does not smooth out the transaction and eliminate costs; in fact, it generates costs and conflicts. Contracts always have to be interpreted; they never provide for their own interpretation. Consequently, conflict is endemic to the construction industry and much of it arises from the contractual relations rather than in spite of the contractual relations. The major resources for seeking to fix diverse interpretations, which always involve different conceptions of interest, are the relations of power/knowledge which are present in the division of labour, particularly the professional division of labour. Occupational identities, knowledges and practices are resources for striving to secure interpretation fixed on one's own terms, rather than those of some other parties to the contract. Consequently, the modes of rationality which are characteristic of the construction industry are deployed around diverse modes of accomplishing the calculations appropriate to 'professional' interpretations. From the contractor's point of view this all occurs within the dominance of the 'profit principle' as a form of life. Indeed, where the reproduction of this principle seems unlikely, for whatever reasons, on any particular project, the indexicality of the contractual documents offers an opportunity for attempts at renegotiation of the contract in order better to secure the profit principle. (All this is discussed at length in Clegg 1975.)

The modes of rationality of French bakers are a contrary case. Here everything hinges on negotiating and securing interpretations of common interest which bind formally non-contractual parties such that at the end of their careers and prior to their retirement they find it quite rational to lend a great deal of their savings in order that some post-apprentice in the trade may be able to buy their business as a going concern. The key mechanism securing reproducibility of this organization form is the trust which they extend to these others, people tied to them only by the experience of working in a bakery, being married and wanting to be their own *boulanger*.

Both trust and contracts are defined by the cultures of local knowledge and local practice. These may be composed out of a complex *pot-pourri* of ingredients. One may be dealing with aspects of a traditional local culture, an occupational or organizational culture or the clashes between them. One may be dealing with the way in which frames of meaning are subject to regulation by legislation, the norms of professional practice or rationalized bureaucracy. Even contracts, seemingly the most rational and transcendent of forms, when studied empirically in local practice, require large elements of trust which may not be forthcoming for all sorts of good economic reasons which have nothing to do with the 'trustworthiness' of the parties but everything to do with substantively rational action.

Elements of trust are frequently at the centre of economic action. (The papers collected in the volume edited by Gambetta [1988] are a valuable resource for understanding the nature of trust, as is the classic text in organization analysis, Alan Fox's [1974] *Beyond Contract.*) Trust, along with a limited range of other devices such as the structuring of member's (and client's, customer's and so on) conceptions of their self-interest in ways which are compatible with organizationally approved actions, serves to produce rationalities conducive to organizational understanding: that is, stable patterns of action extending beyond immediate co-presence and through space and time.

The rationalities which can be called upon tend, in the first instance, to derive from whatever seems to work best in a particular environment. They are culturally available in a particular place and time. Here, elements of the population ecology argument are useful. Innovation may occur for all sorts of contingent reasons and when it does some forms will tend to survive and be reproduced with a greater frequency than will others. Thus, organizations may well persist in displaying the characteristics which attended their formation, as Stinchcombe (1965) suggests. The structure of organizations is 'sedimented' as different concerns and issues are laid down in it. Sedimentation will occur particularly as organizations have to take on functions to deal with aspects of their institutional environment which are externally mandated by authoritative regulation by government, for instance, which seeks to see that organizations comply with some statutory objectives, such as being equal opportunity employers or ecologically acceptable manufacturers or disposers of waste. Frequently, the criteria of regulation are developed in the context of professional practice, as DiMaggio and Powell (1983) have suggested. What survives organizationally may not be most efficient but survives because at some time in the past of the organization it came to be instilled with value in that specific institutional context. This is the essential insight of the institutional school. Things, forms and practices may well be valued for and in themselves, irrespective of their contribution to the efficiency of the organization. Historically one might think of the place that the Latin mass once had in the Roman Catholic Church, or the role that the confessional still plays. Such practices do not necessarily make priests more efficient, but they are valued as legitimate icons in their own right. They are constitutive parts of a ceremonial fabric with an explicable past cultural context.

At the centre of analysis will be organizational agencies. Such agencies may be individuals or they may be collective agencies of some sort which have developed mechanisms for both the calculation and the representation of interests. They are able to make these calculations through the various discursive forms available to them. In particular, one thinks of the articulation of the various scientific, technical and other knowledges which constitute the primary occupational identities and resources of organizational agencies. Other sources of discursive availability will be drawn from whatever regulative (that is, political, legal, economic, accounting and so on) and local frameworks of meaning present themselves, as well as from the many competing sources of value representation which surround any agency.

What are constituted as local frameworks of meaning may be embedded in an infinite variety of contexts. 'Local' refers to specific sites of organizations, sites which empirically offer a plenitude of possible meanings and memberships with which to organize or to resist. In Hong Kong, for instance, it would be an imprudent Chinese organization which did not consult the *feng-shui* specialist in designing its buildings, moving into new offices, choosing a chief executive officer or determining the layout of the furniture or the location of doors and windows. As a visitor at the University of Hong Kong I was once witness to such a ceremony conducted when the department I was attached to moved into new offices in a new building. The ritual consists of sprinkling water around the corners of the room and at the threshold, placing lighted candles in strategic positions, burning 'paper money' (not real currency but ceremonial money for *feng-shui* purposes), offering roast duck and oranges which are subsequently eaten, and conducting a formula of words and actions appropriate to the ceremony. *Feng-shui* rituals may look like the height of irrationalist geomancy to those trained in rationalities such as micro-economic calculation. However, in the Hong Kong local context they enter into the modes of rationality in use in important ways.

It should be clear from the (albeit colourful) *feng-shui* example that in considering local context one is thinking of the discourse of various substantive rationalities which are capable of being regarded as 'ultimate values' of some kind: discourses pertaining to represent the interest of efficiency, of equality, of the market, of the ecology, of *feng-shui*, of a specific ethnicity or place. Indeed, almost any abstractions can be expressed as icons of modernity. Practices in and around organizations will be constructed on the contested terrain of these various knowledges. It is by no means clear that the outcome of these struggles will always be decided in terms of the technically rational, as the success of 'green' values should serve to demonstrate. Whichever values achieve stable articulation as necessary nodal points through which organizational discourse must pass become what Weber referred to as 'principles of dominance' (see Clegg 1989b for a discussion of 'necessary nodal points'). The triumph of efficiency has no necessity attached to it.

What is constituted as efficiency is itself subject, to some extent, to the processes which have been described. Clearly it is not entirely so. It may be difficult to claim that the efficient pacification of a village requires the death of all its inhabitants, but the moral scruples seem not to have been uppermost in some relatively recent history. Similarly, it is difficult to regard questions of efficiency as just an abstract and technical matter, where, for instance, evident distributional and agrarian inefficiencies exist as in much of sub-Saharan Africa. However, as Weber was well aware, efficiency is ultimately a technical term, derived from the discourse of accounting conventions. These will vary widely with national frameworks. As is anthropologically self-evident, these principles of domination are necessarily derived from the complex fabric of the surrounding material culture of members' knowledges and the practices which these knowledges can be claimed to license, to authorize, to enable or to approve. Where these practices can be represented as the principal conduits serving ultimate values, such as efficiency, in the context in question, they will be that much more secure against the strategic play of alternative discursive forms. An empirical specification of these views was presented in Chapter 4 in Fligstein's (1985) findings. That organizational power, expressed in terms of occupational identities and knowledges, was a major factor in organization structuring was supported by data which showed that in different historical periods different departments were likely to control large firms for different reasons.

Discursive forms of knowledge and the practices which are coterminous with them are not random, happenstance nor merely contingent. They are actions produced and reproduced according to rules which are constructed, reconstructed, transformed and innovated through practice. In the same way that an evidently material structure such as a building is an application (and sometimes an extension or innovation) of design, engineering and other construction rules, so an organization form is only a marginally less material structure composed through available rules. Taken together, where these achieve dominance in and as an organization form then we may refer to them as displaying a mode of rationality. From this perspective one can reconsider the issues of organizational form which have been the substantive focus thus far.

Some reiteration is in order at this point. What I have sought to do is the following. First, the book has explored the diversities offered by organizational modernities. Second, it has been argued that this diversity is not explicable in terms of market-based explanations. From the perspective of these accounts, the existence of French bread or the diversity of East Asian organization forms is an embarrassment. Third, while there may be attempts to explain these diversities in terms of cultural reductionism, it is debatable whether this form of reduction is any more appropriate than that of the market. Variations of organization form within common cultural contexts such as post-Confucianism seem to be of more significance than the continuities. Fourth, it has been suggested that organization forms are human fabrications which agencies will structure using whatever discursive rationalities they can secure. These rationalities will vary in their institutional location, drawing not only from occupational identities, or from the regulative framework of law, accounting conventions and so on. In addition, they will also draw on whatever resources find expression in a particular context, local resources which are particular to that context.

It has been suggested earlier that the specificities of local practice should be seen as a reservoir of potential resistance to the contingent pressures of organizations. It would be appropriate to view instances of French artisanal bakery and project managers' strategies on construction sites in this light, as well as the struggles which took place over wages and enterprise unions in the immediate post-war era in Japan. In addition, there are pressures which are institutionally derived. These may go either with or against the grain of some local practices. In one place institutional pressure is closely subsumed to the local warp and weft of the cultural context; elsewhere it derives less from local cultural practices and more from the regulative aspects of the institutional framework as that is nationally defined. In either case, the outcomes tend rather more to organizational diversities than they do to a rationalized convergence on a collective fate inside a common iron cage. We shall explore these issues in the next section.

Ethnicity and family as resources for rationality in East Asia

The East Asian countries which have been considered in Chapter 5 include Taiwan, South Korea and Japan. Taiwan represents a particular case amongst these three. It is an instance of economic action constructed at base out of an institutional value which is defined in terms of a particular aspect of Chinese familial lineage rules. These are based on patrilineage and equal rights of inheritance between sons. While assets are distributed equally, authority is highly age-stratified. The eldest son inherits the mantle of elder from the father. Authority is due to the elder as the first-born. As Hamilton and Biggart (1988: S84) note:

> Because all males remain in the line of descent, the patrilineage quickly expands within just a few generations . . . Equally privileged sons connected to networks of relatives create a situation of bifurcated loyalties, with wealth itself becoming a measure of one's standing in the community of relatives. Accordingly, conflict between sons is ubiquitous, intralineage rivalries are common, and linage segmentation is the rule.

It is from these patrilineal rules that much of the characteristic mode of rationality of Taiwanese organizations is derived. In this respect Taiwan shares a number of features with other notable instances of overseas Chinese economic action, such as in Hong Kong, where the family business is the predominant form.

Historically, as Redding (1990) observes, within the Chinese business community there have been good reasons for keeping business within the family and as far away from rapacious outside interests as possible, particularly those associated with the imperial state and its bureaucracy. Contemporary experience, both on the mainland and in many of the overseas contexts in which Chinese business activity flourishes, would have done little to change this view on the part of many for whom it is now almost instinctive.

Chinese businesses have typically developed on the basis of small family-run firms in which there is strong patrimonial and personalistic direct control, rather than on the more impersonalized, formalized and standardized control of the rational-legal bureaucratic model which we are familiar with from the West (for example, see Wong 1985; Redding 1990). The control is equally personalistic in terms of inter-organizational linkages which are premised on individuals one can 'trust' and who are 'face-worthy' (Redding 1980). These personalistic relations connect backwards to sources of supply and forwards to markets for the organization's product or service, employing a complex web of putting-out and contracting systems, satellite factory systems and distributional systems based on particularistic and personalistic ties (Hamilton and Biggart 1988: S85).

Redding (1990) has referred to the Chinese family business form as 'a family fortress'. Consequently, Chinese family businesses rarely grow in the way that one would credit from a knowledge of either strategy and structure or markets and hierarchies. They are clearly not irrational, but their mode of rationality is derived from a quite different agenda than what one might have thought apparent from reading disembedded accounts of under-socialized agents in a great deal of organization theory.

The Chinese family business is organized with the contingency, or ultimate value, of inheritance as uppermost. The head of the household heads the firm. The central tasks of managerial surveillance and control are kept, wherever possible, within the family. There is a substantial motive for continuous bifurcation or innovation of new enterprises given the combination of familism and patrilineally equal inheritance. As an organization prospers, these profits can be used to start other enterprises which sons or, less frequently, other family members will run. When the founder-father dies, then sons can inherit those assets for which they were stewards during their father's life. In turn, they will follow the same pattern in running their business in relation to their own sons. Principles of divisibility, familial control and strategic management of the asset base in the long-term interests of the family are the structures of dominance within which modes of rationality are constructed.

Redding (1990), amongst others, has referred to Chinese management in terms which suggest a series of concentric circles or boxes within boxes. At the centre are the core family members: these people control the organization and either own it or will inherit it. Next, moving out one degree from the centre there are more distant relatives, friends or people from the same region or locale as the owner(s), employed on the basis of these preconditions for trust and reciprocity. These elements form the upper echelons of Mintzberg's (1983) operational core: the strategic apex of inner family members and immediately below them the middle management ranks of 'trusties'. These people run the organization nepotistically and with a characteristic benevolent paternalism. At a third remove from the strategic apex will be employees such as specialists and staff, depending on the size of the organization. At the furthest limit will be operatives – the unskilled wage labourers.

In many respects the characteristics might be considered to be those of a small family business anywhere, if one were to subtract the inheritance component. However, close observers of the form such as Redding (1990) see its specificity in the fact that characteristics of small scale such as paternalism, personalism, opportunism and flexibility are retained even where organizations grow to a larger scale. What it does not have is as important as what it does have. It is rare to find the same degree of professionalization, specialization, credentialization, careerization, formalization, standardization, legitimization, impersonalization and disciplinization in these organizations, as they are described by Redding (1990), and comparable organizations from the West. It is not just that they are locatable at a different but related point on scales of these variables, Redding suggests, but that these variables are simply not foremost in the way these organizations operate.

What is foremost for overseas Chinese family businesses is the organization as a familial asset base in which control is highly personalized and centralized upon the *paterfamilias*. Familism as the central principle of the operating core negates any wider sharing of trust as a basis upon which decentralization might operate and structure develop. Legitimate authority springs only from ownership, and ownership is a strictly family business. Such an inviolable fortress is particularly dependent upon both the quality of the family's genetic pool and the wisdom of its example as a means of organizational reproduction. This sits together with an equally strong cultural commitment to an autocratic, didactic and patrimonial style as the *modus operandi* of choice. If assets are to remain safe for the family and the family honour and standing thus preserved, then one is under a moral obligation of stewardship in having control of these assets. As a responsibility it cannot be taken lightly and its burden is expressed in terms of an *ethic* of direct control of relationships. Direct control is not simply some primitive form of managerial skill which will be overtaken by technical or bureaucratic control with the full development of modernity (for an account which stresses this sequence, refer to Edwards 1979). Direct control is intentionally striven for. It is also intentionally replicated as sons set up their own businesses in order to constitute the asset base for their next generation. No guarantees exist that elder sons will inherit – if they 'shame-face' or show themselves unworthy in some other way, they will not necessarily do so.

The tensions which patrimonial control can give rise to, between competing members of the same family jockeying for influence over the control of the assets in the succession process, are a source of fission and schism which cannot easily be contained within the fabric of a super-ordinate autocratic control convinced that *he* (it is usually a he but not always) knows best. It is far easier to establish one's own sphere for autonomy/autocracy rather than to battle that of an elder. Consequently the organizations remain relatively small and relatively unstructured but far more centralized than is normal in the West.

Not only are Chinese family businesses a different type of organization in their internal characteristics: they are also different in their external linkages. Intra-organizational linkages are based less on the family and more on clan and regional networks, as well as personal ties, and the maintenance of face within these. It is from these networks and ties that most capital is actually raised, in an informal manner, untouched by legal agreements or contracts. Where these are successful they seem to function in a similar fashion to the 'inner circles' of Western business that Useem (1979) has studied as far as the exchange of information is concerned. Transaction costs are trimmed greatly if the overheads of eternal vigilance over those others with whom one does business can be avoided. Where trust operates effectively, then legally institutionalized surveillance, arbitration and conciliation costs can be avoided. The core organizational activities of producing particular goods or services can be focused upon and budgeted for to a much greater extent.

One consequence of this reliance on trust is greatly to restrict the circles from whom one may draw resources, particularly those of capital. The absence of recourse to institutionally regulated sources of capital, together with the particularism of managerial practices, leads to considerable overhead costs even as transactions are economized. The sheer complexity of managing networks of trust tends to limit their number and thus 'contribute[s] to keeping businesses fairly small and investment patterns directed towards conglomerate accumulations rather than vertical inte-gration' (Hamilton and Biggart 1988: S85). It also militates against the development of highly specialized and expensive technical knowledge-applications in the organization, in terms of both capital resources and skill resources. Firms tend to be small and are unlikely to be capital intensive or to involve multiple discrete knowledge-based skills. The co-ordinative overhead costs associated with these types of organization are avoided.

The overseas Chinese business organizations of places such as Taiwan and Hong Kong are examples of firms whose modes of rationality derive very clearly from the culturally embedded local resources of familism and clanship, which is not to say that they are either inefficient or irrational. There is ample evidence in terms of the usual kinds of economic indicators to demonstrate that they are indeed efficient and the thrust of this analysis is to demonstrate that they are indeed rational. Of course, the conception is of this as one *mode* of rationality. It is one which has its drawbacks, but, as we shall see subsequently, it is not as if seemingly more rational modes are bereft of irrationality – for they are not. Modes of rationality always display some strengths, otherwise it is hard to think how they would survive in any moderately competitive ecology, but this is not to absolve them of weaknesses. The weaknesses of the Chinese family business, with its mode of rationality constructed around an ultimate value of family, surrounded by loyalties derived from clan and locale and a structure of dominance which is heavily personalistic and autocratic, are evident. The degree of particularism makes it difficult for those outside the charmed circles ever to gain admittance.

When seen from an 'inside' perspective some aspects that to an outsider might seem to be weaknesses may, in fact, appear as strengths. For instance, the fact that the majority of organizations constructed according to this mode of rationality are relatively small, and find it difficult to grow and to expand, is hardly a weakness if personal direct control is taken as an ultimate value. However, it does mean one is constantly running up against the limits of personal surveillance from which even a modicum of organizational systematicity, in terms of formalization or standardization, might deliver one.

Another instance of a weakness which may have some strengths is 'factionalism', something which has been observed to be particularly rife. Conflict, as sociologists have long known, has its functions (Coser 1956). Familial factionalism, if not too poisonous and if well managed, may serve as a competitive framework within which rival ideas may flourish, existing practices be made less imperfect and innovation arise. Where the cultural grain and the organizational form together conspire so sharply against upward initiative this may be especially valuable.

Much less dialectical in their implications, however, will be some persistent problems which Redding (1990) identifies, such as the problem of how to arrange managerial succession, where the pool of possible talent is unduly restricted by mechanisms which extend trust only to those who are family. As well as limiting innovation, complexity and size this often shows up in problems in the third generation, whose members have never known the hardships and commitments which their fathers and their fathers' fathers went through in building the assets whose fruits have, perhaps, become taken for granted, and who choose other, more intrinsically interesting and often, in the context, counter-cultural pursuits.

Chinese family business in places like Hong Kong and Taiwan clearly have developed specific forms of organization which trade-off the cultural capital of familism, clan and locale, in order to produce a form which has flourished in the niche of ethnicity in ways which, on a more market- or contingency-based set of expectations, one would not have predicted. Still, as a form, these organizations typically do not develop great complexity or size even though some of them dominate industries, like bicycle transport in Taiwan.

Overseas Chinese organizations in Taiwan and Hong Kong remain small. There is little in the way of external regulation applied to them either directly by the state or indirectly through professional practice which might serve to encourage or promote growth. Both the Taiwanese and Hong Kong states are markedly laissez-faire in their regulation of the business environment, even though they are highly regulatory elsewhere (for instance, in the housing market in Hong Kong, in military, defence and foreign affairs matters in Taiwan). In the examples of overseas Chinese organization which have been considered, the local resources of a specifically 'Chinese' culture are uppermost in framing modes of rationality. The institutional framework is experienced primarily in terms of cultural reserves, rather than as a regulatory environment, sustaining and facilitating certain vocabularies of motive, certain modes of rationality, with certain organizational outcomes.

Institutional frameworks as resources for rationality in East Asia

When we come to consider the other major NICs in the East Asian context it is clear that in South Korea, Japan and Singapore the state is a far more pervasive actor and institutional regulator than is familism. The institutional framework of the state is decisive in the constitution of modes of rationality. In Japan and South Korea state intervention takes an explicitly economic cast, while in Singapore, as well as being involved in major housing subvention, the state is an extremely active practitioner of a moral regulation in which attempts at cultural manipulation are explicit (Wilkinson 1986). In the cases of Japan and South Korea the building-blocks of rationality are located in practices which have a far greater institutional framing in the regulatory context than they do in local reserves of culture.

In some respects the conclusion of the last paragraph may strike one as surprising if one is familiar with some of the Western views of Japanese organizational success. Frequently these have been attributed to culturally specific factors, as we have seen in Chapter 5. What might appear as quite naturally a cultural matter to an outside observer, dazzled by the charms of difference, may in fact be the result of institutional arrangements which have very few roots in a specific culture. One may identify as cultural, and thus relatively unchangeable, something which is in fact far more of an institutional fabrication cut from cloth which displays little specific cultural influence in its design.

For instance, in each of Taiwan, South Korea, Japan and Singapore industrialization has been actively promoted by the state. Initially this was in terms of a product life cycle pattern in which the initial post-war era of import substitution switched to an era of primarily low-wage-labour assembly zones. More recently the transition has been into contemporary export-led growth premised on high technology development (Cummings

1984; Ting 1986). (The city state of Hong Kong, with the PRC cheap labour zone in its backyard, where during the 1980s two and a half million low-level jobs were generated in neighbouring Guandong province, is somewhat different in this respect.) The state policies under which these transformations occurred were in each case somewhat different. Consequently, the impact of state regulation on the availability of vocabularies of motive for constituting modes of rationality differed.

In South Korea the process is very much top-down. Organizations are expected to work within frameworks which government makes available. Planning is centralized, implementation forced, control direct and bureaucratic for public enterprises and routed through financial controls on banks and the supply of credit for the private sector (Hamilton and Biggart 1988: S77; sourced from Bunge 1982: 115; Mason et al. 1980: 257; Westphal et al. 1984: 510). There is no ideology of a liberal, neutral or laissez-faire state. Instead, South Korea has a strongly interventionist, proactive and coercive state actively pushing a very definite policy line on the benefits of 'bigness': state policies encourage economic concentration for large enterprises and government regulation for many medium-sized ones. Clearly, the major reason why organizations are so much bigger in South Korea than elsewhere in East Asia is because the state makes them bigger. The chief contingency in organization growth and size is political will, its effective implementation and regulation. At the organization level modes of rationality would have to be geared towards the all-pervasive facts of state regulation. The strategies which sustain familism in Hong Kong or Taiwan have little play here.

The state in South Korea has a peculiar pervasiveness, born in part out of the fragile legitimacy it has had throughout its existence. South Korea is clearly the least stable of the East Asian NICs and has had the greatest levels of labour and political mobilization. The factors which contribute to this seem to be tied up with aspects both of its route to modern industrialization and its state development. The former has been founded on the creation of very large, centralized urban enterprises, in which an independent unionism has flourished, despite official sanction against it. This labour organization has become a major actor in the struggles for democracy which characterize South Korea. As Koo (1987: 11) has noted, 'Frequent state interventions in labour conflicts led to the politicization of labour relations and to the development of an alliance between the labor movement and other political movements.' Consequently, South Korea has the industrial structure which, of the East Asian economies, is closest to what Marx in the *Communist Manifesto* thought most conducive to proletarian class formation. This has taken place in a nation which has long had a vociferous and highly political student body. Together these social movements confront a state regime which differs significantly from those of the other East Asian countries under consideration.

South Korea was founded in the immediate post-war era in close concert with the leading industrial enterprises and in alliance with a landlord class whose legitimacy was tarnished by wartime collaboration with the Japanese colonialists. Consequently, the South Korean state, suggests Koo (1987), has never enjoyed civil hegemony. It continues to use 'systematic torture' in order 'to intimidate and suppress political opposition . . . carried out with the tacit approval of senior officials' (International Commission of Jurists Report on South Korea, *Sydney Morning Herald*, January 14, 1988: 10). (Not that the other East Asian NICs are immune to charges of considerable official neglect of what are the norms and procedures of their own constitutions with respect to the use of forced confessions, torture and due process, as McCormack 1986 and Igarashi 1986 discuss with respect to Japan.) The state and economic action have been implicated in each other in South Korea from the outset.

While the South Korean state has not enjoyed civil hegemony, this is much less true of the post-war Taiwanese, Japanese and Singaporean states: Hong Kong's legitimacy was premised less on its state form and more on its being an industrially and capitalistically dynamic haven for refugees fleeing from Chinese communism. Civil hegemony does not just happen. State and organizational relations are not necessarily imbued with legitimate authority. It has to be produced and reproduced where it exists. Where it does not have a strong root then indeed a strong state may be a necessity. The East Asian NICs have expended considerable effort on 'manufacturing consent' (Burawoy 1979; see Sugimoto 1986 for Japan and Wilkinson 1986 for Singapore, in particular). With the partial exception of South Korea, with its strong civil movements for democratization, they have achieved considerable success in quelling opposition. Not only that, one should acknowledge with Berger (1987) that they have done so on the basis of profound economic growth and prosperity, which is itself legitimating. The role of the state must enter into specific explanations for the economic success of the East Asian NICs. It is essential to shaping the fabric within which institutional frameworks serve to structure modes of rationality through regulation.

Although it was once the colonial power whose hegemonic sway extended over South Korea, Japan is quite different. The popular outside perception is of 'Japan Inc.', in which the focus is invariably on the Ministry of International Trade and Industry (MITI) and sometimes the Ministry of Finance and Economic Planning. What characterizes the 'Japanese industrial system' is 'constant and quite detailed levels of interaction between executives in the corporate sector and the government ministries, even among low level officials, in an attempt to reach overall consensus on a coherent and long range vision of the forward direction of the economy' (McMillan 1984: 44). The interaction is not between atomistic enterprises and a coercive government. Organizations in the private sector are generally formed into inter-market groups, as we have seen, and these are as cohesive as government organizations. It is the latter, particularly MITI, which administratively guide economic calculation and aid the formulation of modes of rationality. MITI's role with respect to administrative guidance is not simply confined to the better known aspects of 'industry planning' which writers like Johnson (1982) have focused on with respect to industrial decline and renewal (see the discussion in Ewer, Higgins and Stevens 1987, for instance), but reaches down to guide the important small business and subcontracting sector:

> MITI has developed a number of programs to assist the small business sector, including the establishment of the Small Business Promotion Corporation, provision of technical guidance and subsidies for R&D, policies for accelerated depreciation for certain machinery and facilities, programs for management consulting and management education, encouragement of cooperatives formed through prefectural federations of small business associations, regulation of sub-contracting relations, and funding of the Small Business Investment Company. In all there are sixteen major laws on small business in Japan (ten passed since 1961) which both individually and in combination with Japan's Fundamental Law of Small-Medium Enterprises, passed in 1963, form an integrated frame-work for small business development. Not only is the tenor of this legislation interventionist in flavour and biased towards 'eliminating the barriers associated with smallness', it is aimed at making the small sector modern and efficient within the context of the total economy. (McMillan 1984: 59–60)

There are complex sets of stable relations which govern access to financial resources, horizontally, as well as there being vertical integration of satellite subcontractors into the orbit of the big name firms. It is the stability of these relations which appears to be crucial.

A key component of the vocabularies of motive from which modes of rationality may be constructed will be the forms of financial calculation which frame managerial action, the centre of Weber's (1976) classic analysis. In Korea the networks are highly structured from the state downwards, while in Taiwan and Hong Kong they are far more horizontal, working through kin, clan and locale. In Japan straightforward state regulation of banks, channelling semi-public funds directly into manufac-turing, and strong institutional links, including a system of 'stable share-holders' who take up new share issues in manufacturing firms and undertake not to trade in them, help to produce a highly stable framework in which planning can occur. In recent years, however, the relationship with banks has become somewhat weaker. Many firms have begun to rely more on the stock market and on internally generated funds (Kosai and Ogino 1984). Both bank and internal sourcing ensure that stable frame-works for calculation can be constituted at the enterprise level. It is within the *keiretsu* and the inter-market groups that the stable sources of finance and shareholding have been organized, as well as more general matters of strategic policy. Those firms which are members of 'independent groups', groups that are vertically rather than horizontally organized, typically cluster around a big name firm. Such firms organize satellite subcontractors and are interlinked through stable mutual shareholdings with other enterprise groups. At least part of the Japanese answer to the need for integrated financing, manufacturing and market structures thus emerges.

A similar integration is achieved in South Korea with different mechanisms. Here the enterprise groups (*chaebol*) are usually owned and controlled by a single person or family and generally operate in a single industrial sector. They do not rely on stable subcontract relations but vertically incorporate most component producers. While control is associationally negotiated in Japanese firms, in the South Korean enterprise it is familially unified. Consequently while the negotiation of trust and financial stability is achieved in Japan by highly organized joint stockholding, in Korea it is achieved by family control and financing, together with board links to government-controlled financial institutions, the major source of externally generated capital. Family control ensures continuity of purpose and ownership.

Family control also characterizes overseas Chinese organizations, such as are found in Taiwan, but here family sources of finance are of most importance: Orrù, Biggart and Hamilton (1988: 22) report that over 60 per cent of capital is derived from family and friends. Consequently, business groups here are familially interlinked through individual family members holding positions in multiple firms. In Taiwan this occurs within the context of a state which, in respect of the export sector, is an effective support. It offers this support through mechanisms like special tax breaks and export zones (Gold 1986; Amsden 1985) as well as strong regulation of one part of the financial sector, oriented to saving, while another part, oriented to the supply of credit, has been left unregulated. Otherwise state planning of a strong or indicative type appears to be absent, with the consequence that Taiwan has had one of the most polluting and polluted of post-war industrial developments. State planning is not a significant aspect of the Taiwanese industrial landscape (Little 1979).

Across the region there is an extreme variation in enterprise form from the primarily market co-ordinated multiplicity of small, family-controlled and subcontracting Taiwanese firms, characteristic of overseas Chinese business, to the large hierarchically and impersonally controlled Japanese enterprise groups, the even larger South Korean state-financed enterprises or the major sector of Singaporean foreign-owned multinationals. Such variation seems sufficient to suggest that efficient performance cannot be adduced solely to the level of organization variables (Orrù, Biggart and Hamilton 1988). In addition the wide variation in the average size of enterprises in each national economy suggests that contingent organizational variables like size will not readily serve as explanatory factors of performance variables. Measures of typical organization size characteristic of the states in question do not strongly or easily correlate in terms of national growth rates as a measure of the overall effectiveness of the economy. In fact, according to the argument constructed here, the typical enterprise size will depend very much on the state's role in developing the economy, the capital market, regulating inter-organizational relations and so on.

While the market may be important in explanation of Taiwan and Hong Kong, it is of less importance in Japan than an appreciation of the role of the 'industrial system' (McMillan 1984) or, for instance, that of the state corporations in the financing of enterprises in South Korea. Singapore also represents a singular case. Neither the state nor families are the major locus of capital formation due to the preponderance of foreign investment in Singapore. The multinational penetration of Singapore, much of it Japanese as well as British and American, is not mirrored as extensively elsewhere.

It would seem that major contingencies derived from culture, markets, the state and organizational characteristics carry differential explanatory weight in each case, as a different balance of factors comes into play. The picture is of organizations constructed under contingent pressure, where local practices are the ultimate contingency. These practices may be sources of resistance to rationalizing pressures from markets, efficiency, ecology and institutions or they may be facilitative. Everything will hinge on the modes of rationality which agencies in and around organizations construct, the material that is stressed in its fabrication. In one place it may be familism over-determining economic rationalism and pressures towards greater efficiency and goodness of fit of contingencies and structure in the Chinese form; in another it may the economic rationalism which deploys a local peasant culture to reproduce businesses, retirements and *baguettes*; in another it may be the power and strategic control of capital resources by the state which exerts pressures towards the reproduction of extremely large organizations.

Are Chinese family businesses any less rational than South Korean *chaebol*? Is French bread an 'irrational' product in the same way that a Taiwanese bicycle is? Only from a perspective which is ignorant of the rationalities which the agents themselves construct, of the local practices which enter into its fabrication and reproduction.

It remains only to note, of course, that local practices are by no means absent from the seemingly more rational South Korean *chaebol* or Japanese *keiretsu*. The South Korean state developed an authoritarian route to modernization, out of the chaos of a post-colonial civil war which had escalated into a superpower war in all but name. Many of the existing centres of power were compromised by their collaboration with the Japanese colonists. The new state was a strong puppet of the United States in its early creation, fashioned to withstand and to fight communism. Its authoritarian form was re-oriented after the Korean war to the task of economic development, which it sought to 'force' in an authoritarian manner through the 'massification' of national enterprise. Starting war-led modernization almost from scratch, due to the nature of colonial development and the compelling necessities of the Korean war, there were hardly any strong intermediate powers, the anti-communist paranoia hardly permitting legitimate oppositional political actors. Organizations grew and were structured by political diktat, using business and managerial ideologies of efficiency willingly proffered and funded by the appropriate branches of the US state in its fight against communism (Hamilton and Biggart 1988: S82; sourced from Bunge 1982: 115 and Zo 1970: 13–14).

In Japan it had been the pre-war practice, stretching back to before Meiji times, that strong, plural and interlinked economic actors surrounded a relatively weak political centre, one whose primary contribution was the facilitation of these decentred powers (Johnson 1982; Westney 1987). During the 1950s this structure re-emerged with the headless *zaibatsu* of the post-war economic scene, the inter-market groups. As such, they were simply reaching back into the local history of economic custom and practice in Japan rather than responding to market forces. In Taiwan and Hong Kong the state has typically not involved itself greatly with family business, and so there has been little directive power exercised from the centre. Consequently, traditional family business practices have flourished.

Conclusion

In each one of these East Asian countries the picture is of unparalleled economic success in macro-economic terms in the last twenty years or so. In none of these countries has the structuring of organizations unequivocally followed the causal paths towards rationalization that prediction from markets, from efficiency or from contingencies would lead one to expect. In all of these countries diverse modes of rationality have mediated these pressures. In some, such as South Korea, the pressures were largely institutionally transmitted through the state. In others they were largely transmitted through the institutional framing of local culture and practice. The picture is always complicated by the availability, or not, of local discursive resources with which modes of rationality may be constructed, resisted or transformed.

At the heart of rationalization stands the greatest contingency of human achievement: material culture, sometimes resisting, sometimes bending, but never discountable, together with the enveloping frame of the state and national institutions, within which organizational forms are fabricated. The material reviewed shows that across countries there are clear diversities between contemporary forms of organization. The contrasts can be attributed to the different modes of rationality available for fabrication within diverse settings. These differences result from the interplay of local cultures with processes of institutional framing and regulation which derive from the state and other agencies of rationalization. It is from this matrix of possibilities that resources are drawn for power-play within organizations.

The conclusions of this chapter are profoundly disturbing for some orthodox conceptions of the analysis of organizations since the discourse is no longer necessarily tied to the employment contract as an implicit fundamental of analysis and a constitutive element of key variables such as 'size'. Indeed, in a move foreshadowed by some Western analyses of Japan it may be said that a possible object of postmodern organization analysis is presaged. That it might in turn be premised upon pre-modern forms of contracting is merely exquisite irony. Such post-modern objects of analysis will not be contained in the simple legal fictions of the employment contract but will be constituted through a range of other social relations, notably extensive subcontracting and networking, and characterized above all by an extensive de-differentiation of several aspects of organizational life. It is from the analysis of these tendencies, untrammelled by the reductionisms of modernist theory, that a post-modern organization studies might develop.

7

Modernist and Postmodernist Organization

The material reviewed thus far suggests that, when viewed in a comparative context, there are clear diversities between contemporary forms of organization. The contrasts have been attributed to the different modes of rationality available for organizational fabrication in diverse settings. These differences have been attributed to the interplay of local cultures with processes of institutional framing and regulation which derive both from the state and from other agencies of rationalization. It is from this matrix of possibilities that resources are shaped for power-play within organizations.

The previous chapters have advanced an argument with several facets. First, that arguments which seek to use effectiveness to explain the ascendancy of a limited number of organization forms are not quite as universalistic in scope as they might appear to be. Not only can one distinguish significant cases where this does not apply, particularly in the economic success stories of East Asia; these cases themselves conform to no one precise structural form. Rather than there appearing to be a convergence on any one dominant organization form, there appears to be a considerable range of what Cole (1973) refers to as 'functional alternatives' in the context of Japan. Second, it may be said that organizations per se may not necessarily be the sole nor even the most appropriate theoretical object with which to construct a sociology of the organization of economic action. Conceptions of how social organization is embedded in an economic system appear to be an equally appropriate object for analysis, through familialism, subcontracting, formal organization, business groups and so on. As such it is a conception which does not prejudge the organizational form one will find.

It would appear, particularly in organizations in East Asia, that important aspects of this embeddedness may well challenge certain taken-for-granted aspects of what are taken as constitutive features of 'modern' organizations. The modernness of modern organizations resides in the way they may readily be appreciated within a genre of more or less harmonious variations on the theme of Weber's composition of bureaucracy. To suggest that in some respects organizations in Japan or Hong Kong differ from this theme is not to say that they are not recognizably 'organizations'.

A postmodern building, such as the Hong Kong and Shanghai Bank in Hong Kong is still recognizably a building. So it is with organization form. Postmodern organizations would be ones which owe some aspects of their embeddedness to practices and aspects of design which find little resonance in either the modernist theory or the practice of organizations. Taking Japan as the most advanced, materially, of the East Asian societies, it is appropriate to regard aspects of organization design in this country as a hypothetical test-bed for a thesis of organizational postmodernity.

Bureaucracy and Fordism: the modernist mix

As a hypothesis one may entertain the idea that the Japanese variant of East Asian enterprise represents a form of organization which stands to earlier bureaucratic forms of organization as does the postmodern to the modern. The entertainment is no more than hypothetical. Elements of actual organizational practice will be the key. To the extent that these may appear antithetical to modernism, not only in practice but also in theory, then we may find ourselves running up against the limits of our modernist frameworks of understanding.

Modernist organizations may be thought of in terms of Weber's typification of bureaucratized, mechanistic structures of control, as these were subsequently erected upon a fully rationalized base of divided and de-skilled labour. In contemporary literature, following the lead of Gramsci's (1971) reflections in the *Prison Notebooks*, these foundations are usually referred to as those of 'Fordism'. The Fordist labour process base is semi-automatic assembly-line production on the Detroit model. It developed from the 1920s onwards, particularly for mass consumer goods produced in large production runs, although it spread to the 'production of standardized intermediate components for the manufacture of these means of consumption' (Aglietta 1979: 117). The labour process base was intensive, mechanized, divided labour. It consisted of the previous achievements of Taylorism in the application of empirical methods to the study, design and 'de-skilling/re-skilling' of work (see Clegg and Dunkerley 1980: chs 3, 11). However, it added to these what Aglietta (1979: 118) refers to as 'two complementary principles'. These were 'the integration of different segments of the labour process by a system of conveyors and handling devices ensuring the movement of the materials to be transformed and their arrival at the appropriate machine tools'. In other words, it was characterized by the semi-automatic assembly line, organizing work into a straightforward linear flow of transformations applied to raw materials. The second principle 'was the fixing of workers to jobs whose positions were rigorously determined by the configuration of the machine system'. In such a system individual workers lost control over their own work rhythm, and became fully adjuncts to the machine, repeating those few elementary movements designed by engineering departments as the rationalized sum of their formal organizational existence. (Which, of course, is not to deny that there was indeed an extremely rich and culturally embedded 'under-life' of informal organization in the whole system, as writers such as Roy [1958] investigated.)

Fordism was a system of mass production based on both the increases in labour productivity and the wage relation which linked real wage and productivity growth which Taylorism made possible. Productivity gains were translated into wages which enabled the growth of final demand for standardized consumer goods (Albertsen 1988: 344). Mass workers were also mass consumers in the era of 'consumer capitalism' (Jameson 1984), centred on families and homes in the suburbs as locale of reproduction. From these they would drive to work in large, spatially concentrated organizations and drive to consume from similar spatially concentrated 'shopping towns' (as they are known in Australia). The spatial concentration of organizations produced a characteristic tendency towards centre–periphery structures with 'high employment, high wages, and in-migration of labor concentrated in central industrial regions, and unemployment, low wages and out-migration concentrated in the surrounding peripheral areas' (Albertsen 1988: 345). Technologically mature industrial concentrations tended to decentralize to branch plants in the periphery in order to take advantage of cheaper, stable and unskilled labour. (It should be clear that the nature and location of these centre–periphery relations were in a constant process of making and re-making, shaping international, regional and community relations.)

Stretching above the organizational base of Fordist enterprises was a pyramid of control, designed in a classically bureaucratic fashion. At its apex this radiated from the product division to the central organs of calculation and control. In the pyramid of control, according to both the formal theory and the practical application of it in organizational design, authority would reside in individuals by virtue of their incumbency in office and/or their expertise. These offices would be organized hierarchically, with compliance being to superordinate instruction expressed in terms of universal fixed rules. Such rules would be formalized so that any appeal against the rules could be expressed in terms of a 'correspondence principle' linking action and formal rules. The day-to-day principles of control, derived from the hierarchy of offices, would reside in direct surveillance and supervision, as well as the standardized rules and sanctions. Employment would be based on specialized training and formal certification of competence, acquired prior to gaining the job. Great care would be taken with the selection of personnel in order to ensure homogeneity in the organization's reproduction. For these upper levels of control (by contrast to the lower levels of those who were far more controlled than controlling), employment could constitute a career in which either seniority or achievement might be the basis for advancement. The general formality of relations would be buttressed through the ideal of impersonality such that relations would be role based, segmental and instrumental: the primary sources of motivation would be incentive based. This instrumentalism would be carried over into a principle of differential rewards according to the hierarchy of office, in which prestige, privilege and power would be isomorphic with one another.

At the core of the pyramid there would be a maximal division of labour. Intellectual work of design, conception and communication would be differentiated from manual work. The latter would be the work of so many interchangeable 'hands' executing and making possible the designs of superordinate others. These others, the managers, supervisors and administrators of the central work-flow, would be differentiated from the performance tasks. Indeed, in many respects, *differentiation* was the hallmark of the system. There was a maximal specialization of jobs and functions and an extensive differentiation of segmental roles. Forms of expertise would be exclusively held and arranged such that the ideal of the specialist-expert would be the basis for individual or occupational specialist or sub-unit empowerment in the system.

By the 1970s, as Albertsen (1988: 348) puts it,

> the Fordist model began to run out of steam. The crisis of the 1970s turned out to be a crisis of the model itself rather than just another conjunctural swing within its confines. The very conditions which had originally supported the expansion of the model now turned into limits to its further development. A slowdown in productivity growth, fierce international competition, and permanent upward pressures on direct and social wages combined to squeeze the profits and put a brake on the accumulation process. At the same time the downward rigidity of wages prevented social demand from cumulative collapse. So the Fordist model survived, but in a stagnating form marked by a prolonged 'stagflationary' crisis, and also imbued with tendencies working towards its dissolution.

Within organizations productivity slowed down, on this view, because Taylorism had reached its limits – there were no new areas left to rationalize; workers had become more resistant, especially during the prolonged period of post-war full employment, and efficiency gains were being outstripped by increasing costs of surveillance and control associated with the rigid separation of mental and managerial labour. There were related changes in the state sphere and a wholesale 'internationalization' and associated 'de-industrialization' of areas and enterprises which had previously been strongholds of Fordism. Existing centre–periphery relations 'broke up as mature corporations began to decentralize units of standardized manual production to dispersed localities also within the advanced nations, while concentrating managerial and financial functions within large metropolitan areas' (Albertsen 1988: 347). Organizational responses to this changing state became evident in the 1980s and it is in order to explicate these that the concept of postmodern organizations has been coined. In terms of the changing centre–periphery relations, as a concept it is oriented particularly towards understanding the nature of Japanese organizations.

Postmodern organizations?

Whatever else, it is clear that a modernist representation would not accurately capture the organizational patterns of contemporary Japanese organization, which have served in the 1980s as if they were a very beacon of postmodernity, given the role that various representations of them have played in recent debates. For this reason these are sometimes referred to as 'post-Fordist' or 'Fujitsuist' organizations (Kenney and Florida 1988). Mindful of the totality of the picture and not just the technology or work-flow elements, one might prefer to call it postmodernist, in order to index the contrast with Weber's modernist representation. The two tendencies, towards modernism and postmodernism, are not unconnected. Theorists of the 'regulation' school, such as Aglietta (1979), regard Fordism as something which will be increasingly confined to the less developed industries, themselves tending to be located within less developed areas of the world economy, as capitalism becomes ever more internationalized. Within the core enterprises and countries control will become less authoritarian in the workplace as new forms of market discipline substitute for the external surveillance of supervision, changes fostered by extensive deregulation. Internal markets within large organizations will increasingly be created as cost-centres and profit-centres proliferate, and surveillance will be lessened as more flexible manufacturing systems are adopted within which the collective workers become their own supervisors.

For many writers the phenomena which are under discussion here are part of more global tendencies. Lash and Urry (1987), for instance, write of the break-up of 'organized capitalism' and the development of 'dis-organized capitalism', in the variable responses of the United States and some of the West European nations to the end of the post-war boom; Piore and Sabel (1984) write of a 'second industrial divide' opening up in societies as a result of the development of flexible manufacturing systems. What these responses have in common is a focus on some tendencies in the articulation of both production and consumption in some of the advanced capitalist societies. The aim of this analysis is altogether more modest and more specific. It is to focus on these tendencies through the embeddedness of economic action.

What the components of a postmodernist organization might be emerge best in contrast to some familiar features of modernist organization. In common with analyses of postmodernism in other spheres, *de-differentiation* (Lash 1988) is an important component, at least in production. (In consumption, the postmodernist tendency is very much towards greater differentiation.) De-differentiation refers to the reversal of that differentiation process which observers such as Weber (1978) saw as central to the processes of modernity. Postmodernism points to a more organic, less differentiated enclave of organization than those dominated by the bureaucratic designs of modernity. Some highly general tendencies, which will necessarily be subject to subsequent refinement and caution, can serve to represent the scene.

Where modernist organization was rigid, postmodern organization is flexible. Where modernist consumption was premised on mass forms, postmodernist consumption is premised on niches. Where modernist organization was premised on technological determinism, postmodernist organization is premised on technological choices made possible through 'de-dedicated' microelectronic equipment. Where modernist organization and jobs were highly differentiated, demarcated and de-skilled, post-modernist organization and jobs are highly de-differentiated, de-demarcated and multi-skilled. Employment relations as a fundamental relation of organizations upon which has been constructed a whole discourse of the determinism of size as a contingency variable increasingly give way to more complex and fragmentary relational forms, such as subcontracting and networking.

If organization were to mirror art (and there is no reason why it should or should not), Williams (1989: 52) would have us rediscover organiz-ational 'community' in the neglected, alternative tradition of the past century. While he would see in these neglected traditions a democratic imperative, it is by no means clear that this should be so. Communitarian conceptions of organization have had no locational monopoly within the imagination of reformers of a 'left' persuasion. As we have seen in the appeal of post-Confucianism, the familiar image of an imagined organic past can as readily illuminate the contemporary reformers of the 'right'.

Postmodernism does not signal the end of politics or the creation of forms which are emptied of political content. There are for instance, diverse democratic conceptions of this postmodernity. One does not have to be a pessimist to realize that no necessity attaches to the contours that any possible postmodernism might take. An interpretation which sees postmodernist organization as simply another form of totalitarianism may just as well turn out to be appropriate as one which celebrates its pluralism. Eventually these matters will not be decided by analytical judgement alone, but will depend on the triumphs and failures of diverse institutional forms of power/knowledge in the making of the postmodern world. For this reason ideal types of Fordism and post-Fordism, such as that footnoted by Rustin (1989: 56–7), are somewhat misleading (which, to be fair to Rustin, he clearly acknowledges in the body of his analysis): they prejudge the contexts which will shape, and be shaped by, these tendencies.

Aspects of postmodernist tendencies might in some contexts be depen-dent upon an anti-trade-union posture, such as the contemporary United States (where unionization of the workforce is now as low as 17 per cent). Such would not be the case in Sweden where unionization stands at 90 per cent. For some other countries, such as Australia, the prognosis is not so clear.

Some states will be faced with more strategic choices than others in the construction of contemporary capitalisms. Recent research by Calmfors and Diffil (1988) suggests that a key contingency in comparing capitalisms is the type of wage bargaining system which is institutionalized in different national settings. Studies have consistently shown a relationship between this variable and selected macro-economic outcomes such as the levels of unemployment and inflation (Clegg, Boreham and Dow 1986). Three types of arrangement were identified by Calmfors and Diffil (1988). Focussing on inter-employer and inter-union co-operation in wage bargaining they split seventeen OECD countries into those characterized by centralized, decentralized and intermediate bargaining patterns. These types were then related to a range of macro-economic outcomes such as levels of inflation and unemployment. Those countries which were either highly centralized or decentralized in their wage bargaining system consistently out-performed those in the intermediate category. Included in this intermediate category were both Australia and New Zealand, as well as West Germany, Holland and Belgium; Britain, they suggest, probably belongs here as well. These countries clearly have considerable incentive to rethink their strategies in terms of either a more or a less centralized wage bargaining system if they are concerned with achieving more effective macro-economic outcomes. Those countries at either end of the spectrum are necessarily more 'locked into' their design by virtue of not only institutional isomorphism but also the performance advantages that this goodness of fit produces. Those countries which are least isomorphic in their institutional arrangements have the greatest freedom of movement and choice either way.

It is as a consequence of the choices facing countries which are in this intermediate category that the postmodernist organizational debate takes on an important policy dimension. To the extent that there is an elision in the terms of debate, and the concept of postmodern arrangements is aligned only with a 'free' labour market variant of organizational forms, which actually means freedom for a few and restriction to much more repressive conditions for the many, then the terms of debate and choice are unnecessarily restricted. Moreover, an interest in alternative prescriptions would seem ill advised. Consequently, the discussion of Pacific examples such as Japan and the East Asian NICs needs to be balanced with discussion of less 'economically liberal' and more 'social democratic' possibilities such as those which, for example, prevail in Sweden. When posed in these terms the issue of choice becomes even more acute.

If we concentrate only on Japan and the East Asian NICs, the choices, although somewhat inchoate between national strategies, do appear to have some common elements oriented towards re-casting the organizational and industrial relations arena to terms consonant with those which have marked the 1980s revival of neo-conservative liberal analysis. Recipes for success will be sought in deregulation, in de-unionization or enterprise unionism and in state intervention oriented to curbing the excesses of democracy, administrative overload, ungovernability and so on. (For an account of the general arguments consult Clegg, Boreham and Dow 1983: 34–8.) When the political and economic imagination is confronted by the economic success of an example which is in many respects an alternative to these Pacific cases, typified here by reference to Sweden, the implicit choices really do become quite evident.

In Sweden, as in a small number of other OECD countries, there is a relatively well organized labour movement which works through organizations and institutions of bargained corporatism, seeking to impose its policy preferences on employers and government. Lash and Urry (1987: 283) note that

> German and Swedish trade unions have taken a role in the initiation of flexibility in the workplace, in the promoting of job enrichment through the broadening of job classifications. They have in part been able to make flexibility work for labour. British trade unions in their blanket rejection of such change have let employers initiate flexibility in a way that has been very damaging to the interests of workers and unions.

The distinctiveness of the Swedish strategy will be seen to hinge on the central notions of citizenship and representation: on the one hand the deepening and extension of these on a universalistic basis in not only the political but also the economic sphere; on the other hand their restriction within not only the economic but also the political sphere. Consequently, it is through consideration of these issues that one might be attracted to what, in any economically liberal conception of possible organizational postmodernism, would hardly be a promising example.

The next section will contrast possible aspects of modernist and postmodernist organization forms. It will do so from a common perspective: that is, how might each of them handle what have been seen as necessary imperatives of organizational action? A particular strategy will be followed in mounting this contrast. Initially the major point of comparison will be between aspects of contemporary Japanese organization contrasted with a typification of modernist bureaucratic and Fordist organizations. By contrast, occasional reference will be made back to other East Asian examples. It will become clear that the contrast between modernist and putative postmodernist organization has to be conducted across a broad range of dimensions. It concerns not just aspects of skill formation but also capital formation and the way these frame differential possibilities for organizational action through contrasting modes of rationality. In Chapter 8 the focus will at first be on the questions of skill formation, because so much of the contemporary debate has revolved around this issue. To follow this tack is to focus on the technical core of postmodernist organization tendencies. Having already looked at these in the Japanese context the focus here will be in terms of developments in Western Europe, particularly as refracted through West German and Swedish debates. The reason for looking at the matter in this way is quite obvious – it is to enable a shift in focus from issues purely of skill formation to the broader agenda of capital formation. As will become evident from consideration of the Japanese case, stability in and of capital formation is a crucial variable entering into the organizational calculations from which modes of rationality are constructed. As will subsequently become evident from the discussion of Swedish developments, there is more than one way to achieve this particular outcome. There usually is, of course, as that savage but homely metaphor concerned with 'skinning a cat' suggests.

Organizational imperatives

All effective forms of organization must be capable of resolving perennial problems which beset any administratively co-ordinated, recurrent and routine activities which occur between transacting agencies. However, it is by now clear that there is no 'one best way' of doing so. Systematic comparison can be fostered greatly by the application of a common template with which different ways of achieving organization can be compared. Blunt (1989) has argued that all organizations have to find some way of achieving solutions to perennial problems. These can be thought of in terms of seven organizational imperatives which he derives from a larger set constructed by Jacques (1989). The imperatives are:

1   Articulating mission, goals, strategies and main functions.
2   Arranging functional alignments.
3   Identifying mechanisms of co-ordination and control.
4   Constituting accountability and role relationships.
5   Institutionalizing planning and communication.
6   Relating rewards and performance.
7   Achieving effective leadership.

Contemporary Japanese organization can be reviewed under these headings and contrasted with an ideal type modernist, Weberian organization. The point of doing this is not to suggest that Western organizations are just like the modernist ideal type. On the contrary, they may well have moved much closer to the type which will be referred to as putatively postmodernist. However, to the extent that our assumptions for thinking about them remain within the framework which derives from Weberian thought, we may well not recognize them for what they may be. Instead, we may tend to note rather more what they are not.

Mission, goals, strategies and main functions

With respect to strategy Japanese enterprise groups tend not to adopt the conglomerate model which is more common to large firms in the United

States or Britain as the locus of their strategic initiative, preferring instead the *keiretsu* form. This is because Japanese corporations place very little emphasis on merger as a mechanism of growth or diversification of business (Cool and Lengnick-Hall 1985: 8–9; Howard and Teramoto 1981; Kono 1982). As a consequence, as Cool and Lengnick-Hall (1985: 8–9) suggest, organization members *know* what business they are in; they have a deep-rooted and substantive knowledge that a policy of horizontal or vertical acquisitions hardly allows for. One of the reasons why the complex inter-market relations of the *keiretsu* are entered into is to organize those related and ancillary actions which would be internally subject to imperative co-ordination in more typical Western enterprises. In the case of the United States or Britain this centre is likely to be a locus of 'private' calculation which attempts to co-ordinate across a range of economic activities. (Elsewhere in East Asia, such as in the South Korean *chaebol*, the imperative co-ordinator is likely to be the state.) One consequence of having well focused missions, goals, strategies and main functions, it is suggested, is that there usually is a core technology to the organization which is well understood. In consequence, following Emery and Trist (1960) and Tichy (1981), one can propose that 'Since Japanese firms limit their scope to primarily one basic technology, their internal culture tends to be very homogeneous' (Cool and Lengnick-Hall 1985: 9).

De-differentiation of what elsewhere are more likely to be imperatively co-ordinated functions will lead to a lessening of the degree of specialization of functions subordinated to the missions and goals of an organization. Whitley (1990: 64) has suggested that specialization, when associated with relative homogeneity in the nature of employees, will minimize transaction costs. In the Chinese family business this minimization is based upon concentric circles of 'trust' arranged outwards from kin, clan and place. Within Japanese enterprises it is secured through company socialization in the guise of firm-specific training, enterprise unionism and tenure of employment for those in the internal labour market. Some researchers, such as Cole and Tominga (1976), argue that these processes operate to such an extent in Japanese enterprises that modernist assumptions about there being an 'occupational structure' are quite inappropriate. In the internal labour market, instead of a commitment to an occupation per se, they suggest, one finds that because of permanent employment and seniority payment systems, workers tend to be more committed to their organizations than to their occupations.

Dore (1973) tends to regard the development of this institutional framework in Japanese core enterprises as a result of the 'late development' effect. According to Dore (1979) the later that capitalist development occurs the less likely there will have been established a prior system of free wage labour in a capitalist agricultural sector. Consequently the forms of paternalism signified by feudal relations are more likely to be a recent tradition rather than a distant memory. It is from this tradition that he would see organizational commitment and permanent employment deriving. Cole (1978), in contrast, prefers to see the emergence of permanent employment in terms not so much of a living tradition but of an institutional legacy which organizational innovators were able to draw on (see also Cole 1971).

In Chapters 5 and 6, it will be recalled, the creation of the conditions in which the application of this legacy, or 'rational myth', might flourish was seen in terms of the relations of power occurring between organized labour and the employers in both the pre-war *oyakata* system and the resolution of the immediate post-war industrial conflicts. (The latter period is stressed by Sakaiya [1981] in his 'debunking' of 'the myth of loyalty'.) From this perspective, as Marsh and Mannari (1975) have suggested, the internal labour markets which generate organizational commitment are not at all unique to Japan (although the extent of their misrepresentation may be). The misrepresentations are easily gauged. Estimates put as low as 25 per cent the proportion of the labour market which positively benefits from organizational tenure, those male, white-collar, full-time employees of the major, core and big name enterprises (Hamada 1980). The function of these labour market arrangements is clear, however: principally they serve to retain workers who embody valuable skill formation for the enterprise (Jacoby 1979). Retention is achieved through the cumulative advantages which accrue to employees from the higher wages and status flowing from long service under the seniority system. Buttressing these are the scarcity of good job opportunities on the internal labour market and the intense competition that there is for them (Koshiro 1981). These factors explain both the exclusivity and the articulation of permanent employment with the system of subcontracting and outworking, in which the labour of women and retired workers predominates. (Retirement, although now approaching Western norms, until recently occurred at 55. In the absence of a well developed welfare state, 'retirees' have to work, live off earnings or rely on familial support.) The emphasis placed by writers such as Abegglen (1973) and Drucker (1971) on internalized beliefs and values in culturalist accounts is too great and, it is suggested, unwarranted by the texts which are available to Japanese scholars themselves (see Ishikawa 1982; Urabe 1979). Culturalist accounts require replacement with a greater emphasis on a more organizationally materialist context (see Marsh and Mannari 1977; 1980; 1981).

At the centre of de-differentiated specialization of functions and the growth of organizational rather than occupational commitments are technical aspects of production. Technique is not simply a commodity to be bought, but a vital aspect of organization. This is clear in the sense that applied technique includes the human organization or system that sets equipment to work. Equally importantly the concept includes the physical integration of a new piece of equipment into a production process and its subsequent refinement and modification at the hands of the technically skilled workforce. Many manufacturers have come to grief on the belief that technical solutions can be bought pre-packaged. This is to ignore, precisely, that in operation these are always socio-technical solutions. What is at issue is precisely the 'cultural' context in which these solutions have to work. Studies have shown that equipment users rather than makers develop major process innovations (thus stealing a march on their competitors) and that small, imperceptible 'everyday rationalizations' account for the lion's share of productivity gains in an ongoing manufacturing business. Ergas (1987) has referred to this as a 'deepening' model of technological development, in which 'learning by doing' and making the best organizational and technical use of 'what you've got' are far more important than acquiring the latest 'state of the art' process technology (Ewer, Higgins and Stevens 1987: ch. 4). A 'deepening' model of technological development may be contrasted with those discontinuous models of technological development which stress the production of novel technological principles. Discontinuous conceptions of technological change may be termed a 'shifting' model. Kenney and Florida (1988: 140) suggest that in Japan 'the close linkage between production and innovation and a more general legacy of organizational flexibility has resulted in the integration of shifting with deepening'. The achievement of successful integration is very much an institutional question. Where employees have a rooted substantive knowledge of what they are doing, rather than one which is simply a certified mastery of some abstract occupational or analytical techniques, then the institutional conditions appear to be most appropriate for such an achievement.

Japanese organizations achieve integration of research and production through deliberately designed overlapping teams which work in the production complex. Such integration appears to be the key to the simultaneous achievement of 'shifting' and 'deepening'. 'As a result, technologies not only diffuse rapidly and help to rejuvenate mature sectors but large enterprises can quickly penetrate emerging areas either through invention, successful imitation, or knowledge acquisition' (Kenney and Florida 1988: 140). The complex of cross-cutting relations within enterprise groups is used to facilitate this technological innovation. 'Component companies in the corporate family are able to launch joint projects, transfer mutually useful information, and cross-fertilize one another' (Kenney and Florida 1988: 140) using networks which incorporate markets rather than vertical integration.

Deepening requires the combination of technical constraints and complexities, on the one hand, with the constant need to adapt to and anticipate changes in processes and products on the other. One particular organizational feature which facilitates this process is a degree of flexibility in work practices and a skilled and constantly re-skillable workforce (Hoshino 1982c). The organization of enterprises dominated by the modernist characteristics of Fordism, in terms of functional specialization, task fragmentation and assembly line production, is inimical to these requirements. The overlapping work roles, extensive job rotation, team-based work units and relatively flexible production lines which characterize

Japan are far more facilitative. Flexibility emerged out of the modes of rationality which were constructed during struggles in Japanese enterprises in the post-war era.

At the centre of this emergent mode of rationality was the negotiation of long-term employment tenure in the immediate post-war years. This minimized many of the employment inflexibilities which were endemic to modernist bureaucratic and Fordist organizations. Tenure guarantees reduce the rational basis for worker and union opposition to moves to automation or work re-design by management. Where the jobs of members are guaranteed then the rationality of opposition retreats. In such a context, then, it is not surprising to find that skill sharing will occur more frequently and easily, and that job rotation may be used to facilitate both formal skill sharing and informal learning amongst employees (Koike 1987). Long-term employment also allows management to decide rationally to make large scale investments in upgrading the skills of their workforce and in training them, secure in the knowledge that the investment will earn them a return, rather than accrue to someone else who succeeds in poaching the labour away. Where these guarantees are not in place it is always easier and certainly cheaper not to train and not to rely on a production system which requires highly skilled workers. Instead one would work to the lowest common skill denominator – the basis of modernist organization – and minimize the costs of labour turnover not through minimizing the labour transfers but through minimizing training costs and skills.

Arranging functional alignments

Typically, in Weberian bureaucracies, relationships have been settled by hierarchy, giving rise to many of the most characteristic aspects of organizations as they are currently understood. In the case of both the Chinese family businesses and the Japanese enterprise groups many of these hierarchical relationships are arranged through complex subcontracts and the extensive use of quasi-democratic work teams (in the Japanese case) or personalistic networks (in the Chinese case). Each instance uses horizontal relationships to substitute for functional arrangements which more typically are hierarchical in the modernist bureaucracy.

Rather than market and hierarchy being opposed types, as in the Williamsonian formulation, it may be more appropriate to see them as alternative solutions to the problem of how to arrange functional alignment within the enterprise. They are not the only solutions. Hierarchy may also be mediated by elements of quasi-democracy in the use of work teams, without market relations being entertained in the construction of this internal democracy. Whitley (1990: 63) has suggested that enterprise structures which are premised on producing a relatively concentrated range of related products will tend, of necessity, to resort to market relations in order to complement this narrow base, an option which more imperatively co-ordinated organizations will not require. Those with more of a penchant for market relations will 'tend to deal with uncertainty by being highly flexible and evolutionary in their patterns of strategic change'. Internally, one way of achieving this is to emphasize greater elements of democracy and self-management, albeit within structural parameters, in organizational work teams. By contrast, those more oriented to hierarchy will handle organizational change 'by reallocating resources to new activities as opportunities arise' (see also Kagono et al. 1985: 57–87), thus contributing to differentiation and further specialization.

Unlike a large divisionalized Western corporation, Japanese enterprises are unlikely to practise vertical integration of their component suppliers, in order to minimize transaction costs. Instead, they are likely to use the 'just-in-time' (JIT) system where complex market relations with component subcontractors are used to ensure that supplies arrive on the premises where they are needed at the appropriate time. Large inventory stocks are dispensed with, and the circulation of capital in 'dead' buffer stock is minimized. In Japan there are large JIT production complexes spatially organized so that subsidiary companies, suppliers and subcontractors are in contiguous relationships with each other, extending through to tertiary subcontracting relations. Quoting Cusamano (1985), one may note that with respect to Toyota there are as many as 30,000 tertiary, 5,000 secondary and 220 primary subcontractors. Of the latter, 80 per cent had plants within the production complex surrounding Toyota in Toyota City.

Kenney and Florida (1988: 137) see a number of distinct advantages flowing from the JIT system. One is that it displaces wage costs out of the more expensive core to the somewhat cheaper periphery; another is that it leads to stable long-term relations with suppliers which open up multidirectional flows of information between the partners in the subcontracting network. Personnel as well as ideas are freely exchanged. Innovations can be accelerated through the system.

Japanese work organization is premised on self-managing teams rather than workers striving against each other under an individualistic and competitive payment and production system. In Japanese enterprises the functional alignment of activities is achieved by extensive use of the market principle through subcontracting and a (quasi-) democratic principle through self-managed teamwork. (As it takes place within an overall structure of hierarchy and private ownership it is clear why the principle can only be described as quasi-democratic.) Within the self-managing teams work roles overlap and the task structure is continuous, rather than discontinuous, in which the workers themselves allocate the tasks internally (see Schonberger 1982). Production is not accelerated by re-designing work downwards in its skill content, by simplifying it further and separating the workers more one from the other, as in the classical modernist organization under Fordism. This is clear from studies of Japanese organizations in other countries, such as the research by Lincoln, Olson and Hanada (1978) into 54 Japanese-controlled Californian organizations, which found an inverse relationship between functional specialization and Japanese control. Within Japanese organization practices, work in the internal labour market seems to be designed with an eye to the collective worker rather than in opposition to the collective worker. It appears to be designed to facilitate such collective work:

> With work teams, the pace of production can be changed by adding or removing workers, and management and team members can experiment with different configurations for completing specified tasks. In contrast to US mass production where work arrives on a conveyor belt, Japanese workers often move with the production line . . .
>
> Work groups perform routine quality control. This allows Japanese quality control departments to focus on nonroutine aspects of quality control, such as advanced statistical measurement or even work redesign. There is substantial evidence that work groups detect and remedy mistakes much more quickly than designated 'inspectors', saving considerable rework and scrappage. Japanese work organization has led to the integration of quality control and shopfloor problem solving. (Kenney and Florida 1988: 132)

Quality circles have been seen as a major achievement of the Japanese system, and not only because they serve as a substitute for quality surveillance as a separate management function. They include both operatives and staff specialists such as engineers in the same circle, oriented towards not only reducing the wastage rate but also making technological and process improvements. Once more this is related to the 'deepening' of technological development. Quality control is not 'externalized', nor is maintenance, to anything like the same degree as in more traditional modernist organizations. Much of the routine preventive maintenance is done by the operatives who use the machines. Kenney and Florida (1988: 132) note that 'downtime' is considerably less on machines in Japan compared to the United States (the figures cited are 15 per cent compared to 50 per cent downtime). This confirms Hayes's (1981) view that the Japanese succeed because of meticulous attention to every stage of the production process.

The greater flexibility of workers extends to the technological design of work itself. Production lines in Japanese enterprises are organized to be more flexible than the simple linear track of a Fordist factory. They can be easily reconfigured between different product lines (Cohen and Zysman 1987: ch. 9) and do not necessarily conform to the linear layout. Kenney and Florida (1988: 132–3) note that in some industries the lines may be 'U'-shaped or modular, so that operatives can 'perform a number of tasks on different machines simultaneously while individual machines "mind" themselves'. As they note, for such a strategy to succeed, multi-skilling is essential.

Mechanisms of co-ordination and control

Mechanisms of co-ordination and control of the different functions and alignments of the organization depend, in part, on the strategies of power pursued. There are two aspects to this: power in the organization and power around the organization. We shall look at power in the organization first. Within the Chinese family businesses this is clearly premised on familism as in part is the strategic apex of the South Korean *chaebol*. Both of these are modes of *personalization* of power, as opposed to that *impersonalization* (or formalization) which one would anticipate from the Weberian model. This personalization and particularization of power appear to be quite normal throughout much of the Asian region in both business and politics (Pye 1985). Consequently, informal, rational-legal sources of authority appear to be less significant than does the personal mandate.

Closely related to the question of power, whether particularistic or universalistic, personalistic or impersonalistic, will be the more general issue of how authority is relayed. With Whitley (1990) one would anticipate that the greater the particularism/personalism of power then the more diffuse will be the ambit of authority, restricted far less to specific zones and arenas of certified competence. This crops up repeatedly in Aston studies of organizations in Asia which consistently show them to be more centralized than comparable Western organizations (see Donaldson 1986a). The personal authority of ownership relations colours the whole of the organization.

In both Chinese and South Korean organizations family is the major political principle. Family can be trusted, outsiders cannot. Consequently, formal, impersonal structures of co-ordination and control function badly in transmitting 'undistorted communication' in contrast to those which are familially based. Within such a system, relatively high levels of trust within the family can coexist with high levels of distrust between those inside the circle and those who are excluded. Where the family is the basis of trust then more inclusive bases for a moral order will not be appropriate. No basis for trusting outsiders exists. Thus, we find quite different mechanisms for elite co-ordination and control developed between the familial-based South Korean and Chinese overseas business systems and the enterprise-based Japanese system. Both differ sharply from the more purely instrumental strategies of classical bureaucracy.

Japanese organizations are not based on familism. Nor are authority relations of co-ordination and control. In Japan superiors are expected to make their subordinates accept the practice of groupism so that trust is constituted which transcends particularisms, binding each person to the universal love of the enterprise. According to Rohlen (1973), drawing on fieldwork in a Japanese bank, about a third of Japanese organizations give their employees 'spiritual training', akin to techniques of religious conversion, therapy and initiation rites, which emphasize social co-operation, responsibility, reality-acceptance and perseverance in one's tasks. Tanaka (1980) also describes similar phenomena of socialization to and indoctrination in company goals. Organizational commitment would not appear to be left to chance in many cases. In the case of Japan organizational commitment is of most moment for those workers who are secured by the golden chains of the internal labour market. These core employees are securely incorporated as members with benefits. Such benefits are not typically approached where there is a much greater reliance on the external labour market as a source of recruitment. (In some instances, as in the case of skilled labour in New Zealand and Australia for much of the post-war era, this reliance on the external labour market has led to a positive neglect of questions of skill formation.) Where skill formation has not been marginalized, as in the Japanese case of the core internal labour market, then it is important to remember that the benefits are not spread throughout the industrial system. Those workers who are subject to domestic outwork, seasonal working or extended subcontracting will secure none of the benefits of the much vaunted core workers (Dore 1973; McMillan 1984), yet it is upon their 'flexibility' that the system rests. It is a system which works well in securing loyal commitment, by virtue of low turnover and dissent, even if it does not produce markedly more satisfied workers than elsewhere.

Empowerment on the shop-floor appears to be more widespread in Japanese enterprises than it does in the bureaucratically conceived Fordist structures of Western modernity. This is achieved through mechanisms like extensive firm-specific basic training and learning. In part, this is accomplished through being involved in the work teams with more experienced workers. Job rotation also facilitates this learning. Such rotation takes place not only within the work teams but also more widely in the enterprise.

> Workers sequentially master the complexities of different tasks and grasp the interconnectedness among them. By breaking down the communication barriers among work groups, rotation enhances the flow of information between workers and across functional units. Rotation generates a storehouse of knowledge applicable to a variety of work situations and enhances problem-solving capabilities at the enterprise level. (Kenney and Florida 1988: 133)

The empowerment strategies of Japanese enterprises have been identified in a generalized commitment to 'learning by doing' (Kenney and Florida 1988: 133–5). The *kanban* system, which is used to co-ordinate work between different work teams, has been seen as a part of this empowerment. Instead of top-down co-ordination of the workflow in the form of superordinate commands and surveillance, the *kanban* system allows for communication flows which co-ordinate horizontally rather than vertically. Work units use work cards (*kanbans*) to order supplies, to deliver processed materials and to synchronize production activities. Communication is through the cards, laterally rather than vertically, reducing planning and supervision, creating empowerment as workers 'do' for themselves.

Empowerment through widespread use of communication of information has been seen by Clark (1979) to be a key feature of the *ringi-ko* decision-making system, where printed documents circulate widely through the enterprise for comment and discussion. Consequently, when decisions are made after this exposure, snags and sources of opposition will have invariably been 'cooled out', often in ways which are organizationally quite productive. Much the same can be said of the widespread use of 'suggestions schemes', which although not compulsory are so widespread that employees feel obliged to participate in them. (For instance, Kamata [1982], in his exposé of Toyota in the early 1970s, suggested that workers who chose not to 'empower' themselves in this way were punished for it through criticism and smaller bonuses!)

Flexibility and empowerment extend throughout the organization structure. There is a far wider use of management 'generalists' than is typically the case under the Weberian model of specialization and credentialization. Managers will not usually be specialists in accounting or finance, for instance, but will more likely be generalists who can rotate between positions (Kagono et al. 1985). 'Management rotation', state Kenney and Florida (1988: 134), 'results in flexibility and learning by doing similar to that experienced on the shopfloor. This blurs distinctions between departments, between line and staff managers, and between management and workers.' Through this rotation the commitment to a tenure principle and the prevention of organizational arteriosclerosis are maintained simultaneously. Managers who never leave do not have to wait for other managers to retire or die so that they can fill their shoes. Typically, the enterprise will always leave some management slots vacant. Nominal subordinates may discharge managerial tasks. Job titles are thus denotive of seniority not function. Because of rotation and the fact that promotion of a subordinate is not threatening to the status of a superordinate, internal managerial competition is far less than in the Weberian bureaucracy. Managers tend to cross boundaries and share knowledge far more in the normal course of doing their work where the quite rational anxieties induced by more explicitly 'face-threatening' systems are present (Kagono et al. 1985: 116).

Where the traditional Weberian bureaucracy and Fordist production relations are characterized by highly specialized divisions of formalized power and authority, maintained by highly compartmentalized information flows, the situation is quite different in tendencies towards postmodernist organization:

Long-term employment and extremely low rates of labour mobility ensure that shared knowledge remains internal to the enterprise and that leakage is minimal. This provides firms with large collective memories. The Japanese remuneration schedule sets up sizable disincentives to careerism based on information hoarding. Since bonuses hinge on overall corporate performance and wage increases take into account group performance, the ability to share information, and the development of multiple skills, there are very strong incentives for interaction and cooperation. The Japanese firm thus becomes an information-laden organization with problem-solving and regenerative capabilities far exceeding its Fordist counterparts. (Kenney and Florida 1988: 135)

Japanese enterprises have not only developed some productive ways of organizing power internally; they are also somewhat different in terms of their power 'around' the organization, to use Mintzberg's (1983) phrase. Power around the organization concerns the way enterprises are inter-connected between their strategic apices. In the West this takes place primarily through the mechanisms of 'interlocking directorships' (see Clegg, Boreham and Dow 1986: ch. 5) and the share market (see Ingham 1984; Morgan 1989). In these capital-market-based systems long-term horizontal linkages, other than of cross-ownership or predatory behaviour oriented towards that end (or associated strategies), are rare. This is also the case in the state-organized system of South Korea. The nature of interlocking power relations around Chinese family businesses appears more closely to resemble a series of spot-market transactions frequently negotiated between kin, clan or community. In distinct ways each of these systems does little to secure long-term extensive and routinized relations between the strategic apices of distinct firms.

Japanese enterprises operate under relatively stable capital market conditions compared to the highly volatile share-transactions of bundles of 'ownership' which characterize British, United States and many other Western stock exchanges. (By contrast, family and state ownership consolidates stability of capital formation in the South Korean case.) Surprisingly, perhaps, to advocates of 'free' markets this does not result in a lack of dynamism or a neglect of issues of co-ordination and control at the strategic apices of industry in Japan. In fact, it is the facility to achieve high degrees of such co-ordination and control in its complex inter-market organization and state-facilitated integration which many commentators have seen as the strategic edge of Japanese capitalism. In Japan, as we saw in Chapter 6, the role of MITI has been of particular importance in vertically co-ordinating enterprises in the achievement of longer-term, macro-economic, industry-wide planning (Dore 1986). Much of the market uncertainty which has to be organizationally buffered in the West is displaced outside the organization in Japan. The system of financial ownership does not generate as much risk in the first place, while the state handles much of what does occur. Consequently there is no necessity to devise strategies to handle risk or to manage uncertainty which is not likely to occur: resources can be better invested in core activities.

In general, the question of managing state–enterprise relations also arises with respect to power around organizations. No matter how well an organization's strategic actors perceive leadership issues and pursue solutions they must secure organizational dominance and consensus, or at least obedience, for their goals. Moreover, they will have to depend on a national institutional environment if their strategy for the organization is to succeed. The most urgent need will invariably be for sources of long-term credit to finance major new investments, to maintain debt-to-equity ratios consistent with minimal capital costs and to cushion the inevitable destruction of capital that flows from basic innovations in organizational practice. Public policy also enters into this general picture. Financial assistance may be required to meet the 'front end' costs of marketing and establishing distribution and service networks, as well as there being policies to protect the domestic market from other governments' predatory trade strategies, such as dumping and the provision of credit packages on tenders for major development projects. Industrial relations systems that do not put arbitrary limits on technological innovation and the upgrading of work practices will also be required (Williams, Williams and Thomas 1983: see the introduction). Finally, technical inputs of equipment and components, as well as the maintenance of markets, will depend upon insertion into a diversified manufacturing sector in which public policy plays a coherent role in establishing and maintaining linkages. These general conditions are derived from intensive studies of a counter-factual case to that of Japan: the example of 'manufacturing decline' which has been charted for core sectors of the British economy in the post-war period (Williams, Williams and Thomas 1983).

The stability of the enterprise conditions of calculation that develop in these three East Asian examples has not been productive of the formation of high-risk entrepreneurial behaviour as firms launch into speculative and unrelated lines of business. In both Japan and South Korea the role that the state takes in developing industry policy with respect to new and declining branches of industry effectively operates to prevent the arteriosclerosis of national capitalism which might otherwise occur. Despite frequent classically economic liberal claims that government should not be in the business of picking winners, the institutional arrangements for achieving this do seem to work smoothly enough in some countries. The issue is whether or not there should be a strong framework and organizational commitment to instruments of public policy or whether or not there is a belief that such interventions are illegitimate and best left to the mysterious movements of market forces. Even in Hong Kong, which is one of the most economically liberal of places, there is a very strong public policy orientation in the two decisive areas of law and order and the provision of an effective and cheap supply of public housing (Henderson 1989). Clearly, in the maintenance of a competitive national workforce, formed initially on price competitiveness, where there is no well established housing market, the two factors are not unrelated.

Constituting accountability and role relationships

Management involves accountability for role-related actions which it is the manager's responsibility to produce and facilitate in others. The division of labour which achieves this may be more or less complex and more or less individuated. In each of the East Asian economies there is evidence to suggest that both the level of complexity and the degree of individuation of labour are less than is typically the case in a classical Weberian bureaucracy. De-differentiation appears to be operative. Whitley (1990: 65) has suggested that this is in part because of the way skill formation is more intra-organizationally than individually achieved, and thus located in the context of the overall skilling of work groups rather than just the human capital of a competitive individual. Further supporting this sense of group accountability and relationships is a reward system oriented more to teamwork than to individual work. All this is only possible where multi-skilling and flexible skilling are the norm, rather than restrictive skill defensiveness. Where there is a high degree of skill division then more formalized and externalized co-ordination and control will be required. Individual role relationships will tend to be normalized in the calculations which organization agencies make and so management control will be expressed far more in terms of the accountability of individuals.

Institutionalizing planning and communication

Planning and communication of the enterprise strategy are the fifth imperative which Blunt (1989) identifies as essential for organization. In the manufacturing sectors of Britain, the USA and Australia, con-glomerates predominate as a major locus of internalized planning and communication. Whatever the structure, a manufacturing firm's facilities, workforce and distribution network impose their own focus on its tech-nologies and markets, and thus their own limits on rational diversification. Recognizing those limits is a matter of fine judgement; expensive mistakes, resulting from unco-ordinated manufacturing strategies and managerial distraction, can occur even in the cases of integration and diversification motivated solely by manufacturing considerations. They occur much more frequently in the case of mergers and takeovers that represent a second best to internal expansion, and the situation is much worse in the usual case where businesses are acquired with no manufacturing rationale at all. Thus arises the typical conglomerate of, say, twenty or thirty unrelated businesses presided over by a single head office which, however, bears ultimate responsibility for their strategic decision-making. Merger and acquisition do not necessarily produce rational reconstruction on divisional lines but can produce conflicting authority structures based on disparate organization cultures and systems resistant to the new locus of control.

In such a situation the head office's necessary lack of insight into the dynamics of the individual businesses is compounded by its over-reliance on the major formally rational means of control over local management and assessment of business prospects – that is, dependence upon financial calculations and accounting techniques premised on the divisional form. The degradation of subsidiary businesses to 'profit centres' in contem-porary managerial jargon tells the tale plainly enough. Centralized cost-accounting and capital-budgeting systems are the new organs of control to whose simplistic quantifications all complex technical and organizational questions, as well as future production and marketing imponderables, have to be reduced (Standish 1990). 'Profit-centre' managers in their turn submit to the iron law of quarterly or annual return-on-investment (ROI) calculation, which hardly encourages them to become far-sighted captains of industry. Thurow's (1984) investigation of a conglomerate with thirty subsidiaries revealed an average time horizon of 2.8 years, hardly adequate for planning investments in processes with lifespans covering several product-generations! Analysts of manufacturing decline almost unanimously pin point the rise to prominence of ROI calculations as the immediate cause of the sharp decline in expenditure on new process technologies, facilities and research and development.

The adoption of one or other accounting convention as the basis for planning has real material consequences (Standish 1990). The most important general example is the use of modified historic-cost accounting in Britain and Australia which systematically overstates profits by understating the value of real capital, and this in turn may lead to inadequate retention of operating surpluses and the winding down of the assets of the business. Another arbitrary – if formally rational – aspect of accounting practice is the choice and weighting of time-frames. Profit is struck on an annual basis, and the time-frame and weighting of anticipated returns can vary greatly. The financial institutions' separation from, and domination of, manufacturers gives yearly accounts a much greater salience than in countries where financial institutions are made more receptive to manufacturers' requirements, and this in turn highlights the artificial distinction between operating costs and capital outlays.

Current ROI calculations and capital budgeting techniques bear a heavy inherent bias to conservative investment behaviour and short-term management of manufacturing enterprise. The quarterly or annual ROI calculation presents an unambiguous case and a very strong influence on local managerial behaviour because it is the main – and often only – form of control of it available, as well as the measure of its success. It is much easier to improve 'performance' on such measures by decreasing the denominator than by increasing the numerator, which can take a long time, involves risk and has to be discounted for taxation. A profit-centre manager can achieve quicker, surer and easier results by delaying replacement of old or worn-out equipment, replacing equipment eventually with technologically dated or inferior substitutes and skimping on maintenance, research and development and personnel development – in other words, by disinvestment and technological stagnation (Hayes and Garvin 1982: 74; Hayes and Wheelwright 1984: 11–13). In the 1970s, for instance, robots did not meet ROI criteria in either Japan or the USA in the car industry. The Japanese introduced them anyway and thereupon gained market dominance through the much higher quality achieved. As a result, robots were paying for themselves within two and a half years (Thurow 1984).

Even more insidious, perhaps, is the rapid acceptance of capital-budgeting techniques, which involves discounting calculations for assessing strategic investments. The amount and timing of future cash flows resulting from a proposed investment are estimated; then they are discounted by the estimated return on an alternative, external investment of the same size and aggregated to produce a 'net present value'. This procedure provides plenty of room for fudging the figures and building in arbitrary assumptions. In particular it relies on estimating the final cost of the investment, the amount and timing of returns, the rate of return on the alternative investment (the 'hurdle rate') and the rate of real deterioration of items of productive capital. Even if used sensibly, capital-budgeting procedures will tend to discourage major initiatives and indicate strategies aimed at short-term returns. In practice, hopelessly unrealistic assumptions and expectations are often built into these 'analyses', like payback periods of three years or less, and very high, rule-of-thumb hurdle rates that bear no relation to the real cost of capital to the business or actual rates achievable from external placements. (Net present value calculations can, however, be bent the other way, to justify massive strategic overkill with catastrophic socio-economic – and political – consequences. Perhaps the best examples of this mistake were the British National Coal Board, British Steel Corporation and British Leyland, all of which had strikingly similar histories: see Higgins and Clegg 1988.)

Whether one is 'sticking close to the knitting' (Peters and Waterman 1982; Redding 1990) by focusing only on what one knows well, in a family business, or whether one is involved in imperatively co-ordinating only a fairly specific range of business-related activity, as in typical Japanese enterprises, leaving the broader picture to the inter-market relations and to state planning, one is certainly involved in a far more restricted and less audacious exercise of planning than one would be in trying to plan the twenty or thirty unrelated businesses of the typical conglomerate. Planning and communication can take place through abstracted techniques of management control but it is by no means clear that the technical reason implicit in the use of these techniques serves to substitute for more substantively based judgements and planning. The greater degree of substantive as opposed to formal rationality evidenced in Japanese organization, in particular, seems to be an important consideration. Under conditions of more stable enterprise relations the forms of short-term economic calculation which are predominant in Western enterprises do not prove so necessary. Knowledge of the business is more rooted in substantive criteria of operational intimacy rather than merely rational techniques. Practitioners of such technically adept management, the new 'professional managers' of United States business schools, have recently been lambasted both for their failure to conceive strategies and to implement them as well as for their systematic choice of self-defeating strategies (Hayes and Abernathy 1980; see also Hayes and Wheelwright 1984; Hayes, Wheelwright and Clark 1988). Unlike their predecessor who typically worked up through the various functional departments and divisions of the enterprise, gaining 'hands-on' experience, the new manager cultivates a 'fast track' career by job-hopping and scoring up quick symbolic 'wins'. Knowledge of the specific business grounded in its local culture is replaced with an analytic detachment borne of de-contextualized and portable skills gained at business, accountancy or law school. Apart from the formal accomplishments of law, accountancy and financial management, these skills restrict themselves to formalized consumer analysis, market survey technique. matrixes and learning curves. Ignorance of technical contingency is supplemented with 'technology aversion' and an elitism that prevents either being remedied (Pascale 1984). Institutionally cultivated individual career strategies for organizational dominance contribute to organizational decline.

Two prominent analysts of the Harvard Business School, Hayes and Abernathy (1980: 74) have branded these new managers as 'pseudo-professionals' who *systematically* mismanage a manufacturing business. They regard plant as an embarrassing constraint on financial manoeuvrability and try to buy pre-packaged solutions, commonly on an inappropriate and grandiose scale. But what they do well is more damaging than what they do badly. 'Managing by the numbers' collapses time-frames: individual businesses have to show quick returns on minimal outlays or be deliberately run down and liquidated as 'cash cows'; in conglomerates, individual businesses are reduced to bargaining chips, quickly acquired and shed. 'A "successful" American manager doesn't plant or harvest,' Thurow (1984: 23) comments, 'he is simply a Viking raider.' Clearly, such individuals are strategically ill equipped to address the substantive issues of manufacturing management; and obsolescence, lack of fit, quality and labour problems result.

For many writers, the investigation of manufacturing decline stops here, and they propose solutions accordingly. At the most extreme, Pascale (1984: 65) suggests that rationality as such is an ethnocentric cul-de-sac, and the standard business-journal exercise of learning-from-the-Japanese for him boils down to a flight from rationality and emulating the inspired but erratic hit-or-miss business behaviour of Soichiro Honda. 'The givens of organization', he reminds us, 'are ambiguity, uncertainty, imperfection and paradox'; he thus follows the organization theory of March and his associates (Cohen, March and Olsen 1972) towards the conviction that strategic and structural responses carry their own falsehood. The more common remedies are no less fanciful and voluntarist, from exhumation of the Schumpeterian entrepreneur to proposals for corporate cultural revivalism (see Ray 1986) and an evangelical faith in the explanatory purchase of 'economic culture' in its post-Confucian mode, an explanation to which can be attributed both the 'decline of the West' and the rise of East Asia. By contrast, this chapter is recommending consideration of the specificities of substantive practice.

In the case of Japan, writers such as Fox (1980) stress that long-term planning based on market research has been vital in those areas where innovation, and not just importation, of technology has occurred in Japan, such as the consumer electronics industry. Eto (1980) stresses the role of the government in supplying information and technological forecasts, sharing the emphasis which Holden (1980) places on MITI's national industrial policy. In addition, she also stresses the institutional freedom which Japanese firms have to plan long term as well as their emphasis on quality control in the actual production process. (The 'cultural homogeneity' of the workforce is also stressed as being important). Other writers, such as Hoshino (1982a; 1982b; and especially 1982c and 1982d), while sharing the stress on technological innovation, argue that it is characteristics of the organization structure which enable long-term research planning to occur easily, notably the flexibility of the specialist workforce.

Relating rewards and performance

Performance and reward imperatives may be more or less related. Now, this can be achieved in one or other of two contrasting ways. It may be achieved through complex processes of individualization in effort-related bonus systems. Alston (1982), for instance, has noted how these arrangements may give rise to jealousy and rivalry. Alternatively, it may be done through linking rewards not to individual efforts but to organizational success and service. The latter strategy has characterized Japanese management systems. The payment system has been oriented primarily to improving overall organization performance, by tightly coupling length of service to frequent promotion up a ladder of many small gradations. The seniority-based nature of the wages system in Japan, the *nenko* system, has been the major focus of much discussion of the relation between rewards and performance in Japan (see Sano 1977). It should be clear that *nenko seido*, the combination of lifetime employment and seniority-based wages systems, applies only to the core employees, who will be almost entirely males (Matsuura 1981). In common with Matsuura, other writers such as Takeuchi (1982) have argued that the ease of dismissal, low wage and fringe benefit costs and frequent part-time provision of female labour are important in buffering and stabilizing the employment situation of core workers. As we have seen in Chapter 5, the basis of flexibility is disproportionately shouldered by female patterns of labour force participation.

Wages in Japan are not simply based on age alone. Performance elements do enter into the equation. However, they do so in a distinctive way. Bonuses are related to overall group or organizational performance (Dore 1973: 94–110). It has been suggested, for instance, that wages in Japan are determined by mechanisms based largely on profit maximization, while Matsuzuka (1967) has pointed to the closely related variable of organization size in determining wage disparities, as well as age and duration of employment service. One aspect of this size function seems to be that the *nenko* system is surviving in larger firms while it is being eroded in the smaller ones (Tachibanaki 1982). This stress on organizational aspects in wage determination is picked up by Nakao (1980) in the emphasis given to the correlation between high wages and market share (which is itself related to advertising expenditures).

Alston (1982) has suggested that in practice there are two guidelines or rules at work relating rewards and performance in Japan. First, a single individual is never rewarded alone, but the reward is distributed as equally as possible within the work group. Second, he has pointed to the expressive dimension of the reward system, in addition to its instrumental qualities. Group rewards of a symbolic kind like a group photograph or company shield with the group's name on it are important devices used to build up the sense of practical ideological community. However, it is easy to overstress how these rewards relate to job satisfaction. The implicit suggestion is that they do – that non-instrumental rewards are of importance in securing greater commitment, involvement and satisfaction from workers. On these criteria one would anticipate that Japanese workers would exhibit high levels of job satisfaction in comparative surveys. Despite the popular image of Japanese employees as happy and harmonious group workers the reality seems to be that they are not. As Lincoln and McBride (1987: 304) suggest on the basis of their extensive survey of the research literature (citing Odaka 1975; Azumi and McMillan 1975; Dore 1973; Pascale and Maguire 1980; Cole 1979; Naoi and Schooler 1985), a 'particularly perplexing but strong and consistent finding from numerous work attitude surveys is the low level of job satisfaction reported by the Japanese'. This suggests caution in imputing too much in the way of intrinsic superiority from the actor's point of view to Japanese management practices, irrespective of the reasons for this low satisfaction. Interestingly, Cole (1979: 238) suggests that the low rates of Japanese satisfaction are due to the fact that they expect more from work than other nationalities! In view of the available evidence from the questions expressly asked there is little chance of disconfirming this view, although one may be inclined to regard it with a degree of scepticism.

Achieving effective leadership

The global success not only of Japanese enterprise in the 1980s but also of the other NICs of East Asia has been seen by some commentators such as Blunt (1989: 21) as a spur to the renaissance of studies of effective leadership in recent times (for example, Biggart and Hamilton 1987; Conger 1989; Handy 1989; Kotter 1988; Muczyk and Reimann 1987). Leadership is usually defined in terms which relate a 'vision' of the future to some 'strategies' for achieving it, which are capable of co-opting support, compliance and teamwork in its achievement and serve to motivate and sustain commitment to its purpose (after Kotter 1988:

25–6). Hamilton and Biggart (1988) have stressed 'institutional aspects' of leadership – that is, the societal 'principles' or 'values' around which the vision can coalesce.

In the Chinese family business leadership clearly latches on to the larger societal values of familism as they have been engrained in Confucianism, a value which also plays a part, albeit a quite distinct one, in the South Korean *chaebol*. In both types of enterprise structure the familial principle stays close to the power as the power stays close to the family. It does not embrace those who are outside the family, and, as we have seen in the case of Redding's (1990) research, it is by no means a guarantee that leadership will be effective over several generations. In both the Chinese family businesses of Taiwan and Hong Kong, as well as in South Korean *chaebol*, patrimonialism is the basis for rational organization.

Japan is neither patrimonial nor exactly like the Western type of professional bureaucracy, with its upper echelons of 'cosmopolitans' well versed in conflicts with their more 'local' compatriots (Gouldner 1957–8). In fact, Japanese organization is closer in many respects to depictions of an 'organic' structure, where the flexible aspects of the latter are widely distributed over areas of the organization which elsewhere would be more mechanical. The fairly effective neutralization of countervailing sources of leadership from professional bodies and trades unions is an important component of this, as is the considerable attention paid to ensuring that leadership initiatives have broad-based support before they are adopted, through the mechanisms of the *ringi-ko* decision-making structure and the extensive use of generalist managerial job rotation. The 'organic' qualities are clearly important in allowing the adoption of systems of management which, in the absence of less effective leadership in gaining commitment, would hardly be viable. Holding very little in the way of stocks and inventory and relying on components suppliers to supply these 'just in time' for use in production could not operate where supply was liable to frequent bottlenecks, disruption or downright 'guileful' dispositions to milk positions of strategic contingency for what they are worth. The achievement of a situation where this is not the case, in leadership terms, is clearly related to the whole institutional fabric of the enterprise, in terms of phenomena such as the labour market structure and system of rewards.

Some writers, such as Blunt (1989: 22), refer to these institutional aspects of leadership in terms of an extended medical metaphor. Leadership provides organizational values which can serve as a basis for the development of mutual trust and commitment. Organization life which lacks this, which is premised on mistrust, is riddled with cholesterol clogging and incapacitating the system, like an epidemic of modern organizational life. The metaphor is a little too colourful, perhaps, but the general point is quite clear. Those organizations whose members can find no good reason, whatever the basis of the bargain, to trust one another at a modicum will find it extremely hard to work effectively with each other. If nothing else, leadership is about building this basis (Bartolme 1989).

Organization imperatives and organizational representations

The imperatives of organizations have been discussed in terms of a number of dimensions. Representationally these are arranged as in Figure 7.1.

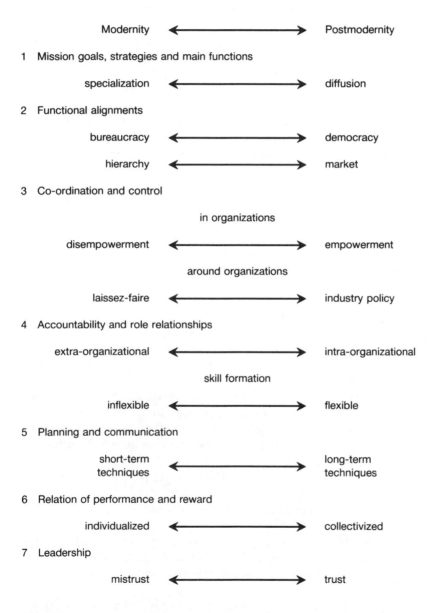

Figure 7.1   *Organizational dimensions of modernity/postmodernity*

The preceding section has suggested some ways in which these dimensions align themselves in Japan. National types of economic embeddedness have not been located on these dimensions, for at least two reasons. First, the descriptive data are, by and large, societal and macro in orientation. They have not been specifically collected as organization-level data, generated from a schema such as this. In this respect the schema is more indicative and sensitizing than anything else – it gives us some clues as to what to look for if we are interested in discovering organization diversities. Second, one would very much doubt whether one would find that all organizations aligned themselves neatly on to national patterns. There are likely to be some nationally based organizations which will be deviant cases in terms of some or other dimension of the imperatives, if only because of the effects of more specific organization contingencies of size or technology, neither of which are considered here.

This framework for enquiry suggests several things. First, organizations which are undoubtedly effective in their own national contexts may be fabricated in quite diverse ways, using distinct local resources to construct their particular response to the organizational imperatives. Second, some of the typical patterns which emerge, those which tend to be more specialized in mission, goals, strategies and functions and to be more oriented towards market relations to handle their functional alignments, for instance, will tend to be a part of a broader economic system in which the isolation of the focal organization makes only limited analytical sense. Indeed, it may well serve to do some injustice and violence to the integrity of the substantive phenomena.

For the future research needs to address the extent to which these dimensions of organization imperatives do form coherent patterns; the extent to which the coherent patterns form national clusters; and the extent to which they relate to more common criteria of organizational analysis such as the Aston measures. If the analysis which has guided this book is correct, then through asking such questions it ought to be possible to begin to address systematically some of the sources of organizational diversity which both modernity and postmodernity present to us in their many authentic ways, rather than trying to push them all into a limited number of boxes made to a dominant pattern. Where that national pattern is distinctly modernist and the data under consideration are putatively postmodernist, this analytical strategy should certainly not be preferred. It may be that what is important is not so much 'strategic choice' within national patterns of organization normalization but the patterns themselves, the way they differ from one another and form more or less coherent, nationally contingent entities. Rather than looking for deviations from pattern, perhaps one should be looking at the patterns produced by the modes of rationality which agents typically find it conventional to construct.

Theoretical arguments in organization analysis have tended to be deterministic. The most obvious examples of this are contingency theories of a 'culture-free' variety (Hickson et al. 1974) but it is also the case with certain kinds of institutional theory, such as in Biggart and Hamilton's (1987: 437) hypothesis that '[l]eadership strategies in any one socio-cultural setting will have strong underlying similarities'. Against either form of determinism one might instead want to argue that contingencies and institutions should be seen as providing the arena in which power-players will seek to utilize whatever resources are available in constructing local organizational practice, shaped to whatever mode of rationality, against the last of organizational imperatives. Organizations are arenas within which some things will tend to hang together and be adopted by power-players as a bundle, while other forms of combination may be far less likely to occur as a coherent package, perhaps because they are less coherent or because the alliance which could make them so lacks a position in the field of power to be able to constitute the necessity of its choices. (For the general theory of 'power' which undergirds this view see Clegg 1989b.) Institutional and contingency matters will enter into this deter-mination. The general theoretical model, in a very simplified form, is shown in Figure 7.2.

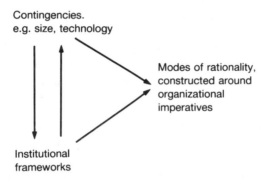

Figure 7.2   *Framing contingent modes of rationality*

The argument of this chapter has been to suggest that a distinctive mode of rationality, which is postmodernist in its opposition to the principles of the Weberian/Fordist organization pattern, may have emerged in some aspects of post-war Japan. Rather than attribute this either to cultural explanations of an over-socialized kind or to market explanations which are under-socialized, the chapter has built upon the earlier discussion of Japanese specificity in order to develop a power/institutions model for this analysis. Some aspects of the power settlement in post-war Japanese enterprises, particularly the enterprise unions, the wage payment systems and the flexibility which these allowed, have been crucial for the emerg-ence of this putative postmodernist form of organization.

Aspects of the institutional framework of Japanese enterprises developed in the pre-war era, notably the tendency to extensive networking within the *zaibatsu*. This tendency was continued in the post-war era of enterprise groups to shape a framework in which developed a quite distinct set of practices and forms of calculation of economic action. It was out of these that what has been hypothesized as postmodernist organization developed.

If Japan represents one possible path towards postmodernity, it is clear that there have been winners and losers in this development. To recap, the winners have been men who were in internal labour markets in the big name companies and the enterprise group networks. The losers have been women and those, more than two-thirds of all workers, who are outside the core labour market. With respect to women, the loss derives not just from a low level of labour force participation but from the nature of employment practices. Extended service is a key factor in remuneration, as we have seen. Because there are very few women who have extended lengths of continuous employment with a single employer, male–female wage differentials are so large in middle age. It is the nature of the workforce participation which varies, with women's work being largely unskilled because they are not employed in the core enterprises and internal labour market, where continuous training and re-skilling are provided to permanent employees (Koike 1981). The labour market is relatively highly segmented, with comparatively less rights for labour and a more arduous regime of work than in the more social democratic OECD states. Longer hours and shorter recreation are the norm, with the annual average working hours of a Japanese worker amounting to more than 2,100: by contrast, in Britain and the USA the average is 1,800–1,900 hours, with about 1,650 the norm in the Federal Republic of Germany (Deutschmann: 1987a). Within the labour market core wages are relatively high, compared internationally – but so are the costs of basic consumer goods and services, with housing, in particular, being inordinately expensive per square metre, compared with OECD averages. Typically, each person occupies far fewer square metres than would be the norm in most other OECD states. Of course, outside Japan, elsewhere in the world, there may also turn out to be losers on a wider scale, those trapped and organizationally outflanked in modernist organization forms as the leading edge turns ever more postmodern.

Conclusion

In this chapter a detailed consideration has been made of the organizational characteristics of the system of economic embeddedness which characterizes contemporary Japanese enterprises. Overall, in addition to matters of more purely technological consideration, which will be a focus of Chapter 8, there appear to be some significant differences when one makes comparison with more typically modernist organizations. Perhaps that is sufficient reason for claiming that postmodern organization forms appear to be implicit in these developments. Certainly, there are evident differences and they may well sketch one political conjecture for postmodern organization premised on stable private capital formation, production-centred strategies of economic calculation and high degrees of labour market segmentation.

The final chapter of this book will hone in on the more restricted echoes of events in Japan which have been sounded in the debate on 'flexible manufacturing systems' in Western Europe, North America and Australia, in order to chart another set of postmodern possibilities.

8

Postmodern Skill and Capital Formation?

Can something which appears to have had a fair degree of institutional specificity and lack of initial purposiveness be generalized to elsewhere in the world? Perhaps it is easiest to consider this question through looking at what has happened when attempts have been made to develop the technical core of the Japanese system elsewhere, through the adoption of flexible manufacturing systems. In many ways this is an acid test, because one is considering how easy it is to generalize technology as one of the most determinate of contingencies. If it cannot be generalized across frontiers then the postmodern organizational thrust will not travel either. The data are mixed in their interpretation, suggesting that these are not purely matters of efficiency but necessarily involve the relation of power and institutions.

Many criticisms have been made of the idea that flexible manufacturing systems may be ushering in a new era of organization. To the extent that these criticisms hit deterministic arguments on the head, they are quite right to do so. Unfortunately, in so doing they often use too blunt an instrument, with equally deterministic effects. Under appropriate environmental conditions, it will be argued, where institutional frameworks of a strongly social democratic type restrict the free play of managerial discretion and labour market functioning, rather than new technologies being introduced to de-skill workers they may be the vehicle both for enhanced skill formation and participation on the part of the organization's labour force and for changed conditions of capital formation. Or they may not.

Turning Japanese? Debates on flexible manufacturing as the technical core of postmodern organization

There are three broad positions in the debates on flexible manufacturing systems. These positions may be characterized as one of neo-romanticism, one of neo-managerialism and one of neo-Marxian critique. A fourth position has been argued for throughout this book. Unlike the other positions it begins from no a priori assumption about whether or not flexible manufacturing is 'a good thing' but looks instead to analysing how, and through what variables, configurations of power/institutions structure empirical instances.

Neo-romanticism

The neo-romantic argument derives from the contribution of Piore and Sabel (1984), with their insistence that we are at a critical divide in human history, one whereby the utopian aspects of community, lost with the nineteenth century demise of craft work in domestic industry, may be regained. The romanticism resides in this retrospective vision. At base their theory is consumption-driven. It contrasts the modernist regime of mass consumption through standardized markets premised on mass production bureaucracies organized around low-trust relations, with changes which began to occur in the late 1970s. By this time a conjuncture of several factors made the absolute ascendancy of the older production regime impractical. Amongst these factors were numbered the continuing post-1974 recession and the increased competition from not only Japan but also the other NICs we have considered in previous chapters. It was from Japan in particular that the new ideas were to gain their legitimacy.

What was in question was the 'mass' base in both production and consumption of the previously ascendant system of organizing economic action. On the one hand Japanese manufacturers seemed to be outflanking Western manufacturers with their emphasis of high quality and product differentiation; on the other hand the West seemed unable to respond competitively to the extent that it remained wedded to a mass production, low profit margin and standard product system. Moreover, aspects of the mass production system itself seemed to be increasingly dysfunctional – notably the costs associated with inventories and fault rectification.

The market changes emanating from Japanese product competition are the key to understanding flexible manufacturing in the Piore and Sabel account. A more consumer-oriented and differentiated market meant that flexible organizations would steal a competitive edge. The term 'flexible specialization' is thus introduced to characterize such organizations. The 'flexible' aspect refers to the restructuring of the labour market and the labour process, while the 'specialization' aspect refers to the ascendancy of niche or specialist markets and marketing, as opposed to mass markets. The 'push' of the latter is seen to require the response of the former. Changes to more differentiated consumption cause production changes away from organizations based on tight managerial control through surveillance, de-skilling and mechanization (Smith 1989: 204). As Sabel (1982: 220) initially proposed it, these changes would be in the direction of a new type of 'high technology cottage industry' in which craft forms of production would be enveloped by new forms of technology, fostered by local state initiatives. The Benetton-type models of Emilia–Romagna are the paradigm case. In the collaboration with Piore (Piore and Sabel 1984) this is extended somewhat to include not only high technology cottage industry but also restructuring mass production industry which is adopting new technologies and new practices. Smith (1989: 210–11) sees a contemporary romanticism at work in Piore and Sabel's (1984) adoption of the ideology of 'corporate community and solidarity'. The focus is not on small business and craft production but on the engineering, industrial relations and production restructuring of Boeing, General Electric, GM and Ford to meet the Japanese challenge. At the heart of this restructuring will be flexible specialization enabling a new organicism as a haven in the hitherto heartless world of large organizations. They propose that organization is increasingly coming to be characterized by flexible, market-responsive manufacturing based on generalist skills and technologies rather than highly differentiated ones. Later still, in Katz and Sabel (1985) and Piore (1986) the major blockages to the realization of this new organicism are argued to be labour institutions which have not changed to accommodate the new production systems, as they have in West Germany and Japan. The synthesis of worker and employer interests in the 'flexible specialization' typology, suggests Smith (1989: 210), is resolved in favour of the employers. With Pollert (1988) he is equally sceptical about the extent to which there is a marked tendency towards product diversification in mass production industries such as industrial foodstuffs.

The determinism of the neo-romantic argument is in seeing the product market as determining organization restructuring and the spread of flexible specialization.

Neo-managerialism

The neo-managerialist writers are preponderantly British, characterized by the work of writers such as Cross (1985) and the National Economic Development Office (NEDO) Report of 1986. Whereas the neo-romantics tend to emphasize the forces of consumption and the product market, and the neo-Marxians tend to emphasize the forces and associated relations of production, the neo-managerialist school takes on board both production and consumption as forces pushing towards flexibility.

The emphasis on consumption is similar to that found in Piore and Sabel (1984). In order that organizations have the flexibility to respond to changing market conditions they have had to develop a core of committed and flexible employees, on the model of 'Japanization'. Consequently, employment security has been developed for the strategically contingent elements of the workforce at the same time as there has been a peripheralization of other workers into casualized or part-time employees who are mainly female (see the excellent discussion by Lever-Tracy [1988]). Company-specific skills are developed for the core workers; as a corollary of this employers invest heavily in training costs which they protect, as an investment, through offering the core workers security, retraining and every opportunity to integrate into an organization culture. Peripheralized workers by contrast are usually unskilled and enjoy none of the benefits of those in the primary sector. Management is simply responding to changed patterns of rational choice in the market by changing its rational choices concerning the arrangement of organization and pro- duction relations.

Neo-Marxian critiques in the debate on flexible specialization

The neo-Marxian critique connects concerns which have found expression in the 'labour process' debate, particularly in Britain, with the more recently developed debate on flexible specialization. In doing so it has taken off from a number of contributions from French theorists of the 'regulation' school, notably the seminal contribution of Palloix (1976). From this perspective the phenomenon which writers like Piore and Sabel concentrate on does not represent a 'great divide' between epochs, but rather some significant shifts of emphasis which never the less occur within the same framework. For this reason they refer to neo-Fordism rather than to post-Fordism. The phenomena of more collective working and skill enhancement are seen as new techniques of control, in which managerial prerogatives remain unchallenged and in which work-group autonomy becomes an internalization into the collective workers of what has hitherto been external surveillance (Coriat 1980: 40). Company interests will predominate in any restructuring, these writers suggest.

Old and familiar themes about the incorporation of workers, their integration into the organization and the cunning of capital in coming up with new technology to further the intensive exploitation of the workforce: these are the themes which come through the neo-Marxian literature on new forms of flexible manufacturing. Neo-Fordism, for writers like Aglietta (1979), represents a capitalist solution to scientific management's greatest problem, from the capitalist's point of view. The problem is how to regain, re-utilize and re-control the worker's formally excluded but tacitly traded-on knowledge of the production process, and use it in order to further capitalist restructuring.

For the neo-Marxian school the major explanatory focus, not surpris- ingly, is on production relations rather than product markets. Neo-Fordism solves the contradictions which the previous Fordist regime developed and was unable to resolve. The major contradiction was that the Fordist regime had reached the limits of its ability to increase productivity. Without somehow re-integrating the active consent and knowledge of the workers back into the production process Fordism had run up against the obstacle of its own design. This became apparent as labour productivity began to slow down in the 1960s and 1970s, as the long post-war boom wound down. It was in those countries which developed new forms of accumulation regime, based on enhanced participation by the workers, notably Japan, that productivity increases were gained. This pointed the way to a new accumulation regime which had effected a temporary resolution of the contradictions of capitalism as they had developed in the previous regime. At its core was the material technology of new productive forces, the flexible manufacturing technology of CAD/CAM, for instance, as well as changed relations of production which incorporated rather than alienated the worker.

A number of critiques of the idea that organization through flexible specialization offers anything that is at all postmodern have been developed in the neo-Marxian literature. Amongst these are contributions by Williams et al. (1987), Pollert (1988), Bramble (1988) and Hyman (1988). Some common issues in the critiques will be focused on here, drawing on Badham and Matthews (1989). Pollert (1988), for instance, in common with Shaiken, Herzenberg and Kuhn (1986) in the United States and Bramble (1988) in Australia, argues that in practice (rather than in the general theory of writers like Piore and Sabel [1984]) microprocessor technology has been used to de-skill work under the guise of flexibility. The tendency is to see new technology in the service of some old objectives of class exploitation.

At the core of these neo-Marxian critiques is the grave suspicion that flexible specialization is simply yet another instrument by which capital can further the exploitation of workers. It will do this through speeding up the pace of work and intensifying it, increasing work-related mental stresses and physical strains; through creating a new labour aristocracy of core, skilled workers and a growing periphery of de-skilled workers who receive none of the high trust/high power/high responsibility trade-offs of those incorporated in the core. The union movement is thus seen to be split as the workforce is split, between those prepared to go down the 'new realist' route of flexibility and those who, unable or unwilling to make single-industry deals or become quasi-enterprise unions, can only represent workers whose position is in relative decline. Above all, the critics condemn 'technocratic optimism' but unfortunately they often do so through 'relapse into old ideological stances' as Badham and Matthews (1989: 247) suggest.

Flexible manufacturing, power/institutions

It is now widely recognized that there is more than one way to achieve goodness of fit between technology and structure, and that the way chosen may well be for reasons of power as much as of efficiency (for example, Child 1984; Child and Tayeb 1983). The intersection of institutional factors with power in the delimitation of these choices comes out quite clearly in comparative work on 'flexible manufacturing systems' (FMS). These are automated self-contained cells of machine tools controlled by computers (Computer Numerically Controlled – CNC – machines) which are increasingly used in Japan as the technological base of flexible manufacturing (Jaikumar 1986). The technology of FMS is not confined to Japan, however, although their utilization is much greater in this country than elsewhere, other than Sweden. (Why Sweden should be so far advanced in its adoption is another question for which there really is not the space to provide an answer here. Suffice to say, however, that where a conjunction of power/institutions has made Swedish labour amongst the most powerful and expensive in the world, then Swedish employers have ample incentive to minimize its cost in their enterprises.)

In the United States Kenney and Florida (1988: 140–1) point to the fact that there are half the number of FMS systems compared to the situation in Japan. Japanese systems had much higher rates of capacity utilization (84 per cent as opposed to 52 per cent, with some used untended on a third shift bringing utilization up to 92 per cent). What was most striking was the quite different ways in which the same technology was being used in the two countries:

> US corporations were not using FMS to accomplish what it is supposed to. The US companies used FMS to produce relatively standardized parts rather than to produce high volumes of a wide range of parts. The average number of parts produced by FMS in the United States was 10; in Japan it was 93. The annual volume per part in the United States was 1.727 versus 258 for Japan. In effect, US corporations were using FMS to mass produce parts. (Kenney and Florida 1988: 141)

Technology does not mean the same thing when inserted in a modernist as opposed to a postmodernist system. In the United States FMS was used to further the de-skilling of workers, to increase management's power relative to them and to produce large batches of a standardized product. Child (1987) has emphasized that it is unlikely that FMS will produce much organizational difference in such cases of large-batch standardized production, particularly, one might add, where the product is one with a low profit margin. It will be only in those cases where there is product variability that one would anticipate significant changes in organizational structuring. The crucial consideration appears to be whether or not the changes in product and methods of production are unpredictable, as Badham and Matthews (1989: 223) suggest. In line with this point, case studies conducted by Shaiken, Herzenberg and Kuhn (1986) in the United States demonstrate that this new technology has been used to diminish the autonomy and the responsibility for planning of shop-floor workers. In Japan the situation has been quite different even though the technology is the same. There it has been used to further re-skilling rather than de-skilling, has been harnessed to multi-level and multi-skilled work teams and has allowed shop-floor operatives to become involved in doing routine computer programming. In short, it has been used to transform workers into 'think-workers' (see Jaikumar 1986). The reasons for these differences should be apparent. Kenney and Florida (1988: 142) spell them out clearly enough:

> Japan's response to restructuring has in large measure been determined by the organizational and institutional arrangements that first emerged in manufacturing. By creating the social space and flexibility in which organizational innovation could occur, Japanese industrial organization has paved the way for a synthesis of production and innovation and for integrating new technologies into manufacturing.

The analytical point is obvious. Technology, like any other organizational contingency, will not necessarily determine anything. Technological determinism has been a stalwart of organization studies, but clearly it is now time to put the old horse out to grass. It has been flogged near to death and there is little life left in the beast, particularly when exposed to the recent debates on 'new production systems' (Badham and Matthews 1989). What is at issue are situational contingencies and their fabrication in specific modes of rationality. As Badham and Matthews (1989: 201) put it, these contingencies will not have determinate and predictable effects on work organization, even when they appear to empower workers unambiguously:

> For example, effective control over broader production plans and work scheduling, health and safety, forms of social interaction (working conditions) or pay, job security and career paths (employment conditions) may be reduced by a decrease in the individual or collective bargaining power of workers – due to increased unemployment, a lack of an external labour market for acquired skills, a decline in the competitive strength of the enterprise, the use of new technology to replace worker skills, reductions in legislative safeguards, increased managerial strength, a drop in the membership, finances and organizational strength of trade unions, or changes in political parties or politics.

It will depend upon the framework of institutions and power as to how elements in organizational practice, such as technology, are actually fabricated into modes of rationality. A further case can make the point. Sorge et al. (1983) studied the adoption of CNC machine tools in a range of British and West German organizations. They matched the organizations and found that some of the difference in the way in which CNC affected skill polarization and equity could be attributed to organization contingencies such as batch production and firm size. However, there were broader national differences which cut across these. In Germany, in the context of institutional commitments to co-determination, CNC was used in such a way that it developed a common team focus between foremen, chargehands, workers and planners, in a postmodernist prefiguration. In Britain, quite the reverse: here it was used in such a way as to maintain departmental and personnel group autonomy. As Sorge and Streeck (1988: 26) suggest, what is required is 'a concept of how a society or economy is populated by technical and organizational types, and how this population changes over time'.

From the accounts and original source material available in English, it would appear that the approach which Sorge and Streeck (1988) call for, is, in fact, best developed in the West German literature, particularly as it has developed around the contributions of Kern and Schumann (1984a). Useful accounts in English include Kern and Schumann (1987), Littek and Heissig (1989), Hoss (1986) and Campbell (1989). Campbell (1989) is the most detailed. West Germany has been a rich site for a number of organization studies which have built on the fundamental insights of the Aix school into the importance of national institutional differences in the structuring of organizations, paying particular attention to systems of education and training and industrial relations in shaping organizational workforce contingencies (Maurice, Sorge and Warner 1980; Sorge et al. 1983; Sorge and Streeck 1988; Lane 1988). In addition, in the contributions of Kern and Schumann (1984a; 1984b) it has also had an empirically well grounded discussion of the flexibility debate.

Initially conceived as a study which would follow up work they had done a decade earlier on de-skilling in West German industry, Kern and Schumann's (1984a) *Das Ende der Arbeitsteilung?*, which translates as *The End of the Division of Labour?*, in fact found that in the automobile, machine tool and chemical industries new social phenomena of enhanced skill formation and restructuring were under way. Whereas in the past, under what the literature is wont to call Fordist auspices, the intelligence of the worker was only tacitly acknowledged, often oppositional and frequently marginalized, new forms of restructuring in the core sectors of the economy are producing new forms of work organization and 'new production concepts' in which the intelligence of the workers is implicated and enhanced rather than opposed: 'The skills and expert competences of the workers are productive forces that should be more fully utilized' (Kern and Schumann 1984a: 19; translated in Campbell 1989: 255). This is occurring through a re-skilling of production work into tasks requiring broad and multi-skilled personnel. In the automobile industry this is due to task restructuring into more integrated processes; in the machine tool industry it is due to the opportunities for skill enhancement opened up by CNC machines; in the chemical industry the production workers are becoming more professionalized, developing a 'more comprehensive knowledge and competence in the mechanical as well as the chemical area, so that more extensive repairs and corrections can be made without calling in specialist teams' (Campbell 1989: 256). In common is a process of enhanced and concentrated skill formation creating a new type of worker through greater training, one who is qualitatively different from the craftsperson ideal, by virtue of being far more tightly coupled into an overall structure of managerial control.

Several factors are utilized to explain this shift, including the stress now familiar from Piore and Sabel (1984) on the product market. However, implausible romances concerning craft labour are avoided and additional factors are highlighted. These include changes in the labour market, due to the development of structural unemployment, which strengthen managerial control. Rather than utilizing this in the oppositional way of the past, at least in the core sectors of major, high-margin organizations in the economy, the emergence of new technology, through a major increase in the ratio of constant capital to the variable capital of labour power, means that a more facilitative attitude towards the latter is possible. Indeed, it is necessary if costly interruptions to production are to be avoided and because the new processes require a far more skilled workforce – even in the interstices of the new technology (Campbell 1989: 257). However, this restructuring cuts two ways: just as a core of more privileged workers are produced, others, by virtue of industry and organizational location, and perhaps as a result of discriminatory characteristics and human capital formation deficiencies on their part, will be consigned to the underside of the new labour market segmentation. The two tendencies are not unconnected as aspects of capitalist restructuring.

One aspect of the Kern and Schumann (1984a) argument is the need to recognize that there are political struggles in and between management as to whether new production concepts will be introduced. They advocate that the labour movement, rather than opposing change, should seek strategic alliances with the progressive forces in management, and hasten the development of the productive forces and social relations in and of production. In effect, what they are recognizing is that the traditional Marxian conception of the politics of production as being a zero-sum game is no longer very useful. Under conditions in which returns both from and to labour depend far more on the formation of skills and capital than they do on extensive exploitation of brute labour power, the zero-sum conception of the labour process as a locus of class struggle has little other than a rhetorical purpose to play. Not only can the politics of production give way to the production of politics in the political arena, through the practices of political trade unionism and bargained corporatism (see Clegg, Boreham and Dow 1986; Boreham, Clegg and Dow 1986), also, at the workplace level negotiations may produce win-win situations for both labour and capital in terms of the conditions under which they operate. Certainly, such changes do not seem to hasten the revolutionary impulse or refresh the jaded palate of those many workers blasé to the requirements of class struggle. The past history of labour relations and democratic politics in the advanced societies should serve to make us very sceptical about not only the potential of past politics and modes of struggle but also the extent to which there is any broad-based support that these are desirable. Nor should one readily have recourse to traditional concepts of hegemony to save the argument from the indifference of those who have been represented as the key agents of history, as has been argued at length elsewhere (Clegg 1989b).

Kern and Schumann's (1984a) suggestions for how trade union policy should be developed with respect to the opportunities of 'flexibility' call for the following strategies:

1 concerted use of the broadened total mass of skilled functions associated with the new technologies in order to establish complex work definitions for as many workers as possible.
2 influence over the entry requirements for the new areas in order to lessen competition and division in the workforce.
3 creation of appropriate and satisfactory replacement jobs for those displaced when new technologies are used to abolish restrictive jobs.
4 development of training processes based on a comprehensive concept of qualification, distinct from the process-specific demands of individual situations in the workplace. This implies an orientation to autonomous professional work and an acceptance of the applicability of the acquired knowledge and skills outside the workplace.
5 disclosure and regulation of new performance demands, in order to prevent any one-sided determination on the part of management and to avoid any blocking of the possibility of more comprehensive job definitions as a result of pressures for intensification. (Campbell 1989: 261)

Campbell (1989: 273) makes some salient criticisms of implicit aspects of Kern and Schumann's (1984a) approach. They are dealing with tendencies, and whether or not these tendencies will be epoch-making is a matter of empirical rather than theoretical conjecture. Too much emphasis should not be placed on the managerial control of the labour process: labour may well be a marginal cost in many high-technology industries and hardly the central focus of strategic attention. Not only are questions of managerial control and labour 'autonomy at issue but complex issues of production more generally.

Analytically, the writers who have come closest to capturing the distinctive processes involved in the technological core of the new production systems, conceived as the central focus of putative postmodern organizations, are Badham and Matthews (1989). Building on the work of writers including Child (1987), Perrow (1970) and Sorge and Streeck (1988), they construct a model of three dimensions which will be at the centre of any bargaining between representatives of management and labour in struggles over the shape of postmodern organization. What they suggest, in fact, is those types of organization in which struggle might strategically seek postmodern outcomes around the technical core. Whether or not this will be part of a more general organizational postmodernization, as has been suggested above, will depend not simply on the structuring of power in the organization but also on its structuring around the organization, through the nature of the institutional framework in which the organization is constituted. However, their insights are valuable because they enable one formally to model the conditions which should be sought in the technical core if post-Fordist production regimes are to be established as a basis for postmodernist possibilities. After briefly discussing the former we can move to a broad sketch of the possibilities for the latter.

Badham and Matthews (1989: 207) construct a model in three-dimensional space, built around the degree of product innovation, process variability and labour responsibility – see Figure 8.1. Product innovation is identified by the frequency with which products are changed and the degree of variation between products. Process variability is identified by the frequency and degree of changes in production methods, and the degree of difficulty, in terms of the learning time that new systems require, that such switches entail (Badham and Matthews 1989: 212). The dimensions are conceived as capable of changing independently of each other, although being only relatively autonomous; that is, they are not wholly independent but each sets variable limits upon the other.

Conditioning the limits of relative autonomy of these two dimensions are the power/trust relations which Fox (1974) conceptualizes as mediating between management control and employee consent. As is well known, these can be highly variegated from high trust/high discretion configurations down to the low trust/low discretion configuration which is so conducive to a 'vicious cycle of control' (see Clegg and Dunkerley 1980: ch. 9).

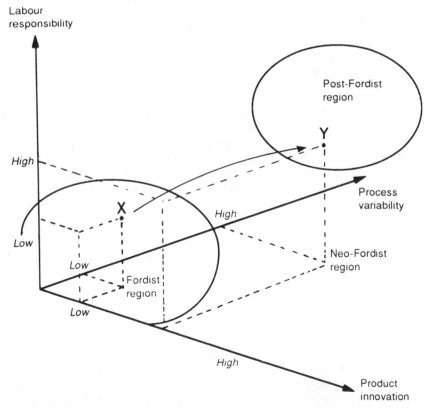

Figure 8.1   *Badham and Matthews's production system model (Badham and Matthews 1989: 207)*

A number of environmental variables will affect the calibration of organizational control as more or less premised on the polarities of either high trust/high autonomy/high responsibility or low trust/low autonomy/ low responsibility. Conditioning the use of these will be not only specific substantive features of the occupational groups in question, such as their strategic contingency, but also more general aspects of the political configuration, particularly as these are focused on conceptions of 'citizenship rights'. These can be more or less restricted with respect to the spheres of industrial and economic democracy. The obvious case in point would refer to Sweden (see Clegg, Boreham and Dow 1986: ch. 9), where these rights are most extensive. Together with questions of labour market structure (solidaristic vs segmented), the issue of citizenship will be closely related to the organizational capacities of the labour movement, and issues of how much organizational slack is available in the resources which they, and other participants, are prepared to commit to the organizational arena in question.

Any organization, sector or industry could be characterized in terms of this model, in terms of either its production process (where it actually is operating at any given point in time) or its production strategy (where its preferred operating point would be at some future point in time). The concept of production process refers to the performance of a number of functions associated with design, co-ordination and manufacture (Kaplinsky 1984). These functions include 'the combination and organization of raw materials, equipment and personnel to design, plan and manufacture a product' (Badham and Matthews 1989: 209).

The notion of production strategy represents the outcome of those processes which determine the boundedly rational calculation of more or less coherent and preferred goals by the mandators of the organization. A decisive element in the setting of limits and possibilities on the boundedness of the incremental processes involved in formulating these strategies will, of course, be the power of other strategic actors in and around the organization, as well as the institutionalized acceptance of what is possible, desirable and rational in terms of the cultural capital implicated in the process. The sources of these are many, involving not just state organization specifications (such as might derive from instrumentalities responsible for health and safety, equal opportunity, restructuring and so on) but also coming from professional/occupational conceptions of rational desiderata, as well as from other key actors such as the various media of information transmission in consultancies, universities, journals and magazines. Some researchers, such as Perez (1985), would include in this list of institutional factors over-arching architectonic forces which are regarded as clustering distinct 'techno-economic paradigms' around key points in long waves of technological innovation. Postmodernity would thus be characterized through the structuring and keying provided by the relative availability and cheapness of new microelectronic information technology, much as the availability of cheap oil was the architectonic point of the previous long wave. One does not have to accept this more macro perspective in order to see that it is through processes of power/institutions that possible rationalities which connect processes and strategies are negotiated and fought over. The 'long wave' view merely provides an epochal explanation of the availability of modes of rationality in their historical specificity.

In the model (Figure 8.1), point X represents a production process with medium levels on all three dimensions, while Y represents a production strategy whose preferred options are high on each dimension. Given these notions of production process and strategy the model is amenable to an overall conceptualization in terms of embedded modes of rationality. Crucial to these will be the negotiation of not just material aspects of production, such as product innovation and process variability, but the far more complex and indeterminate matter of labour responsibility, or what Fox (1974) terms power/trust relations. It is on this axis that the relative success or failure of the two more material dimensions will depend.

Specific points linking production processes and strategies will point to specific modes of rationality structuring organization around the technical core. In the model as illustrated three distinct modes are represented: the Fordist, the neo-Fordist and the post-Fordist, each associated respectively with consistently low, medium and high positions on the three dimensions. With this model in mind, much of the dispute which has occurred in the literature falls into place. Those theorists such as Pollert (1988) who regard flexible manufacturing systems as simply another instrument of worker control, de-skilling and labour degradation may well be accurately characterizing their use when implemented under a neo-Fordist mode of rationality, as Badham and Matthews (1989: 208) suggest: 'Aware of the flexible potential of new technologies, and of the need for limited forms of worker responsibility, managerial strategies in this area will be focused on further developing technology in a direction that overcomes short term needs for increased worker skills and responsibility.'

The interest of a labour movement, one would anticipate, would be in moving as much of national enterprise as possible towards the post-Fordist axis. In the next section post-Fordist issues of skill formation and production more generally will be rejoined with issues of capital formation. It will be recalled from Chapter 7 that this issue stood at the heart of possible Japanese postmodernization tendencies in organizations, because it created the conditions for stable forms of enterprise calculation. Institutionally, these conditions of stability can be fabricated under quite distinct conditions.

The practice of Swedish social democracy: other postmodern possibilities?

Let us get to Sweden by way of Australia, as this route enables consideration of an important analytical point. Australia has recently seen a most fascinating instance of institutional isomorphism in practice. This has resulted in the publication of a document called *Australia Reconstructed* (ACTU/TDCS 1987). The document was the product of a joint 'Mission to Western Europe' by the Australian Council of Trades Unions, the peak organization of labour, and the Trade Development Commission Secretariat, a public service body. The 'mission' was to go and learn from overseas practice in selected Western European countries how Australian manufacturing industry and related economic policy might best be developed, to the advantage of Australian wage earners. *Australia Reconstructed* is an extremely clear and interesting example of the general salience of the power/institutions approach that has been argued for in this book. It represents a conscious attempt at institutional isomorphism through mimesis of, in particular, Swedish and West German practices, combined with a clear understanding that these can only be achieved through both institutional politics in the Federal Government and in the judicially independent Industrial Relations Commission (the centralized wage-fixing, arbitration and conciliation body) as well as local politics pursued through various organizations, the media and the union movement. As the ACTU/TDCS mission to Western Europe recognized in *Australia Reconstructed*, West Germany and Sweden offer the most interesting instances for isomorphism on the part of what one might term a postmodernist labour movement: one no longer obsessed with the politics of production as a zero-sum game between omnipotent capital and labour resistance. Sweden is actually the most interesting of the two countries because the policy agenda of hypothetical postmodernization has progressed furthest there, to challenge the fundamental differentiation of labour/capital, within one of the world's most efficient and effective economies. Sweden points the way forward to a set of possibilities in which not only relations in production are subject to a degree of de-differentiation but also relations of production, through mechanisms of collective capital formation. The former theme has been picked up in Australia and has been reflected in the ACTU push for flexible award restructuring and broadband skill formation, pursued through the Industrial Relations Commission, in which unions have been prepared to bargain for increased flexibility for productivity agreements and wage restructuring (see Badham and Matthews 1989: 227–32). In fact, the strategy pursued seems remarkably similar to that proposed by Kern and Schumann, as it was reviewed in the previous section. At the time of writing, the concern with de-differentiation through collective capital formation, although it has been discussed by some at the peak of the union movement, has not made its way on to the formal agenda. It is to Sweden that we must look to see the furthest development of these ideas, building on an aspect of strategy already identified as important in the Japanese case.

Capital formation is decisive for organizational action: its effective achievement is a prerequisite for organizational survival. In the previous chapters, one factor which has been identified as being important in accounting for Japanese organizational success in economic terms has been the absence of institutional inducements to organizational strategies predicated on a mode of rationality in which short-term financial, rather than organizationally substantive, criteria predominate. It will be recalled that this did not entail that, in consequence, the financial well-being of organization was neglected. On the contrary, certain benefits were argued to flow from a substantive concern with organizational activity rather than one merely focused on the simulacra of paper transactions. The stability of capital formation was a vital aspect in structuring the overall picture of Japanese enterprise in a distinct configuration compared to the modernist norm. However, in addition to the practice of stable private capital formation, debates and practice in Sweden have also been oriented towards the theory and practice of collective capital formation. Collective capital formation, in so far as it represents a further de-differentiation of organizational relations from the modernist norm, presents an intriguing set of postmodernist possibilities, in which the capital/labour difference would be superseded.

Collective capital formation is not a new idea. It has been a central plank of many in the labour movement since its inception. What distinguishes recent Swedish approaches to the topic is the way they have been oriented towards the constitution of capital flows which gradually and transformatively become channelled to a greater extent through passage points defined in obligatory terms as 'necessary nodal points' (Clegg 1989b) by wage earners rather than capital holders. Collective capital formation can take many forms. It is not the same thing as those notions of individual employee ownership which are current in the United States inspired notions of Employee Stock Ownership Plans (ESOPs) (Meade 1982; Weitzman 1984), or Mrs Thatcher's visions of a 'shareholders' democracy' or a 'people's capitalism' (Clarke 1989). Notions of collective capital formation are somewhat different to this.

Matthews (1989: 166), in an important overview of contemporary and historical approaches to collective capital formation, notes a range of collective funds schemes. These can include pension/superannuation funds, which are forms of deferred income to wage earners, usually jointly controlled by unions and employers; wage funds, savings out of wages used for investment; development funds, raised by special categories of taxes, for instance on imports, and usually administered under tripartite government, employer and union control; wage earners' funds, which are equity raised from collective profit sharing, usually under union control; training funds, which are usually financed directly from firms but expended under joint union–employer control; and social funds, which are levied on specific activities or sectors. In the context of this chapter the primary interest is wage earners' funds and their development in Sweden. Although one should acknowledge that the collective funds idea first seems to have been proposed in West Germany in the 1950s (Matthews 1989: 173), it is in Sweden that it has been most developed.

Collective capital formation in Sweden has sought to bring the investment function under 'socialized' auspices directly through representation via the mechanisms of economic democracy (see Clegg and Higgins 1987). Such a conception stands in stark contrast to discredited notions of state or public ownership (see Tomlinson 1982). However, as a concept it is not without its critics, notably in the work of Ramsay and his colleagues (Ramsay 1977; 1983a; 1983b; Ramsay and Haworth 1984). The corpus of work by Ramsay is of considerable critical importance in at least two respects. First, it debunks a great deal of liberal-humanist concern gesticulating at 'radical reform'. Second, it demonstrates how organizational reforms have often been attempts (albeit inefficient and ineffective ones) at securing consent and building it into otherwise unchanged forms of control. However, Ramsay's essentialism wields too blunt an instrument in his amorphous notion of domination, something that rules out crucial differentiations between policies pursued through deceptively similar reforms. He thus uses a Marxist argument to reject reforms as such – including ones which derive their impetus from a wider critique. He and Haworth write:

> in the actual creation of socialist relations, a change in ownership relations (or to Marxist hands on the levers of a state 'machine') in isolation from other transformations has little meaning. The division of labour (particularly of mental and manual work), the experience of control at the workplace, the production of goods for use rather than exchange, and the very relations embodied in the nature of the state must all be transformed. To seek incremental changes as if these dimensions were separate spheres or their development could be raised notch by notch is, we believe, an absurdity as a means to create socialism in the real world of class struggles. To change ownership and leave the division of labour intact and unchallenged for example, merely recreates capitalist relations at the workplace. . . . [W]orkers cannot hope to transform their position in isolation from the political economy of the system in which they live, produce, and trade their labour and the wages received in return for it. (Ramsay and Haworth 1984: 314)

Certainly in Britain there has been little to celebrate in the public corporation that constitutes a monument to a traditional obsession with nationalization (although as Tomlinson [1982] and Williams et al. [1985] show, its failure owes more to poor socialist policy than to the capitalist demon). Fundamental problems arise out of this widespread assumption that the division of labour belongs to the essence of capitalism and that it must also go when the latter is abolished; or at very least it must be so completely 'transformed' as to lose its presently ubiquitous features of complexity, scale and hierarchy. This view of the division of labour overtotalizes the power of capitalism in ascribing to it a seamless functional unity, establishes unrealistic criteria for organizational change and thus prejudges all organizational reform. At times the prejudice takes explicit aprioristic form. For example, Ramsay and Haworth (1984: 311) justify their rejection of the Swedish wage earners' funds scheme for collective ownership of capital (to which we shall return) because 'if it should come to constitute a real threat to capital, the latent forces of repressive domination could be marshalled to eradicate or neutralize it'. It sounds like *Catch 22* (Heller 1962; Perry 1984): defeat is the ultimate test of the system-transforming potential of any reform. Logically, reformism cannot impinge on the essence of capitalism.

The argument here is both more modest and more realistic: hypothetically, a degree of de-differentiation would be such as to represent a significant break with the modernist tendencies of past organizationally dominant forms. It does not take the overthrow or the absence of the phenomenon of the division of labour for one to admit that new social possibilities are posed. A significant change of direction in major tendencies of differentiation may be sufficient.

Ramsay and Haworth fail to distinguish between the form and intent of a particular proposal, like industrial democracy or wage earners' funds, and the fragments of legislation and actual changes in routine practice in which it has to be implemented over time. Stop the clock at any moment and the results may not seem too impressive when measured against an ideal. However, as Etzioni (1960) advised us long ago, organizational goals are better judged in terms of the effectiveness of their achievements by reference to past or competitor performance, rather than by reference to some ideal model. Only over the long term and in hindsight can one ever know where a line of development was leading, and even that knowledge needs revising from time to time as the historian's craft requires. The point of the ideal is not to stand in judgement on poor realities but to provide a 'provisional utopia', an achievable vision of a better future (Tilton 1984). Ramsay and Haworth's critique of reformist organizational creativity never comes to grips with the internal organizational dynamic, and the evidence against reformist proposals is purely circumstantial: they are products of the state; they appear when the (essentially capitalist) economy is in 'crisis' (presumably to save it from the latter), when the all-powerful bourgeoisie does not crush them; and so on. This leaves them with an awkwardness they are at pains to underplay but which they muse over explicitly at one point in their article (Ramsay and Haworth, 1984: 311): why do those articulated capitalist interests (who positively embrace so much organization theory) wax so histrionic against reformist proposals like wage earners' funds?

Ramsay and Haworth take up the Swedish wage earners' funds proposal to illustrate the vanity of reformism. In the Swedish reformist tradition, the concept of collective capital formation comes from Ernst Wigforss, the social democratic party's main theoretican (and the country's treasurer 1925–6 and 1932–49) who fundamentally reworked Bernsteinian revisionism (Higgins 1985a; 1985b). The doctrinal shift which Wigforss introduced illuminates not only the thrust of the recent fund proposal, but also the trajectory of the political unionism that launched it as part of the attempt to transform capitalism through piecemeal organizational redesign.

It is worth recalling here why Bernstein in particular took upon himself the odium of challenging 'orthodox Marxism' in the international Marxist movement, for we would argue that many present-day Marxist theorists are caught in the same intellectual bind and political limbo as the old orthodoxy (even if they have done more than their forebears to raise their predicament to the level of an art form!). Working from deterministic theses about inevitable class polarization and crisis under capitalism, the orthodoxy announced three 'guarantees' of history – capitalism's self-destruction, the working class's coming demographic dominance and, given continued agitation and propaganda, socialist political dominance on that demographic basis (Salvadori 1979). For the orthodox, be it noted, it was capitalism's macro-economic irrationality that would precipitate the terminal 'crisis' of mature capitalism: at the point of production the bourgeoisie ran a tight ship whose presumed technical sophistication and organizational efficiency would fall like ripe fruit into socialist laps. (This belief, of course, underpinned Lenin's conversion to Taylorism.)

In hindsight, this last point was an astonishing and self-defeating concession. For Western labour movements this concession has left the bitter and enduring legacy of complicity in economic-liberal policy, with which it shares the implicit assumption that any capitalist organization necessarily spells effective enterprise (Higgins 1985a; 1985b). Secure in the belief that the final, cataclysmic crisis of capitalism was only just around the corner, 'orthodox Marxism' also remained secure in its disinclination to concede the importance of organizational questions. Its fatalistic vision led inexorably to a politics of abstention.

Bernstein demolished the 'guarantees of history' to make way for a new interventionist socialist politics. His classic *Evolutionary Socialism*, though concerned mainly with an argument about social democracy's wider political role, contains suggestive obiter dicta on organizational questions (Bernstein 1961: 139; see also 163). But Bernstein stopped halfway. His attack on determinism did not extend to upsetting the orthodox assumption that capitalism had still to mature – that is, still had a progressive future – before it would be meaningful to propose transformative (as opposed to ameliorative) policies. Pending this mystical maturation, reformist interventions such as social policy or industrial democracy rested on a merely ethical-liberal basis. In other words, Bernstein stopped short of a critique of capitalism's organizational effectiveness and thus could not forge the link between democratization and economic renewal.

This is precisely the link that Wigforss latched on to in the 1920s. Armed with Marx's conceptualization of capitalism's 'irrationality', Wigforss imbibed the lessons of the then ongoing 'rationalization movement' which uncovered – albeit sympathetically – the organizational roots of industrial dislocation and inefficiency in the capitalist enterprise. Two of the themes which the movement articulated drew Wigforss's attention. First, forms of financial calculation in the enterprise conflicted with the technical and organizational preconditions of an efficient manufacturing process.

Second, typical authority relations and reward systems tended to produce inefficient work practices. Wigforss concluded that these disorders were systemically induced, flowing inescapably from two aspects of private ownership of industry – the profit principle and the necessarily authoritarian forms by which, as Weber (1978) had already noted, the outside owners' interests and prerogatives were imposed on a working collectivity. Here, then, was a whole new dimension of 'critique' in addition to the critique of capitalism's macro-economic irrationality.

Where Bernstein had talked about 'organized capitalism', Wigforss (later joined by his colleague, Gunnar Myrdal) repeatedly took up the cudgels against capitalist 'disorganization' (see especially Myrdal and Myrdal 1934; see also Eyerman 1985). For Wigforss, these considerations completely reversed social democracy's programmatic presuppositions. Capitalism no longer had a progressive future and socialists had no business tinkering with ameliorative reforms while awaiting the great day of maturation (or 'crisis') and leaving capital in control of the enterprise and resource allocation. The former had now to be democratized and the latter brought under social control. Socialism, in his celebrated phrase, had to be brought forward as 'the working hypothesis' of day-to-day policy-making rather than left to Sunday outings to Utopia. Transformational reforms had to go on the immediate agenda. Wigforss was to bring together the issues of organizational effectiveness and control. 'It is a curious blindness', he wrote, 'not to see that the organization of economic life is at the same time a question of forms of control' (Wigforss 1981: IX: 63).

In the 1920s, leading elements of the Swedish union movement agreed with Wigforss that contemporary forms of capitalism constituted a deteriorating basis for the organization of the modern industry it itself had created. The labour movement presented itself not simply as a challenger to capital's control of the economy and enterprise, but more particularly as the bearer of sounder organizational principles and social priorities upon which to place a more advanced economy and enterprise (de Geer 1978; Hadenius 1976). None of this, of course, could make any sense to Marxists of an older school who still assumed that efficiency belonged to the essence of capitalism. Not unlike some modernist managers and management theorists then and now, they equated greater managerial control of the labour process with higher productivity, and they inevitably mistook the pursuit of organizational efficiency as subservience to capitalism, as class collaboration. Two perverse contemporary contrasts to Wigforssian social democracy make this point plain enough. In the early 1920s, while Wigforss himself was trying to generate an offensive for industrial democracy, that bastion of orthodox Marxism, Lenin, was introducing Taylorism into the USSR – its bourgeois credentials sufficed to establish its claim to technical efficiency. In the first years of the Depression, while Wigforss was leading the onslaught against economic liberalism in Sweden, in Britain the leftist Labour leader and Prime Minister, Macdonald, was defending laissez-faire as 'old, sound socialist doctrine' and declaring that his party was 'not concerned with patching up the rents in a bad system, but with transforming Capitalism into Socialism' (cited in Winch 1969: 123–4). The actual outcome of posing socialism's choices in this way are too notorious to be laboured here.

The labour movement that consolidated its ascendancy in Sweden from the 1930s onwards did not attempt to build its programme overnight. Rather, whether intentionally or not, they set themselves only such tasks as they could solve (Marx 1968). The early tasks thus posed were none the less impressive – reorganization of public economic management and of the labour market and intervention in the distribution of access to education and health care. But in the 1950s and 1960s Wigforss kept prodding the movement towards its central task, reorganization of the economy itself along social democratic and collectivist lines in order to eradicate 'that economic organization, those forms of property rights and control over the material foundations of social life as a whole, which we are accustomed to call bourgeois' (Wigforss 1981: IX: 430). He revamped this central task in terms of 'economic democracy' as a counterweight to the widespread complacency that held up welfarism as the harbinger of 'post-capitalist' society, a complacency which begged the whole question of economic organization.

Wigforss broke down this central task into two interdependent parts – democratization of work life (industrial democracy) and democratization of control over productive resources (economic democracy). His work during the 1920s on the former anticipated the labour movement's offensive into worklife organization from the beginning of the 1970s. Strategically this was an offensive informed by the inseparable objectives of worklife democratization: on the one hand greater productive efficiency than capitalist managerial authoritarianism could achieve, and on the other hand the intention of making workers fully fledged 'citizens' in economic as well as political life (Wigforss 1981: V: 387). In the mid-1950s, in aid of economic democracy, he advocated experimentation with collective capital formation in terms that prefigure the Swedish union confederation LO's wage earners' fund proposal of 1976.

It is highly significant that both these initiatives were triggered by the greater salience that capitalist 'disorganization' assumed with the end of the long boom, as well as with the coming of the conglomerate and other forms of centralization and internationalization of capital. Both represent a serious, in some cases a mortal, threat to an industrial economy as such, with industrial disinvestment and technological dependence at home, and relocation of vital aspects of now internationalized production processes to the less democratic Newly Industrializing Countries.

Contemporary Sweden involves a combination of organized labour's high profile in economic decision-making, with free enterprise (90 per cent of Swedish industry is privately owned) and state surveillance and co-ordination (mechanisms exist for capital to be channelled in particular directions – especially into product development and new technology).

Sweden owes its distinctiveness almost entirely to the nature of its political institutions and the policies which have been pursued through them, particularly with respect to what has been the governing party in Sweden for most of the past fifty years. The Swedish Social Democratic Party (SAP) was founded in 1889 as an affiliate of the Second International. Like the German parent party, the Swedish social democrats began with an uncomfortable mixture of Marxist and Lassallean strategic perspectives which was gradually subordinated to a distinctively Swedish strategy, albeit under the guise of German 'orthodox' and then 'revisionist' Marxism until the 1920s. On the conventional interpretation of social democracy's history (Tingsten 1967), the movement's political trajectory was a long 'maturation' process, culminating in the 1930s, from revolutionary Marxism to welfare liberalism. Undoubtedly the latter years of the party's first generation leadership up to the mid-1920s were marked by hesitation; but far from the latter stemming from forsaken socialist goals, it signalled confusion over how to pursue those goals under the newly-won universal suffrage (Higgins 1988). Neither the political problem nor its novel solution figures in the conventional historiography, but the solution underpinned the party's subsequent unique political success.

The definitive formulation of social democracy's problem in the 1920s, and the strategic re-orientation to overcome it, as was argued above, came primarily from the work of Ernst Wigforss. It will be recalled how his analysis focused on the inability of the social democratic party to attain an electoral majority while it failed to challenge orthodox public economic management and thus colluded in the typically free-market outcomes of macro- and micro-economic inefficiency and social inequity. Mass unemployment was the most topical such outcome. The party could only aspire to majoritarian rule if it contested free-market economic rationality by proposing the comprehensive reform of macro- and micro-economic institutions in the overt pursuit of efficiency, equity and democracy as mutually reinforcing goals (Higgins 1985b; 1988). On this basis the party launched its spectacularly successful electoral offensive in 1932, in the aftermath of which it has been in government ever since, with the exception of the non-socialist interregnum of 1976–82. The electoral success of the SAP is based mainly on the fact that the majority of Swedes associate the party not only with the beginnings of their economic success but also with its continuation (see Himmelstrand et al. 1981). Even many Swedish business people have faith in the economic practices that have become institutionalized and tend to be suspicious of change. Industrial leaders – for example Curt Nicolin, a former chairman of the Swedish employers' federation (SAF) – have gone on record as saying that they prefer to deal with a social democratic government because 'they have a better understanding of the rules of the game' on the labour market. That this is so might strike an outsider as remarkable, given the nature of the policies which the SAP has followed, if not always consistently. These policies, as we shall see, have had major organizational implications. The Wigforssian politics of contesting free-market economic rationality have not only made the Swedish social democrats the West's most successful electoral party, but have also moulded what have become distinctively Swedish institutional innovations and proposals: indicative planning, the public orchestration of economic development, a direct role for organized labour in macro-economic management, and industrial and economic democracy. In contrast to settings in which organized labour has been remote from the institutional environment in which policies are formed, this context has generated a set of institutional innovations whose diffusion would produce a fascinating case not only of 'isomorphism' but also of organizational transformation on a societal scale. The institutional implications flow right to the heart of power relations in private sector organizations: the structuring of organizational relations around an axial principle of private capital ownership of the means of production, and the strategic attempt to subordinate other relations to the service of this axial principle (see Clegg and Dunkerley 1980: ch. 12). The carrier of this subversive institutionalism has been the labour movement.

The Swedish blue-collar union movement (LO), from at least the 1920s and especially since the late 1940s, has been an important institutional locus of a politics of economic rationality which has had profound implications for the structuring of organization relations. It has also been uniquely successful amongst its Western counterparts, both in terms of union density (around 90 per cent), institutional development and its direct part in public and 'private' economic management, and in overtaking its affiliated party as the labour movement's major policy initiator. It took up this latter role in the late 1940s, and did so by developing its own distinctive policy regime (the Rehn–Meidner model adopted in 1951), in order to perpetuate full employment while at the same time counteracting inflationary pressures at their source, in substantively irrational investment behaviour – rather than in what is presumed conventionally to be their source in wage movements (Higgins and Apple 1983; Higgins 1985a).

Consider some examples of these institutional innovations. In the late 1930s, for instance, the social democrats pioneered an investment reserve fund mechanism to re-phase and promote investment during recessions. The scheme became operative in the 1950s, and allows Swedish firms to retain pre-tax profits in frozen Central Bank accounts. The government 'releases' the funds in downturns, and provided the firms then invest them appropriately, they do not attract tax. The National Labour Market Board (*Arbetsmarknadsstyrelsen*), which has a majority of union delegates, exercises a degree of influence over these releases. The main activities of this important state organ consist in retraining, relocation of labour and job creation, all of which also constitute indirect levers into investment decisions. One can see that through institutional forms such as this the probability of employers being able to introduce 'flexibility' under anti-labour auspices would be remote, as would be the possibility that labour would oppose such restructuring.

The Labour Market Board is an offshoot of the Department of Employment, but there are also regional labour market councils and the local labour exchanges, the latter operating with what Rothstein (1985) refers to as 'street level bureaucracies'. The term is appropriate in this context. The SAP, in pursuit of an 'active' labour market policy, has from the early post-war period broken the tradition of meritocratic recruitment of bureaucrats in order to put individuals who are more in sympathy with their policies into contact with concrete labour market problems at the grass-roots level. Rothstein describes this as 'cadre activity' on the part of the social democrats. Certainly it has to be seen as determination on the part of the social democrats to make inroads into the 'conservative' civil service in order to accommodate better their reform programme, especially in the areas of the labour market, education and agriculture.

The labour movement invests the Labour Market Board with great importance, particularly for its support of the broader policy ambition of keeping wages high, even if this forces weak firms to the wall. Indeed, precisely because it does force weaker firms to the wall: as the Rehn–Meidner model problematized wage differentials, why should it be the case that low-wage workers subsidize inefficient firms? The labour market policies board deals with any problems of redeployment (rather than unemployment). The national board handles macro-level planning and industrial relocation; the regional boards concentrate on job creation, retraining and redeployment in the regions; and the labour exchanges are equipped (and financed) to deal effectively and sympathetically (from the labour point of view) with individual cases.

Despite arguments to the contrary (Rothstein 1985) this is not just a case of the social democrats filling the various levels of public administration with their party nominees, but rather of a highly specific institutional model being implemented, with these boards made up, at both national and county levels, of nominees from government, employers and unions plus other interest groups, where appropriate. In recent years policy has returned to 'economic realism' in the denial of public money to declining industries after the non-socialist government's lavish support of doomed industries like shipbuilding. Instead, a network of local investment corporations has been set up to solicit private investment and these, incidentally, have tended to be over-subscribed.

Meanwhile, in the case of larger problems, such as those encountered in the formerly highly successful shipbuilding industry, Sweden's large companies have been mobilized into the breach, with some financial encouragement. In the case of the closing down of the large Uddevalla shipyard, a new Volvo plant was built, and in the more recent case of the Kockums yard at Malmö, a new Saab plant is planned. The future may be more difficult because, as a Ministry of Industry official pointed out, there is not an endless supply of possibilities on this scale. As a counter example, it is interesting to note that in 1987 when the Dannemora and Grängesberg iron ore mines were threatened with closure the government compromised its policy and underwrote a five-year extension. To some extent this highlights the status of miners as a special case almost everywhere, but it also reflects the relatively small scale of the problem with only about a thousand jobs to be protected. From a different perspective, in the case of Uddevalla and Malmö it should be noted that the result is 'state of the art' technology for Volvo and Saab, already known for their innovation in manufacturing technology and organization (Sandkull 1986).

The original Rehn–Meidner model and its institutional ramifications (above all, the pension funds and the labour market planning apparatus) successfully sought to perpetuate full employment and economic dynamism under socially equitable and increasingly democratic conditions. It tackled the main enemy of the full-employment economy – inflation – at its source in the irrationality of unregulated private investment behaviour. High wages and wage equalization featured as centrepieces, and the model prescribed a direct and growing role for the union movement in policy-making and implementation. But from the beginning of the early 1970s many LO strategists and union activists perceived a need to take the model a great step further. The original model had served well in the stable, expansionary conditions of the long boom, and while Swedish industry was in the hands of competent industrialists. But, as this model stood, it was less well equipped to deal, from the 1970s, with the international economic contraction and destabilization, on the one hand, and the internationalization of financial markets on the other – a change that made Swedish industry subject to predatory financial interests and their anti-manufacturing forms of calculation. The Swedish union movement responded to these new conditions by extending the model.

It did so by mounting two simultaneous campaigns, for industrial democracy and for economic democracy in the form of wage earners' funds (Higgins and Apple 1983). Both arose out of the movement's penchant for collectivist and democratic solutions rather than a relapse into economic-liberal atavism. Both industrial democracy and wage earners' funds proved non-negotiable with the employers' federation (SAE) and thus necessitated resort to both legislation and intense mobilization of the rank and file. A series of statutes, known as the Aman laws, redefined the rights of shop stewards, safety committees and employees in general, as well as imposing obligations on employers to accept worker directors and to disclose and negotiate over all corporate plans affecting their workforces. Despite employer resistance, the industrial-democracy campaign has left its mark in the qualitatively heightened ability of local union organizations (backed by central union resources) to enter into corporate planning and decision-making. They do so as the bearers of a substantive industrial rationality which is often at loggerheads with the paper entrepreneurialism of the new major players on the capital market (Higgins 1987).

The second union campaign from this period, the wage earners' fund proposal, shared the same rationale, attacking the problems of capital formation at root. Although its original pretext was to cream off and thus sterilize a proportion of excess profits that otherwise stimulated wage drift, a major motive of the funds was to secure the re-investment of those profits in industry at a time when the country's capital resources were being diverted into speculative and purely financial placements. More broadly, the proposed reform aimed partially to fulfil the traditional social democratic goal of democratizing economic life, in this instance by bringing the all-important function of resource allocation under gradually increasing social control. In the event, a failure of political will on the part of the social democratic party, in the face of sustained opposition, resulted in the enactment of a wage earners' fund scheme that was too watered down to achieve any of these ambitions. However, the present scheme may prove the precursor of democratic reforms in capital formation that come closer to fulfilling the original ambitions of the wage earners' fund concept.

Two streams of development in particular influenced the proposal of a wage earners' fund as a source of collective capital formation. One had been the success of the pensions funds, the major LO initiative of the 1950s. The other had been the fact that as a result of following a wages and incomes policy which stressed solidaristic rises for the lowest paid in order to minimize differentials in the economy, by the mid-1970s the highest paid workers in the core sectors of the economy had, through their wage restraint, handed the employers profits which they would not otherwise have had. Meidner, the LO's chief economist, came up with the wage earners' fund scheme as a way of putting these 'super-profits' to productive and long-term purpose.

The basic idea was that a series of wage earners' funds would be created through the simple mechanism of shares being issued in firms in proportion to their profit level, which would be lodged in funds invested across regions and industry.

> The idea was that as the funds acquired an increasing proportion of the equity in a firm, they would be able to nominate directors to the board, subject to the consent of the unions representing workers in that firm or group of firms. (The voting rights were to be 50 per cent to local unions and 50 per cent to the funds.) The beauty of this scheme was that, with one proposal, many of the labour movement's objectives were advanced: the funds would promote equality and industrial democracy; they would reduce the trend to capital accumulation in a few hands; they would redistribute wealth; and they would complement the solidaristic wages policy. (Matthews 1989: 174–5)

Ownership and control of Swedish industry would gradually pass into the wage earners' funds, at a rate dependent upon the percentage level that the profits tax was set at. For instance, if it were set at 20 per cent then effective control would be ceded in about 20 or 25 years; if it were set as low as 5 per cent it could take up to 75 years. Considerable opposition during the election campaigning of 1979 to the original Meidner proposals led to only a watered-down version of the funds being introduced in 1984. These represented regional funds set up under rules which provided that proportions of both wage rises and company profits should be put into five funds for investment under tripartite control in Swedish industry.

All these institutional arrangements contribute to a system of sticks and carrots intended to draw capital into the renewal and expansion of the manufacturing sector, where they have stimulated investment levels and shared up substantively rational forms of calculation. Collective capital formation, empowered and democratized labour and a high-wages-forced national manufacturing rationality (rather than a rationality premised on internationally comparatively lower wages and/or much longer hours of work by segmented and divided workers) are the hallmark. The key to this close contingency or elective affinity is the extension of institutions of representation throughout society, rather than their restriction. A distinct framework has been produced within which action is calculated and modes of rationality may be formed.

The 'Swedish model' is not culturally specific but institutionally produced. Such developments are institutionally feasible at national levels, despite the increasing interdependence of national economies and their susceptibility to economic factors outside their control (Bruno and Sachs 1985; Hicks 1987). In fact, these international interdependencies make national institutional factors of more, not less, importance. Some of these institutional conditions are, in principle, capable of replication elsewhere. A party of labour in government, a strong and centralizing union structure and peak tripartite institutions in which priorities and policy commitments can be hammered out concerning wages, investment, skill and capital formation, and industry policy all point to the possibility of developing a broader organizational world. It would be a different organizational world, in some formal respects not too dissimilar to the modernist organizations we know so well. In some other important respects, however, it would be different. It would be a world of organizations replete with political possibilities for postmodern development. It would be an organizational world of enhanced skill formation and de-differentiation, facilitated in its further realistic development by the de-differentiation of the relations of private capital formation as a modernist hallmark. Its political choices would thus hardly be those of the 'New Right', but neither would they be those of the 'New Left' commitment to ideals inspired by the creed of collectivist organizations (see Rothschild-Whitt 1979; and the critique in Clegg and Higgins 1987).

The choices proposed could be politically possible, technically feasible and organizationally practicable. They would have the potential to extend opportunities for more fully formed economic citizenship to a far greater extent than has been the case with the much more restricted modernist project. They would locate us positively within the possibilities of postmodern times.

Conclusion

The sketch proposed here is one in which there would be an enhancement of general representational rights in organizations. The other major postmodern alternative which has been considered would be one in which an enclave of privileged workers would be formed on highly exclusivist principles of social identity, such as gender, ethnicity and age, characteristics which were tightly coupled to the processes of skill formation. Japan stands as a practical example of how this might be organized through processes of 'Nipponization' occurring on a global scale.

If these alternative postmodern conditions to those argued for here were to be generalized then one might anticipate that privileged individuals might easily be seduced by the organizational benefits on offer. It would not be too hard for such privileged individuals to be relatively indifferent to the majority. Indeed, they would be fortunate that they too were not condemned to the margins of postmodernity. On these margins everyday life would be hard-pressed, compared to the enclave of privilege. Indeed, not only the returns from work but also the conditions of its pursuit would be an everyday struggle against the dark side of that dialectic which illuminates privilege as it blights indifference. Postmodernity would be a series of privileged enclaves stockaded within the bleak vistas of modernity. Their status would be utterly dependent on the exclusion of others from the prizes secured, precisely because such definitions of an exclusive good are 'positional' (Hirsch 1978): if they are widely available to all they cease to have any exclusivity for the few who once held them. Working within privileged and exclusive labour market segments, residing within a set of exclusive life-style options, commuting between them, briefly transgressing the boundaries which demarcate the sacred from the profane: is that life in the postmodern age for the fortunate few whom 'market forces' favour? Highly differentiated rights in work would be the basis of possibilities for participation in citizenship more generally, as one bought or was excluded from the options available.

Paradoxically, we are individually much freer to choose postmodernist seduction (and repression and exclusion for others, by implication) than we are postmodernist enlightenment: the latter demands far more than sustained individual effort in a fiercely competitive labour market for admission to the ranks of the organizationally seduced. It requires concerted political will to shape and transform the institutions of policy in which those relations of organization power are normally constituted. Realistically it may well be that such a strategic initiative and momentum are far too idealist or too difficult to occur. Maybe they will simply lack sufficient institutional expression, even over the long sweep of possible futures. It is, after all, much more pleasurable to be seduced than to be spurned and disappointed, to enjoy *one's* rights. While one enjoys them, why should one presume to worry about those of others one doesn't know and, under the prevailing conditions, probably wouldn't care to know? Moreover, it is unlikely that those within the arena of privilege will be obliged to listen for as long as any dissenting voices remain organizationally outflanked, outside the stockade. The very existence of fierce competition for admittance to enclaves of privilege, together with appropriate policies of containment for those who neither resign nor compete but who seek to change the rules of the game, should suffice to secure this outflanking. Postmodern organization, as a mechanism of outflanking, may well function rather more to define, confine and confirm limits rather than to transcend them.

It does not have to be like that. There is an alternative. Postmodernism can be about possibilities denied by the project of modernity. Yet no necessity attaches to the future of organizational diversities. The view of this book has been that everything depends upon the indeterminate outcomes of struggles for meaning and power in and around organizations, struggles which take place under quite distinct national and institutional patterns. Cross-national learning is possible but it is not easy. It is never simply a case of taking an element out of context and applying it, hoping to get the desired result. It is certainly never a simple matter of organizational design as an intentional process – this is the rationalist illusion of the modernist age. Leaving illusion aside, organizational modernity is giving way to possibilities of organizational postmodernity at the leading edges of the capitalist world; yet, to reiterate: no necessity attaches to the outcomes of these possibilities. National institutional frameworks and specific organizations, whether they go down the more strongly collectivist and solidaristic path outlined in Sweden or develop along the segmented and more exclusivist route of Japan, are capable of constructing diverse frameworks within which these possibilities might be fought.

In the face of possibilities TINA tendencies in organization studies are of an increasingly limited analytical value. However, they may well serve other purposes. These are, perhaps, best appreciated through regarding them less in terms of what they depict and rather more in terms of what they do. Once one can evacuate all other contenders from an intellectual field of power and their representations from the organizational field of force which they interpret, then a privileged path is cleared in which interpretation, with all its necessary pluralities and ambiguities, becomes legislation. Possibilities would be narrowed. To argue that such tendencies are analytical delusions, one would submit, is an important first line of defence against the practical triumph of absolutism in whatever guise.

References

Abbott, A. (1989) 'The New Occupational Structure: What Are the Questions?', *Work and Occupations*, 16(3): 273–91.

Abegglen, J. C. (1958) *The Japanese Factory*. Glencoe, Ill.: Free Press.

Abegglen, J. C. (1973) *Management and Worker: The Japanese Solution*. Tokyo: Sophia University Press.

Abegglen, J. C. and G. Stalk Jr. (1985) *Kaisha: The Japanese Corporation*. New York: Basic Books.

Abercrombie, N., S. Hill and B. S. Turner (1980) *The Dominant Ideology Thesis*. London: Allen and Unwin.

ACTU/TDCS (Australian Council of Trade Unions/Trade Development Council Secretariat) (1987) *Australia Reconstructed*. Canberra: Australian Government Publishing Service.

Aglietta, M. (1979) *A Theory of Capitalist Regulation*. London: New Left Books.

Albertsen, N. (1988) 'Postmodernism, Post-Fordism, and Critical Social Theory', *Environment and Planning D: Society and Space*, 6: 339–66.

Albrow, M. (1970) *Bureaucracy*. London: Pall Mall.

Aldrich, H. E. (1972) 'Technology and Organizational Structure: A Re-examination of the Findings of the Aston Group', *Administrative Science Quarterly*, 17: 26–42.

Aldrich, H. E. (1979) *Organizations and Environments*. Englewood Cliffs, NJ: Prentice-Hall.

Allen, V. L. (1975) *Social Analysis*. London: Longman

Alston, J. P. (1982) 'Awarding Bonuses the Japanese Way', *Business Horizons*, 25(5): 46–50.

Amsden, A. H. (1985) 'The State and Taiwan's Economic Development', pp. 78–106 in P. B. Evans, D. Rueschemeyer and T. Skocpol (eds), *Bringing the State Back In*. Cambridge: Cambridge University Press.

Anderson, B. (1983) *Imagined Communities: Reflections on the Origins and Spread of Nationalism*. London: Verso.

Attewell, P. (1977) 'The De-skilling Controversy', *Work and Occupations*, 14(3): 323–46.

Azumi, K. and C. J. McMillan (1975) 'Worker Sentiment in the Japanese Factory: Its Organizational Determinants', pp. 215–29 in L. Austin (ed.), *Japan: The Paradox of Progress*. New Haven, Conn.: Yale University Press.

Badham, R. and J. Matthews (1989) 'The New Production Systems Debate', *Labour and Industry*, 2(2): 194–246.

Barnard, C. (1938) *The Functions of the Executive*. Cambridge, Mass.: Harvard University Press.

Bartolme, F. (1989) 'Nobody Trusts the Boss Completely – Now What?', *Harvard Business Review*, 67(2): 135–42.

Bauman, Z. (1982) *Memories of Class: The Pre-History and After-Life of Class*. London: Routledge and Kegan Paul.

Bauman, Z. (1987) *Legislators and Interpreters*. Cambridge: Polity Press.

Bauman, Z. (1988a) 'Viewpoint: Sociology and Postmodernity', *Sociological Review*, 36(4): 790–813.

Bauman, Z. (1988b) ' Is There a Postmodern Sociology?', *Theory, Culture and Society*, 5: 217–37.

Bauman, Z. (1989) 'Sociological Responses to Postmodernity', *Thesis Eleven*, 23: 35–63.

Baumol, N. (1967) *Business Behaviour, Value and Growth*. New York: Macmillan.

Beck, S. and J. Child (1978) *Mastering the Art of French Cooking* (Vol. 2). Harmondsworth: Penguin.

Belussi, F. (1989) 'Benetton – a Case Study of Corporate Strategy for Innovation in Traditional Sectors', pp. 116–33 in M. Dodgson (ed.), *Technology Strategy and the Firm: Management and Public Policy*. Harlow: Longman.

Benedict, R. (1946) *The Chrysanthemum and the Sword: Patterns of Japanese Culture*. Boston, Mass.: Houghton Mifflin.

Berger, P. (1987) *The Capitalist Revolution*. London: Wildwood.

Berger, P. and T. Luckmann (1967) *The Social Construction of Reality*. Harmondsworth: Penguin.

Berle, A. A. and G. C. Means (1932) *The Modern Corporation and Private Property*. New York: Macmillan.

Bernstein, E. (1961) *Evolutionary Socialism*. New York: Schocken.

Bertaux, D. and I. Bertaux-Wiame (1981) 'Artisanal Bakery in France: How It Lives and Why It Survives', pp. 121–54 in F. Bechofer and B. Elliot (eds), *The Petite Bourgeoisie: Comparative Studies of the Uneasy Stratum*. London: Macmillan.

Biggart, N. W. and G. G. Hamilton (1985) 'The Power of Obedience', *Administrative Science Quarterly*, 29: 540–9.

Biggart, N. W. and G. G. Hamilton (1987) 'An Institutional Theory of Leadership', *Journal of Applied Behavioral Science*, 23(4): 429–41.

Blau, P. M. (1955) *The Dynamics of Bureaucracy*. Chicago: University of Chicago Press

Blau, P. M. (1956) *Bureaucracy in Modern Society*. New York: Random House.

Blau, P. M. and R. Schoenherr (1971) *The Structuring of Organizations*. New York: Free Press.

Blau, P. M. and W. R. Scott (1963) *Formal Organizations: A Comparative Approach*. London: Routledge and Kegan Paul.

Blau, P. M., C. M. Falbe, W. McKinley and P. K. Tracy (1976) 'Technology and Organization in Manufacturing', *Administrative Science Quarterly*, 21: 20–40.

Blunt, P. (1989) 'Strategies for Human Resource Development in the Third World', opening address to *The International Human Resource Development Conference*, University of Manchester, June 25–8.

Bond, M. and G. Hofstede (1988) 'The Confucius Connection: From Cultural Roots to Economic Growth', *Organizational Dynamics*, 16: 4–21.

Boreham, P., S. R. Clegg and G. Dow (1986) 'The Institutional Management of Class Politics: Beyond the Labour Process and Corporatist Debates', pp. 186–210 in D. Knights and H. Willmott (eds), *Managing the Labour Process*. Aldershot: Gower.

Boulding, K. (1956) 'General Systems Theory: The Skeleton of Science', *Management Science*, 2: 197–208.

Bourdieu, P. (1984) *Distinction: A Social Critique of the Judgement of Taste*. London: Routledge and Kegan Paul.

Bramble, T. (1988) 'The Flexibility Debate: Industrial Relations and New Management Production Practices', *Labour and Industry*, 1(2): 187–209.

Braverman, H. (1974) *Labor and Monopoly Capital: The Degradation of Work in the Twentieth Century*. New York: Monthly Review Press.

Brinton, M. C. (1989) 'Gender Stratification in Contemporary Urban Japan', *American Sociological Review*, 54(4): 549–64.

Brittain, J. W. and J. H. Freeman (1980) 'Organizational Proliferation and Density Development Selection', pp. 291–338 in J. B. Kimberley, R. H. Miles and Associates (eds), *The Organizational Life Cycle: Issues in the Creation, Transformation, and Decline of Organizations*. San Francisco: Jossey-Bass.

Bruno, M. and J. D. Sachs (1985) *Economics of Worldwide Stagflation*. Cambridge, Mass.: Harvard University Press.

Bunge, F. M. (1982) *South Korea: A Country Study*. Washington, DC: United States Government Printing Office.

Burawoy, M. (1979) *Manufacturing Consent: Changes in the Labor Process under Capitalism*. Chicago: University of Chicago Press.

Burns, T. and G. M. Stalker (1961) *The Management of Innovation*. London: Tavistock.

Burrell, G. and G. Morgan (1979) *Sociological Paradigms and Organizational Analysis*. London: Heinemann Educational Books.

Calmfors, L. and J. Diffil (1988) 'Bargaining structure, corporatism and macro-economic performance', *Economic Policy*, 6(1): 13–62.

Campbell, I. (1989) 'New Production Concepts? – the West German Debates on Restructuring', *Labour and Industry*, 2(2): 247–80.

Caves, R. E. and M. Uekusa (1976) *Industrial Organization in Japan*. Washington, DC: Brookings Institute.

Chandler, A. D. (1962) *Strategy and Structure: Chapters in the History of the American Industrial Enterprise*. Cambridge, Mass.: MIT Press.

Chandler, A. D. (1977) *The Visible Hand: The Managerial Revolution in American Business*. Cambridge, Mass.: Harvard University Press.

Chandler, A. D. (1984) 'The Emergence of Managerial Capitalism', *Business History Review* 58: 473–502.

Channon, D. F. (1973) *The Strategy and Structure of British Enterprises*. Boston, Mass.: Division of Research, Graduate School of Business Administration, Harvard University.

Child, J. (1972) 'Organization Structure, Environment and Performance: The Role of Strategic Choice', *Sociology*, 6: 1–22.

Child, J. (1982) 'Discussion Note: Divisionalization and Size – a Comment on the Donaldson/ Grinyer Debate', *Organization Studies*, 3(4): 351–3.

Child, J. (1984) *Organization: A Guide to Problems and Practice*. London: Harper and Row.

Child, J. (1987) 'Information Technology, Organization and the Response to Strategic Challenge', paper presented at the opening session of the 8th EGOS (European Group for Organization Studies) Colloquium, Antwerp, July.

Child, J. and A. Keiser (1979) 'Organization and Managerial Roles in British and West German Companies: An Examination of the Culture-Free Thesis', pp. 251–71 in C. J. Lammers and D. J. Hickson (eds), *Organizations Alike and Unlike: International and Inter-Institutional Studies in the Sociology of Organizations*. London: Routledge and Kegan Paul.

Child, J. and R. Mansfield (1972) 'Technology, Size and Organization Structure', *Sociology*, 6: 368–93.

Child, J. and M. H. Tayeb (1983) 'Theoretical Perspectives in Cross-National Organizational Research', *International Studies of Management and Organization*, 12: 23–70.

Chua, W.-F. and S. R. Clegg (forthcoming) 'Professional Closure', *Theory and Society*.

Clark, R. (1979) *The Japanese Company*. New Haven, Conn.: Yale University Press.

Clarke, T. (1989) 'Socialized Industry: Social Ownership or Shareholding Democracy?', pp. 485–512 in S. R. Clegg (ed.), *Organization Theory and Class Analysis: New Approaches and New Issues*. Berlin: De Gruyter.

Clawson, D. (1980) *Bureaucracy and the Labor Process: The Transformation of US Industry 1860–1920*. New York: Monthly Review Press.

Clegg, S. R. (1975) *Power, Rule and Domination: A Critical and Empirical Understanding of Power in Sociological Theory and Organizational Life*. London: Routledge and Kegan Paul.

Clegg, S. R. (1977) 'Power, Organization Theory, Marx and Critique', pp. 1–40 in S. R. Clegg and D. Dunkerley (eds), *Critical Issues in Organizations*. London: Routledge and Kegan Paul.

Clegg, S. R. (1979) *The Theory of Power and Organization*. London: Routledge and Kegan Paul.

Clegg, S. R. (1981) 'Organization and Control', *Administrative Science Quarterly*, 26(4): 545–62.

Clegg, S. R. (1988) 'The Good, the Bad and the Ugly', *Organization Studies*, 9(1): 7–13.

Clegg, S. R. (1989a) 'Radical Revisions: Power, Discipline and Organizations', *Organization Studies*, 10(1): 97–115.

Clegg, S. R. (1989b) *Frameworks of Power*. London: Sage.

Clegg, S. R., P. Boreham and G. Dow (1983) 'Politics and Crisis: The State of the Recession', pp. 1–50 in S. R. Clegg, G. Dow and P. Boreham (eds), *The State, Class and the Recession*. London: Croom Helm.

Clegg, S. R., P. Boreham and G. Dow (1986) *Class, Politics and the Economy*. London: Routledge and Kegan Paul.

Clegg, S. R. and D. Dunkerley (1980) *Organization, Class and Control*. London: Routledge and Kegan Paul.

Clegg, S. R., D. Dunphy and S. G. Redding (eds) (1986) *The Enterprise and Management in East Asia*. Hong Kong: Centre of Asian Studies, University of Hong Kong.

Clegg, S. R. and W. Higgins (1987) 'Against the Current: Organizations, Sociology and Socialism', *Organization Studies*, 8(3): 201–22.

Clegg, S. R. and W. Higgins (1989) 'Better Expert than Orthodox: Reply to Shenkar', *Organization Studies*, 10(2): 253–8.

Clegg, S. R., W. Higgins and T. Spybey (1990) '"Post-Confucianism", Social Democracy and Economic Culture', pp. 18–46 in S. R. Clegg and S. G. Redding (eds), with the assistance of M. Cartner, *Capitalism in Contrasting Cultures*. Berlin: De Gruyter.

Clegg, S. R. and S. G. Redding (eds), with the assistance of M. Cartner (1990) *Capitalism in Contrasting Cultures*. Berlin: De Gruyter.

Cohen, M. D., J. G. March and J. P. Olsen (1972) 'A Garbage Can Model of Organizational Choice', *Administrative Science Quarterly*, 17(1): 1–25.

Cohen, S. and J. Zysman (1987) *Manufacturing Matters: The Myth of Post-Industrial Society*. New York: Basic Books.

Cole, R. E. (1971) *Japanese Blue Collar: The Changing Tradition*. Berkeley, Calif.: University of California Press.

Cole, R. E. (1973) 'Functional Alternatives and Economic Development: An Empirical Example of Permanent Employment in Japan', *American Sociological Review*, 38: 424–38.

Cole, R. E. (1978) 'The Late-Developer Hypothesis: An Evaluation of its Relevance for Japanese Employment Practices', *Journal of Japanese Studies*, 4: 247–68.

Cole, R. E. (1979) *Work, Mobility and Participation*. Berkeley, Calif.: University of California Press.

Cole, R. E. and K. Tominga (1976) 'Japan's Changing Occupational Structure and its Significance', pp. 53–95 in H. Patrick (ed.), *Japanese Industrialization and its Social Consequences*. Berkeley, Calif.: University of California Press.

Colebatch, H. (1988) 'Review of L. Donaldson (1985) *In Defence of Organization Theory: A Response to the Critics*', *Australian Journal of Management*, 12(2): 307–10.

Collingon, R. and D. Cray (1980) 'Critical Organizations', *Organization Studies*, 1(4):349–66.

Collins, R. (1980) 'Weber's Last Theory of Capitalism: A Systematization', *American Sociological Review*, 45: 925–42.

Conger, J. A. (1989) 'Leadership: The Art of Empowering Others', *Academy of Management Executive*, 3(1): 17–24.

Cool, K. O. and C. A. Lengnick-Hall (1985) 'Second Thoughts on the Transferability of the Japanese Management Style', *Organization Studies*, 6(1): 1–22.

Cooper, R. and G. Burrell (1988) 'Modernism, Postmodernism and Organizational Analysis: An Introduction', *Organization Studies*, 9(1): 91–112.

Coriat, B. (1980) 'The Restructuring of the Assembly Line: A New Economy of Time and Control', *Capital and Class*, 11: 34–43.

Coser, L. A. (1956) *The Functions of Social Conflict*. London: Routledge and Kegan Paul.

Crenson, M. A. (1962) *The Un-politics of Air Pollution: A Study of Non-Decisionmaking in the Cities*. Baltimore, Md: Johns Hopkins University Press.

Cross, M. (1985) *Towards the Flexible Craftsman*. London: Technical Change Centre.

Crozier, M. (1964) *The Bureaucratic Phenomenon*. London: Tavistock.

Cummings, B. (1984) 'The Origins and Development of the Northeastern Asia Political

Economy: Industrial Sectors, Product Cycles, and Political Consequences', *International Organizations*, 38: 1–40.

Cusamano, M. (1985) *The Japanese Automobile Industry: Technology and Management at Nissan and Toyota*. Cambridge, Mass.: Harvard University Press.

Cutler, A., B. Hindess, P. Q. Hirst and A. Hussain (1979a) *Marx's Capital and Capitalism Today*. Volume 1. London: Routledge and Kegan Paul.

Cutler, A., B. Hindess, P. Q. Hirst and A. Hussain (1979b) *Marx's Capital and Capitalism Today*. Volume 2. London: Routledge and Kegan Paul.

Cyert, R. M. and J. G. March (1963) *A Behavioural Theory of the Firm*. Englewood Cliffs, NJ: Prentice-Hall.

de Geer, H. (1978) *Rationaliseringsrörelsen i Sverige*. Stockholm: SAIS.

Deutschmann, C. (1987a) 'The Japanese Type of Organization as a Challenge to the Sociological Theory of Modernization', *Thesis Eleven*, 17: 40–58.

Deutschmann, C. (1987b) 'Economic Restructuring and Company Unionism – the Japanese Model', *Economic and Industrial Democracy*, 8(4): 436–88.

DiMaggio, P. (1988) 'Interest and Agency in Institutional Theory', pp. 3–21 in L. G. Zucker (ed.), *Institutional Patterns and Organizations*. Cambridge, Mass.: Ballinger.

DiMaggio, P. and W. Powell (1983) 'The Iron Cage Revisited: Institutional Isomorphism and Collective Rationality in Organizational Fields', *American Sociological Review*, 48(2): 147–60.

Donaldson, L. (1982) 'Divisionalization and Size: A Theoretical and Empirical Critique', *Organization Studies*, 3(4): 321–38.

Donaldson, L. (1985a) *In Defence of Organization Theory: A Response to the Critics*. Cambridge: Cambridge University Press.

Donaldson, L. (1985b) 'Organizational Design and the Life Cycle of Products', *Journal of Management Studies*, 22(1): 25–37.

Donaldson, L. (1986a) 'Size and Bureaucracy in East and West: A Preliminary Meta Analysis', pp. 67–91 in S. R. Clegg, D. Dunphy and S. G. Redding (eds), *The Enterprise and Management in East Asia*. Hong Kong: Centre of Asian Studies, University of Hong Kong.

Donaldson, L. (1986b) 'Research Note: The Interaction of Size and Diversification as a Determinant of Divisionalization – Grinyer Revisited', *Organization Studies*, 7(4): 367–80.

Donaldson, L. (1987) 'Strategy, Structural Adjustment to Regain Fit and Performance: In Defence of Contingency Theory', *Journal of Management Studies*, 24(2): 1–24.

Dore, R. (1973) *British Factory, Japanese Factory: The Origins of National Diversity in Industrial Relations*. London: Allen and Unwin.

Dore, R. (1979) 'More about Late Development', *Journal of Japanese Studies*, 5: 137–51.

Dore, R. (1983) 'Goodwill and the Spirit of Market Capitalism', *British Journal of Sociology*, 34: 459–82.

Dore, R. (1986) *Flexible Rigidities*. Stanford, Calif.: Stanford University Press.

Drucker, P. F. (1971) 'What We Can Learn from Japanese Management', *Harvard Business Review*, 49: 110–22.

Dunford, R. (1988) 'Scientific Management in Australia: A Discussion Paper', *Industry and Labour*, 1(3): 505–15.

Dunphy, D. (1986) 'An Historical Review of the Literature on the Japanese Enterprise and its Management', pp. 334–68 in S. R. Clegg, D. Dunphy and S. G. Redding (eds), *The Enterprise and Management in East Asia*. Hong Kong: Centre of Asian Studies, University of Hong Kong.

Durkheim, E. (1957) *Professional Ethics and Civic Morals*. London: Routledge and Kegan Paul.

Durkheim, E. (1964) *The Division of Labour in Society*. New York: Free Press.

Dyas, G. P. and H. T. Thanheiser (1976) *The Emerging European Enterprise – Strategy and Structure in French and German Industry*. London: Macmillan.

Edwards, R. (1979) *Contested Terrain: The Transformation of Work in the Twentieth Century*. New York: Basic Books.

Emery, F. and E. J. Trist (1960) 'Socio–technical Systems', pp. 83–97 in C. Churchman and M. Verhulst (eds), *Management Science, Models and Techniques*. Volume 2. Oxford: Pergamon.

Ergas, H. (1987) 'Does Technology Policy Matter?', pp. 191–245 in B. Guile and H. Brooks (eds), *Technology and Global Industry*. Washington, DC: National Academy Press.

Eto, H. (1980) 'Problems and Lessons of Japanese Technology Policy', *R & D Management*, 10(2): 49–59.

Etzioni, A. (1960) 'Two Approaches to Organizational Analysis', *Administrative Science Quarterly*, 5: 257–78.

Etzioni, A. (1961) *The Comparative Analysis of Complex Organizations*. New York: Free Press.

Etzioni, A. (1975) *The Comparative Analysis of Complex Organizations* (2nd Edition). New York: Free Press.

Ewer, P., W. Higgins and A. Stevens (1987) *Unions and the Future of Australian Manufacturing*. Sydney: Allen and Unwin.

Eyerman, R. (1985) 'Rationalizing Intellectuals: Sweden in the 1930s and 1960s', *Theory and Society*, 14: 777–87.

Fayol, H. (1949) *General and Industrial Management*. London: Pitman.

Fligstein, N. (1985) 'The Spread of the Multidivisional Form among Large Firms, 1919–1979', *American Sociological Review*, 50(3): 377–91.

Ford, J. D. (1980) 'The Administrative Component in Growing and Declining Organizations: A Longitudinal Analysis', *Academy of Management Journal*, 29(2): 203–9.

Foucault, M. (1977) *Discipline and Punish: The Birth of the Prison*. Harmondsworth: Penguin.

Fox, A. (1974) *Beyond Contract: Work, Power and Trust Relations*. London: Faber and Faber.

Fox, B. (1980) 'Japan's Electronic Lesson', *New Scientist*, 88: 517–20.

Freeman, J. (1982) 'Organizational Life Cycles and Natural Selection Processes', *Research in Organizational Behaviour*, 4: 1–32.

Freeman, J. and M. T. Hannan (1975) 'Growth and Decline Processes in Organizations', *American Sociological Review*, 40: 215–22.

Gambetta, D. (ed.) (1988) *Trust: Making and Breaking Co-operative Relations*. Oxford: Blackwell.

Gamble, A. and P. Walton (1973) *From Alienation to Surplus Value*. London: Human Context Books.

Goffman, E. (1959) *The Presentation of Self in Everyday Life*. New York: Doubleday Anchor.

Gold, T. B. (1986) *State and Society in the Taiwan Miracle*. New York: Sharpe.

Gordon, A. (1985) *The Evolution of Labour Relations in Japan*. Cambridge, Mass.: Harvard University Press.

Gouldner, A. W. (1954) *Patterns of Industrial Bureaucracy*. New York: Free Press.

Gouldner, A. W. (1957–8) 'Cosmopolitans and Locals: Towards an Analysis of Latent Social Roles', *Administrative Science Quarterly*, 2: 281–302; 444–80.

Gouldner, A. W. (1959) 'Organizational Analysis', pp. 400–28 in R. K. Merton, L. Broom and C. Cottrell (eds), *Sociology Today*. New York: Basic Books.

Gramsci, A. (1971) *Selections from the Prison Notebooks*. London: Lawrence and Wishart.

Granovetter, M. (1985) 'Economic Action and Social Structure: The Problem of Embeddedness', *American Journal of Sociology*, 91: 481–510.

Grinyer, P. H. (1982) 'Discussion Note: Divisionalization and Size – a Rejoinder', *Organization Studies*, 3(4): 339–50.

Grinyer, P. H. and M. Yasai-Ardekani (1981) 'Strategy, Structure and Bureaucracy', *Academy of Management Journal*, 24(3): 471–86.

Grinyer, P. H., M. Yasai-Ardekani and S. Al-Bazzaz (1980) 'Strategy and Structure, the Environment and Financial Performance in 48 United Kingdom Companies', *Academy of Management Journal*, 23: 193–220.

Grumley, J. (1988) 'Weber's Fragmentation of Totality', *Thesis Eleven*, 21: 20–39.

Hadenius, A. (1976) *Facklig Organisationsutveckling. En Studie av Landsorganisationen i Sverige*. Stockholm: Rabén och Sjögren.

Haferkamp, H. (1987) 'Beyond the Iron Cage of Modernity? Achievement, Negotiation and Changes in the Power Structure', *Theory, Culture and Society*, 4(1): 31–54.

Hage, J. (1965) 'An Axiomatic Theory of Organizations', *Administrative Science Quarterly*, 10: 289–320.

Hage, J. and M. Aiken (1970) *Social Change in Complex Organizations*. New York: Random House.

Hall, R. H. (1962) 'Intraorganizational Structure Variation: Application of the Bureaucratic Model', *Administrative Science Quarterly*, 7: 295–308.

Hall, R. H. (1963) 'The Concept of Bureaucracy: An Empirical Assessment', *American Journal of Sociology*, 69: 32–40.

Hall, R. H. (1989) 'Review of L. G. Zucker (ed.), *Institutional Patterns and Organizations: Culture and Environment*', *Contemporary Sociology*, 18(1): 54–6.

Hall, R. H., J. E. Haas and N. J. Johnson (1966) 'An Examination of the Blau-Scott and Etzioni Typologies', *Administrative Science Quarterly*, 12: 118–39.

Hall, R. H., J. E. Haas and N. J. Johnson (1967) 'Organization Size, Complexity and Formalization', *American Sociological Review*, 32: 903–12.

Hamada, T. (1980) 'Winds of Change: Economic Realism and Japanese Labor Management', *Asian Survey*, 20: 397–406.

Hamilton, G. G. and N. W. Biggart (1988) 'Market, Culture, and Authority: A Comparative Analysis of Management and Organization in the Far East', pp. S52–95 in C. Winship and S. Rosen (eds), *Organizations and Institutions: Sociological Approaches to the Analysis of Social Structure. American Journal of Sociology*, 94, supplement. Chicago: University of Chicago Press.

Handy, C. (1989) *The Age of Unreason*. London: Hutchinson.

Hannan, M. and J. Freeman (1977) 'The Population Ecology of Organizations', *American Journal of Sociology*, 82(5): 929–40.

Hannan, M. T. and J. Freeman (1984) 'Structural Inertia and Organizational Change', *American Sociological Review*, 49(2): 149–64.

Hannan, M. T. and J. Freeman (1988) 'The Ecology of Organizational Mortality: American Labor Unions, 1836–1985', *American Journal of Sociology*, 94(1): 25–52.

Harrington, M. (1977) *The Twilight of Capitalism*. London: Macmillan.

Harvey, E. (1968) 'Technology and Structure of Organizations', *American Sociological Review*, 35: 247–59.

Hayek, F. A. (1944) *The Road to Serfdom*. London: Routledge and Kegan Paul.

Hayek, F. A. (1960) *The Constitution of Liberty*. London: Routledge and Kegan Paul.

Hayek, F. A. (1967) *Studies in Philosophy, Politics and Economics*. London: Routledge and Kegan Paul.

Hayes, R. H. (1981) 'Why Japanese Factories Work', *Harvard Business Review*, 59(4): 56–66.

Hayes, R. H. and W. Abernathy (1980) 'Managing our Way to Economic Decline', *Harvard Business Review*, 58(4): 67–77.

Hayes, R. H. and D. A. Garvin (1982) 'Managing as if Tomorrow Mattered', *Harvard Business Review*, 60(3): 70–80.

Hayes, R. H. and S. C. Wheelwright (1984) *Restoring our Competitive Edge: Competing through Manufacturing*. New York: John Wiley.

Hayes, R. H., S. Wheelwright and K. Clark (1988) *Dynamic Manufacturing: Creating the Learning Organization*. New York: Free Press.

Heller, J. (1962) *Catch 22*. London: Corgi.

Henderson, J. (1989) 'The Political Economy of Technological Transformation in Hong Kong', *Comparative Urban and Community Research*, 2 :102–55.

Heydebrand, W. V. (1989) 'New Organizational Forms', *Work and Occupations*, 16(3): 323–57.

Hicks, A. (1987) 'Socialism: Scientific and Utopian', *Contemporary Sociology*, 16(5): 661–4.

Hickson, D. J. and C. McMillan (eds) (1981) *Organization and Nation: The Aston Programme IV*. Aldershot: Gower.

Hickson, D. J., D. S. Pugh and D. C. Pheysey (1969) 'Operations Technology and Organization Structure: An Empirical Reappraisal', *Administrative Science Quarterly*, 14: 378–97.

Hickson, D. J., C. R. Hinings, C. A. Lee, R. E. Schneck and J. M. Pennings (1971) 'A Strategic Contingencies Theory of Intra-Organizational Power', *Administrative Science Quarterly*, 16: 216–29.

Hickson, D. J., C. R. Hinings, C. J. McMillan and J. P. Schwitter (1974) 'The Culture-Free Context of Organization Structure: A Tri-National Comparison', *Sociology*, 8: 59–80.

Hickson, D. J., C. J. McMillan, K. Azumi and D. Horvath (1979) 'Grounds for Comparative Organization Theory: Quicksands or Hard Core?', pp. 25–41 in C. J. Lammers and D. J. Hickson (eds), *Organizations Alike and Unlike: International and Inter-Institutional Studies in the Sociology of Organizations*. London: Routledge and Kegan Paul.

Hickson, D. J., R. J. Butler, D. Cray, G. R. Mallory and D. C. Wilson (1986) *Top Decisions: Strategic Decision-Making in Organizations*. Oxford: Blackwell; San Francisco: Jossey-Bass.

Higgins, W. (1985a) 'Political Unionism and the Corporatist Thesis', *Economic and Industrial Democracy*, 6(3): 349–81.

Higgins, W. (1985b) 'Ernst Wigforss: The Renewal of Social Democratic Theory and Practice', *Political Power and Social Theory*, 5: 207–50.

Higgins, W. (1987) 'Unions as Bearers of Industrial Regeneration: Reflections on the Australian Case', *Economic and Industrial Democracy*, 8(2): 213–36.

Higgins, W. (1988) 'Swedish Social Democracy and the New Democratic Socialism', pp. 69–90 in D. Sainsbury (ed.), *Democracy, State and Justice: Critical Perspectives and New Interpretations*. Stockholm: Almqvist an Wiksell International.

Higgins, W. and N. Apple (1983) 'How Limited Is Reformism?', *Theory and Society*, 12(3): 603–30.

Higgins, W. and S. R. Clegg (1988) 'Enterprise Calculation and Manufacturing Decline', *Organization Studies*, 9(1): 69–89.

Himmelstrand, U., G. Ahrne and L. Lundberg (1981) *Beyond Welfare Capitalism*. London: Heinemann.

Hindess, B. (1987) *Freedom, Equality and the Market: Arguments on Social Policy*. London: Tavistock.

Hinings, C. R., D. J. Hickson, J. M. Pennings and R. E. Schneck (1974) 'Structural Conditions of Intra-Organizational Power', *Administrative Science Quarterly*, 19(1): 22–44.

Hinings, C. R., S. R. Clegg, J. Child, H. Aldrich, L. Karpik and L. Donaldson (1988) 'Offence and Defence in Organization Studies: A Symposium', *Organization Studies*, 9(1): 1–32.

Hirsch, F. R. (1978) *The Social Limits to Growth*. London: Routledge and Kegan Paul.

Hirsch, P. M. (1986) 'From Ambushes to Golden Parachutes: Corporate Takeovers as an Instance of Cultural Framing and Institutional Integration', *American Journal of Sociology*, 91(4): 800–37.

Hobsbawm, E. J. (1975) *The Age of Capital, 1848–1875*. London: Weidenfeld and Nicolson.

Hofstede, G. (1980) *Culture's Consequences: International Differences in Work Related Values*. Beverly Hills, Calif.: Sage.

Holden, C. (1980) 'Innovation: Japan Races Ahead as the US Falters', *Science*, 210: 751–4.

Hoshino, Y. (1982a) 'The Japanese Style of Management; Technical Innovation (Part I)', *Sumitomo Quarterly*, 7: 15–18.

Hoshino, Y. (1982b) 'The Japanese Style of Management; Technical Innovation (Part II)', *Sumitomo Quarterly*, 8: 15–18.

Hoshino, Y. (1982c) 'The Japanese Style of Management; Technical Innovation (Part III): Staff Motivation, Job Mobility Are Keys to Japanese Advance', *Sumitomo Quarterly*, 9: 19–22.

Hoshino, Y. (1982d) 'The Japanese Style of Management; Technical Innovation (Part IV): Creative Technology Needs New Environment', *Sumitomo Quarterly*, 10: 8–10.

Hoss, D. (1986) 'Technology and Work in the Two Germanies', pp. 231–72 in P. Grooting (ed.), *Technology and Work: East-West Comparisons*. London: Croom Helm.

Howard, N. and Y. Teramoto (1981) 'The Really Important Difference between Japanese and Western Management', *Management International Review*, 3: 19–30.

Hughes, E. C. (1939) 'Institutions', pp. 283–346 in R. E. Park (ed.), *An Outline of the Principles of Sociology*. New York: Barnes and Noble.

Hyman, R. (1988) 'Flexible Specialization: Miracle or Myth?', pp. 48–60 in R. Hyman and W. Streeck (eds), *Trade Unions, Technology and Industrial Democracy*. Oxford: Blackwell.

Ichimura, S. (1981) 'Japanese Firms in Asia', *Japanese Economic Studies*, 10(1): 31–52.

Igarashi, F. (1986) 'Forced to Confess', pp. 195–214 in G. McCormack and Y. Sugimoto (eds), *Democracy in Contemporary Japan*. Sydney: Hale and Iremonger.

Imai, M. (1969) '*Shukko, Jomukai, Ringi* – the Ingredients of Executive Selection in Japan', *Personnel*, 46(4): 20–30.

Ingham, G. (1984) *Capitalism Divided? The City and Industry in British Social Development*. London: Macmillan.

Inkson, J. K., D. S. Pugh and D. J. Hickson (1970) 'Organization Context and Structure: An Abbreviated Replication', *Administrative Science Quarterly*, 15: 318–29.

Ishida, H. (1981) 'Exportability of the Japanese Employment System', pp. 99–111 in *Industrial Policies, Foreign Investment and Labour in Asian Countries, Proceedings of the Asian Regional Conference of Industrial Relations*. Tokyo: Japan Institute of Labour.

Ishikawa, A. (1982) 'A Survey of Studies in the Japanese Style of Management', *Economic and Industrial Democracy*, 3(1): 1–15.

Jacoby, S. (1979) 'Origins of Internal Labor Markets in Japan', *Industrial Relations*, 18(2): 184–96.

Jacques, E. (1951) *The Changing Culture of a Factory*. London: Tavistock.

Jacques, E. (1989) *Requisite Organizations*. Arlington, Va: Casson Hall.

Jaikumar, R. (1986) 'Postindustrial Manufacturing', *Harvard Business Review*, 64(6): 69–76.

Jameson, F. (1984) 'Postmodernism, or the Cultural Logic of Late Capitalism', *New Left Review*, 146: 53–93.

Johnson, C. (1982) *MITI and the Japanese Miracle*. Stanford, Calif.: Stanford University Press.

Johnson, T. (1972) *Professions and Power*. London: Macmillan.

Jones, L. and I. Sakong (1980) *Government, Business and Entrepreneurship in Economic Development: The Korean Case*. Cambridge, Mass.: Harvard University Press.

Kagono, T., I. Nonaka, K. Satakibara and A. Okumura (1985) *Strategic vs Evolutionary Management: A US/Japan Comparison of Strategy and Organization*. Amsterdam: North-Holland.

Kahn, H. (1979) *World Economic Development: 1979 and Beyond*. London: Croom Helm.

Kamata, S. (1982) *Japan in the Passing Lane*. New York: Pantheon.

Kaplinsky, R. (1984) *Automation: The Technology and Society*. London: Longman.

Karpik, L. (1972a) 'Sociologie, Economie, Politique et Buts des Organisations de Production', *Revue Français de Sociologie*, 13: 299–324.

Karpik, L. (1972b) 'Les Politiques et les Logiques d'Action de la Grande Enterprise Industrielle', *Sociologie du Travail*, 1: 82–105.

Karpik, L. (1977) 'Technological Capitalism', pp. 41–71 in S. R. Clegg and D. Dunkerley (eds), *Critical Issues In Organizations*. London: Routledge and Kegan Paul.

Karpik, L. (1978) 'Organizations, Institutions and History', pp. 15–68 in L. Karpik (ed.), *Organization and Environment: Theory, Issues and Reality*. Beverly Hills, Calif.: Sage.

Katz, D. and R. L. Kahn (1966) *The Social Psychology of Organizations*. New York: John Wiley.

Katz, H. C. and C. F. Sabel (1985) 'Industrial Relations and Industrial Adjustments in the Car Industry', *Industrial Relations*, 24(2): 295–315.

Kawashini, H. (1986) 'The Reality of Enterprise Unionism', pp. 138–56 in G. McCormack and Y. Sugimoto (eds), *Democracy in Contemporary Japan*. Sydney: Hale and Iremonger.

Kenney, M. and R. Florida (1988) 'Beyond Mass Production: Production and the Labor Process in Japan', *Politics and Society*, 16(1): 121–58.

Kern, H. and M. Schumann (1984a) *Das Ende der Arbeitsteilung? Rationalisiering in der Industriellen Produktion*. Munich: Verlag C. H. Beck.

Kern, H. and M. Schumann (1984b) 'Work and Social Character: Old and New Contours', *Economic and Industrial Democracy*, 5: 51–71.

Kern, H. and M. Schumann (1987) 'Limits of the Division of Labour, New Production and Employment Concepts in West German Industry', *Economic and Industrial Democracy*, 8: 151–70.

Kerr, C. J., T. Dunlop, F. Harbison and C. A. Myers (1973) *Industrialism and Industrial Man*. Harmondsworth: Penguin.

Ketcham, R. (1987) *Individualism and Public Life*. Oxford: Blackwell.

Koike, K. (1981) 'A Japan–Europe Comparison of Female Labour-Force Participation and Male-Female Wage Differentials', *Japanese Economic Studies*, 9(2): 3–27.

Koike, K. (1987) 'Human Resource Development and Labor Management Relations', pp. 289–330 in K. Yamamura and Y. Yasuba (eds), *The Political Economy of Japan*. Volume 1: *The Domestic Transformation*. Stanford, Calif.: Stanford University Press.

Kolko, G. (1963) *The Triumph of Conservatism, 1900–1916*. New York: Free Press.

Kondratieff, N. D. (1979) 'The Long Waves in Economic Life', *Review*, 11(4): 519–62.

Kono, T. (1982) 'Japanese Management Philosophy: Can It Be Exported?', *Long Range Planning*, 3: 90–102.

Koo, H. (1987) 'Industrialization and Labor Politics in the East Asian NICs: A Comparison of South Korea and Taiwan', paper presented to the American Sociological Association Annual Meetings, Chicago, August 17–22.

Kosai, Y. and Y. Ogino (1984) *The Contemporary Japanese Economy*. London: Macmillan.

Koshiro, K. (1981) 'The Quality of Working Life in Japan', *The Wheel Extended: A Toyota Quarterly Review*, special supplement, 9: 1–8.

Kotter, J. P. (1988) *The Leadership Factor*. New York: Free Press.

Kuhn, T. S. (1962) *The Structure of Scientific Revolutions*. Chicago: University of Chicago Press.

Lane, C. (1988) 'Industrial Change in Europe: The Pursuit of Flexible Specialization in Britain and West Germany', *Work, Employment and Society*, 2(2): 141–68.

Lash, S. (1988) 'Postmodernism as a Regime of Signification', *Theory, Culture and Society*, 5(2–3): 311–36.

Lash, S. and J. Urry (1987) *The End of Organized Capitalism*. Cambridge: Polity Press.

Lawrence, P. and T. Spybey (1986) *Management and Society in Sweden*. London: Routledge and Kegan Paul.

Lee, H.-K. (1987) 'Enterprise Groups in Korea', *Shoken Keizai*, 162: 10–14.

Lever-Tracy, C. (1988) 'The Flexibility Debate: Part Time Work', *Labour and Industry*, 1(2): 210–41.

Lincoln, J. R. and K. McBride (1987) 'Japanese Industrial Organizations in Comparative Perspective', *American Review of Sociology*, 13: 289–312.

Lincoln, J. R., J. Olson and M. Hanada (1978) 'Cultural Effects on Organizational Structure: The Case of Japanese Firms in the United States', *American Sociological Review*, 43: 829–47.

Littek, W. and U. Heissig (1989) 'Work Organization under Technological Change: Sources of Differentiation and the Reproduction of Social Inequality in Processes of Change', pp. 289–314 in S. R. Clegg (ed.), *Organization Theory and Class Analysis: New Approaches and New Issues*. Berlin: De Gruyter.

Little, I. M. D. (1979) 'An Economic Reconnaissance', pp. 448–507 in W. Galenson (ed.), *Economic Growth and Structural Change in Taiwan*. Ithaca, NY: Cornell University Press.

Littler, C. R. (1980) 'Internal Contract and the Transition to Modern Work Systems: Britain and Japan', pp. 157–85 in D. Dunkerley and G. Salaman (eds), *The International Yearbook of Organization Studies 1979*. London: Routledge and Kegan Paul.

Littler, C. R. (1982) *The Development of the Labour Process in Capitalist Societies*. London: Heinemann Educational Books.

Lorenz, E. H. (1988) 'Neither Friends nor Strangers: Informal Networks of Subcontracting in French Industry', pp. 194–210 in D. Gambetta (ed.), *Trust: Making and Breaking Co-operative Relations*. Oxford: Blackwell.

Loveridge, R. and A. L. Mok (1979) *Theories of Labour Market Segmentation: A Critique*. The Hague: Martinus Nijhoff.

Lukes, S. (1974) *Power: A Radical View*. London: Macmillan.

Lyotard, J.-F. (1984) *The Postmodern Condition*. Manchester: Manchester University Press.

Macpherson, C. B. (1962) *The Political Theory of Possessive Individualism: From Hobbes to Locke*. Oxford: Clarendon Press.

Maier, C. S. (1970) 'Between Taylorism and Technocracy: European Ideologies and the Vision of Industrial Productivity in the 1920s', *Journal of Contemporary History*, 5: 27–61.

Mandel, E. (1975) *Late Capitalism*. London: New Left Books.

Marceau, J. (1989) 'The Dwarves of Capitalism: The Structure of Production and the Economic Culture of the Small Manufacturing Firm', pp. 198–212 in S. R. Clegg and S. G. Redding (eds), with the assistance of M. Cartner, *Capitalism in Contrasting Cultures*. Berlin: De Gruyter.

March, J. G. and H. A. Simon (1958) *Organizations*. New York: John Wiley.

Marcuse, H. (1964) *One-Dimensional Man*. London: Routledge and Kegan Paul.

Marris, R. (1964) *The Economic Theory of 'Managerial' Capitalism*. London: Macmillan.

Marsh, R. M. and H. Mannari (1975) 'The Japanese Factory Revisited', *Studies in Comparative International Development*, 10(1): 31–43.

Marsh, R. M. and H. Mannari (1977) 'Organizational Commitment and Turnover: A Prediction Study', *Administrative Science Quarterly*, 22(1): 57–75.

Marsh, R. M. and H. Mannari (1980) 'Technological Implications Theory: A Japanese Test', *Organization Studies*, 1(2): 161–83.

Marsh, R. M. and H. Mannari (1981) 'Technology and Size as Determinants of the Organizational Structure of Japanese Factories', *Administrative Science Quarterly*, 26(1): 33–57.

Marsh, R. M. and H. Mannari (1989) 'The Size Imperative? Longitudinal Tests', *Organization Studies*, 10(1): 83–96.

Marx, K. (1968) *Marx and Engels: Selected Works*. London: Lawrence and Wishart.

Marx, K. (1976) *Capital* (Vol. 1). Harmondsworth: Penguin.

Mason, E. S., M. K. Kim, D. H., Perkins, K. S. Kim and D. C. Cole (1980) *The Economic and Social Modernization of the Republic of Korea*. Cambridge, Mass.: Council of East Asian Studies, Harvard University.

Matsuura, N. F. (1981) 'Sexual Bias in the *Nenko* System of Employment', *Journal of Industrial Relations*, 23(3): 310–22.

Matsuzuka, H. (1967) 'Industrialization and the Change of Wage Structure in Japan', pp. 111–13 in N. Uchida and K. Ikeda (eds), *Social and Economic Aspects of Japan*. Tokyo: Economic Institute of Seijo University.

Matthews, J. (1989) 'The Democratization of Capital', *Economic and Industrial Democracy*, 10(2): 165–194.

Maurice, M. (1976) 'Introduction: Theoretical and Ideological Aspects of the Universalistic Approach to the Study of Organizations', *International Studies of Management and Organization*, 6: 3–10.

Maurice, M., A. Sorge and M. Warner (1980) 'Societal Differences in Organizing Manufacturing Units: A Comparison of France, West Germany and Great Britain', *Organization Studies*, 1(1): 59–86.

Mayer, J. P. (1956) *Max Weber and German Politics*. London: Faber and Faber.

Mayo, E. (1933) *The Human Problems of an Industrial Civilization*. New York: Macmillan.

Mayo, E. (1975) *The Social Problems of an Industrial Civilization*. London: Routledge and Kegan Paul.

McCormack, G. (1986) 'Crime, Confession and Control', pp. 186–94 in G. McCormack and Y. Sugimoto (eds), *Democracy in Contemporary Japan*. Sydney: Hale and Iremonger.

McMillan, C. J. (1984) *The Japanese Industrial System*. Berlin: De Gruyter.

Meade, A. (1982) *Stagflation*. Volume 1: *Wage Fixing*. London: Allen and Unwin.

Merton, R. K. (1940) 'Bureaucratic Structure and Personality', *Social Forces*, 18: 560–8.

Meyer, J. and B. Rowan (1977) 'Institutionalized Organizations: Formal Structure as Myth and Ceremony', *American Journal of Sociology*, 83: 340–63.

Mills, C. W. (1940) 'Situated Actions and Vocabularies of Motive', *American Sociological Review*, 5: 904–13.

Milton-Smith, J. (1986) 'Japanese Management Overseas: International Business Strategy and the Case of Singapore', pp. 394–412 in S. R. Clegg, D. Dunphy and S. G. Redding (eds), *The Enterprise and Management in East Asia*. Hong Kong: Centre of Asian Studies, University of Hong Kong.

Mintzberg, H. (1979) *The Structuring of Organizations*. Englewood Cliffs, NJ: Prentice-Hall.

Mintzberg, H. (1983) *Power in and around Organizations*. Englewood Cliffs, NJ: Prentice-Hall.

Mo, T. (1978) *The Monkey King*. London: Abacus.

Moore, B. (1968) *The Social Origins of Dictatorship and Democracy*. Harmondsworth: Penguin.

Moore, J. (1983) *Japanese Workers and the Struggle for Power 1945–1947*. Madison, Wisc.: University of Wisconsin Press.

Morgan, G. (1986) *Images of Organizations*. London: Sage

Morgan, G. (1989) 'Ownership and Management Strategy', pp. 175–91 in S. R. Clegg (ed.), *Organization Theory and Class Analysis: New Approaches and New Issues*. Berlin: De Gruyter.

Muczyk, J. P. and B. C. Reimann (1987) 'The Case for Directive Leadership', *Academy of Management Executive*, 1(4): 301–11.

Murakami, Y. (1984) '*Ie* Society as a Pattern of Civilization', *Journal of Japanese Studies*, 10(2): 281–363.

Murakami, Y. (1986) 'Technology in Transition: Two Perspectives on Industrial Policy', pp. 211–41 in H. Patrick (ed.), with the assistance of L. Meissner, *Japan's High Technology Industries: Lessons and Limitations of Industrial Policy*. Seattle, Wash. and London: University of Washington Press.

Muto, I. (1986) 'Class Struggle in Post-War Japan', pp. 114–37 in G. McCormack and Y. Sugimoto (eds), *Democracy in Contemporary Japan*. Sydney: Hale and Iremonger.

Myrdal, A. and G. Myrdal (1934) *Krisis i Befolkningsfragan*. Stockholm: Rabén & Sjögren.

Nakane, C. (1973) *Japanese Society*. Harmondsworth: Penguin.

Nakao, T. (1980) 'Wages and Market Power in Japan', *British Journal of Industrial Relations*, 18(3): 365–8.

Naoi, A. and C. Schooler (1985) 'Occupational Conditions and Psychological Functioning in Japan', *American Journal of Sociology*, 90: 729–51.

NEDO (National Economic Development Office) (1986) *Changing Working Patterns*. London: NEDO.

Numazaki, I. (1987) 'Enterprise Groups in Taiwan', *Shoken Keizai*, 162: 15–23.

Numazaki, I. (forthcoming) 'State and Business in Postwar Taiwan: Comment on Hamilton and Biggart', *American Journal of Sociology*.

Odaka, K. (1963) 'Traditionalism and Democracy in Japanese Industry', *Industrial Relations*, 3(1): 95–103.

Odaka, K. (1975) *Toward Industrial Democracy: Management and Workers in Modern Japan*. Cambridge, Mass.: Harvard University Press.

Offe, C. (1976) *Industry and Inequality*, translated and with an introduction by J. Wickham. London: Edward Arnold.

Orrù, M., N. W. Biggart and G. G. Hamilton (1988) 'Organizational Isomorphism in East Asia: Broadening the New Institutionalism', *Program in East Asian Culture and Development Research Working Paper Series No. 10*. Davis, Calif.: Institute of Governmental Affairs, University of California.

Palloix, C. (1976) 'The Labour Process: From Fordism to Neo-Fordism', pp. 46–67 in

Conference of Socialist Economists (eds), *The Labour Process and Class Strategies*. London: Stage 1.

Parsons, T. (1951) *The Social System*. New York: Free Press.

Parsons, T. (1956) 'Suggestions for a Sociological Approach to the Theory of Organizations', *Administrative Science Quarterly*, 1: 63–85, 225–39.

Parsons, T. (1966) *Societies: Evolutionary and Comparative Respectives*. Englewood Cliffs, NJ: Prentice-Hall.

Pascale, T. (1984) 'Perspectives on Strategy: The Real Story Behind Honda's Success', *Californian Management Review*, 26(3): 47–72.

Pascale, R. T. and M. Maguire (1980) 'Comparisons of Selected Work Factors in Japan and the United States', *Human Relations*, 33: 433–55.

Perez, C. (1985) 'Microelectronics, Long Waves and World Structural Change: New Perspectives for Developing Countries', *World Development*, 13(3): 441–63.

Perrow, C. (1967) 'A Framework for the Comparative Analysis of Complex Organizations', *American Sociological Review*, 32: 194–208.

Perrow, C. (1970) *Organizational Analysis: A Sociological View*. London: Tavistock.

Perrow, C. (1981) 'Markets, Hierarchies and Hegemony: A Critique of Chandler and Williamson', pp. 371–86 and 403–4 in A. Van de Van and W. Joyce (eds), *Perspectives on Organizational Design and Behavior*. New York: John Wiley.

Perrow, C. (1984) *Normal Accidents: Living with High-Risk Technologies*. New York: Basic Books.

Perrow, C. (1986) *Complex Organizations: A Critical Essay* (3rd Edition). New York: Random House.

Perry, N. (1984) 'Catch, Class and Bureaucracy: The Meaning of Joseph Heller's *Catch 22*', *Sociological Review*, 32(4): 719–41.

Peters, T. J. and R. H. Waterman Jr. (1982) *In Search of Excellence*. New York: Harper and Row.

Pfeffer, J. (1981) *Power in Organizations*. Boston, Mass.: Pitman.

Pfeffer, J. and G. R. Salancik (1978) *The External Control of Organizations*. New York: Harper and Row.

Piore, M. J. (1986) 'Perspectives on Labor Market Flexibility', *Industrial Relations*, 25(2): 156–66.

Piore, M. J. and C. F Sabel (1984) *The Second Industrial Divide: Possibilities for Prosperity*. New York: Basic Books.

Pollert, A. (1988) 'Dismantling Flexibility', *Capital and Class*, 34(1): 42–75.

Pugh, D. S. (ed) (1971) *Organization Theory: Selected Readings*. Harmondsworth: Penguin.

Pugh, D. S. (1988) 'The Aston Research Programme', pp. 123–35 in A. Bryman (ed.) *Doing Research in Organizations*. London: Routledge and Kegan Paul.

Pugh, D. S. and D. J. Hickson (1976) *Organizational Structure in its Context: The Aston Programme I*. London: Saxon House.

Pugh, D. S. and C. R. Hinings (eds) (1976) *Organizational Structure – Extensions and Replications: The Aston Programme II*. Aldershot: Gower.

Pugh, D. S. and R. L. Payne (eds) (1977) *Organizational Behaviour in its Context: The Aston Programme III*. Aldershot: Gower.

Pye, L. (1985) *Asian Power and Politics: The Cultural Dimensions of Authority*. Cambridge, Mass.: Harvard University Press.

Ramsay, H. (1977) 'Cycles of Control: Worker Participation in Sociological and Historical Perspective', *Sociology*, 11: 481–506.

Ramsay, H. (1983a) 'An International Participation Cycle: Variations on a Recurring Theme', pp. 257–317 in S. R. Clegg, G. Dow and P. Boreham (eds), *The State, Class and the Recession*. New York: St Martins.

Ramsay, H. (1983b) 'Evolution or Cycle? Worker Participation in the 1970s and 1980s', pp. 203–26 in C. Crouch and F. Heller (eds). *International Yearbook of Organizational Democracy*, 1. London: John Wiley.

Ramsay, H. and N. Haworth (1984) 'Worker Capitalists? Profit Sharing, Capital Sharing and Juridical Forms of Socialism', *Economic and Industrial Democracy*, 5(3): 295–324.

Ray, C. (1986) *Social Innovation at Work: The Humanization of Workers in Twentieth Century America*, Ph.D., University of California, Santa Cruz.

Redding, S. G. (1980) 'Cognition as an Aspect of Culture and its Relationship to Management Processes: An Exploratory View of the Chinese Cases', *Journal of Management Studies*, 17: 127–48.

Redding, S. G. (1990) *The Spirit of Chinese Capitalism*. Berlin: De Gruyter.

Reed, M. (1989) 'Deciphering Donaldson and Defending Organization Theory: A Reply to Lex Donaldson's Review of *Redirections in Organizational Analysis*', *Australian Journal of Management*, 14(2): 255–60.

Robins, J. A. (1985) 'Ecology and Society: A Lesson for Organization Theory from the Logic of Economics', *Organization Studies*, 6(4): 335–48.

Rohlen, T. (1973) '"Spiritual Education" in a Japanese Bank', *American Anthropologist*, 75: 1542–62.

Rohlen, T. (1974) *For Harmony and Strength: Japanese White Collar Organization in Anthropological Perspective*. Berkeley, Calif.: University of California Press.

Rostow, W. W. (1978) *The World Economy: History and Prospect*. Austin, Tex.: University of Texas Press.

Rothschild-Whitt, J. (1979) 'The Collectivist Organization: An Alternative to Rational-Bureaucratic Models', *American Sociological Review*, 44: 509–27.

Rothstein, B. (1985) 'The Success of the Swedish Labour Market Policy: The Organizational Connection to Policy', *European Journal of Political Research*, 1: 153–65.

Roy, D. (1958) '"Banana Time": Job Satisfaction and Informal Interaction', *Human Organization*, 18: 158–68.

Rustin, M. (1989) 'The Politics of Post-Fordism: Or, The Trouble with "New Times"', *New Left Review*, 175: 54–78.

Sabel, C. F. (1982) *Work and Politics*. Cambridge: Cambridge University Press.

Saha, A. (1989–90) 'Basic Human Nature and Management in Japan', *International Minds*, 1(2): 11–17.

Sakaiya, T. (1981) 'Debunking the Myth of Loyalty', *Japan Echo*, 8(2): 17–29.

Salvadori, M. (1979) *Karl Kautsky and the Proletarian Revolution 1880–1938*. London: New Left Books.

Sampson, A. (1976) *The Seven Sisters*. London: Coronet.

Sandkull, B. (1986) 'Industry, Government and the Public – the Public Role of Big Corporations', pp. 59–75 in R. H. Wolff (ed.), *Organizing Industrial Development*. Berlin: De Gruyter.

Sano, Y. (1977) 'Seniority-Based Wages in Japan – a Survey', *Japanese Economic Studies*, 5(3): 48–65.

Schonberger, R. J. (1982) *Japanese Manufacturing Techniques*. New York: Free Press.

Scott, J. (1979) *Corporations, Classes and Capitalism*. London: Hutchinson.

Scott, W. R. (1981) *Organizations: Rational, Natural and Open Systems*. Englewood Cliffs, NJ: Prentice-Hall.

Scott, W. R. (1987) 'The Adolescence of Institutional Theory', *Administrative Science Quarterly*, 32(4): 493–511.

Scott, W. R. and J. W. Meyer (1983) 'The Organization of Societal Sectors', pp. 129–54 in J. W. Meyer and W. R. Scott (eds), *Organizational Environments: Ritual and Rationality*. Beverly Hills, Calif.: Sage.

Selznick, P. (1943) 'An Approach to a Theory of Bureaucracy', *American Sociological Review*, 8: 47–54.

Selznick, P. (1948) 'Foundations for a Theory of Organizations', *American Sociological Review*, 13: 23–35.

Selznick, P. (1949) *TVA and the Grass Roots*. Berkeley, Calif.: University of California Press.

Selznick, P. (1957) *Leadership in Administration*. New York: Harper and Row.

Shaiken, H., S. Herzenberg and S. Kuhn (1986) 'The Work Process under More Flexible Production', *Industrial Relations*, 25(2): 167–83.

Shelley, M. W. (1969) *Frankenstein: Or, The Prometheus Unbound*. London: Oxford University Press.

Shenkar, O. (1984) 'Is Bureaucracy Inevitable? The Chinese Experience', *Organization Studies*, 5(4): 289–306.

Shenkar, O. (1989) 'Rejoinder to Clegg and Higgins: The Chinese Case and the Radical School in Organization Studies', *Organization Studies*, 10(1): 117–22.

Shimada, H. (1977) 'The Japanese Labor Market after the Oil Crisis (1)', *Japan Labor Bulletin*, 16: 7–10.

Shirai, T. and H. Shimoda (1978) 'Interpreting Japanese Industrial Relations', pp. 242–83 in J. T. Dunlop and W. Galenson (eds), *Labor in the Twentieth Century*. New York: Academic Press.

Silin, R. H. (1976) *Leadership and Values: The Organization of Large-Scale Taiwanese Enterprises*. Cambridge, Mass.: East Asian Research Center, Harvard University.

Smith, A. (1961) *An Enquiry into the Nature and Causes of the Wealth of Nations*. Indianapolis, Ind.: Bobbs-Merrill.

Smith, C. (1989) 'Flexible Specialization, Automation and Mass Production', *Work, Employment and Society*, 3(2): 203–20.

Sorge, A. and W. Streeck (1988) 'Industrial Relations and Technical Change: The Case for an Extended Perspective', pp. 19–47 in R. Hyman and W. Streeck (eds), *New Technology and Industrial Relations*. Oxford: Blackwell.

Sorge, A., G. Hartmann, M. Warner and I. Nichols (1983) *Microelectronics and Manpower in Manufacturing*. Aldershot: Gower.

Standish, P. E. M. (1990) 'Accounting: The Private Language of Business or an Instrument of Social Communication?', pp. 122–41 in S. R. Clegg and S. G. Redding (eds), with the assistance of M. Cartner, *Capitalism in Contrasting Cultures*. Berlin: De Gruyter.

Stanton, A. (1989) *Invitation to Self-Management*. London: Dab Hand Press.

Starbuck, W. H. (1981) 'A Trip to View the Elephants and Rattlesnakes in the Garden of Aston', pp. 167–97 in A. H. Van de Van and W. F. Joyce (eds), *Perspectives on Organizational Design and Behavior*. New York: John Wiley.

Stinchcombe, A. (1965) 'Social Structure and Organizations', pp. 142–93 in J. G. March (ed.), *Handbook of Organizations*. Chicago: Rand McNally.

Sugimoto, Y. (1982) 'Japanese Society and Industrial Relations', pp. 1–20 in H. Shimada and S. Levine (eds), *Industrial Relations in Japan*. Melbourne: Japanese Studies Centre.

Sugimoto, Y. (1986) 'The Manipulative Basis of "Consensus" in Japan', pp. 65–75 in G. McCormack and Y. Sugimoto (eds), *Democracy in Contemporary Japan*. Sydney: Hale and Iremonger.

Sugimoto, Y. and R. Mouer (1985) *Images of Japanese Society*. London: Routledge and Kegan Paul.

Suzuki, Y. (1981) 'The Strategy and the Structure of Top 100 Japanese Industrial Enterprises 1950–1970', *Strategic Management Journal*, 1: 265–91.

Tachibanaki, T. (1982) 'Further Results on Japanese Wage Differentials: *Nenko* Wages, Hierarchical Position, Bonuses and Working Hours', *International Economic Review*, 23(2): 447–62.

Taira, K. (1961) 'Characteristics of Japanese Labor Markets', *Economic Development and Cultural Change*, 10: 150–68.

Taira, K. (1980) 'Colonialism in Foreign Subsidiaries: Lessons from Japanese Investment in Thailand', *Asian Survey*, 20(5): 373–95.

Takamiya, S. (1969) 'Characteristics of Japanese Management and its Recent Tendencies: Effectiveness of Japanese Management', pp. 394–405 in *The Proceedings of the 15th CIOS International Management Congress*. Tokyo: Kogakusha.

Takeuchi, H. (1982) 'Working Women in Business Corporations – The Management Viewpoint', *Japan Quarterly*, 29(3): 319–23.

Takezawa, S. (1966) 'Changing Workers' Values and Implications of Policy in Japan', pp. 327–46 in L. E. Davis and A. B. Cherns (eds), *The Quality of Working Life*. New York: Free Press.

Tanaka, H. (1980) 'The Japanese Method of Preparing Today's Graduate to Become Tomorrow's Manager', *Personnel Journal*, 59(2): 109–12.

Tayeb, M. (1988) *Organizations and National Culture*. London: Sage.

Taylor, F. W. (1911) *Principles of Scientific Management*. New York: Harper.

Taylor, I., P. Walton and J. Young (1974) *The New Criminology*. London: Routledge and Kegan Paul.

Taylor, L. and P. Walton (eds) (1971) *Images of Deviance*. Harmondsworth: Penguin.

Therborn, G. (1976) *Science, Class and Society*. London: New Left Books.

Therborn, G. (1986) *Why Some Peoples Are More Unemployed than Others*. London: New Left Books.

Thompson, J. D. (1967) *Organizations in Action*. New York: McGraw-Hill.

Thurow, L. (1984) 'Revitalizing American Industry: Managing in a Competitive World Economy', *Californian Management Review*, 27(1): 9–40.

Tichy, N. (1981) 'Networks in Organizations', pp. 386–408 in P. Nystrom and W. Starbuck (eds), *Handbook of Organization Design*. New York: Oxford University Press.

Tilton, T. A. (1984) 'Utopia, Incrementalism and Ernst Wigforss' Conception of a Provisional Utopia', *Scandinavian Studies*, 56(1): 36–54.

Ting, W. (1986) 'International Product Life Cycle Myths and High Technology Developments in Newly Industrializing Asia', pp. 229–46 in S. R. Clegg, D. Dunphy and S. G. Redding (eds), *The Enterprise and Management in East Asia*. Hong Kong: Centre of Asian Studies, University of Hong Kong.

Tingsten, H. (1967) *Den Svenska Socialdemokratins id Utvelckling*. Volumes 1–11. Stockholm: Aldus/Bonniers.

Tomlinson, J. (1982) *The Unequal Struggle? British Socialism and the Capitalist Enterprise*. London: Methuen.

Touraine, A. (1988) 'Modernity and Cultural Specificities', *International Social Science Journal*, 118: 443–57.

Tsurumi, Y. (1976) *The Japanese Are Coming: A Multinational Interaction of Firms and Politics*. Cambridge, Mass.: Ballinger.

Ueda, Y. (1987) 'Enterprise Groups in Japan', *Shoken Keizai*, 162: 23–7.

Urabe, K. (1979) 'A Critique of Theories of the Japanese-Style Management Systems', *Japanese Economic Studies*, 7(4): 33–50.

Useem, M. (1979) 'The Social Organization of the American Business Elites and Participation of Corporate Directors in the Government of American Institutions', *American Sociological Review*, 44: 553–72.

Van de Ven, A. H. and A. Delbecq (1974) 'A Task-Contingent Model of Work-Unit Structure', *Administrative Science Quarterly*, 19: 183–97.

Vlastos, S. (1986) *Peasant Protests and Uprisings in Tokugawa Japan*. Berkeley, Calif.: University of California Press.

Vogel, E. (1979) *Japan as Number One: Lessons for America*. Cambridge, Mass.: Harvard University Press.

von Bertalanffy, L. (1968) *General Systems Theory: Foundations, Development, Applications*. New York: Brazillier.

Walmsley, G. and M. Zald (1973) *The Political Economy of Public Organizations*. Lexington, Mass.: D. C. Heath.

Weber, M. (1920) *Gesammelte Aufsätze zur Religionssoziologie*. Tübingen: J. C. B. Mohr (Paul Siebeck).

Weber, M. (1923) *General Economic History*, translated by F. H. Knight. London: Allen and Unwin.

Weber, M. (1947) *The Theory of Social and Economic Organization*, translated by T. Parsons and A. M. Henderson, with an introduction by T. Parsons. New York: Free Press.

Weber, M. (1948) *From Max Weber: Essays in Sociology*, translated, edited and with an introduction by H. H. Gerth and C. W. Mills. London: Routledge and Kegan Paul.

Weber, M. (1949) *The Methodology of the Social Sciences*, translated and edited by E. A. Shills and H. A. Finch. New York: Free Press.

Weber, M. (1958) *Gesammelte Politische Schriften*. Tübingen: J. C. B. Mohr (Paul Siebeck).

Weber, M. (1968) *Economy and Society: An Outline of Interpretive Sociology* (3 Vols), edited and with an introduction by G. Roth and C. Wittich. New York: Bedminster Press.

Weber, M. (1976) *The Protestant Ethic and the Spirit of Capitalism*, translated by T. Parsons and with a new introduction by A. Giddens. London: Allen and Unwin.

Weber, M. (1978) *Economy and Society: An Outline of Interpretive Sociology* (2 Vols), edited by G. Roth and C. Wittich. Berkeley, Calif.: University of California Press.

Weick, K. E. (1979) *The Social Psychology of Organizing*. 2nd edition. Reading, Mass.: Addison-Wesley.

Weitzman, M. (1984) *The Share Economy*. Cambridge, Mass.: Harvard University Press.

Westney, D. E. (1987) *Imitation and Innovation: The Transfer of Western Organizational Patterns to Meiji Japan*. Cambridge, Mass.: Harvard University Press.

Westphal, L. E., Y. W. Rhee, L. S. Kim and A. H. Amsden (1984) 'Republic of Korea', *World Development*, 12: 505–33.

Whitley, R. (1990) 'East Asian Enterprise Structures and the Comparative Analysis of Forms of Business Organization', *Organization Studies*, 11(1): 47–74.

Whyte, W. H. Jr. (1956) *The Organization Man*. New York: Simon and Schuster.

Wigforss, E. (1981) *Skrifter i Urval*. Stockholm: Tiden.

Wilkinson, B. (1986) 'Emergence of an Industrial Community? The Human Relations Movement in Singapore', pp. 111–28 in S. R. Clegg, D. Dunphy and S. G. Redding (eds), *The Enterprise and Management in East Asia*. Hong Kong: Centre of Asian Studies, University of Hong Kong.

Williams, K., A. Cutler, J. Williams and C. Haslam (1987) 'The End of Mass Production?', *Economy and Society*, 16(3): 405–39.

Williams, K., C. Haslam, T. Cutler, A. Wardlow and J. Williams (1985) 'Accounting Failure in the Nationalized Enterprises – Coal, Steel, and Cars since 1970', Mimeo, Department of Economic History, University of Wales, Aberystwyth.

Williams, K., J. Williams and D. Thomas (1983) *Why are the British Bad at Manufacturing?*. London: Routledge and Kegan Paul.

Williams, R. (1989) 'When Was Modernism?', *New Left Review*, 175: 48–53.

Williamson, O. E. (1963) 'A Model of Rational Managerial Behavior', pp. 237–52 in R. M. Cyert and J. G. March (eds), *A Behavioral Theory of the Firm*. Englewood Cliffs, NJ: Prentice-Hall.

Williamson, O. E. (1975) *Markets and Hierarchy: Analysis and Antitrust Implications*. New York: Free Press.

Williamson, O. E. (1981) 'The Economics of Organization', *American Journal of Sociology*, 87: 548–77.

Williamson, O. E. (1983) 'Organization Form, Residual Claimants and Corporate Control', *Journal of Law and Economics*, 36: 351–66.

Williamson, O. E. (1985) *The Economic Institutions of Capitalism*. New York: Free Press.

Willis, P. (1977) *Learning to Labour: How Working Class Kids Get Working Class Jobs*. London: Heinemann Educational Books.

Wilson, H. T. (1983) 'Technocracy and Late Capitalist Society: Reflections on the Problem of Rationality and Social Organization', pp. 152–238 in S. R. Clegg, G. Dow and P. Boreham (eds), *The State, Class and the Recession*. London: Croom Helm.

Winch, D. (1969) *Economics and Policy*. New York: Walker.

Wong, S.-L. (1985) 'The Chinese Family Firm: A Model', *British Journal of Sociology*, 36(1): 58–72.

Woodward, J. (1958) *Management and Technology*. London: HMSO.

Woodward, J. (1965) *Industrial Organizations: Theory and Practice*. London: Oxford University Press.

Woodward, J. (1970) *Industrial Organizations: Behaviour and Control*. London: Oxford University Press.

Wornoff, J. (1982) *Japan's Wasted Workers*. Montclair, NY: Allanheld.

Wrong, D. H. (1961) 'The Oversocialized Conception of Man in Modern Sociology', *American Sociological Review*, 26: 183–93.

Yamada, A. (1969) 'Japanese Management Practices – Change is on the Way as Traditional Habits are Challenged', *Conference Board Record*, 6(11): 22–3.

Young, R. C. (1988) 'Is Population Ecology a Useful Paradigm for the Study of Organizations?', *American Journal of Sociology*, 94(1): 1–24.

Zald, M. (ed.) (1970a) *Power in Organizations*. Nashville, Tenn.: University of Vanderbilt Press.

Zald, M. (1970b) *Organizational Change: The Political Economy of the YMCA*. Chicago: University of Chicago Press.

Zo, K.-Z. (1970) 'Developments and Behavioural Patterns of Korean Entrepreneurs', *Korea Journal*, 10: 9–14.

Zucker, L. G. (1977) 'The Role of Institutionalization in Cultural Persistence', *American Sociological Review*, 42: 726–43.

Zucker, L. G. (1983) 'Organizations as Institutions', *Research in the Sociology of Organizations*, 2: 1–47.

Zucker, L. G. (ed.) (1988) *Institutional Patterns and Organizations: Culture and Environment*. Cambridge, Mass.: Ballinger.

Zwerman, W. (1970) *New Perspectives on Organizational Theory*. Westport, Conn.: Greenwood.

Index

DATE DUE

HIGHSMITH 45-220